T0309056

Ruins to Riches

In 1945, Germany and Japan lay prostrate after total war and resounding defeat. By 1960, they had the second- and fifth-largest economies in the world, respectively. This global leadership has been maintained ever since. How did these 'economic miracles' come to pass, and why were these two nations particularly adept at achieving them? Ray Stokes is the first to unpack these questions from comparative and international perspectives, emphasising both the individuals and the companies behind this exceptional performance and the broader global political and economic contexts. He highlights the potent mixtures in both countries of judicious state action, effective industrial organisation, benign labour relations, and technological innovation, which they adapted constantly – sometimes painfully – to take full advantage of rapidly growing post-war international trade and globalisation. Together, they explain the spectacular resurgence of Deutschland AG and Japan Incorporated to global economic and technological leadership, which they have sustained to the present.

Raymond G. Stokes is Professor of Business History and Director of the Centre for Business History in Scotland at the University of Glasgow. His extensive publications on business, environmental, and technological history include co-authoring *The Business of Waste* (Cambridge University Press, 2013) and *Building on Air* (Cambridge University Press, 2016).

Ruins to Riches

The Economic Resurgence of Germany and Japan after 1945

Raymond G. Stokes

University of Glasgow

CAMBRIDGE
UNIVERSITY PRESS

Shaftesbury Road, Cambridge CB2 8EA, United Kingdom

One Liberty Plaza, 20th Floor, New York, NY 10006, USA

477 Williamstown Road, Port Melbourne, VIC 3207, Australia

314–321, 3rd Floor, Plot 3, Splendor Forum, Jasola District Centre,
New Delhi – 110025, India

103 Penang Road, #05–06/07, Visioncrest Commercial, Singapore 238467

Cambridge University Press is part of Cambridge University Press & Assessment,
a department of the University of Cambridge.

We share the University's mission to contribute to society through the pursuit of
education, learning and research at the highest international levels of excellence.

www.cambridge.org
Information on this title: www.cambridge.org/9781316514528

DOI: 10.1017/9781009083669

First published 2024

Printed in the United Kingdom by TJ Books Limited, Padstow Cornwall

A catalogue record for this publication is available from the British Library

Library of Congress Cataloging-in-Publication Data
NAMES: Stokes, Raymond G., author.
TITLE: Ruins to riches : the economic resurgence of Germany and Japan after 1945 /
Raymond G. Stokes, University of Glasgow.
DESCRIPTION: Cambridge, United Kingdom ; New York, NY : Cambridge University
Press, 2024. | Includes bibliographical references and index.
IDENTIFIERS: LCCN 2023048701 | ISBN 9781316514528 (hardback) |
ISBN 9781009083669 (ebook)
SUBJECTS: LCSH: Germany – Economic conditions – 1945–1990. | Germany –
Economic conditions – 1991– | Japan – Economic conditions – 1945–
CLASSIFICATION: LCC HC286.5 .S76 2024 | DDC 338.943–dc23/eng/20231107
LC record available at https://lccn.loc.gov/2023048701

ISBN 978-1-316-51452-8 Hardback

To Anne, with love, appreciation, and gratitude

CONTENTS

Part IV Navigating Waves of Globalization, 1990 to the Present

CHARTS AND FIGURES

Chart

Figures

ACKNOWLEDGEMENTS

I have wanted to write this book for a long time. The idea started to take shape in conjunction with my general examinations for the PhD at The Ohio State University, where Professors Alan Beyerchen, James Bartholomew, Mansel Blackford, and June Z. Fullmer supervised complementary fields in German history, Japanese history, business history, and history of science and technology, respectively. I am grateful for their guidance and support in the exam, and also for Alan Beyerchen's continued interest in my subsequent career. Since then, the interests reflected in that examination have formed the foundation for my research and, even more so, of my teaching: over the past decades, I have taught variations of a comparative course on the development of national systems of innovation in Germany, Japan, and the United States in the twentieth century to hundreds of students in the United States and the United Kingdom. And all the while, I have been thinking about writing this book.

I am delighted finally to have the opportunity to do so, prompted by an approach from the Peters Fraser + Dunlop (PFD) agency. Tessa David and others at PFD – most recently Laurie Robertson, who took over from Tessa in mid-2020 – have worked closely with me to develop and refine the detailed proposal for the book, for which I am very grateful.

Our work paid off when the proposal was accepted by Cambridge University Press following positive – and also extraordinarily helpful – reviews from two anonymous referees. Michael Watson, Head of Trade Publishing at Cambridge University Press, managed that process, and has since provided excellent advice and feedback on the manuscript as it developed. I would like to thank him and his team, and also the reviewer of the penultimate manuscript I submitted in December 2022, whose invaluable comments and small corrections I have tried to incorporate into the final version of the book, which has been carefully copy-edited by Steven Holt, to whom I am grateful.

During the writing process, I benefited from a full year of research leave from my usual duties in the subject area of Economic and Social History at the University of Glasgow, which enabled me to complete it on time. Christine Leslie, administrator of the Centre for Business History in Scotland, has provided invaluable long-term support in managing the Centre and its finances throughout. Profound thanks to her. A number of colleagues and friends also provided crucial feedback on the proposal, partial drafts of the manuscript, and/or ideas about the project. Thanks in particular to Phillips O'Brien, Neil Rollings, Chris Miller, Jeff Fear, Niall Mackenzie, Hugh Murphy, Brian M. Linn, Ralf Banken, Valerio Cerretano, Sean Vanatta, Jonathan Stokes, Nikolas Stokes, Donald Mackinnon, Louis Joyner, Fred Hay, and David Gunn, as well as my late colleague and collaborator Stephen Sambrook.

I owe my deepest debt of gratitude, however, to my wife, Anne, who not only provided helpful comments and criticism from the start of the project through to the final manuscript, but also edited repeated drafts for style and clarity. I dedicate this book to her, with love, appreciation, and gratitude.

INTRODUCTION

Signs of revolutionary change can appear in the most ordinary of places.

On 14 April 1978, in the rolling hills of Westmoreland County, Pennsylvania, not far from Pittsburgh, the first Volkswagen Rabbit emerged from the German carmaker's massive new assembly line. Plain-vanilla white and designed to meet the specific environmental and safety requirements of the US market, the car was presented to a crowd of about 1,000 dignitaries and workers, including Milton Shapp, the Governor of Pennsylvania. He was joined on the rostrum by Toni Schmücker, the CEO of Volkswagen AG, who had flown in from the firm's headquarters in Wolfsburg, Germany. The factory's first Rabbit came to rest on a gold carpet where an employee snapped on its final part, a plastic grill. It was promptly dispatched to the VW Museum back in Germany. Schmücker announced proudly that 'Today, Volkswagen becomes the fifth American automobile producer.'[1]

Just over four years later, in November 1982, the first North American-made Honda, a modest looking slate-grey Accord, made its appearance in the Japanese automaker's sprawling new factory built in the cornfields bordering rural Marysville, Ohio, a short distance from the state's capital, Columbus. The ceremony that marked the first Japanese car ever produced in the United States was a muted affair. Participation was restricted largely to a few visiting company dignitaries and the factory's own local managers and workforce. But, in keeping with midwestern American tradition, a high school marching band provided musical accompaniment. And, in marked contrast to the first Rabbit, which was sent back to VW headquarters in Germany, Marysville's initial Accord remained in the United States and was later donated to the Henry Ford Museum in Detroit.[2]

The two plants represented, respectively, the first and second overseas auto manufacturing facilities located in the United States since 1931, when Rolls-Royce shuttered its Springfield, Massachusetts, factory. And they spearheaded a decades-long invasion of the US by foreign – primarily German and Japanese – automobile producers in the context of the oil crises of the 1970s, the emerging globalisation of trade and technology, and constant competition for foreign investment among the US states.

However, the two most striking aspects of the initial transplants were where they came from and what that meant. After all, just over a generation before VW and Honda began producing cars in the United States, Germany and Japan lay defeated and prostrate, their populations decimated and their economies in tatters in the wake of the world war they had started recklessly and lost absolutely.

Volkswagen's fate in 1945 was uncertain, its eventually iconic Beetle one of the symbols of the limitless ambitions of the Third Reich for its own 'Aryan' people over all others. The firm's automobile output before and during the war had been negligible, but its factory buildings and equipment were practically brand new. VW therefore formed a likely potential target for punitive Allied occupation policies. Honda, on the other hand, had yet to produce even one automobile in 1945: it did so only in 1963, nearly two decades after the end of the Second World War. During the conflict, Honda's founder had failed as a piston-ring manufacturer; just after the war ended, he got busy designing a prototype of a modest motor bike for eventual production.

The inauspicious beginnings after 1945 were not restricted to the auto industry in the two defeated nations. Indeed, for the rest of the 1940s, there were few industrial sectors where recovery seemed imminent, and this could happen only once the countries' desperate straits in infrastructure, housing, and supply of basic necessities were addressed. Nevertheless, already by 1960, the Federal Republic of (West) Germany, formed in 1949, boasted the second-largest economy in the capitalist world, while Japan ranked fifth. Both, moreover, had completed the journey from pariah to loyal ally of the world's political, economic, and technological leader: the United States. This was a relationship that remained fundamental in the decades that followed as the two countries retained – and in Japan's case substantially improved – their positions among the world's dominant economies into the twenty-first century. Indeed, in 2020, Japan and Germany ranked third and fourth, respectively, among the top economies in the world in terms of total gross domestic product (GDP), behind the United States and China, and ahead of India and the United Kingdom.[3] Their per capita GDP was even more impressive compared with most of these other large economies.

What accounts for these massive, rapid, and sustained transformations, and why, among all nations, were the Germans and the Japanese particularly adept in bringing them about? *Ruins to Riches* answers these questions: first, by focusing on major actors from the public and private sectors who were responsible for realising the West German and Japanese 'economic miracles'[4] during the 1950s and propelling them forward in the decades that followed; and second, by placing these internal developments in international political and economic context. In doing so, the book highlights a potent mixture of subtle state action, effective industrial organisation, benign labour relations, key companies, and fundamental technologies, all of which took flight in tandem with growing post-war international trade and globalisation. Together, they stood at the heart of the spectacular resurgence of Deutschland AG and Japan Incorporated to global economic leadership in the post-war period.

* * *

Germany and Japan are located nearly half the world away from one another, with vastly different languages and histories. Germany is largely landlocked, with no real natural borders. This accounted in large part for wild fluctuations in its political boundaries from the first German unification in 1871 through to 1990. The lack of natural borders was especially pronounced in flat, mostly sandy Prussia, the German state that brought about that first unification. It also goes a long way towards explaining both the ascendancy of the military in the decades that followed and the closely related constant threat of war as latecomer Germany sought to find its 'place in the sun' by seeking out overseas colonies.

Japan, on the other hand, is an island nation, which attempted to isolate itself from any outside influences for over two-and-a-half centuries from the early seventeenth century. Its era of splendid isolation ended abruptly in the 1850s, when Japan succumbed to the might of western countries, which threatened invasion. The Japanese avoided the implementation of the threat by signing the humiliating 'unequal treaties', obviously under duress. Thereafter, the focus was on undoing the treaties by enacting the slogan of Japan's new ruling elites: 'Rich Nation, Strong Army'. The new rulers had come to power in a revolution masquerading as the Meiji 'Restoration', which transformed politics, the economy, business, and technology in the island nation. The political boundaries of the Japanese home islands, however, did not change very substantially, either during this period of upheaval or afterwards.

Despite clear differences between Germany and Japan, then, military elites in both exercised an unhealthy influence over the countries' politics, both domestic and foreign. Both countries suffered from severe social tensions associated with rapid industrialisation. And what is more, for these and other reasons, the leaders of both countries were more than willing to go to war in order to achieve their ambitions.

In 1914, under the disastrously mistaken illusion that Germany would win swiftly, the Reich led its allied Central Powers to war, which resulted in defeat by 1918. Adolf Hitler's Third Reich attempted to reprise the folly in 1939, with even more disastrous results. Most see these as two entirely separate conflicts. Winston Churchill and others, however, have characterised the two world wars taken together as the Second Thirty Years' War, although this is, of course, a Eurocentric conception. To them, like the first Thirty Years' War, which lasted from 1618 to 1648, the two world wars constituted a single struggle punctuated by periods of peace and with changing alliances, which resulted in the devastation of central Europe and the emergence of two strong flanking powers. France and Russia emerged triumphant in 1648, the United States and the Soviet Union in 1945.

The Japanese Empire, for its part, went to war with China in 1937, and with most of its other near neighbours (mostly colonies of western powers) in the years that followed, culminating in a brazen attack on the US fleet anchored in Pearl Harbor on 7 December 1941. Not surprisingly, the United States declared war on Japan in retaliation. The attack on Pearl Harbor thus represented a *va banque* strategy in a conflict that the bigger, richer, and better equipped country was bound to win. This applied, too, to Germany, which declared war on the United States shortly after Pearl Harbor, making this a truly global conflict.

Germany and Japan, then, caused the Second World War and were defeated in it. Their economies have also both performed spectacularly in its aftermath. But they have much more than that in common. In terms of economic development, for example, both were early-late industrialisers (Japan later than Germany). This meant that they were able to learn from earlier industrialisers – most importantly Britain, but also the Low Countries, parts of France, and, for Japan, Germany and the United States. Being a follower, however, also entailed the need to play catch-up, especially with regard to technology, finance, and industrial organisation.

Limited access to natural resources beyond abundant water supplies was another characteristic common to both Germany and Japan. Certainly, the German area also featured high-quality coal, especially in the Ruhr District. But neither the Germans nor the Japanese possessed adequate quantities of iron ore, cotton, or many of the other basic commodities essential to the first industrial revolution. And, as the age of petroleum dawned in the early twentieth century, with implications for defence technologies and mass motorisation, it soon became obvious that the two countries had virtually no domestic reserves of oil. This was confirmed definitively and much to their chagrin in the course of intensive – and very expensive – exploration for petroleum in the 1930s.

Of course, Germany and Japan were not alone among early – or even early-late – industrialisers in being short of some key natural resources domestically. In fact, only the United States boasted magnificent arrays and vast quantities of most commodities crucial for industrial production. The British, French, Belgians, and Dutch, however, could expand their 'domestic' raw materials base starting already in the seventeenth century through imperial conquest. By the late nineteenth century, each of them held a large clutch of lucrative colonies, which served both as suppliers of crucial raw materials and as markets for goods manufactured in the metropole. Germany and Japan, however, by industrialising late, also arrived late to this increasingly frenzied carving up of most of the world outside Europe and North America. As a result, they were able to gain only limited colonial holdings (although some, such as Germany's takeover of Shantung Province in China in the late nineteenth century and Japan's incorporation of Taiwan, the Korean peninsula, and eventually Manchuria into its empire in the first decades of the twentieth century, proved important economically). What is more, this latter-day imperial expansion occurred at the price of the Germans and Japanese coming into conflict with the established imperial powers, although neither country shrank back much from that.

However, neither Germany nor Japan relied exclusively on imperial expansion to overcome hindrances associated with their limited domestic supplies of raw materials. Keen cultivation of foreign trade was one fruitful way forward, and both Germany and Japan engaged increasingly in that during the 'first globalisation' from the late nineteenth century until the outbreak of the First World War. Thereafter, however, significant impediments to foreign trade arose because of economic disruption and deglobalisation, culminating in a severe rise in protectionism around the world from the late 1920s. Regardless, though, right from the outset, heavy reliance on foreign trade by Germany and Japan stood in marked contradiction to their willingness to engage in acts of brinkmanship and bellicosity.

Ingenuity was the second major alternative to imperial expansion for overcoming heavy reliance on other countries for supplies of natural resources and, indeed, for the reliance on foreigners for the intangible, knowledge-based inputs required for industrial production. Germany performed particularly well in this domain through its development, starting in the 1860s, of a world-beating organic chemicals industry, which produced substitutes for imported dyestuffs and eventually fertilisers and other materials. Moreover, and at least as importantly, the new industry manufactured entirely new products for which there was apparently insatiable demand, including striking new colours for dyestuffs never before seen in the natural world as well as wonder drugs, such as aspirin. More broadly, however, Germany pioneered the *institutionalisation* of ingenuity as the first country to harness the interaction of government, universities, and industry in what is now known as the 'triple helix' of a national system of innovation. Japan lagged behind Germany in the first half of the twentieth century in establishing its own national system of innovation. But development in this direction was nevertheless swift. What is more, the Japanese proved highly effective in their ability to develop domestic capabilities in sectors as diverse as steelmaking, shipbuilding, and electrical generation and distribution.[5]

Following the defeat of the Axis powers in 1945, Germany and Japan shared the experience of military occupation, with especially important input from the United States and its representatives. One of the most significant impacts here was a fundamental reorientation of the political economy of each of the defeated powers, which was undertaken under the tutelage and watchful eye of the US Americans. By the 1950s, at the insistence of the occupiers, and with the generally willing collaboration of key opinion formers and policymakers among the occupied, Japan and the newly created West Germany had transformed themselves, profoundly and permanently, from national-security states to trading nations. Gone was the overriding impact and influence of the military, with the concomitant heavy emphasis on cutting-edge technologies, along with generally high levels of social tension and confrontational industrial relations. What replaced them was a commitment to keeping the peace, low levels of social tension, and consensual industrial relations, all with a primary emphasis on commerce, civilian technologies, and (generally, and until recently) incremental innovation.

Since the Second World War, both Germany and Japan have achieved unparalleled success in four main areas: realisation of the potential of effective innovation systems that emphasise applications; manufacturing; fostering of human capital through highly effective education and training systems; and coordination of all of this through generally constructive (if sometimes problematic) cooperation among social groups from politics, industry, trade unions, education, and science and technology. Little wonder that Germany and Japan are the exemplars of what social scientists specialising in analysis of the 'varieties of capitalism' have called coordinated market economies (CMEs).[6]

* * *

Not long after the late Thomas Parke Hughes published *Networks of Power*, his masterly 1983 study of the emergence of the electric-power industry in Germany, the United States, and Britain up to 1930,[7] I asked him informally about the challenges of doing comparative history. He replied that he found it extremely difficult, not least because 'things are often almost the same, but at the very same time so very different'. So it is here, not least because, in addition to being similar yet different, Germany and Japan share strong bilateral links with the United States, which serve as a conduit for mutual interaction. In many ways, therefore, Germany and Japan have a lot in common. But they are by no means identical. Indeed, what drives the narrative in the chapters that follow is the tension arising from the remarkable similarities, but also the striking differences, between these two countries as they navigated the second half of the twentieth century and passed into the twenty-first century. One task in what follows will be to tease out some of the 'finer varieties of advanced capitalism', at least as manifested in these two leading exemplars of CMEs.[8] The other is to demonstrate that the characteristics of capitalism were not static in either country, even after the so-called 'zero hour' that tolled at their defeat in 1945.

In other words, throughout the book – and here is where this account diverges strongly from those presented by proponents of varieties of capitalism – the emphasis will be on how the two countries have *become* what they are, on contingency rather than inevitable outcomes, and on continuities as well as change. After all, attaining economic and technological success and global influence in the post-war period was not foreordained for Germany and Japan. Nor has the road to such success and influence been smooth. And their economic performance has sometimes disappointed, most recently, for example, Japan's sustained low levels of GDP growth. Alongside this, the challenges of unabated globalisation have been particularly taxing for these countries, with their massive dependence on foreign trade and imported raw materials and, increasingly, energy, a dependence that pre-dated 1945 and continues to the present. Other problems, too, have their origins in the pre-1945 era, but, unlike the countries' natural resource endowments, were self-inflicted. The highly chequered pasts of prominent figures in Germany and Japan, for example, resulted in frequent scandals well into the 1970s, while the very same tight socio-political and economic networks that were at the centre of the countries' pre-war economic and technological successes as well as their respective 'economic miracles' at times involved shadowy and illicit practices. Environmental challenges that came to the fore during the extremely rapid growth in both countries in the post-war period, too, often had origins that pre-dated 1945.

***

Boiled down to its essence, this book starts from what seems to me an uncontroversial observation: in spite of impressive economic and technological successes through the first four decades of the twentieth century, it became abundantly clear by 1945 that the German and Japanese brands of capitalism had not worked out very well at all. Both countries had indeed industrialised more or less effectively. But they remained relatively poor compared with Britain and the United States. They also suffered from extreme social tensions. These factors were both cause and effect of the countries entangling themselves in a war that they could not win, and which made their social and economic situations horrendous, at least initially. Yet, in stark contrast, from the early 1950s onwards, German and Japanese forms of capitalism have played out surprisingly well, with increasing levels of wealth, which was distributed more equitably, and substantially eased social tensions, all of this without any bellicose behaviour. What is more, this remarkable performance has been sustained over an extraordinarily long period of time.

The primary question posed here, then, is this: *Why, in general, have things worked out so much better the second time around?* The chapters that follow seek to provide an answer to that simple question, and they are grouped in four parts, arranged for the most part chronologically. Part I explains the rapid recovery of the German and Japanese economies in the immediate aftermath of the Second World War in 1945 and the (re-)construction of political, social, and economic networks by the early 1950s that enabled that recovery. Part II explores the next stage in that process between about 1950 and 1973: how West Germany and Japan came to rank among the richest nations on earth by the early 1970s. Part III then turns to consideration of the period 1973 to 1989, when some of the consequences of becoming so rich so fast came home to roost, and Germany and Japan coped with political, economic, and environmental crises. And Part IV analyses how the two countries sustained their respective economic miracles as they navigated waves of globalisation and other international challenges from 1990 until 2022.

The subtitle of the book refers to the 'economic resurgence' of the two countries since 1945, something that resonates with the widespread reference to their 'economic miracles' in the post-war period. I have used this concept in this introduction, and, in many of the part and chapter titles that follow, there is frequent use of terms associated with miracles, magic, and the supernatural. This sits somewhat uncomfortably, of course, with the fact that the book is fundamentally dedicated to explanation and elucidation. But rest assured that there is no resort in the narrative that follows to explanations involving wizardry or the occult. The terms and imagery have in fact been chosen advisedly. There must, after all, be a sense of wonder at the spectacular accomplishments of these two countries in the global economy, business, and technology, achievements which are envied by many, and which some have tried to emulate. At the same time, there must and will also be due recognition of the many scandals and transgressions that have accompanied these successes, demonstrating some of the foibles of the societies that produced them.

Part I

NO MERE INCANTATION
Rising from the Ashes of Defeat, 1945 to the Early 1950s

1 # FROM FOE TO FRIEND
The Allied Military Occupation of Germany and Japan

Descent into Chaos

Novelist Thomas Pynchon called it 'The Zone'.[1]

When Allied forces converged on Nazi Germany in spring 1945, the 'Thousand-Year Reich' dissolved into chaos after just twelve years of existence. The Nazi Party – and the government it controlled – evaporated, practically overnight. Business and the economy ground to a halt. As Germany surrendered to the Allies on 8 May 1945, longstanding power relationships had already been fundamentally disrupted. There was no clear indication of what might emerge in their place.

Officially, the defeated nation, after having its pre-war borders moved westwards at the insistence of the Soviets, was divided into four zones of occupation. It was presided over, although only nominally at first, by the British, the Americans, the French, and the Soviets: the victorious Allied powers. In practice, however, late spring and summer 1945 constituted a nightmarish journey through a lawless land for many. It was an odyssey enacted against the backdrop of cities bombed to rubble (Figure 1.1), energy shortages, and limited availability of food and other necessities. About 6 million of those who made their way through the ravaged landscape were malnourished and exhausted foreign forced labourers and slaves. They sought to return home to France, Belgium, Italy, Poland, or one of the other war-torn countries of central and eastern Europe.

Figure 1.1 British troops survey bombing damage in Berlin, 1945. United Archives/Getty Images

Streaming in droves in the other direction were millions of ethnic German refugees. Viewed as potential pawns in causing yet another war, they were dispossessed and driven from places such as the Sudetenland in Czechoslovakia, Silesia in Poland, and the Volga region in the Soviet Union. Between 1945 and 1950, about 12 million of them ended up in the four zones of occupation, which, by 1949, became the two post-war German states.

These millions of unwilling nomads trudging through the post-war German landscape were joined by hundreds of willing wanderers who were in much better physical condition. They also had a clear mission. The swarms of expert teams of scientists, engineers, and businessmen from the Allied countries moved into The Zone in the immediate aftermath of German defeat to try to make sense of the situation – and to exploit it for their own ends.

Dutch-American atomic scientist Samuel Goudsmit from the Manhattan Project led a group of experts in the crucial 'Alsos Mission'.

He and his team entered Germany even before the fighting ended to make sure the Americans and their Allies knew just how far the Nazi atomic bomb effort had progressed. The Mission also guaranteed that the Americans were first to reach top German physicists such as Werner Heisenberg and Otto Hahn, denying them to their erstwhile allies, the French. Then, under the umbrella of Operation Epsilon, American and British specialists spirited Heisenberg, Hahn, and eight other high-ranking German physicists away to Cambridgeshire in England in July 1945. There, the scientists were interned in Farm Hall, a large country house specially kitted out with electronic bugs so that Allied experts could eavesdrop on their conversations.[2]

The Allied specialists duly recorded the German scientists' initial gasps of disbelief when informed that the first atomic bomb had been dropped on Hiroshima on 6 August 1945. Then, after Heisenberg and the others discovered that the news was in fact true, Allied eavesdroppers heard the physicists excitedly try to figure out just how the bomb worked. The exchanges confirmed what the Alsos Mission had already established: the Germans had not got very far with their nuclear weapons project, despite having the lion's share of the best physicists in the world.

Meanwhile, Operation Paperclip hoovered up rocket scientists and aeronautical engineers, including the notorious head of the V-2 ballistic missile programme, Wernher von Braun, whose creations were responsible for a reign of terror in Antwerp and London in the latter stages of the war. Many of these scientists and engineers were transferred to the United States – illegally, and in spite of their clear Nazi credentials. Even their involvement in the use of slave labour at the Dora underground concentration camp, where V-2s were built, did nothing to impede the transfer. Instead, within days of being rounded up in Germany, von Braun and the other 'rocket scientists', who would later play vital roles in the development of ballistic missiles and in training aeronautical engineers in the United States, were on covert flights to America. There, they were provided with American passports and, eventually, given security clearances.[3]

Von Braun ultimately played a key role in the US space programme and was instrumental in ensuring that Americans would be the first to walk on the moon in 1969. And he worked alongside other Nazi-era scientists brought to the United States for the same purpose. Arthur Rudolph, the developer of the Saturn V rocket that lifted the

Apollo astronauts into outer space, was one of them. When his role in working thousands of concentration camp inmates to death in the V-2 programme finally came under public scrutiny in the early 1980s, Rudolph fled the United States for his native Germany – notably, neither this revelation nor Rudolph's flight from justice resulted from any remorse on the part of the US government for having recruited him in the first place. Hubertus Strughold, the 'father of space medicine', was also part of the NASA team. Strughold gained some of his insights from data gathered in experiments done on concentration camp inmates and prisoners of war in the Third Reich. Ironically, many of these scientist-refugees from Nazi Germany first plied their trade in Huntsville, Alabama, in the Deep South, where the nascent US civil rights movement was gathering momentum.[4]

At the same time, enormous numbers of experts seconded to Allied military units from industry descended on the defeated nation.[5] Their task was to collect detailed data on the state of German technology and business. Urgent aid in prosecuting the ongoing war against Japan again formed the initial justification, but taking commercial advantage was certainly another motivation. Companies such as Imperial Chemical Industries (ICI), DuPont, and Union Carbide, for instance, were keen to find out about wartime developments of new plastics and other substitute materials at German chemical firm IG Farbenindustrie AG. Meanwhile, engineers at Ampex, a firm only established in 1944, were anxious to learn all they could about the magnetic tape-recording technology pioneered at IG Farben in the 1930s. Partly with the help of information gathered in Germany, the American company went on to develop sophisticated reel-to-reel tape-recording hardware in conjunction with Bing Crosby and other prominent musicians.

It was immediately obvious to the experts that many ideas developed in Nazi Germany had great commercial value. Tensions therefore soon emerged among the Allied powers as they scurried to secure the most lucrative technologies. Even more intense competition emerged in the area of national security, as the former Allies scrambled to get their hands on the cream of the crop of German engineers and scientists. The 'brain chase', as one French scholar has termed it,[6] was not a business for the faint-hearted. None of those involved was above kidnapping, intimidation, or bribery to get what they wanted. Human war booty like Wernher von Braun was highly prized – and rightly so. Without him, the Americans might not have won the space race. Had the Soviets got to von Braun first, perhaps it would have been them, and not the Americans, planting their flag among the moon's craters in 1969. If only for this reason, no moral scruples could stand in the way of getting hold of – or holding onto – such highly valued individuals, even if they were deeply tainted with the crimes of the Nazi regime. Teams of German engineers and scientists located in the Soviet zone discovered this to their chagrin in October 1946, when they were awoken early in the morning and spirited away to the Soviet Union in the last major operation of this sort. Indeed, throughout this early occupation period, the Soviets and Americans competed most intensely.[7] The Cold War in science and technology got off to a quick start by late spring 1945, even before the Second World War itself had ended.

* * *

Chaos and disunity in defeated Germany were only to be expected at the end of a long and brutal war. For this reason, the Allies deliberately planned to avoid these anticipated problems by devising schemes to ensure an orderly transition to peace, plans which were agreed at the highest level in conjunction with the military victory. The last of the European war's major Allied conferences was held at the resort of Yalta in the Soviet Crimea in February 1945, three months before Germany officially surrendered. There, the leaders of the Big Three met in the magnificent Livadia Palace, the 116-room summer retreat of the last Russian Czar, Nicholas II. Confident of impending Allied victory over Nazi Germany, Josef Stalin, Franklin D. Roosevelt, and Winston Churchill faced one another across a round table in the largest and most luxurious chamber of the Italian Renaissance-style villa.

Amidst portraits of members of the Russian Imperial dynasty, with Churchill puffing on his trademark cigar and Roosevelt and Stalin chain-smoking cigarettes, the three most powerful men in the world set about redrafting the map of central and eastern Europe – carefully, radically, and fundamentally. First, they moved German borders westwards by awarding large swaths of East Prussia to Poland. Newly recreated Poland, in turn, had its former borders relocated to the west into what used to be parts of Germany. The Polish territory evacuated in the east was then ceded to the Soviet Union. In the process, the wartime Allied leaders carved out a Soviet sphere of influence in central and eastern Europe that would last until the 1990s.[8]

As confirmed at Yalta, the Big Three planned to divide defeated Germany among themselves into separately governed zones of occupation. They would guarantee administrative, economic, and political coordination among the zones through an Allied Control Council. Meanwhile, Germany's capital, Berlin, located deep in the Soviet zone of occupation, would itself be divided into separate zones. The western Allies would have access to Berlin from their occupation zones via road, rail, and air, through designated corridors in the Soviet zone. It was as simple as that. What could possibly go wrong?

***

It was not long, of course, before the fog of combat and rapidly changing political circumstances conspired to disrupt these carefully formulated plans. American forces overshot their agreed zonal boundaries during the last of the fighting in Germany. The United States therefore had boots on the ground well inside the Soviet zone by the time Germany surrendered in May 1945. And, when the Americans withdrew to their designated zone a month later, the Soviets' initial pleasant surprise rapidly turned into deep consternation. Russian troops discovered that US forces had taken the opportunity when withdrawing to their own zone to relocate dozens of experts and managers from Zeiss, the high-tech optics company, confirmation again of the start of a cold war in science and technology. The former Zeiss employees evacuated from the headquarters in Jena eventually set up a West German firm to rival East German Zeiss.[9]

In the meantime, British diplomats had begun to worry that the Americans might pull out entirely from Europe soon after the war's end, just as they had after the First World War. Fearing Soviet domination would ensue, Churchill made a bold suggestion. Calling his counterparts together, he convinced his US allies and the reluctant Soviets to grant a fourth zone of occupation in Germany to France. Churchill was delighted with the result, of course. He neglected, however, to ensure that the French received an invitation to the final wartime Allied conference in Potsdam, just outside Berlin. There, in July and August 1945, the plot thickened when there were fateful changes at the helm of two of the Big Three countries. Stalin remained the one constant presence at the Potsdam conference. But Harry S. Truman replaced FDR, who passed away in April. Churchill himself went home about halfway through the conference and never returned. A Labour electoral victory in summer 1945 instead saw a new British Prime Minister, Clement Attlee, join Stalin and Truman in Potsdam. The three leaders agreed in the Potsdam Declaration of 26 July 1945 to treat the four zones of occupied Germany as a single economic unit. But the French, who had of course not been party to the Declaration, did not feel obliged to comply.[10]

**

The Potsdam Declaration also involved a commitment on the part of the Big Three to join forces to defeat Japan. The Soviets duly declared war against the Japanese on 9 August, revoking a longstanding cease-fire agreement from the middle of September 1939. Nonetheless, it was blindingly obvious to all that the Soviet motivation for this declaration of war stemmed more from a desire to gain influence over the post-war occupation of Japan than from a sense of solidarity with the western Allies. It was in any case clearly hastened by the American atomic bomb attacks on Hiroshima and Nagasaki on 6 and 9 August 1945. Japan's surrender shortly after the Nagasaki attack, on 15 August (and only six days after the Soviet declaration of war) meant that there was no time for anyone other than the Americans to take control of the defeated country.

What US occupation forces encountered in Japan in the immediate aftermath of the war was, in many ways, at least as dismal and harrowing as what they had experienced earlier in Germany. A relatively poor country with limited natural resources compared with the other major combatants, Japan had squeezed its people harder than any of the others, especially in the final stages of the war. Many therefore emerged from the conflict weak and malnourished, and food and energy shortages prevailed even after the fighting ground to a halt. Just as in Germany, bombing had destroyed masses of housing stock (Figure 1.2). And many Japanese, displaced because of the requirements of war production, due to bombing destruction, or because they had served in the armed forces either at home or abroad, wandered, apparently aimlessly, through the desolate landscape.[11]

In contrast to Germany, there were far fewer foreign workers in post-war Japan. The Japanese war economy had been every bit as brutal as the German one, mercilessly exploiting foreign labourers,

Figure 1.2 Emperor Hirohito inspecting bombing damage in Tokyo, 1945. Universal Images Group/Getty Images

who were frequently enslaved. And some of these foreign workers were located in Japan, especially in coal mining, where about a third of the workforce were Koreans and an additional 10 per cent Chinese prisoners of war.[12] But mining was the exception. Unlike Germany, where workers were mostly imported to work in the factories of the Reich, Japan primarily used – and often used up – foreign workers *in situ* in their home countries to provide food, raw materials, and some manufactured goods vital to the war effort. Unlike in Germany, then, where refugees from a wide range of ethnic groups roamed the landscape, there were only Japanese, Korean, and Taiwanese displaced people in Japan at the end of the war.

Again, though, the millions of civilians and former soldiers travelling through Japan's post-defeat desolation were joined by hundreds of well-fed and highly motivated Allied investigators. They went about their work just as they had done in Germany, although there was virtually no interest in spiriting away Japanese engineers and scientists to Allied countries. There was also far less focus on possible technology transfers. And, while there was a major effort, as in Germany, to uncover just how much progress Japan had made towards building an atomic bomb (the clear answer was not much),[13] this and all other investigations were carried out almost exclusively by Americans. Officially, the occupation of Japan was a combined Allied effort, just as in Germany. In practice, though, it was completely different: the Americans were virtually unhampered in doing exactly as they pleased.

Taking Control: Punishment in Peacetime

Despite Germany's and Japan's different circumstances immediately after the end of the war, the two occupations had much in common. And this was not at all surprising. The Second World War had been a savage 'war without mercy' both in Europe and in the Pacific, one in which racism and ethnic cleansing loomed large.[14] Inevitably, it had to end in a peace without mercy. Accordingly, as victory by Allied forces over the Thousand-Year Reich and Japan became increasingly certain, members of the Allied coalition prepared to impose a draconian peace. The Americans, the only combatant nation unaffected directly by fighting on their home turf, proved particularly industrious planners. While there were, of course, variations in emphasis between them and their Allies, all plans for the initial post-war occupation of Germany and Japan were predicated on punishment.[15]

But how best to punish? Allied officials entering the defeated nations were well supplied with a list of excellent answers to that question.

- First of all, don't repeat the mistakes made after the First World War. Make sure that the Germans and Japanese know unequivocally that they lost. And ensure that the military occupation lasts long enough to emphasise the point.
- Second, root out National Socialism and Nazis, as well as extreme Japanese nationalism and ultranationalists.
- Third, get rid not only of weapons and ammunition, but also of the ability to produce them in future.
- Fourth, destroy massive concentrations of economic power embodied in monopolies and cartels. This was a particularly high priority for the Americans, especially those who had cut their teeth in President Franklin Roosevelt's New Deal.

These four principles underpinned all the directives issued to the American military governor in Germany – initially General Dwight

D. Eisenhower – as implemented and transformed by his deputy and eventual successor, pragmatic logistical wizard General Lucius D. Clay. The same basic directives were issued to their British, French, and Soviet counterparts in Germany. And in the Pacific, a very similar set of guidelines went to mercurial, arrogant, and highly opinionated General Douglas MacArthur, the Supreme Commander of the Allied Powers (SCAP) in Japan.

The devil, though, lay in the detail. Everyone could agree, for example, that it would be wise to rid Germany of Nazis and Japan of ultranationalists. But who were these pariahs? The Nazi Party at least had a central file, so, on the face of it, identifying Party members should have been easy. For many Soviet and French officials, however, all Germans were Nazis, in spirit if not in formal affiliation. They thus saw absolutely no need to go to the bother of poring through files to determine membership. Strict supervision to prevent the Germans from any further mischief marked the only sensible way forward.

The Americans, on the other hand, realised that the Party register was a start rather than an endpoint for identifying Nazis. Mere membership was far too crude a criterion. Did the person really believe in Nazi ideology, or did they join the Party simply because a lot of other people were doing so, or perhaps because their business demanded it? To answer these questions, Germans in the US zone had to complete a questionnaire, the *Fragebogen*, which they submitted to a review board. The board then conducted hearings to determine whether the person was indeed a Party member, and, if so, at what level of commitment (true believer, fellow traveller, etc.). If cleared, the person was issued a so-called *Persilschein*, a certificate of ideological cleanliness (or, perhaps, whitewashing) named after the well-known laundry detergent. Needless to say, the process was all very complicated and time-consuming. Before long, the denazification effort was abandoned, even in the US zone. In Japan, things were even more complex, not least because there was not even a central registry of ultranationalists to consult in order to get the ball rolling.

For the economy, the punishment to be meted out seemed much more straightforward. Joint Chiefs of Staff directive 1067 (JCS 1067) for Germany (along with parallel directives issued by the other occupying powers) and JCS 1380 for Japan carried specific instructions on what was *not* to be done. The Military Governor, for instance, was explicitly barred from undertaking measures to resuscitate the defeated nations' economies. There were also direct orders to destroy war-related industries and to prohibit any production or research and development related to atomic energy or aeronautical engineering.

But destruction of war-related industries proved extraordinarily difficult, not least because, like Nazis or ultranationalists, such industries were in practice extremely hard to detect, let alone pinpoint. Tank production? Certainly, this should be eliminated. However, tanks were produced in the same kind of factories, by the same people, and using the same machines, materials, and skills, which were deployed in the production of any other vehicle. And vehicle manufacturing was sorely needed for the purposes of the occupation. Dynamite? Here, production prohibition seemed a no-brainer, except for the fact that explosives were in fact essential for removal of debris, civil engineering (for instance bridge and tunnel construction), and the reopening of coal mines. And what about synthetic petroleum products made from coal, which had fuelled the German air force and, to a lesser extent, Japanese military aircraft? A production ban appeared even more sensible. Synthetic fuel plants, though, could easily be retrofitted to refine heavy petroleum oils into motor fuels for use in the civilian economy, thus saving foreign exchange that would otherwise be expended on imported finished petroleum products and lowering the costs of the occupation. Consequently, punishing properly, severely, and uniformly proved far more difficult than Allied planners had envisaged, although that did not stop them from implementing a broad set of programmes designed primarily for that purpose.

These programmes of punishment slowed and eventually stopped, however, when the fundamental fragility of the economies of the defeated countries became obvious. But what is more notable is their surprising – and fully unintended – consequences. For the ultimate implications of these initiatives resounded far beyond the occupation period for the economy and society in both countries, and indeed the world.

Divide and Prosper

The subtitle of Joseph Borkin and Charles Walsh's bestselling 1943 book, *Germany's Master Plan*, said it all: 'The story of an industrial offensive'.[16] The two authors, prominent trustbusters in Franklin Roosevelt's New Deal administration, insisted in their analysis that the conflict was caused by the global ambitions of large German firms.

These companies represented a dangerous and overwhelming concentration of economic power. It was a view endorsed in the foreword by no less a light than Thurman Arnold, then head of the US Justice Department's Antitrust Division.

The central character in Borkin and Walsh's drama was IG Farbenindustrie AG, by most measures the largest chemical company in the world at the time. IG Farben formed Borkin's obsession for decades: he later characterised it as his 'Moby Dick'.[17] And the story Borkin told remained consistent across the decades: by virtue of pioneering work in new and challenging technologies undertaken by its chemists and engineers in the 1920s and 1930s, the IG supplied the Nazi war machine with vital strategic goods. This enabled the Nazi leadership to dream of domestic self-sufficiency in materials that had previously been imported. The firm's strategically crucial output included synthetic fuels and rubber made from domestic German coal.

Not incidentally for American-based trustbusters such as Borkin and Walsh, the German behemoth also cooperated closely until the late 1930s with DuPont and Standard Oil of New Jersey (Esso), powerful US firms hungry for German technology and willing to pay in cash or kind for access to it. Indeed, cooperation between the IG and Esso beginning in the 1920s provided substantial funding for the development of the IG's synthetic fuels technology, which later fuelled Luftwaffe planes. The very same ties with Esso later enabled imports of the anti-knock compound tetraethyl lead, an essential additive to enrich the Luftwaffe's aviation fuel. Through its international ties, IG Farben thus put the finishing touches on the Nazi war machine, enabling it to stand poised for war.

During the conflict, the IG and its top managers also became intimately involved in the exploitation of the chemical industry in occupied Europe. More ominously still, they were implicated in some of the most heinous crimes of the Nazi era. These included the use of slave and forced labour in most IG factories and, chillingly, the establishment of a large IG Farben plant near the Nazi death camp at Auschwitz. The IG factory there was constructed and operated by an enslaved workforce. Underfed and severely mistreated, the workers were housed in a purpose-built concentration camp that was owned by the firm, but operated by the Nazi Party's notorious SS.

The putative role played by Germany's largest chemical firm in quite literally fuelling the war, along with the company's clear involvement in carrying out some of the darkest horrors that accompanied it, placed the IG squarely in the sights of Allied occupiers. The Americans in particular soon converged on two main objectives: to break up the chemical behemoth into successor companies that were smaller and much less powerful; and to prosecute top IG managers for crimes committed during the Nazi period.

* * *

Initial US plans for the breakup of IG Farben were radical.[18] The Americans insisted, for example, on dismissal of all Nazi-era managerial staff. They also intended to set up separate companies not just for each factory, but for each sub-plant *within* every factory. But such radical reforms could be realised only through close cooperation with the other occupiers because the bulk of the disgraced firm's assets lay outside direct US control. The headquarters and main factories of BASF, another of the world-class German chemical companies that had formed the IG, for instance, were in the French zone of occupation, while those of Bayer, another world beater, lay in the British zone. And many of IG Farben's newest, largest, and most highly integrated factories were in the Soviet zone or in newly reconstituted Poland. Policy towards the IG and its personnel in each of the other zones thus diverged substantially from US wishes, not least because each former ally saw commercial advantages in fostering close technological and business links with 'their' part of the IG.

Sometimes wildly differing interests among the Allies and the complexity of the firm itself, then, combined to ensure that the breakup of IG Farben was not completed until the early 1950s. By then, the Cold War and the East/West division of Germany intervened to help shape the final outcome. The Soviets, true to form, nationalised the factories in their zone. In West Germany, on the other hand, extensive jockeying among the other three powers, joined eventually by strong German interests, resulted in the establishment of a small number of large companies rather than the large number of small ones championed initially by radical American trustbusters. What is more, the main successor companies in the west corresponded broadly to the IG predecessor companies. These included Hoechst, BASF, and Bayer, among others, as well as a rump corporation, IG Farbenindustrie AG in Liquidation. IG in Liquidation was essentially a troubled asset company. It pursued, ever more hopelessly, compensation for property seizures in communist East Germany and Soviet-dominated central and eastern Europe. And, more importantly, it served as a lightning rod protecting the eventually very large and powerful chemical-producer successors of the IG against claims for compensation from Jewish and other forced and slave labourers.[19]

Ironically, the breakup of the chemical behemoth, motivated by Allied desires to punish and disempower, had precisely the opposite effect. The successors of the IG in West Germany, for the most part recreations of strong firms that had existed prior to the establishment of the gigantic corporation, resumed long and distinguished traditions in technology and world trade. Here, they benefited handsomely from the streamlining of operations caused by the breakup of the previously unwieldy IG. By the 1960s, the three major successors all ranked among the top five chemical firms in the world by sales. What is more, they were effectively absolved by virtue of the intercession of IG Farben in Liquidation of any responsibility for the corporation's criminality during the Nazi period.

* * *

The second key American objective for the post-war treatment of the IG was to bring the firm's managers to justice. Achieving this seemed well in hand, at least by 1948. In 1947, US prosecutors had managed to put all members of the IG management board on trial before an American court in Nuremberg. And their efforts yielded some clear successes: more than half of the twenty-three defendants were found guilty the following year.[20] Top IG manager Otto Ambros, for example, was sentenced to eight years' imprisonment for slavery and mass murder by virtue of being in charge of IG Farben's factory at Auschwitz. This was, of course, far more severe than the slap on the wrist that was the norm for those convicted of white-collar crimes.

But, despite this apparent success, there is no doubt that American officials soon felt stymied in their search for justice. As the US prosecutor at the trial, Josiah DuBois, later claimed, the sentences imposed on most of those found guilty were 'light enough to please a chicken thief'. And even Ambros, who began serving his relatively long sentence in 1948, was pardoned by the US High Commissioner in Germany, John McCloy, in 1951, along with other industrialists who had been convicted of war crimes. Ambros had served just over two years' internment. The pardon formed part of a general rehabilitation of German business elites in the context of the Cold War.[21]

Worse still, although Ambros never subsequently held a position in one of the large IG successors, he remained an active participant in the German and international chemical industry until not long before his death in 1990. He served as a board member of several German companies and as a consultant for such firms as W. R. Grace in America and The Distillers Company in the United Kingdom. What is more, he and the other members of the IG managing board maintained close contacts with one another and with the leaders of the key successor companies. In fact, they met up socially on a regular basis until at least the end of the 1950s. One such dinner meeting of the 'members of the managing board of the former IG Farbenindustrie', held on 6 February 1959, was hosted by Carl Wurster, the chairman of the board of BASF, a major IG successor firm. Virtually all of those tried at Nuremberg attended that dinner, accompanied by their wives. Ambros and his spouse sat close to Dr Ulrich Haberland, the CEO of Bayer AG, another of the main IG successors.[22]

* * *

The breakup of IG Farben was protracted and messy. It was also one of the few examples of trustbusting of a large German firm, not least because of Allied disunity in Germany. The same did not hold for Japan, where the Americans were firmly in the driver's seat. There, decartelisation and trustbusting were widespread and thoroughgoing, extending to the breakup of all of the former *zaibatsu* (the sprawling financial and industrial conglomerates that had carried out Japanese military production). But the outcome of this process, which was also fundamentally punitive in motivation, was the opposite of what was intended, just as it had been in Germany.

The breakup of the Riken, the Institute for Physical and Chemical Research, illustrates this well. A peculiarly Japanese institution, the Riken was at once a product of Japan's relative backwardness compared with the United Kingdom, the United States, and Germany for most of the twentieth century and, on the other hand, a prime example of Japanese institutional innovation.

Japan started industrialising rapidly in the last third of the nineteenth century, with most growth coming from incremental improvements in traditional manufacturing industries and from textiles.[23] But great strides were also made in technologically sophisticated industries, such as electric power and, crucially, military-related industries. The pace and extent of these advances, however, depended heavily on ideas and implements borrowed from abroad, especially from Germany and the United States. Both Germany and America provided a range of goods to Japan, including, most importantly, the precision tools fundamental to industrialisation and technical development in all sectors. Moreover, many of the new technologies were science-based. Germany, as the leading global scientific power in physics, chemistry, and other theoretical sciences, was consequently a particularly valued partner for the Japanese.

Then came the First World War. Japan, far removed from the fighting in Europe, viewed the conflict as an opportunity to realise a long-cherished goal of seizing Shantung Province, a German colony in China. For this reason, the country joined the war on the side of the Allies. Japan was therefore cut off from German science (although the Allied blockade had this effect in any case), and leading figures in government, industry, and universities cast about for a way to address the deficit.

The Riken formed the centrepiece for dealing with the dilemma.[24] Founded in 1917, the new organisation was modelled heavily on the German Kaiser Wilhelm Society, which comprised several prestigious institutes, such as the Kaiser Wilhelm Institute for Physics, established in 1914 and directed from 1917 by no less a figure than Albert Einstein. But Japan was not wealthy enough to afford a suite of institutes, and its scientific basis was still far more modest than Germany's. So, the Japanese improvised institutionally, in the process creating something completely new.

A non-profit foundation, the Riken was funded initially by a start-up grant from the government. It brought the physical and chemical sciences under one roof. Furthermore, because ongoing funding presented existential difficulties from the outset, Riken personnel quickly established much closer relationships with industry than was typical at the Kaiser Wilhelm institutes. They did so initially by selling patents. When that did not prove lucrative enough to support its scientific ambitions, though, the Riken established its own manufacturing operations.

Through this, and under the leadership of the cerebral aristocrat Viscount Masatoshi Okochi (1878–1952) between 1921 and

1946, it played a pivotal role in promoting what Okochi called 'scientific industry'. Okochi championed this essentially technocratic concept in his writings, although somewhat more modestly in the Riken's actual industrial operations. However, his strong advocacy of flexible mass production systems, continuous improvement, and focus on quality presaged the later Toyota system. What is more, during Okochi's directorship of the Institute, by the late 1930s, the Riken employed about 1,800 people directly. It also owned (and often operated) some 60 high-tech subsidiaries with around 40,000 employees. By then, the Riken was one of the most powerful economic actors in Japan, and it accordingly played a crucial role in Japan's war effort. Not surprisingly, then, the Americans considered the Riken a *zaibatsu*, and they targeted it for breakup.

As was the case with IG Farben, though, disentangling the Riken was a long and complex process, although simplified dramatically by the American monopoly over occupation policy in Japan. The ultimate outcome, however, was similar. What started out as punitive action by the occupation forces led ultimately to the breakup of an unwieldy firm into leaner and ultimately more competitive successors. The Riken itself continued to exist, although at the price of losing its director, Okochi, and all of its manufacturing operations. After the breakup, it instead focused on its original mission: basic (and some applied) research into physics and chemistry. The Riken's manufacturing subsidiaries became independent companies, some of which were very successful indeed. The most prominent of them was Ricoh, eventually a world beater in electronic printing and copying.

Mass Production, Quality Production, and the Kamikaze Origins of the Bullet Train

The Luftwaffe's Junkers Ju 88-series airplanes served as workhorses in Germany's air war between 1939 and 1945. They rained down terror and destruction in the Battle of Britain, when the Third Reich was in the ascendancy. And their pilots did their utmost to protect the country against relentless Allied air assaults when Nazi Germany was in steep decline. The Japanese air force's Mitsubishi A6M Zero played a similarly iconic role in the Pacific War.

These and other aircraft deployed by the two main Axis powers in the Second World War were the products of visionary engineering and design, firmly grounded in sophisticated aeronautical science and engineering. Manufacturing airplanes in quantity required extremely high levels of precision, specialist metalworking, and strict quality control that only a handful of nations could generate. It also required substantial innovations in what we would now call outsourcing and supply chain management. After all, mass production of aircraft depended invariably on multiple suppliers, who had to be trained, coordinated, and monitored carefully and effectively. The airplanes produced were the highest-quality outputs of a well-oiled industrial system. They were also a large part of the reason why the Axis armed forces were so dominant in the first part of the war; and why, later, Germany and Japan could for a time stave off inevitable impending defeat.

The Allies knew this all too well. And so, the military governors in post-war Germany and Japan imposed a wholesale ban on production of aircraft and on aeronautical research and development, immediately and for the foreseeable future. A key industry and its scientific establishment, which employed thousands, including many highly qualified engineers and scientists, ceased to exist, suddenly and entirely.

One important question followed immediately. What would – or should – happen to this key industry's technical personnel if they could no longer ply their trade? There were two distinct groups here. On one side stood a relatively small number of elite designers and engineers. On the other stood a fairly large number of firms that constituted aviation industry supplier networks, along with their relatively large number of employees. Their fates would prove somewhat different in post-war Germany and Japan.

* * *

As we have seen, even before the fighting had completely ceased, the elite 'rocket scientists' and aeronautical engineers of the Third Reich occupied a prominent position on Allied target lists for what became known as 'intellectual reparations'. The United States managed to capture or lure some of the most prominent members of this small group through Project Paperclip and other initiatives. The Soviets, too, after some delay, managed to recruit – through a combination of sometimes very sweet carrots and often severely wielded sticks – teams of second- and third-tier aeronautical engineers to reshape and reinvigorate the post-1945 Soviet aviation and space programmes.[25]

The influence of the scientists and engineers who moved following Germany's defeat to the United States or the Soviet Union on the military-aviation capabilities of the two Cold War adversaries would be difficult to underestimate. As Tom Bower put it, the first direct military confrontation between the Americans and the Soviets in the Korean War of 1950–1951:

> can be viewed, on the technical level, as a trial of strength between two teams of Germans: those hired by America and those hired by the Soviet Union. The aerial dogfights between Soviet MiG-15s and American F-86 Sabres – both designed by German engineers – dispelled for many their doubts about the expediency of Germany's scientific expertise.[26]

These elite German designers and engineers had a pronounced impact on military aviation in the United States and the Soviet Union, in large part because they were plugged into new or existing *domestic* supply and production networks in America and the USSR. In contrast, the German supplier and production networks from the wartime aviation industry, which was now banned, remained in-country, now unmoored from their main customers. After a short hiatus, the networks reconstituted themselves in West Germany, but this time in the service of the automobile industry, which was engaged in quality mass production by the early 1950s.

For instance, a largely intact Ju 88 supplier network consisting of a number of small- and medium-sized producers of specialised parts began working with Daimler Benz not long after the war's end to develop the auto firm's mass-production system.[27] Together, they manufactured large numbers of high-quality Mercedes automobiles in the 1950s and 1960s. Mercedes-Benz, BMW, and Audi therefore joined Volkswagen (which, initially through the good offices of the British occupation authorities, began to realise its potential as a mass producer through the iconic Beetle) in delivering an automotive industry that was, and still remains, the envy of the world.

* * *

Allied restrictions on Japanese aircraft production resulted in a similar outcome to that seen in Germany, despite taking a slightly different path. This was mainly because the Japanese aviation industry was less well developed than the German one, and rocket technology in particular had not made much progress there. Lingering racism no doubt played a role as well. In any event, the Americans showed little interest in Japanese aeronautical engineers and designers. And so, the members of this elite group stayed in their home country rather than decamping (or being forcefully decamped) to the United States.

Banned in Japan from working in the industry in which they had cut their teeth, however, these designers and engineers were now available for employment in the Japanese automotive industry. They brought to the table experience in, and ideas about, precision manufacturing, advanced materials, and quality control. They and advocates of science-based industry, such as Okochi from the Riken, had dreamt of even more sophisticated design, manufacturing, and quality assurance than had been possible to achieve during the war. Indeed, in the last stages of the conflict and in its immediate aftermath, these men began to formulate many of the building blocks of the Toyota system for inventory and quality control. For this reason, they were also highly receptive to the innovations of American wartime manufacturing, including W. Edwards Deming's statistical quality control systems, which were as neglected by post-war American manufacturers as they were embraced by the Japanese.[28]

Moreover, as in Germany, dense networks of parts suppliers in Japan had been trained, directed, and disciplined during the war in high-quality precision manufacturing by the large airplane producers. These networks, which had once enabled quality mass production of aircraft, were now available to work as suppliers to nascent automobile producers, including Nissan, Mitsui, Toyota, and, eventually, Honda. In Japan, as in Germany, then, an unintended consequence of Allied punishment of aviation was the fostering of another leading light of global engineering: the Japanese automotive industry.

Still, not all of the elite designers and engineers from the aviation industry could be accommodated in the still embryonic Japanese automobile sector in the late 1940s and early 1950s. The prohibition of airplane production thus had another surprising, yet highly significant, effect – on the rail industry.[29] Japanese railways, locomotives, and rolling stock constituted a key target for Allied bombers. The need for reconstruction following the war was acute. In addition, officials in charge of the state-owned Japanese National Railway (JNR) and its affiliated Railway Technical Research Institute (RTRI) grew increasingly alarmed about levels of unemployment among engineers in the immediate post-war period. The result was that JNR and RTRI appointed a substantial number of engineers and designers previously employed in the aircraft industry.

JNR and its research institute became increasingly ambitious during the occupation period. The focus changed from mere reconstruction to radical new technological departures, involving high-speed trains in particular. The aeronautical engineers soon proved not just handy to have around, but absolutely essential. In fact:

> At least four laboratory leaders with wartime experience in aeronautics contributed markedly to bullet train development. For instance, Tatsuo Yamamura, a wind tunnel technician in the Central Aeronautical Research Institute during the war, led a laboratory that developed electric motors for the high-speed train. The laboratory leader Ikuro Kumezawa, a wartime army engineer, developed the wiring mechanism that fed electric power to the bullet train.... At the RTRI, Doctor Tadanao Miki drew upon his wartime experience as a designer of dive-bomber[s].... His application of theoretical aerodynamics to the design of the streamlined car was a recipe for the bullet train that established its high-speed world record run in 1963.

The fourth laboratory leader was Dr. Tadashi Matsudaira, who had devised solutions to problems associated with severe flutter affecting high-speed, agile aircraft during the Second World War. He directed a team that devised the air suspension system vital for stability of bullet train rail cars.[30]

And so, even as the best and brightest German aeronautical engineers were busily designing and building jets, ballistic missiles, and spacecraft in their newfound American homes, then, the cream of Japanese aeronautical engineering was enacting one of the world's wonders in post-war transport infrastructure, the bullet train (*Shinkansen*). It was a performance that marked an important step in the unfolding of the post-war Japanese economic miracle.

The Enemy of My Enemy

On 22 June 1948, months of secret planning culminated in an operation carried out not only with military discipline and precision, but also with practically instant and long-lasting success. The objective was to replace the discredited Nazi-era Reichsmark (RM) in the western zones of occupation in Germany with a new currency, the Deutschmark (DM). Each person in the western zones received a basic allocation of DM 40 in crisp new banknotes, which had been printed in the United States, in exchange for RM 40; an additional DM 20 per person would follow. This ensured, for the briefest of moments to be sure, widespread economic equality. All other currency instruments (such as bank accounts) were exchanged at a much less favourable rate, on average DM 6.5 per RM 100. Almost immediately, shops began a brisk trade in goods that, since the war, had often been available only on the black market, and then only in exchange for alternatives to currency such as cigarettes. After the currency reform of June 1948, this 'Lucky Strike' economy disappeared. It was replaced by the first stirrings of what became the West German *Wirtschaftswunder*, or economic miracle.[31]

At about the same time, in mid-1948, aid from the United States began flowing into Europe under the Marshall Plan. Formally known as the European Recovery Programme, the Marshall Plan was announced by US Secretary of State George Marshall at a graduation ceremony at Harvard University on 5 June 1947. It provided essential dollars for the purchase of food, fuel, and machinery. Because of the conditions attached to the aid, moreover, western European countries also accumulated substantial funds in banks for industrial reconstruction, which provided much-needed investment in infrastructure, technology, and production plants. After some deliberation, the Americans included the western zones of Germany in the funding. They did so chiefly because the initial punitive policies in defeated Germany had given way to encouraging reconstruction.

The German currency reform and the Marshall Plan constituted the ultimate outcome of growing tensions between the western Allies and the Soviets. The Cold War that had started in science and technology already in spring 1945 gradually pervaded all interactions between the two opposing and gradually hardening blocs.

As the Cold War unfolded, the French, British, and American occupiers in Germany were driven closer together. Led by the wealthy and powerful Americans, the first step in this direction was taken already in 1947, when the British and American zones were combined into the Bizone. The addition of the French zone in 1948 then established what some called, perhaps in a nod to the Marx Brothers, 'Trizonia'.

The subsequent trizonal currency reform of June 1948 startled the Soviets, who responded angrily by closing off all rail and road access for the western Allies to Berlin with immediate effect. Within a few short weeks, as the suspension of land access to the former German capital escalated into a full-scale Berlin crisis, the American-led Airlift began supplying the city's western sectors with food and fuel. During most of the days that followed, and for virtually all of the next year, one plane landed every 45 seconds with their deliveries at the massive, monumental, Nazi-constructed Tempelhof airfield located in the city's American sector. Right up to the end of the Berlin crisis on 12 May 1949, the Soviets were unwilling to breach the letter of the agreements they had signed at Yalta and Potsdam regarding air access to Berlin. And so, astonishingly, Russian air-traffic controllers worked alongside their American, British, and French counterparts guiding the endless string of planes into Tempelhof.

The Soviets did, however, counter the western German currency reform directly by introducing a hastily improvised new currency, the *Ostmark*, into their zone. Germany was now divided in two economically. Political confirmation of the division followed in autumn 1949 with the formal creation of the Federal Republic of (West) Germany, a liberal democracy and capitalist economy dominated by elite groups from government, business, and banking from the pre-1945 period who had been restored to positions of power, and the (East) German Democratic Republic, a Soviet-style planned economy.

The establishment of two German successor states, each dominated by one of the main protagonists of the Cold War, stabilised political tensions in Europe to a large extent. The end of the first Berlin crisis in May 1949 attested to this. In the meantime, the primary battlefield for the Cold War moved to East Asia, where Soviet-backed Chinese communist forces managed to gain control of mainland China, establishing the People's Republic of China (PRC) on 1 October 1949. The still very new PRC, supported again by the Soviets, then moved militarily, in 1950, into the Korean peninsula, a former Japanese colony. General Douglas MacArthur, the Supreme Commander of the Allied Powers in Japan, took charge of US-led United Nations forces opposing the Chinese advance.

The upshot of all of this was that Japan became a key strategic location for US forces, serving in effect as a stationary aircraft carrier for American fighter jets and bombers. Procurement of food, other supplies, and some manufactured goods to sustain those US forces, moreover, stimulated the Japanese economy, providing much-needed foreign exchange. The Japanese, the previous archenemies of the United States in the Pacific, now also became trusted friends and allies of the Americans, supported – as the West Germans were by the Marshall Plan – by a number of aid programmes. Like the elites who had been restored to power in West Germany, they were partners whose opposition to communism was unimpeachable. And, not coincidentally, the Japanese, like the Germans, were already well along the road towards reconstruction, and they were now poised to enact their own sustained and extraordinarily successful economic miracle.

2 THE MIRACLE MAKERS
(Re-)Constructing Cooperative Capitalism

Nearly a century before the Second World War ended, pioneering political economist John Stuart Mill provided a cogent 'explanation of what has so often excited wonder, the great rapidity with which countries recover from a state of devastation'. Mill elaborated on the idea in a widely quoted passage from his 1848 *Principles of Political Economy*:

> An enemy lays waste a country by fire and sword, and destroys or carries away nearly all the moveable wealth existing in it: all the inhabitants are ruined, and yet, in a few years after, everything is much as it was before. This ... has been a subject of sterile astonishment ... [but] there is nothing at all wonderful in the matter. What the enemy have destroyed, would have been destroyed in a little time by the inhabitants themselves: the wealth which they so rapidly reproduce, would have needed to be reproduced and would have been reproduced in any case, and probably in as short a time. Nothing is changed, except that during the reproduction they have not now the advantage of consuming what had been produced previously.[1]

Mill's proposition anticipated what has become known as the 'reconstruction thesis', which economists and economic historians have used to explain Germany's and Japan's rapid recovery after 1945, and, most recently, to forecast rapid recovery from the economic devastation wrought by the COVID-19 pandemic.[2]

The long-term fallout of the pandemic that started in 2020 is still uncertain, but, at first glance at least, Mill and the proponents of the reconstruction thesis seem to have got it spot on in anticipating what would happen after 1945. The United States, of course, emerged from the Second World War physically unscathed and, in its aftermath, America led the world in technology, economic growth, and standard of living. However, West Germany and Japan were already by 1950 well on track to catch up with the United States. The speed with which that happened was breathtaking: both countries featured average GDP growth of nearly 9 per cent per year during the 1950s, while the US economy grew at about one-third that rate. And, although West Germany moderated considerably from this torrid pace in the 1960s, Japan – still somewhat poorer – carried on. Japan's GDP growth averaged nearly 10 per cent per year during the 1960s.

The numbers are objects of wonder, or perhaps, as Mill put it, of 'sterile astonishment'. And there might be some mileage in describing what happened as 'economic miracles'. But the post-war economic bounce-back for Germany and Japan was most certainly not a preordained conclusion, as proponents of the reconstruction thesis seem to imply. Nor was it a disembodied natural economic phenomenon. An economy, after all, is not a rubber band that, after being stretched, returns to its natural shape. Indeed, the German and Japanese economic miracles, such as they were, can only be explained through reference to people, to the hard work and skills of Germans and Japanese from all levels of society, as Mill recognised in a passage that is far less frequently cited:

> The possibility of a rapid repair of their disasters mainly depends on whether the country has been depopulated. If its effective population have not been extirpated at the time, and are not starved afterwards; then, with the same skill and knowledge which they had before, with their land and its permanent improvements undestroyed, and the more durable buildings probably unimpaired, or only partially injured, they have nearly all the requisites for their former amount of production. If there is as much of food left to them, or of valuables to buy food, as enables them by any amount of privation to

remain alive and in working condition, they will in a short time have raised as great a produce, and acquired collectively as great wealth and as great a capital, as before; by the mere continuance of that ordinary amount of exertion which they are accustomed to employ in their occupations.[3]

In other words, to explain the economic miracles in Germany and Japan after the Second World War, we need to pay close attention to the miracle *makers*, who drew upon 'skill and knowledge'. We also need to examine the networks that existed before and during the war. For what was at work was a fundamental refashioning of previously existing German and Japanese cooperative capitalism into something more suited both to the emerging post-war capitalist economic order and, not at all incidentally, to peaceful existence within it.

Constructing Capitalism with a Conscience in Western Germany, 1945–1966

Cigar-chomping, affable, and rotund – a 1963 newspaper article described him as 'roly-poly'[4] – West Germany's first Minister of Economics Ludwig Erhard (Figures 2.1 and 2.2) seemed to have come straight out of central casting as the symbol of the country's newfound prosperity in its economic miracle. Erhard was born in 1897 in Fürth, a small city in Bavaria. Following a commercial apprenticeship, he was drafted into the German Army in 1917, where he was seriously wounded. After the war had ended and he had recovered, Erhard entered Frankfurt University as a mature student in 1922, earning a doctorate in 1925. He subsequently started work as a lecturer at a commercial college and as a consumer marketing researcher in the Institute for the Economic Monitoring of German Finished Goods.[5]

Erhard continued to work in consumer research throughout the remainder of the Weimar Republic and into the Nazi period. For most people, these were harrowing times, in both economic and political terms. But, for an economist, the times were above all else *interesting*: inflation; depression; collapse of trade; increasing restrictions on foreign exchange, prices, labour; planning; war and destruction. Germany experienced this whole macabre range not just in theory, but in bleak practice. Erhard kept his head down for the most part during the Nazi period and the war. But he grew increasingly disillusioned

Figure 2.1 West German Economics Minister Ludwig Erhard, smoking a cigar and reading *Prosperity for All*, 1957. Keystone/Hulton Archive/ Getty Images

with authoritarian attempts to control and direct the economy in the service of political ideology. He pursued ideas about this and about post-war German economic reconstruction from 1942 as founder and director of the Nuremberg-based and industry-financed Institute for Industry Research, the forerunner of the influential Ifo Institute think-tank. His thoughts crystallised in a 1944 memo on 'War Financing and Debt Consolidation', which built upon the then politically hazardous assumption that Germany was about to lose the war. The memo attracted the attention of Carl Goerdeler, who managed, before being executed for his role in the 1944 plot to assassinate Adolf Hitler, to pass on word of it to fellow members of the German resistance.

The 1944 memo and further studies undertaken by Erhard and others at the institute in the latter stages of the war also constituted a ready-made treasure trove of data and recommendations for Erhard to pass on when occupation officers from the American Army assumed

Figure 2.2 West German Economics Minister Ludwig Erhard inspecting a model of a nuclear power station at the Hannover Industrial Fair, 1957. Keystone/Hulton Archive/Getty Images

control of Bavaria in the middle of April 1945. Ludwig Erhard was not shy in coming forward to them, and, clearly well informed and (at least as importantly) unencumbered by any hint of Nazi Party allegiance, he was attractive to the occupiers. They appointed him, in quick succession, to a number of prominent positions. He served first as Economic Advisor to the Military Government for Middle and Upper Franconia, and then, from 22 October 1945, as Minister for Trade and Commerce (Economics Minister) for the Bavarian State Government. The US Military Governor for Germany, General Lucius Clay, made the latter appointment, but Erhard's ideas proved less popular with his state government colleagues, and his term of office ended in December 1946, after Bavaria's first democratic elections.

Even before he left the Bavarian Cabinet, though, Erhard was angling for other means to influence post-war developments. He founded the Institute for Economic Observation and Policy Advice in Munich in the middle of July 1946, as a successor to his Nuremberg-based wartime Institute for Industry Research. Less than a year later, it was renamed the South German Institute for Economic Research, with a remit broadened to the whole of the US Zone of Occupation in Germany and, effectively, to the other western zones of the recently defeated country, as well as to its international economic relationships. Erhard astutely promoted the applied economics research of the Institute through intensive development of close academic contacts and relationships with nascent German state government officials, the occupation authorities, and, not incidentally, members of the press.

Cultivation of strong relationships with the military occupiers of Germany – and with the Americans in particular – was certainly essential to Erhard's success in gaining influence and eventually control over economic policy and practice in West Germany. Through his lobbying efforts, Erhard manoeuvred himself into appointment as Director of the Economic Administration of the Bizone (the combined British and American zones of occupation) in 1948. Effectively, he became Economics Minister of the area, a post he continued after the establishment of the Federal Republic of Germany in autumn 1949. Erhard served as West Germany's first Economics Minister for nearly fourteen years thereafter until he became West German Chancellor in 1963.

In spite of Erhard's cultivation of friendly relationships with the occupiers, he also proved willing to clash with Germany's foreign proconsuls at crucial junctures. A key instance occurred when the occupiers of the western zones decided to introduce the Deutschmark in their territories in June 1948. The currency reform, devised by a group of economists, including two German émigrés to the United States and the Detroit banker Joseph M. Dodge, and supported by Erhard, effectively divided Germany in two economically.[6] Erhard, however, went well beyond this in his proposals for economic reform, insisting on additional (and simultaneous) radical changes to the emergent western German economic system. Disregarding strongly worded advice to the contrary from top occupation officials, Erhard managed to augment the currency reform's impact by simultaneously lifting price controls and other regulations that had been in place during the Nazi period. It was a risky move, but the reforms, combined with the new Deutschmark, had the effect of stabilising the western German economy until the Korean War boom of 1950 stimulated what became known as the West German economic miracle.[7]

For Erhard, dismantling economic controls and deregulation were central planks of his emerging notion of the 'social market economy'. He pursued this course consistently into the 1950s, for example, by bringing about the end to rationing and price controls for motor fuels in spite of resistance from the British occupiers in 1951.[8] Indeed, certainly until the late 1950s, Erhard's accent was always on the *market* in his pursuit of the social market economy.[9] But the social aspect was also an essential ingredient of West German capitalism with a conscience, although other actors were far more important than Erhard in realising that part of his programme.

* * *

Erhard's boss for fourteen years starting in 1949 was a central figure here. Konrad Adenauer, who served as West German Chancellor, was known simply as 'the Old Man', not so much out of affection as simply as a bald statement of fact – he had assumed his first important political office as mayor of Cologne in 1913, before the start of the First World War. Politically experienced and yet sidelined by the National Socialists during the Third Reich, he was a shoo-in for reappointment as Cologne's mayor by the post-war military government until forced out of office owing to consistent opposition to British occupation policies. He was consequently on the outs not only with the Nazis, but also with the occupiers. This made Adenauer a very attractive politician for many Germans as they slowly regained control over their own affairs.

Although he quarrelled both with the Nazis and with the Allied occupation authorities, Adenauer was actually a powerful force for unifying diverse actors in the interest of West German reconstruction. He was a central figure in the reconfiguration of the Weimar Republic's exclusively Roman Catholic Centre Party by incorporating Protestants into the more inclusive Christian Democratic Union (CDU), and, in Bavaria, the Christian Socialist Union (CSU). The CDU/CSU, moreover, worked carefully under Adenauer to facilitate the integration of German refugees from the east, for instance from Silesia, which became part of Poland after 1945. Even more importantly, however, very early in his post-Second World War chancellorship, the Old Man shrewdly reached out to Germany's age-old archenemies, the French. In doing so, he helped forge a bilateral relationship that has stood at the heart of European integration ever since, providing a crucial context within which Germany could be economically powerful without becoming politically – and militarily – dangerous.[10]

Adenauer's relationship with the post-war head of the German Trade Union Congress, tall, broad-shouldered Hans Böckler, was equally unlikely. And it was similarly crucial. The two concluded an agreement enabling the realisation of industrial codetermination in West German heavy industry, which was eventually extended to all major industrial firms in the country. Under this system, workers are guaranteed representation through their trade unions on the non-executive boards of corporations, in exchange for limiting wage demands and strike action. Some consider codetermination to be one of the cornerstones of post-1945 German cooperative capitalism. After all, it has provided the mechanism for linking pay rises to increased productivity (thus helping ensure low levels of inflation), giving workers a vested interest in the health of the firms that employ them, and promoting unusually long periods of industrial contentment. The contrast to the generally confrontational and frequently hostile industrial relations that existed in Germany until 1945 could not be greater.[11]

* * *

Although there was no problem in post-1945 Germany finding trade unionists 'unencumbered' by links to the Nazi Party, finding businesspeople and bankers who were squeaky clean was much more difficult.

The fundamental issue was this: 'by the time the war was over in 1945, companies of all sizes had been tied inextricably to the crimes of the Third Reich'.[12] Indeed, every large German company – and many medium- and small-sized ones – had been involved in enabling the German war effort by supplying it with vital weapons, machines, and/or services. To do so, all of them had come to rely to some degree on forced, and sometimes slave, labour. Moreover, some had even gone so far as to co-locate factories next to concentration camps, most notoriously the IG Farben chemical plant at Auschwitz. Members of the IG Farben board of directors, as well as some top managers from heavy industry and banks, had even been put on trial for these and other crimes committed during the Nazi period – and some of them had been found guilty.[13]

Many more industrialists and financiers would have met the same fate had they been put on trial as well. But they were not. And those who had been found guilty were often soon pardoned. This was mainly because American policymakers deemed German industrial and economic recovery an essential prerequisite not only for western European reconstruction in general, but also for solving the closely related issue of countering Soviet communist influence as the Cold War gathered pace. Industrialists, in their individual companies and through trade associations, also fought a highly effective rear-guard action to facilitate rehabilitation by developing a coherent – if also fundamentally flawed – narrative in which they fashioned themselves as unwilling victims of Nazi policies who had acquiesced only under alleged threats of incarceration or even death.[14]

As industrialists told these tall tales, in alignment with US-led western capitalist interests, managers and their employees in hundreds of German firms of all sizes and in a wide range of sectors resumed production, innovation, and export. It was not, however, a story of each company pursuing its own narrow self-interest, resulting in general prosperity, even if this may well have conformed to Ludwig Erhard's worldview as a free marketeer. No, what was essential to West German cooperative capitalism was coordination. Representatives of sectoral and industry-wide peak associations and of major banks; top-ranking politicians and government officials led by Erhard and Adenauer; and trade unionists, including Böckler, worked together to form a first post-war version of Deutschland AG. It was one in which bankers and industry association officials – as well as most of the banks and associations themselves – provided continuity from pre-1945 (and often pre-1933) Germany into the new Federal Republic.

Interlocking and hierarchical, Germany's industrial associations have provided a focal point for coordination of business investment, collection of statistics, sharing of information about technology, and mobilisation of business influence on politics since the nineteenth century. Generally staffed and run by men who had worked in industrial firms, they had offered a ready-made and effective bureaucracy that the Nazi state apparatus drew upon for industrial planning and policy implementation during the Third Reich, first in the service of recovery from the depression and then for preparing and conducting the war effort. They continued their work after 1945, this time in the service of civilian industries and post-war recovery.

A prominent example is W. Alexander Menne, the president of the trade association for the chemical industry from the late 1940s. Menne, born in 1904, had trained as a banker before starting a career as a manager in the chemical industry. He served in London on the board of a chemical producer from 1929 to 1939 before returning to Germany just before the war started. As a member of the managing board of a chemical firm with plants in Westphalia and Hamburg, Menne, like many other industrialists in the Third Reich, was recruited into the service of the Reich Ministry for Armaments and Munitions, where he was responsible for camouflage paints and fire-protection coatings. In 1943, however, he was accused of high treason and other crimes against the state and the war effort and taken into custody by the Gestapo. He spent most of the rest of the war in jail.[15]

The incarceration must have been unpleasant in the extreme, but it served Menne in good stead after May 1945, as did his excellent command of English acquired during the decade he spent in London. In 1946, he convinced the British occupation authorities (and, shortly afterwards, the Americans as well) to allow him to form a chemical industry trade association in the western zones, which became the basis for the West German Association of the Chemical Industry (Verband der chemischen Industrie, VCI). Menne led the VCI until 1956. In the meantime, he played a crucial role as an advisor to the federal government in the final phases of the breakup of IG Farben between 1949 and 1951. He parlayed this role, in turn, into a seat on the managing board of one of the major IG Farben successors, Hoechst AG, a post he held until 1970. And, beyond that, Menne served as a member of the German Bundestag between 1961 and 1969, representing the liberal Free Democratic Party. Between 1965 and 1969, he chaired the Party's Committee for the Economy and Issues Related to Family and SME Firms (the so-called *Mittelstand*).[16]

Menne was therefore a central linking figure between industry, banking, and politics during the first decades of West Germany's existence. He was also one of the founders in 1949 of the peak association of German industry, the Bundesverband der deutschen Industrie. Menne served as its vice president from its establishment until 1968, a period during which his roles in the VCI, Hoechst AG, and the German federal parliament often overlapped.[17]

* * *

The other pillars of German cooperative capitalism as it emerged in the Federal Republic after 1949 were its large, universal 'D' banks, the Deutsche Bank, the Dresdner Bank, the Darmstädter Bank, and the Deutsche Industrie- und Handelsbank. These banks had a similar function as lynchpins of earlier versions of German capitalism from the middle of the nineteenth century through the Third Reich and into the post-war period. Soft-spoken networker Hermann Josef Abs emerged as a central figure here. Starting in 1938, Abs sat on the board of the largest of the 'D' banks, the Deutsche Bank. Following a short hiatus after being dismissed from all his positions when the Allies placed him in the automatic arrest category after the war, Abs resumed his role on the Deutsche Bank's supervisory board.

By the time the Federal Republic of Germany came into existence, therefore, Abs had become one of the most influential figures in the German economy. The federal government, for instance, appointed him as its commissioner for the re-establishment of the BASF chemical firm, which was refounded in 1952 as one of the main successors to IG Farbenindustrie AG. Abs, who had also sat as the Deutsche Bank's representative on the IG Farben board between 1938 and 1945, was then elected the first chairman of BASF's non-executive supervisory board.[18] In this and other board memberships, he personally ensured coordination of investment and strategy among many of West Germany's largest corporations as they re-entered and reconquered global markets after the war. Indeed, by the 1960s, he sat on the supervisory boards of as many as twenty-four of them.

* * *

The men – and it was almost invariably men – who formed the networks of cooperative capitalism in West Germany, then, were people who had come of age professionally just before and during the Third Reich. Many of the companies and organisations they led or represented also predated 1945. A number of dimensions differentiated the post-war from the pre-war situation, however. Dreams of economic self-sufficiency, or autarky, went out the window, along with industrial paternalism. This was in part owing to strong pressure from the occupation authorities, especially the Americans. But there was also an undeniable realisation of the need for fundamental reform in the aftermath of the catastrophe of German defeat in the war and a genuine willingness among all interest groups to do something about it, not least through incorporating trade unionists into the coordination process. The interests of finance, business, and high politics were no longer the sole shapers of the German economy; labour now had a strong voice, too.

Refashioning Japanese Cooperative Capitalism in the Aftermath of War

Months of pummelling of the Japanese home islands from Allied bombers culminated on 6 and 9 August 1945 in the devastating atomic bomb blasts at Hiroshima and Nagasaki. A few days later, at noon on 15 August, the dazed and downtrodden Japanese people sat in front of their radios. Often gathered in groups around a single receiver, they were transfixed. They had, after all, never heard their Emperor speak before during the nearly twenty years of his reign. And his message, delivered in a high-pitched voice and stilted language as their radios crackled with static, stunned them even more. Emperor Hirohito never used the words 'defeat' or 'surrender' in his speech, yet everyone who heard the broadcast knew its import. Japan had been defeated. It was now time to surrender. The Emperor put his subjects on notice that they would now have to 'endure the unendurable and bear the unbearable'.[19]

Even though he refused to use the 'd' word, Hirohito, the once and future head of the Japanese state, played a crucial, if largely symbolic and ceremonial, role in the process of 'embracing defeat' in the months and years that followed. After Japan's unconditional surrender, US Military Governor General Douglas MacArthur kept Hirohito on the 'Chrysanthemum Throne', seeing the Emperor as both a force for stability and a hope for achieving the General's desired Christianisation of the country. Reticent, aloof, and reclusive, Hirohito sought accommodation with the American occupiers, the eventual protectors of his nation. And, although the Emperor did little to realise MacArthur's dream of widespread Christianisation, he did play a key part in convincing Japanese bureaucrats and citizens that the new constitution, written in English by the occupiers and translated into Japanese, was not a humiliation, but instead a badge of pride ... even though – indeed perhaps precisely *because* – it explicitly rejected previous militaristic traditions.

* * *

In the sombre interregnum between the Japanese Emperor's broadcast to the nation on 15 August 1945, the formal surrender on board the US battleship *Missouri* on 2 September, and the subsequent arrival of American troops to start the Allied occupation, Tokyo's governmental quarter buzzed with activity. The buildings there, constructed of brick, mortar, and stone, had mostly survived the onslaught of bombing late in the war. They were still standing at least, in direct contrast to the wooden and paper houses in the Japanese capital's residential and hospitality districts, which had been razed to the ground by Allied incendiary bombs. In the aftermath of the war and before the arrival of the occupiers, dozens of small fires raged between the intact ministerial buildings. However, they were not, this time, the result of bombing. Instead, they were the work of hundreds of bureaucrats as they scurried to burn the files that documented their planning and actions during the war.[20]

One young man, Saburo Okita, threaded his way through the conflagration, doing his level best to thwart the bureaucrats' efforts by saving as many documents from the flames as possible. An electrical engineer turned economist, Okita had mobilised data demonstrating alarming declines in Japanese steel production already at the end of 1942 to try to convince Prince Fumimaro Konoye, an advisor to Emperor Hirohito, that it was only a matter of time before the economy would collapse. It was a dangerous line of argument at the time, not unlike the one developed in Nazi Germany by Ludwig Erhard. In Okita's subsequent work in 1944 and 1945 in the Research Division of the Ministry of Greater East Asia, he argued, among other things, for a reallocation of resources away from manufacture of metals – which was dependent on overseas raw materials subject to increasing disruption from Allied submarines – and instead towards domestic food production.

Unofficially, he simultaneously organised a group of about thirty economists, engineers, and political scientists to develop secret plans to mitigate imminent economic disaster following Japanese defeat. Okita's group of thirty met formally for the first time in the still-intact Ministry of Greater East Asia building in Tokyo on 16 August 1945. As he later pointed out, to aid in their planning, he and his compatriots needed the:

> documents being burnt in courtyards and other places [that] included mobilization documents, production capacity surveys and many basic economic materials.... Consequently I went

along to those places where documents were being burnt and secretly brought some home.[21]

Okita moved to the Research Bureau of Japan's Ministry of Foreign Affairs following the dissolution of the now superfluous Ministry of Greater East Asia. As he did so, he and his band of brothers continued their work, now formally constituted as the Special Study Committee on Post-war Economic Rehabilitation. Their March 1946 report on 'Basic Problems for the Economic Reconstruction of Japan' and its revised edition of September of the same year was 'instrumental in setting the course of the post-war economic rehabilitation' of Japan.[22]

A strong set of first principles and fundamental objectives lay behind the report's detailed findings: the Japanese economy in future needed to be peaceful. That, in turn, required that it be demilitarised as well as becoming more egalitarian and more internationalised. The Study Committee's basic message therefore reinforced and amplified US occupation policy, which, when implemented, 'undertook to dissolve Japanese capitalism as hitherto constituted'. The specific planks of the Committee's proposed programme involved economic planning, diffusion of modern technology, freedom from military spending, and measures to level up society as well as to preserve labour peace. In essence, they constituted the basic tenets of Japanese strategies for high-speed growth in the post-war period.[23]

Okita and his fellow economists had functioned inside policy-making elites during the war. Yet, not unlike Ludwig Erhard in Nazi Germany, they operated well outside the mainstream. And, although the Study Committee's 1946 suggestions differed in many ways from Erhard's Social Market Economy, there was nevertheless a shared view among key economic analysts in both defeated nations that fundamentally wrong-headed policies had led to defeat and destruction in 1945. Economic direction therefore required profound, even radical, reform. In the Japanese case, as in the German one, the would-be reformers would have to hitch their wagons to policy initiatives commissioned by the occupiers. In Japan, one such set of reforms aimed to curb inflation. Known as the 'Dodge Line', the measures were eventually introduced in Japan in 1949. Not incidentally, the name came from the same Detroit banker, Joseph M. Dodge (Figure 2.3), who had been instrumental in the West German currency reform of mid-1948.[24]

Figure 2.3 Detroit banker Joseph Dodge and General Douglas MacArthur, Supreme Commander for the Allied Powers (SCAP), meeting at Tokyo airport to discuss the Japanese budget, November 1949. Bettmann/Getty Images

Domestically, moreover, the Japanese reformers did not only have to bring on board reform-minded elites and other groups pushing for reform, including organised labour and farmers. They also needed active support from some of the very same people who had formulated and pursued the wrong-headed policies that ended so disastrously. And this in turn meant that the objectives of the reformers were not always realised, and, if they were, they were not necessarily achieved in the way originally envisaged. Again, the parallels with post-war Germany are striking, although the extreme centralisation of the Japanese government in contrast to German federal structures led to very differing pathways towards translating the reform vision into practice.

* * *

Chalmers Johnson, a prominent analyst of the post-war Japanese political economy, neatly summarised the puzzling persistence of one highly influential group from before 1945: 'For reasons that are none too clear, the occupation authorities [in Japan] ... never singled out the civilian bureaucracy as needing basic reform.' And so, although some wartime ministries such as the Ministry for Greater East Asia were abolished, most of those who administered and staffed them remained in post. In fact, it is estimated that only about fifty high-level Japanese ministerial bureaucrats were purged in the aftermath of the war. And many of the wartime ministries remained in place, even if they were sometimes renamed.[25]

A case in point is the Ministry of Commerce and Industry (MCI). Created in 1925, the MCI and its officials worked during most of its existence in close cooperation with the armed forces and *zaibatsu* industry groups to plan and carry out Japan's war of aggression. In fact, it was renamed the Ministry of Munitions (MoM) during the war. The MCI/MoM's partners in crime in the military and (to a lesser extent and for a limited time) industry fell victim to the occupation. This gave officials of the newly created – but essentially merely renamed – Ministry for International Trade and Industry (MITI), founded in 1949, considerably more freedom of manoeuvre than had previously existed.

MITI was a small ministry with a limited budget, but it enjoyed outsized importance in development and implementation of industrial policy in post-war Japan, particularly in relation to crucial export markets. Staffed by a relatively small number of highly capable and well-respected officials and with very little money at its disposal, MITI exercised its power mainly through identifying promising technology transfer and business opportunities, especially abroad, and giving guidance on coordination of production and investment in equipment. In other words, the Ministry gave a lot of advice, backed by minimal resources in funding and foreign exchange.

There is no denying that MITI did not always get things right. For example, Ministry officials tried their level best to dissuade Soichiro Honda (Figure 2.4) from entering the automobile market in the late 1950s and early 1960s. It also tried to push the Japanese car industry more generally towards a particular form of product development (the 'People's Car Concept' of 1955) and a highly concentrated industry structure (the 'Three Production Groups Concept' of 1961). In these cases, MITI's plans failed, primarily owing to Honda's stubbornness and to broad opposition to the two reform concepts from the

Figure 2.4 Soichiro Honda, 1963. The Asahi Shimbun/Getty Images

auto industry. And the outcomes in these cases were almost certainly for the best. But MITI often *did* get it right. What is more, although the actions of Ministry officials fell far short of Soviet-style economic planning, their excellent administrative guidance was a significant factor in the impressive and sustained development of Japanese industry in the post-war period.[26]

* * *

While the Japanese bureaucracy survived largely intact and unreformed into the post-war period, two other pillars of pre-1945 Japanese society did not. With the compliance and complicity of the domestic government, Allied occupiers attacked and dismantled highly contentious pre-war systems of landholding and industrial relations.

Misery and poverty in the Japanese countryside as a direct result of tenant-farming and sharecropping had long formed a source of serious social tension, and this became especially explosive in the 1920s and 1930s.[27] The land reform of October 1946 led to the compulsory purchase from landlords of all of Japan's farmland at prices already eroded by inflation. What is more, the compensation would soon be watered down still further through continued and rampant inflation until 1949. The land was then sold to tenant-farmers at the same knock-down prices (which had already been diluted by additional inflation). Strict limits were placed on the size of each landholding, and even stricter ones on the proportion of the landholding that could be rented out to tenant-farmers.

Landowners were therefore essentially expropriated. It was a profound and breathtaking change, something that perhaps only General Douglas MacArthur, an American Republican with impeccable anti-communist credentials, could have brought about. Former landowners were naturally disgruntled. But they stood little chance of getting the law rolled back even after the end of the occupation owing to the very large number of former tenant-farmers whose votes tended to migrate away from support of left-wing parties towards conservative parties. Essentially, then, with one fell swoop the land problem – which had long been recognised by the Japanese, but which they had been unable to solve owing to vested interests – was largely set aside, creating a large constituency of people deeply invested in democracy and conservative party politics.[28]

* * *

Like the fundamental reforms to landholding, the American occupation authorities in post-war Japan promoted a thoroughgoing overhaul of the system of industrial relations, which was eventually accepted and even embraced by Japanese governmental authorities and business. US officials encouraged the formation of trade unions along American lines and their inclusion in tripartite (government, business, trade union) decision-making. This had clear limits, however, as demonstrated to the chagrin of communist trade unionists trying to organise a general strike in early 1947: General MacArthur intervened personally two weeks before it was scheduled to occur to prohibit it.

In other words, through both the encouragement of inclusion of organised labour as a partner in decision-making and the simultaneous discouragement of direct worker interference in (let alone takeover of) management, western Allied policy had similar impacts in immediate post-war Germany and Japan. However, while German trade unions organised nationally across companies in individual industries and eventually achieved input into the strategies of large companies through codetermination, industry- and national-level unions in post-war Japan functioned mainly as conduits for information and coordination of strategy.

The main focus of activity in Japan, for large firms in particular, was enterprise unions, each of which operated largely independently. Moreover, membership generally extended across different jobs in the firm, and the company's trade union included both blue- and white-collar employees. These more or less elite enterprise unions – which have been much less common and far less powerful within small- and medium-sized enterprises – have served as a functional equivalent to the German codetermination system. Already by the 1950s, and continuing into the 1980s and beyond:

> [i]n the large firms the unions are not only accepted by management as an unalterable fact with which an unwilling management has to reckon; they are attributed a highly positive role in strengthening work morale and loyalty to the company which then in turn enables the company, through the higher productivity achieved, to pay higher wages and fringe benefits.[29]

The impact of this thoroughgoing reform of systems of land-holding and industrial relations cannot be overestimated. And the reforms also played a major role in realising the vision of Okita and others of an economy that was at once peaceful and prosperous, not least because inequality had diminished dramatically. As Mark Metzler, one of the most insightful historians of the political economy of the twentieth century, especially in Japan, has pointed out:

> War and occupation ... initiated a levelling process that was subsequently carried to its fullest extent by high-speed economic growth. The result was that a society characterised by ferocious social and economic inequality was converted into one of the most socially and economically egalitarian in the world.[30]

* * *

As in Germany, businesspeople and bankers in Japan constituted the most problematic social groups in the post-war period, apart, of course, from the top brass of the armed forces and the most senior politicians responsible for causing and carrying out the aggressive and destructive war. Those active in industry and finance – especially in large firms and banks – were heavily implicated in the German and Japanese war machines, the very opposite of 'unencumbered'. Yet, they were also required for economic reconstruction and resurgence: as John Stuart Mill recognised so long before, their 'skills and knowledge' formed an essential prerequisite for recovery.[31]

Just as was the case in Germany, initial occupation policy in Japan emphasised the first of these two contradictory facts, that is, that large firms and banks were responsible for the catastrophe that ended in defeat in 1945. As the occupation dragged on, the Cold War intensified, and the occupied became more powerful participants in domestic politics and the economy, the stress moved to the second. As a result, initial plans both in western Germany and in Japan to break up large concentrations of economic power were implemented half-heartedly, or not at all. In the case of Japan, for instance, among large-scale financial institutions, only the Imperial Bank was disbanded, and the banking system and many of its individual components therefore remained largely intact. Certainly, a large number of the business groups around these banks, the *zaibatsu*, were indeed broken up, in the end many more than in West Germany. However, in the Japanese case a substantial proportion of them reformed at the beginning of the 1950s as bank-based industrial groups known as *keiretsu*.[32]

This is not to say that nothing changed in post-1945 Japan. In fact, just as was the case in Germany, the changes to Japanese capitalism were profound. For example, although some *zaibatsu* groups later reconstituted themselves as *keiretsu*, the firms that were broken up and/or fundamentally reorganised 'constituted the most advanced and technologically efficient parts of the [pre-1945 Japanese] economy'. They included, among others, Mitsui, Mitsubishi, Riken, and Shibusawa, taken together 'the industrial and commercial core of Japan's [pre- and post-war] economic order'.[33] There was therefore both considerable organisational and human continuity and, at the same time, an element of 'divide and prosper' in the realisation of Allied – and especially American – occupation policy towards business both in Japan and in Germany. The result in both cases was a fundamentally refashioned system of cooperative capitalism. Both deployed state-sponsored and bank-centred coordination and corporate cooperation, especially among large-scale firms, in investment and other strategies, although the Japanese variant tended towards industrial groups, whereas the West German one relied more heavily on trade and industry associations.

* * *

Most of the fundamental reforms to German and Japanese capitalism were in place by about 1950, as were the networks that would prove essential to producing the economic miracle. However, we need to bear in mind that the renewed and reformed systems of cooperative capitalism did not function well immediately; in fact, the West German and Japanese economies languished as the 1940s drew to a close. Two things proved essential: first of all, major reforms of manufacturing in firms of all sizes in both countries to enable improvements in output and quality; and, second, vastly increased domestic consumption – and, later, crucially – worldwide demand for all sorts of products as the US-led capitalist world entered the Golden Age.

Part II
MAKING MIRACLES, 1950–1973

3 MANUFACTURING MIRACLES I
Forging Alternative Fordisms

People operating in more or less effective networks provide a crucial basis for improvements in the economy and society. Their abstract aspirations, dreams, relationships, and ideas, however, are ephemeral unless they find concrete expression in tangible objects. After all, despite a fervent embrace of globalisation, offshoring, and a service-oriented economy during the past several decades, especially in the United States and Great Britain, the COVID-19 pandemic has made one thing quite clear: virtually complete reliance on overseas sources of goods is not in anyone's interest. Manufacturing matters.

The Germans and the Japanese, whether politicians, soldiers, engineers, or businesspeople, have long understood this. What is more, from the middle of the nineteenth century through to 1945, they recognised – perhaps just a bit too well – the close linkage between advanced industrial development and political and military power. Consequently, industrialisation in both countries up to 1945 was skewed towards military production and technology, much of which was carried out by large firms. After 1945, that would clearly have to change, not least because there was widespread agreement – and not just among US trustbusters active in occupied Germany and Japan and academic and applied economists such as Alexander Gerschenkron, Josef Schumpeter, and Hiromi Arisawa – that the economic structures of the two countries were fundamentally unhealthy.[1]

Nevertheless, making the transition after 1945 from heavily military to predominantly civilian production proved less of a stretch for large firms in Germany and Japan than might have been expected. And there was one main reason for this: by the middle of the twentieth century, it had become almost impossible to distinguish clearly between arms-related and civilian-oriented industry. Chemicals, fuel, vehicles, machines of all sorts, electrical equipment – manufacture of these and many other things was as necessary for a properly functioning civilian economy as for one engaged in war. The balance of specific products and the markets for them might be different, but many of the products and virtually all of the production processes were identical.

In other words, opportunities for recovery and growth abounded for manufacturing industry in both countries as the 1950s loomed. At the same time, however, wartime production had also served as a stress test for large-scale, high-tech industry, with the experience highlighting one overriding issue in each case. In Germany, large-scale firms built on long traditions and experience to produce high-quality goods for the war effort. But they had considerable difficulty manufacturing in quantity, and even more so in maintaining adequate levels of quality in the process. Most Japanese companies, on the other hand, found quality production challenging during the war regardless of quantity.

The issues of how large-scale firms in the two countries made the transition from military to civilian manufacturing in the immediate post-war period, as well as how they developed high-quality mass-production regimes, are best illustrated by cases from that most salient of mid-twentieth-century industries, automobiles. Making a car is challenging. Making a car well is even more demanding. Making a lot of very good cars is an extraordinary feat. Quality mass production of automobiles tests and reflects the limits of the firm that accomplishes it, and at the same time those of the broader economy in which the company operates. For cars are not only sophisticated and intricate objects to design and build. Their production is also the place where the strengths and weaknesses of many companies, large and small, converge, most immediately in the mechanical engineering industries. But large swaths of the chemical, petroleum, electrical, and, ever increasingly, electronic industries are heavily involved, too.

Ramping Up Quality Production in Post-war West Germany

During the war, Nazi planners and German industrialists often made a virtue of their ability to produce high-quality weapons, claiming, sometimes explicitly but more often implicitly, that this was in some way superior to quantity production. In the final analysis, though, in a war of attrition, the winner is almost invariably the side with the most stuff. Quality, after all, is at best of secondary importance, especially if the stuff is just going to be blown up. Although some see things differently, the consensus, then, is that the vast quantitative superiority of the Allies in armaments constituted a major factor in their ultimate victory over both Germany and Japan.

Still, in spite of the rhetoric about preferring quality to quantity production during the war, Adolf Hitler and the Nazis clearly admired American mass production. Henry Ford, for instance, was one of the few non-Germans awarded the Grand Cross of the Eagle Order. This was mostly because of his contributions to the assembly line, large-scale production, and mass consumption. But Ford's extremely reactionary and racist views did not hurt his chances for recognition by the Nazis either.[2] In any case, the great admiration for US-style mass production translated into a strong compunction to imitate it. Hitler and many other Germans at the time believed the resulting mass output would provide 'Aryans' in the 'People's Community' with vast arrays of consumer goods and a considerably improved standard of living.[3]

To that end, the Nazi regime actively fostered a range of initiatives meant to produce and supply consumer durables to the broad public. First came the 'People's Radio' (*Volksempfänger*), followed by the 'People's Refrigerator' (*Volkskühlschrank*). Finally came the *pièce de résistance*, the People's Car, or Volkswagen.[4]

Achieving this vision of mass car ownership for members of the 'People's Community' would require mass production. And where better to learn about that than in America, where Ford's River Rouge plant provided a state-of-the-art model? Ferdinand Porsche and other planners of the project duly visited the plant in 1936, and again in 1937. On the second trip, moreover, the troupe hired away at least a dozen of Ford America's skilled workers and engineers to help realise the project at a greenfield site in Wolfsburg, which is still the company's headquarters. They also aped Ford's early strategy of making only one model, which in turn was available to order 'in a single color, a dark bluish gray'.[5]

'Available to order' – the phrase is used here advisedly, because there was a deep gulf between the vision of a mass-produced automobile designed and manufactured by a German-owned firm and its output. True, the company actually did build a massive factory. And it was equipped with the latest machines, dedicated machine tools, and specialised jigs required for producing interchangeable parts at scale to feed an insatiable assembly line.

However, the factory was not quite finished during the Nazi 'peacetime' period, in large part owing to shortage of finance. Before the assembly line could ratchet into production, the gigantic outlays already made by the Nazi Party-backed DAF trade union on behalf of the state had to be substantially supplemented through income. The solution was an inversion (and some might say a perversion) of the instalment (or hire-purchase) plan. Instead of getting their cars and paying for them with interest over several years, members of the 'Volkswagen Savers' scheme ordered their cars, agreeing to pay instalments of 25 Reichsmark (RM) a month for four full years *before* they took delivery of their vehicle. But they never did. The Wolfsburg factory, not only incomplete but also unsuited to most war production, stood idle during most of 1939 and 1940. After that, it manufactured a grand total of about 64,000 jeep-like vehicles for the military along with a mixture of mostly low-tech items such as camp stoves. Indeed, the integrated factory envisioned by Nazi planners became a series of co-located, but largely unrelated, manufacturing operations.

To call the project a disappointing and disastrous waste would be far too kind. The 336,000 disgruntled Volkswagen Savers, not one of whom received the dark bluish-grey automobile they had ordered and paid for, no doubt wholeheartedly agreed, even if by the end of the war the material and human consequences of the conflict and the Holocaust provide a stark illustration of the distance between the Savers' misfortune and true misery.[6]

* * *

To fully understand the story of the Volkswagen during the Nazi period and in the post-war period, we need longer-term context. For, despite the dynamism of many sectors of German industry in the late nineteenth and early twentieth century, automobiles had lagged far behind. Initial innovative impulses, especially in internal-combustion engines, came from Karl Benz, Gottlieb Daimler, and the eponymous Rudolf Diesel. But early technological leadership fell victim to poor roads; low levels of buying power; high motor-vehicle taxes; and a dense, efficient, and affordable rail network. Germany therefore fell far behind other industrialised countries in levels of motorisation. By the end of the 1920s, there were about five times as many automobiles per capita in Britain and France than in Germany. In fact, as late as 1935, even the Irish Free State had a higher motor vehicle density than Germany. One implication of the relatively small numbers of cars in Germany was that they tended to be owned by well-off people, who usually did not drive themselves. Bizarrely, this meant that a 1934 Nazi projection of added employment from increased motorisation indicated that nearly a quarter of the 1.1 million new jobs created would be 'Chauffeurs, Drivers, etc.'[7]

To make their business viable, German manufacturers therefore focused almost exclusively on the luxury market. That changed to some extent in 1929, when subsidiaries of American firms introduced some mass-production techniques. General Motors (GM), for instance, acquired Adam Opel in Russelsheim in spring of that year, while Ford established its first full-scale German auto factory in Cologne later in 1929 (Ford had started an assembly plant in Berlin earlier in the 1920s). Still, although vehicle production in Germany increased somewhat with the output of the American carmakers' subsidiaries, the timing of their arrival – at the very outset of the Great Depression – was awful. The market picked up somewhat in the context of the so-called National Socialist economic recovery from the depression, not least because motorisation was one of the regime's key policy levers. But output still lagged. Making the Volkswagen was supposed to change that in the late 1930s. It did not. Production of the fabled People's Car never really got off the ground before 1945.[8]

***

But it did after the war. And the initial impetus came not from German managers, but from the British occupation authorities, specifically from Major Ivan Hirst. An officer with the Corps of Royal Electrical and Mechanical Engineers (REME), Hirst took charge at Wolfsburg in August 1945. He was just twenty-nine years old when he arrived at the facility and remained in the top spot – with a brief hiatus in early 1947, after which he returned as a civilian – until autumn 1949. For, despite his youth, he came to the job with considerable experience in logistics, especially with regard to keeping military vehicles operational under combat conditions through improvisation and, sometimes, just simple force of will.

Upon arrival in Wolfsburg, the plain-spoken, pipe-smoking Yorkshireman encountered a plant that had suffered some bombing damage. But it was largely intact. Most buildings were unmarred. And, even more importantly, the plant's dedicated and sophisticated machine tools and jigs were undamaged, having been either spirited off to safety during the latter stages of the war or protected under cover in Wolfsburg's reinforced sub-basements. Critically, the factory had its own electricity-generating plant, which was also in working order.[9]

At first, however, there was no production. Instead, Hirst and the REME focused on repairing and maintaining vehicles from Allied military units. The long-term future of the factory hung in the balance for some time while it stood on the list of facilities slated for dismantling. But it was the only automobile factory in Germany with substantial intact production capacity, and the need for vehicles to support the military occupation was great. This quickly translated into an order for 20,000 VW Beetle saloons, along with several hundred other vehicles, for delivery by July 1946. Indeed, the need was so great that, already by September 1945, the order from British Military Government doubled.[10]

Manufacturing 40,000 vehicles was a highly ambitious target – challenging, to put it mildly. But Hirst set about organising the factory's Nazi-era managers and workers to produce automobiles in quantity to satisfy demand. The only other potential mass producers were Ford and Opel (GM). Ford's American owners were at the time highly dubious about the future of the German market for cars and so resisted any investment. GM took the same view. What is more, having taken a very large tax write-off in the United States during the war for the loss of its Opel subsidiary, GM was reluctant to engage in any activity in Germany that might entail substantial additional tax liabilities. The calculations of the American giants were far off target, but the upshot was that the Wolfsburg plant and its main product, the Porsche-designed, Nazi-era People's Car, became the only game in town for mass production of automobiles.[11]

As part of this decisive change in direction, and to help reduce the costs of the occupation, British military officials decided, once production had resumed at pace in late 1946, to turn the day-to-day management of the factory over to Germans. As part of the initial reorganisation, Hirst was deployed elsewhere, but was back in post in March 1947, although this time as a civilian.[12]

Hirst knew that his tenure was limited, while at the same time movement towards longer-term expansion of the factory was becoming pressing. Increasingly dissatisfied with the German managers under him, he turned instead to a promising engineer with considerable experience in the motor industry. Heinrich (Heinz) Nordhoff, born in 1899, had worked on developing airplane engines for BMW following his training at the Technical University Berlin before being hired by General Motors when it acquired Adam Opel in 1929. Nordhoff served as Opel's service manager before he became the firm's commercial technical director in 1936.

The war provided Nordhoff, along with many other men of his age and experience, with opportunities for advancement. In 1942, he was named Economic Leader for the War Effort (*Wehrwirtschaftsführer*), with overall charge of the main Opel truck plant in Brandenburg, east of Berlin. He fled west in 1945 ahead of the advancing Soviet armed forces, but his wartime position initially prevented him from gaining employment in the British zone. Still, the fact that he had not joined the Nazi Party worked in his favour. So, in 1947, he wrangled a post as customer service manager at the Opel dealership in Hamburg. It was, though, at a considerably lower level of responsibility than the ones he had held previously.[13]

Hirst invited Nordhoff to Wolfsburg to interview for the post of technical director in October 1947. The two got on well – it no doubt helped that Nordhoff, having worked for an American firm, spoke English. Hirst later recalled that 'Nordhoff was clearly a man who understood what happened in a factory and he knew where we required assistance. He did not like the Beetle. He had a grasp of the financial side and certainly the commercial side.' Hirst decided 'that [Nordhoff] should take the top job' instead of the one for which he had been interviewed. In late autumn 1947, Nordhoff did so. The mutual good feelings between Hirst and the new managing director from the interview soon evaporated, however. Hirst later described his relationship with his new director general during the last year and a half or so of his tenure in Wolfsburg as 'close, but cold'. Nordhoff moved quickly to assert his authority against British military government officials.[14]

* * *

Nordhoff 'did not like the Beetle'. That was a strange thing to say for someone interviewing for the post of technical director of the factory making that automobile and that automobile alone. And perhaps this should have tipped Hirst off that, talented though Nordhoff might be, he spoke his mind, refusing to be cowed by a notional superior. But it is also likely that Hirst mostly agreed with Nordhoff's assessment. The first post-war Beetles were plagued with quality problems owing to poor materials – headlights often shattered – and workmanship – doors and bonnets often did not shut properly. This was something Hirst himself had started to address. Organisational problems also beset the factory as it struggled to implement sophisticated and smooth assembly-line production. More generally, though, even the highest-quality specimens of the early Beetle were noisy and uncomfortable. Still, although Nordhoff began his tenure in Wolfsburg in 1948 by carping that the Beetle 'had more things wrong with it than a dog has fleas', he also recognised from the outset that 'he had inherited "a diamond very much worth our while polishing"'.[15]

And polish it he did – from his arrival in January 1948 through the mid-1960s. As Steve Tolliday has pointed out:

> One of the undoubted foundations of VW's success between 1948 and 1965 was Nordhoff's single-minded pursuit of a single-model policy, to an extent that made him almost more Fordist than the first Henry Ford.[16]

Incremental improvements in quality and design went hand in hand with full implementation of assembly-line mass production at the Wolfsburg plant (Figure 3.1). Output increased from fewer than 20,000 Beetles in 1948 to more than 10 times that number in 1954. By 1961, the Wolfsburg factory was turning out more than a million vehicles a year, about 80 per cent of them Beetles. The plant by that time also produced a small number of other car models along with about 170,000 Transporter vans. Exports rose in tandem from about 4,500 cars in 1948 to just under 109,000 vehicles in 1954. By the early 1960s, VW exported over half of its now prodigious output.[17]

Figure 3.1 Volkswagen Beetle production line, 1952. Mirrorprix/Getty Images

Dramatic growth in sales and exports, coupled with Nordhoff's insistence on paying only limited dividends to the German federal government as the effective owner of the firm, meant that the company's cash reserves grew exponentially. Financing of investments therefore came almost exclusively from retained earnings rather than from borrowing.

Nordhoff would not have accomplished all of this without his single-minded strategy; nor could he have done it without his very high level of organisational and managerial ability. But, not surprisingly for a man who had honed his skills as a *Wehrwirtschaftsführer* in a critical industry, keeping his factory operating during most of the war, he also possessed enormous capacity for improvisation and pronounced political (if not necessarily diplomatic) skills. For instance, in the early 1950s, he parlayed his firm's status as a state-owned enterprise, his extensive network of government connections, and the power that came with being a large employer (not incidentally, of workers who were also key voters) to gain essential and additional allocations of steel. Later, in contravention of governmental attempts to control inflation, Nordhoff quietly negotiated a separate agreement with workers in his factory that awarded them higher wages and a shorter work week.[18]

Erhard fumed at Nordhoff's uncooperative behaviour, writing in November 1959 to his ally, the recently appointed Minister of State Property Fritz Lindrath: 'The behaviour of the management of VW ... holds the danger of influencing views on our economic order.'[19] As a fierce proponent of the free market, Erhard's solution to the perceived threat was predictable: privatisation.[20] And VW was a big and symbolic enough screen on which to project one of Erhard's dreams, that of 'people's shares' – widely dispersed ownership by ordinary Germans – in the people's automobile. It was precisely for this purpose, in fact, that Lindrath had been appointed to head the Ministry of State Property in 1957, following a strong CDU/CSU showing in federal elections that reinforced Erhard's already unassailable position.

There were a lot of complexities involving competing claims for ownership between the CDU/CSU federal government and the state of Lower Saxony (where Wolfsburg was located), which was dominated by the Social Democratic Party (SPD). Nevertheless, a finely balanced final decision on privatisation came in 1961. Volkswagen would be partially, not fully, privatised. (That was to come later.) Forty per cent of the shares would remain in public ownership, half allocated to the federal government and half to that of Lower Saxony. Sixty per cent of the shares could be purchased in small amounts by a large number of individual Germans, with lower-income citizens given a substantial discount to acquire their shares. Measures were also put in place to ensure that shares had to be held for a lengthy amount of time, and that they would be held only by German nationals. Moreover, 1961 brought a settlement that awarded cash or vouchers to the Volkswagen Savers, thus ending the spectre of a huge cash outlay for the firm, while at the same time giving the automaker access to a hitherto blocked DAF trade union bank account from the Nazi era.[21]

Part-privatised and with the Saver problem solved, VW remained under the leadership of Heinz Nordhoff until his sudden death in April 1968, shortly before he was due to retire. During the 1960s, the company also continued to churn up considerable cash, based primarily on sales – and especially exports – of its flagship Beetle automobile. At the same time, some of the limits to Nordhoff's longstanding and mostly successful strategies became evident. The VW boss's cautious assessments of market growth in the 1950s led to limited investment in renewing and expanding plant and equipment, which eventually led to an inability to meet demand fully. His laser focus on the single model, the Beetle, also entailed neglect of design and product development capacity, even as demand grew for new models in maturing automobile markets. At the same time, pre-tax profits, which had reached 15 per cent or more during the mid-1950s, declined even as production costs rose. To add to the miserable forecast, the German subsidiaries of American multinationals Ford and GM began making up ground they had lost in the decade following the war, in the process challenging VW in its home market.[22]

The end of the Nordhoff era in spring 1968, then, coincided with a crisis in the firm as its managers struggled to define and deliver a new strategy. The company's crisis, moreover, took place in the context of West Germany's first post-war recession and a rise in unemployment, which some have characterised as the end of the economic miracle.[23] Nevertheless, we know that both the firm and the German economy itself survived not only the crisis of the 1960s and 1970s, but also several crises since. And this is in no small part because of the success of Volkswagen and other firms in West Germany during the first twenty-five years after the end of the war.

Through its successful adaptation of Fordist mass-production methods, VW played a major role in ending Germany's status as a laggard in car ownership. When Nordhoff took the reins in 1948, West Germany had 228 inhabitants for every car on the road, at a time when the United Kingdom's ratio stood at 25 per car. By 1964, the West German figure, at 6.8 inhabitants per car, was practically equivalent to that of the United Kingdom (6.3). Car ownership in Germany and the United Kingdom had therefore risen enormously by the mid-1960s, although both remained below that of France (4.9) and well behind that of the United States (2.8).[24] As popular as the Beetle was, of course, it was not the only model of car on West Germany's increasingly busy roads. But VW certainly played a significant role in demonstrating to the German subsidiaries of American multinationals that it was worth engaging in mass production in Germany. Moreover, Volkswagen's adoption of mass-production methods while maintaining quality also exercised a demonstration effect on Germany's traditional luxury automakers, including Mercedes-Benz and BMW. VW's successful embrace of mass production also stimulated its many suppliers to follow its lead.

Building Better in Post-war Japan

In 1954, Columbus, Ohio-based supermarket chain Big Bear Corporation decided to expand into the booming discount-store business by acquiring Harts Stores. Big Bear's managers immediately set a course for rapid expansion for their new acquisition. Locals frequenting the discounter in its midwestern outlets celebrated Harts' low prices. But they rarely did so without simultaneously mocking the quality of the stores' products. Even in the late 1960s, they joked sardonically about 'Harts' fall-aparts'. The reason? 'Everything's made in Japan.'

'Made in Japan.' Since the 1980s, that phrase has become a watchword for quality and elegant design. But, like the phrase 'Made in Germany' in the middle of the nineteenth century, there was a time when it was a synonym for 'cheap and shoddy'. The midwesterners who commented sarcastically on Japanese-made goods through to the late 1960s were therefore not far wrong. What they saw – and often bought – in discount stores like Harts was as low in quality as it was in price. And it was not infrequently imported from Japan. Even then, though, a revolution in high-quality production was well under way in the Asian country, although it was initially visible only in products available on the Japanese domestic market. The first fruits of the revolution were most evident in Japan's automobile and consumer electronics industries, but it was happening on all fronts. In other words, the change did not happen quite so rapidly as it seemed to many contemporaries in the United States and elsewhere: there was, as usual, a lag between reputation and reality. In fact, the roots of the revolution stretch back into the 1920s.

We have encountered Masatoshi Okochi (1878–1952) before. In 1917, when Japan was cut off from access to German basic scientific research because of the Great War, he helped establish the Japanese Institute for Physical and Chemical Research, known as the Riken. He then served as its director between 1921 and 1946. Under his directorship, the Riken became not just a research institute, but also an industrial conglomerate that operated a number of companies to exploit the inventions and improvements of its research staff. Latterly, this was in the service of the war effort.

Okochi, however, was far better at devising ideas for innovation and industrial development than he was at implementing them. His thinking, disseminated in a range of influential pamphlets and books beginning in the 1920s, focused on 'scientific industry', which to him 'meant the continuous development of new products and production methods or equipment, and the raising of wages while lowering commodity prices to stimulate demand'. The influence of the modus operandi of the first Henry Ford is obvious here, just as it was in Nazi Germany around the same time: Okochi emphasised the virtuous circle that could be engendered both for the economy and for society at large by new technology, higher wages, and lower prices. He also warned of the dangers of what he called 'passive capitalism'. This was epitomised in the actions of British industrialists and managers in the aftermath of the country's successful First Industrial Revolution, when they pursued capital preservation and short-term profits rather than taking risks and engaging in research and development. In other words, there was also more than a hint here of Thorstein Veblen's contemporary critique of capitalism and simultaneous promotion of technocracy. And Okochi shared this stance with many other engineers of the period, including many of those who supported the National Socialist motorisation project in Germany.[25]

Okochi's vision involved a pathway towards developing and sustaining competitiveness for Japan as it caught up with those countries that had industrialised earlier. Elements of his programme included, first of all, long-term and continuous investment in developing and deploying the latest technologies. Second, he proposed extensive use of unskilled labour from Japanese villages, which the latest technologies would enable. The wages of these unskilled workers, moreover, would lift the villagers out of poverty. The mutually beneficial effects of these two strands would, then, finally, lead to production of goods that were at once low in cost and high in quality.[26]

Okochi was unable to put his ideas into practice. But, as Michael Cusumano has written, '[i]t is particularly striking how commonly accepted many of [Okochi's] ideas became in post-war Japan'. Indeed, Okochi's thoughts were implemented to stunning effect in Japanese industry, most spectacularly in automobiles, but also in consumer electronics and many other areas. And they were complemented by the implementation of the ideas of an American statistician about how best to ensure quality, especially during mass production.

* * *

In 1950, Japan produced a grand total of 1,600 passenger cars, a minuscule output for a nation whose population in that year was well over 84 million. The industry's diminutive size resulted as much from the extremely low buying power of the Japanese public as it did from technological backwardness. Neither of these constraints, though, could impede a posse of fully fifteen automakers from pursuing the holy grail of producing large numbers of motor cars during the 1950s and beyond. Indeed, the carmakers also resisted strong pressure from the Japanese state to merge in order to create two or three decent-sized firms that would be viable both domestically and internationally, each of which would focus on a particular segment of the industry.[27] Instead, they competed with one another for a foothold in the market. And, astonishingly, by the early 1980s, eleven of the fifteen still existed, although they varied considerably in size and market share. By then, however, Japanese domestic production of passenger cars had soared to just under 7 million, which also accounted for about a third of world production.[28]

By the early 1980s, industrialists, academics, pundits, and policymakers marvelled at the Japanese manufacturing system, their discussions peppered with talk of 'just-in-time' production methods, quality circles, and even the odd Japanese word such as *kaizen* (continuous improvement). Almost all of them, moreover, were primarily interested in what might be learned directly and immediately from the Japanese and applied to improvement of manufacturing practice in other countries, especially in the United States. How and why Japanese practice came about in the first place seemed far less urgent questions. Yet much about the particular and to some extent peculiar take on mass production developed by the Japanese cannot be understood without knowing where it came from.[29]

Attention from abroad often focused on the Toyota Motor Company as one of the most prominent practitioners of the Japanese art of manufacturing. And that is not surprising, given that Toyota was one of its co-creators. But, before Toyota made automobiles, its founder was engaged in a distantly related field, that of textile machinery. The Toyoda Automatic Loom Company, Ltd, was established in Nagoya in November 1927 by Sakichi Toyoda to exploit his latest invention, an automatic loom, along with his son Kiichiro's invention of an automatic shuttle replacement mechanism. The company's high-speed loom was a worldwide success, prompting engineers from Platt Brothers, an established English machine building firm, to extol the wizardry of the 'magic loom'.[30]

Sakichi, born in 1867, was himself largely self-taught as a machine maker, but his son, Kiichiro, studied engineering at Tokyo University, Japan's most prestigious academic institution. The younger Toyoda's ambitions were correspondingly high. He prevailed upon his father to use part of the enormous profits from sales of the automatic loom to set up an automotive section within the company to pursue his dream of manufacturing a motor car without any foreign assistance. Kiichiro's first passenger car was completed in 1935. With it, he had achieved his aim in one important respect: the automobile was indeed designed and built in Japan without foreign help. But, in another crucial way, his achievement highlighted the limits of Japanese industry: it was assembled primarily from parts imported from the United States.[31]

The timing, moreover, could not have been worse for the fledgling automaker. In response to growing levels of Japanese aggression in the Far East in the 1930s, the United States increased restrictions on exports to Japan. In 1937, the aggression culminated with the outbreak of the Second Sino-Japanese War – effectively the start of the Second World War for Japan. This in turn meant that domestic production was subsumed almost exclusively into the war effort. Toyoda's automotive section turned to the less technologically demanding production of trucks for the army. It was, however, also a move that exercised a major impact on the company's future: truck production required development of capabilities within the firm for manufacture of parts as well as active encouragement of a network of parts suppliers in Nagoya and its environs.[32]

In the short term, however, in the aftermath of war and defeat, that future looked very much in doubt. The firm faced severe financial difficulties and extensive labour troubles immediately after the war, which threatened it with bankruptcy in 1949. Intervention by the Bank of Japan to write off debt and a change in management of human resources averted receivership, however. And, as part of these changes, a new, more labour-friendly president, Taizo Ishida, was brought on board to replace Kiichiro. Ishida joined forces with Shotaro Kamiya, who already in 1935 had moved to Toyota from General Motors Japan to head Toyota's sales operation. Kamiya presided over Toyota Motor Sales Company, an independent but closely linked firm that would prove an important factor in the success of its sister manufacturing company.

Of far greater significance for Toyota Motor Company, however, were dramatic changes in production organisation and technology. Ishida instigated and oversaw them in conjunction with other top Toyota managers, including Taiichi Ohno, who is accredited with inventing the just-in-time system. The changes arose in large part as a creative response – often using experience from loom manufacturing – to some of the peculiarities and challenges of Japanese economic development up to the early 1950s, which were particularly evident in the case of the automobile industry. For instance, Toyota, like VW in Germany, faced a domestic market with limited buying power, although the problem was much greater in Japan. Furthermore, Toyota and other fledgling Japanese automakers were initially even more reliant than VW on their domestic market, since their recourse to export markets was far more circumscribed. A key challenge, then, was to develop a variation on the mass-production regime pioneered in the United States by Henry Ford and perfected by General Motors that would enable economies of scale stemming from standardised mass production, while simultaneously permitting the manufacture of smaller quantities of individual models.[33]

What was Toyota's solution? Essentially, the firm embraced '"limited volume production" (*genryo seisan*)', a clear departure from the blind pursuit for their own sake of the economies of scale and productivity gains that were central to Fordism. Alongside this modified Fordist mass production, Toyota focused on quality. The company accordingly invested heavily in highly specialised machines and machine tools for operations that were common to all of its manufacturing processes, while simultaneously using new or existing universal machine tools to enable production of small numbers of each of a wide variety of models. The specialised tools and machines also allowed Toyota to use plentiful, low-cost, unskilled and semi-skilled workers, and its managers worked carefully with trade unions to develop a commonly held company spirit.

Unskilled and semi-skilled workers were also among those employed by Toyota's suppliers, most of which were based in Aichi prefecture near its main factory complex. Working closely with those subcontractors and suppliers, Toyota developed its just-in-time and *kanban* inventory control systems to economise on storage and inventory costs. All aspects of the company's operations and those of its suppliers were, furthermore, subject to strict quality-control measures. By the

Figure 3.2 The one-millionth Corolla produced by Toyota, 1970. The Asahi Shimbun/Getty Images

1980s, this 'Toyota system' or 'Toyota way' included automatic defect detection, total quality control, and continuous improvement (*kaizen*).[34] 'Made in Japan' had become something far different from what it was to Harts' midwestern American customers in the 1960s (Figure 3.2).

* * *

Toyota may have been the exemplar of the Japanese obsession with quality, but it was not alone in this, neither in the automotive sector nor in other large-scale manufacturing. And the company was neither the sole nor even the most important originator of many of the quality-control techniques eventually associated with what became known as the 'Toyota system'. For this, we have to look at the contribution of an American, W. Edwards Deming.

Born in 1900, Deming trained as an undergraduate in engineering before moving on to graduate study in mathematics and physics. He completed his PhD in mathematical physics at Yale University in 1928. Deming then worked briefly in industry before turning to government employment, first in the US Department of Agriculture. He subsequently moved to the Bureau of the Census, where he pioneered the development of several new statistical techniques, especially involving sampling. Fighting the Second World War required rapid ramping up of production across many industries, some quite new. During this build-up, Deming became affiliated with the War Production Board. Beginning in 1942, he organised training courses on statistical quality-control techniques for engineers and managers involved in munitions production.[35]

The work of Deming and others during the war, where quality and precision were of utmost importance for production of airplanes, electronics, and other high-tech munitions goods, seemed less relevant to American industry in the immediate post-war period. After all, they had learned all they needed to know during the war, hadn't they? And demand was so buoyant, both at home and abroad, that American manufacturers could sell just about anything they produced at a profit. But Deming and his ideas found a ready and willing audience in Japan. He arrived there for the first time in 1947 at the behest of US military government officials to provide advice to them and the Japanese authorities on preparations for the 1951 census. During his initial visit to Japan, however, Deming also came into contact with leading Japanese scientists, engineers, and managers, who were profoundly interested in his thoughts on how to improve manufacturing. These contacts resulted in 1950 in an invitation from the president of the Japanese Federation of Economic Organisations to address the Industry Club in Tokyo. In his address, Deming reprimanded them severely, insisting that they and they alone were responsible for the woeful state of Japanese manufacturing industry, and that nothing would change until they took personal responsibility for making things better.[36]

His unvarnished indictment of Japanese managers presaged Deming's messaging during his subsequent career as a management guru: indeed, by all accounts, he often admonished American managers in exactly the same way once they began to seek his advice in the early 1980s in the face of stiff competition from Japanese industry. Deming's philosophy was eventually codified in his '14 points of management', twelve 'obstacles to success', and the related 'seven deadly sins of management'. The latter include, for instance, 'emphasis on short-term profits' and 'evaluation of performance, merit rating, and annual reviews of performance'.[37] Clearly, at least part of his message fell on deaf ears when managers in the United States finally rediscovered Deming's preachings in the 1980s. But, aside from some general – and sometimes empty and often ignored – management advice, Deming had some concrete and extremely useful things to offer the Japanese manufacturing community, which is why they invited him repeatedly to advise and address them in the years that followed his speech to Tokyo's Industry Club in 1950. As Deming himself admitted, none of them was particularly original. But, taken together, they were. And they were also very powerful.[38]

Specifically, what Deming brought to the table – and Japanese managers devoured – was a collection of statistical methods and tools for sampling developed from the 1930s onwards that producers could apply to quality control. Underlying all of them was a conception of manufacturing as a unified process. Previous regimes of quality control, still prevalent at the time, relied on more or less careful inspection of the final product. But, as Deming and others realised, by then it was far too late. Finding out when and where the quality problems arose became virtually impossible, which meant that correcting them was impossible too. In contrast, statistical quality control applied to every stage of the manufacturing process allowed precise and timely identification of the emergence of quality issues. It also enabled managers and workers to intervene immediately.[39]

Managers and engineers in the United States may have ignored Deming and his quality-control techniques until the late 1970s and early 1980s, but Toyota and other Japanese manufacturers took his advice to heart. And they took it much further. They enlisted workers on the production line in their dogged pursuit of quality, flexible mass production, seeking their advice in quality circles and going as far as to empower individual workers to bring the assembly line to a halt when quality was being endangered. And they married measures to ensure and enhance quality with initiatives that promoted cost-savings and efficiencies such as just-in-time production and strict inventory control, as well as others – such as imaginative application of combinations of universal and dedicated machines – that permitted the advantages of mass production in smaller production runs. The result, eventually, was the Japanese lean production system. By the 1980s, virtually every manufacturer in the industrialised world was eager to emulate it.

* * *

The diffusion of flexible and quality mass-production techniques throughout large-scale German and Japanese business in the 1950s in the service of the civilian economy formed an essential precondition for the countries' re-entry into – and conquest of – world markets starting in the 1950s. Large, technologically adept firms forged the path in this direction, although they subsequently needed to consolidate these capabilities and to develop new ones, especially in product design. But it was not only large-scale firms that had to change and adapt to compete effectively in the post-war world. To transform the German and Japanese political economies, fundamental changes were also required in small- and medium-sized enterprises, which were often far less developed technologically. And that meant confronting one of the most intractable problems of economic development, industrial dualism, with all of its negative social and political fallout.

4 MANUFACTURING MIRACLES II
From Humble Craftsmen to World Beaters

Diagnosing Dualism

Reminiscing in June 1949 about the post-war occupation with one of his compatriots, a former official from the American military government doubted the extent to which the economy could ever be modernised:

> Now, one thing is, you hear this coming from military government people so often, 'Well, [they] don't know how to do anything. Their methods are antiquated. They have no machinery for this particular thing', and so on, without realizing that their own economy would be further hampered and in many ways totally destroyed if they permitted the full ramifications of the Machine Age to enter their economy in certain fields.... You have got so many people in such a small space, doing so many things, that they would destroy themselves if they adopted modern ways.... We can't say to them, do it the American way.[1]

The official's statement would not be at all surprising if it applied to occupied Japan. But it did not. Walter L. Dorn and Ernest Karl (Doc) Neumann, two midwestern Americans of German descent,[2] were in conversation about Germany. The country was widely admired for the efficiency and technological sophistication of its industry, evidenced, for example, by the development of synthetic fuel, jet aircraft, the V-2 rocket, radar, and highly advanced if ultimately unsuccessful research into nuclear weapons.[3] Yet here was a man, well schooled in the country's capabilities and foibles through extensive experience on the ground, who was highlighting its other, less well-known side. For, in spite of being among the most advanced industrial nations in the world in some areas, Germany, like Japan, still lagged considerably behind the United States in the application of 'modern' machines and technologies, in certain sectors at least. Indeed, in terms of technology, scale, efficiency, and organisation, there was not one Germany, but two. And the laggard Germany – which was small, backward, and inefficient – was going to require considerable reform. There, as in Japan, the challenge lay in resolving the contradiction between the advanced and the lagging sectors by rendering them complementary.

* * *

The key issue that Dorn and Neumann grappled with was what has come to be known as industrial (or economic) dualism. According to this notion, any economy tended to split in two different directions as it developed. On one side stood a set of industrial sectors that were technologically advanced, capital-intensive, and highly productive. They often comprised large firms that were associated with the military. On the other side stood a set of technologically backward, labour-intensive, low-productivity sectors, composed often of smaller companies that tended to be civilian in orientation. Historian Jürgen Kocka put it colourfully in his analysis of the emergence of German large-scale enterprise: the 'largest enterprises ... function[ed] as islands of modernity in a sea of traditional small- and medium-sized enterprises'. The two sets of sectors thus coexisted, perhaps even in a symbiotic relationship with one another.[4] Moreover, the distance between them tended to be greater in countries that developed later.

Because of Japan's later development, industrial dualism was more pronounced and chronic there than in Germany. The problem thus attracted direct and sustained attention from the late 1940s through the 1960s from a number of leading economists, including, for instance, Ichiro Nakayama. As late as 1961, in fact, Nakayama 'identified economic dualism as the most serious threat to Japan's future'.[5] Again, though, there was little clarity about how to tackle that threat.

A consensus soon emerged, however, that industrial dualism was not just puzzling; it was potentially very dangerous. As Alexander Gerschenkron, the great theoretician of economic 'backwardness' argued, 'mild dualism could be overcome'; but 'he warned that the greater the gap between the developed and "backwards" portions of the economy, the greater the likelihood of social tensions and repressive regimes'.[6] All of which, of course, lent considerable urgency to finding a solution to it.

Ironically, of course, there had in fact been considerable movement for some small- and medium-sized firms during the war towards substantially higher levels of technological performance and productivity. Supplier networks that had been developed to serve larger, technologically sophisticated producers, especially in the aircraft industry, forced SME companies to up their game. But this mechanism for doing away with dualism disappeared in defeat. And rightly so: the catastrophic consequences of the direct linkage of industrial and technological development to warfare more than offset any positive gains arising from it. Only gradually, and in the context of fundamental reorientation towards civilian technologies, did companies resurrect these networks. As a result of proactive company action on the one hand and various combinations of state policy and support on the other, industrial dualism narrowed dramatically between the 1950s and the 1970s both in Germany and in Japan.

West Germany and the Cultivation of the Manufacturing *Mittelstand*

Admiration for West German economic performance has waxed and waned over the years. Throughout, however, and certainly since the 1970s, one central focus has been on learning exactly 'how Germany became Europe's richest country'.

A segment of a US Public Broadcast System (PBS) programme that aired in February 2012 tackled precisely that question. Surprisingly and counterintuitively, the report made no mention whatsoever of the performance of large, high-profile firms such as Thyssen-Krupp, Volkswagen, or BMW. Instead, the broadcast focused on more modest manufacturing firms from the so-called *Mittelstand* (usually small- to medium-sized and owned and managed by a single family over several generations). It also underscored the importance of the apprenticeship and other support systems that have enabled many of them to become world beaters in manufacturing. As a result, they make and export a wide array of goods, including home cleaning appliances, specialist electric plugs for nuclear-power facilities, displays for petrol station forecourts, laser-cutting machines, and equipment for digging tunnels for subways, motorways, and train lines.[7]

The first firm profiled in the segment, family-owned Herrenknecht AG, based in the Black Forest in southwestern Germany, specialises in building these tunnel-digging machines, which are massive, sophisticated, and very expensive. Presenter Margaret Warner posed an obvious question to Martin Herrenknecht, the CEO of the 4,000-employee-strong company and the son of an upholsterer who had employed only 12: 'What accounts for this astonishing growth and success?' Herrenknecht responded by pointing to centuries-long craft traditions in the Black Forest region and to the people who perform and maintain them. 'Before let's say 300 years we built cuckoo clocks, and today we build tunnel-boring machines.'

'That's quite an evolution,' Warner replied laconically, before moving quickly on to profile other highly successful *Mittelstand* companies in Germany.[8]

* * *

'Quite an evolution' is right. But, if this has been the German pathway to untold riches, the many who would like to follow it will surely need to know more specifics about exactly *how*. After all, Herrenknecht's father's twelve-employee upholstery operation from the first post-war decades in West Germany sounds suspiciously like part of the 'antiquated' industries that 'Doc' Neumann identified in his conversation with Walter Dorn in June 1949. However, the performance of the firm under Herrenknecht junior clearly refuted Neumann's prediction that embracing 'the full ramifications of the Machine Age' would result in an economy that was 'totally destroyed'. In fact, Martin Herrenknecht and other such entrepreneurs have helped to create an extremely prosperous country, and, contrary to Neumann's expectations, they did not simply 'do it the American way'.[9] The path by which his and other companies in the *Mittelstand* grew from small craft- and artisan-based operations to thriving, highly internationalised, and technologically sophisticated enterprises was a long one. Oddly enough, it does start with cuckoo clocks and other such modest manufactured goods. But there was a lot that happened between making cuckoo clocks and the establishment of the world-renowned *Mittelstand* during the three decades immediately following 1945.

* * *

Among the worst-affected casualties of German industrialisation in the late nineteenth and early twentieth centuries were the country's large numbers of craftsmen and artisans, known as *Handwerker*.[10] Many, including those in the Black Forest, were located far away from the centres of large-scale industrialisation and were thus marginalised geographically. The large number of such enterprises involved in manufacturing, moreover, lagged behind larger companies in productivity and access to capital and markets, with consequent impoverishment. And this process was particularly noticeable among skilled artisans and craftspeople such as weavers, shoemakers, furniture makers, and some machine makers, whose skillsets were often displaced through mechanisation, simplification, and centralisation in factories. We would now call them the technologically unemployed. These people shared an experience of deep oppression with the industrial working class; but their interests and self-understanding were at odds with those of industrial workers.

Gerschenkron and others highlighted the political consequences of this sharp and rapid erosion of economic and social status when discussing emergent industrial dualism in developing economies. Their observations held for industrialising Germany as well. Disaffected and impoverished artisans and craftsmen formed one of the most receptive constituencies for the nascent National Socialist movement in the 1920s, and support from within this group only grew over time. It was, therefore, ironic that the group constituted one of the great losers in the Third Reich as the exigencies of war preparation, and then war itself, favoured the fortunes of large-scale firms.

The Nazi period, however, was also one during which important – and arguably to some extent quite positive – changes to the situation of artisans and craftspeople took place. For one thing, Nazi-era legislation enshrined in law the right of craft chambers and guilds to provide training and certification of competence for artisans and craftspeople, while at the same time recognising these chambers and guilds as fully sovereign organisations in public law. Following a brief period of interruption immediately after the war, and after the removal of some of the original wording in the legislation referring among other things to the importance of the 'leadership principle', the modernisation measures undertaken during the Nazi era were gradually adopted in West Germany. By 1953, they applied to the whole of the Federal Republic. Large parts of the much-vaunted German training and apprenticeship system thus gained full recognition and standing, providing a firm basis for its subsequent development and influence.

Moreover, in spite of all of its ultimately disastrous impact on Germany and its victims and adversaries, Nazi spending on armaments, especially for airplane and vehicle production related to the war, also had a positive impact on some small- and medium-sized craft-based enterprises. It did so primarily by placing urgent and non-negotiable demands on these firms to manufacture high-quality and precision-made parts. This of course did not apply by any means to all firms. Indeed, many of them remained in the civilian sector and therefore subject to shortages of raw materials and overall neglect during the Third Reich. But, for those craft-based, relatively small-scale, and often family-owned companies that did participate as subcontractors and suppliers to large munitions firms during the period, the overall impact of the Nazi-era experience was to narrow the gulf between large-scale and smaller-scale enterprise in terms of quality, precision, and productivity.[11] And this occurred in spite of the fact that the reorientation of production away from munitions and towards civilian needs after the war was sometimes wrenching and took some time.

By the early to mid-1950s, then, many craft-based companies were well positioned to compete effectively in the post-war economy. Although they were dotted throughout much of West Germany, many of them were located in regions with long craft traditions, including the German states of Baden-Württemberg and Bavaria. Not incidentally, these states also featured clusters anchored by important and fast-growing automobile manufacturers, including Mercedes-Benz in Stuttgart and BMW in Munich.

A classic example of a firm that made the journey from craft-based producer to specialist parts suppliers for larger producers after 1945 is Dräxelmaier, based in Upper Bavaria. The family firm was established in 1875 to produce leather goods, including Lederhosen and shoes. It expanded by vertically integrating, establishing its

Figure 4.1 The Goggomobil, 1956. Interfoto/Alamy

own tannery, for instance, and investing in its own electrical power-generation station. The company also pioneered telephone ordering systems and bank payment methods, and it branched out into related areas, including production of outdoor equipment such as ski helmets. Its products were in demand even during the Nazi period, and it continued plying its trade into the 1950s. Then, looking for new markets, Fritz Dräxelmaier, Sr, identified an opportunity in the booming automotive trade, which would allow his firm to capitalise in the producer-goods sector on its experience in production of quality consumer goods involving considerable hand-working. A short business trip in 1958 to the premises of Fritz Glas GmbH, which had introduced the bestselling Goggomobil microcar (Figure 4.1) in 1955, yielded a contract to produce 50,000 cable harnesses. Creating a new company for the new business called Eldra, Fritz Dräxelmaier, Sr, and especially his wife Lisa, after whom the new firm was named (Lisa **Dra**exelmaier), mobilised previous experience by simplifying manufacturing operations and employing an army of mostly female workers. The women initially toiled from home to fulfil the initial Goggomobil order. Eldra's order book grew steadily thereafter, and the firm soon branched out into production of other parts, such as interior panels, again for the auto industry. It is now one of the main suppliers of such items to high-end carmakers such as BMW.[12]

Other craft-based firms also made the journey to become internationally successful specialist producers. Many of them design and manufacture machines or testing equipment, for instance, which they sell to other businesses, large- or small-scale, and are thus also involved in what is now known as B2B sales. A prominent example is Trumpf GmbH & Co. KG in Ditzingen, near Stuttgart, in the state of Baden-Württemberg. The company was founded in 1923 to produce portable and hand-held metal-cutting machines and accessories for them. The specialty soon earned the company a nickname: 'the nibbling king'. And, during the 1950s and 1960s, it gradually grew both in sales and in workforce. Although still in the traditional business, it moved into design and production of larger-scale, stationary machines. From the late 1960s, however, the firm developed competences in emerging numerical-control, and then laser-cutting, technologies, which soon enabled it to become a global player.[13]

Other such firms, though, do not produce primarily for manufacturers, but instead specialise in manufacture of final products for the consumer market, in what is now known as B2C sales. Some have in the meantime even become household names, such as Kärcher, based in Winnenden, also near Stuttgart, in the state of Baden-Württemberg. Founded in 1935, the family firm found its first major market supplying heaters to warm up the engines of Luftwaffe airplanes. Then, immediately after the war, the company employed 40 workers to produce low-tech space heaters and handcarts, with the workforce growing to about 140 by 1948. Searching for new markets, the firm developed the first in a range of steam-cleaning appliances by 1950, before eventually moving into what it now calls 'connected cleaning' – sometimes expensive, but generally affordable, high-quality electric appliances for domestic use that it sells the world over.[14]

Another household name is the family firm now known as Andreas Stihl AG & Co. KG. Founded in 1926 in Waiblingen in Württemberg, the company has specialised from the outset in portable chainsaws, with its first major product a gasoline-powered saw operated by two persons that was introduced in 1929. The primary market initially was the government-dominated forestry management service. By 1941, the firm employed a workforce of 340, with demand buoyed by the need for woodcutting for the war effort. After the war, the company developed its technology further, making lighter chainsaws that were highly effective both for foresters and for farmers. Stihl, too, has effectively managed new product and global market development, especially since the 1970s.[15]

The success of these and other *Mittelstand* firms in building on their strengths to reinvent themselves by adapting to new markets and adopting new technologies during the quarter-century after the end of the Second World War was striking. And the entrepreneurship of individual family managers was not the only factor at work here. Family ownership itself lent a long-term perspective to the firm, which was reinforced by the German laws on inheritance, especially regarding taxation. The long-term perspective, moreover, was buttressed through stability of financing by means of longstanding relationships with local savings banks, known as *Sparkassen*, or regional banks, known as *Landesbanken*.[16] The firms were also supported in crucial ways by the states in which they were located, with Baden-Württemberg and Bavaria particularly strong in provision of advice and market intelligence to *Mittelstand* firms, many of which therefore retained their headquarters and primary production site in small towns in those federal states.[17]

* * *

Other factors promoting the success of these firms included the apprenticeship system and strong craft and artisanal organisations developed prior to 1945, which sustained consistently high levels of training, quality, and certification. Moreover, a pioneering institutional innovation played an essential role in enhancing the innovative capacity of these relatively small firms. In 1949, the same year the Federal Republic was established, the Fraunhofer Society was created. Its mission was applied research carried out primarily on behalf of private companies, many of which were too small to sustain their own research and development units. Financing of basic infrastructure and operations for the Fraunhofer Society came from state governments, joined eventually by the German federal government, and the Society's outlets then performed research and development work commissioned by companies on a contract basis. Although the Fraunhofer Society had few employees and faced calls that it be wound up in the mid-1950s, the governments of the states of Baden-Württemberg and Bavaria – tellingly, from the south and southwest of the country – waded in to guarantee its continued existence and contribution to the survival and growth of *Mittelstand* enterprise in Germany to the present.[18]

Despite all of these tailwinds propelling *Mittelstand* companies forwards during the quarter-century following the end of the war, however, it was not all smooth sailing. Indeed, when the economic miracle drew to a close with the first post-war recession in the late 1960s, followed by oil crises, slow growth, and general inflation in the 1970s, many of them faced existential questions about structure, governance, products, and markets. Making cuckoo clocks – or traditional cutting machines – could only take these companies so far, no matter how much more efficiently they did so. And it was their response to these challenges in the 1970s and beyond – including jettisoning old product lines and starting up new ones, sometimes in entirely new companies, such as Herrenknecht GmbH, founded in 1977 – that made them the companies admired the world over today.

Levelling Up Small- and Medium-Sized Enterprises in Japan

Japan has no equivalent to the *Mittelstand*, in spite of what seems to have been a solitary attempt by *The Economist* in 2008 to shoehorn the country's small- and medium-sized sectors into that category by using the German term.[19] But neither *Mittelstand* nor its functional (if imprecise) rendering in English – small- and medium-sized enterprises (SMEs) – applies easily to Japan. Indeed, when the Japanese Ministry of Agriculture and Commerce first introduced such distinctions among business and industries by size in 1911, the categories referred not to the number of employees, but rather to the level of technology deployed, and they were also specifically applied to the textile industry. In this designation, small firms were traditional, mostly home-based weaving operations, while medium ones involved mills using power looms.[20]

Nevertheless, but not surprisingly, the Anglo-Saxon – and especially US American – usage of SME was introduced to Japan through legislation during the occupation. On 1 August 1948, General Headquarters (GHQ) issued a directive establishing the Small and Medium Enterprise Agency within the newly created Ministry of International Trade and Industry (MITI). The law creating the agency specifically highlighted 'the fact that sound and healthy independent small-business concerns will make the national economy sound and healthy', with one of the aims being 'to prevent the concentration of economic power and to secure the fair opportunities for carrying out economic activities'.

The American occupation authorities thus transferred to the Japanese situation their national proclivity for viewing smaller companies positively, while looking with suspicion on overwhelming concentrations of economic power. At the same time, the Americans were perfectly comfortable with large firms, as long as they faced competition. The basic principle was that a preponderance of smaller business units and competition among larger ones were two sides of the same coin, both essential to the preservation of liberal democracy.[21] The occupation forces imposed this view in Japan even though the US conception of SMEs did not necessarily apply there. Japanese SMEs, after all, were often family firms, but not always. If engaged in manufacturing, they were much more likely to be directly linked to a large-scale enterprise as a supplier and/or subcontractor. And they were much more likely to be of relatively recent vintage – many were founded after the Second World War.

This is not to say that there were not small- and medium-sized business units in pre-1945 Japan. Indeed, there were. As in other countries, small retail shops, food stands, and restaurants, as well as other traders in hospitality and other services, made up the bulk of them. But importantly, just as in Germany, there were also many craft-based, artisanal sole traders or small companies. They were especially prevalent in sectors such as textiles, apparel, casting and metalworking, brewing, and food processing. And, although many of these craftsmen and small companies are of relatively recent vintage, many have long and distinguished traditions, some of which have been able to thrive over many decades and even centuries.

However, industrialisation harmed a great deal of traditional Japanese small manufacturing operations, just as it did in Germany, with impoverishment and technological unemployment a result for many of those involved in them. These social and economic pressures had inevitable political effects. Small-scale entrepreneurs, along with the much larger and even more downtrodden Japanese peasantry, drifted to the right. By the late 1920s and early 1930s, many supported right-wing radical would-be reformers in government and especially the military.

During the Second World War, the contribution of many of these small- and medium-sized operations proved vital to the war effort, in particular as suppliers to larger armaments firms. In studies conducted in the early 1940s, Japanese economists estimated that just under three-quarters of all workers were employed by firms with fewer than 100 employees. Companies with five or fewer employees accounted for fully half of all workers, while those employing thirty or fewer accounted for nearly two-thirds. In other words, given that virtually all of Japan's economy had to be mobilised in the service of the war effort, small and very small businesses were absolutely essential. One of these economists, H. Arisawa, however, noted that, in 1940, productivity at these smaller firms was on average considerably lower than at larger ones. Still, levels of subcontracting increased as the war proceeded. And the learning, discipline, and technological improvements that accrued to smaller firms through functioning as suppliers to larger firms, especially in the demanding aviation, communications, and vehicle sectors, went some way towards bridging productivity gaps between large and some small companies.[22]

After the war, many of these pre-war trends continued, albeit with some lag and adjustment owing to the reorientation of the economy to civilian production and high levels of inflation. Many new small firms were also established by former employees of plants involved in war production and by returning soldiers. The Dodge Line of 1949 brought inflation under control, but at the cost of higher unemployment and a large number of bankruptcies, not least among the new entrants. The Korean War boom starting in 1950 offset this to some degree, although the temporary economic slowdown at its end also brought with it considerable bankruptcies among smaller firms, again with a pronounced effect on newly formed ones. During the early 1970s, about half of small business establishments continued to be in the wholesale and retail sector, with a further 20 per cent in services. About 15 per cent were involved in manufacturing, and about 5 per cent in construction. Notably, however, small manufacturing operations accounted for about a third of all employees among small-business establishments, approximately the same as for wholesale and retail. About 14 per cent of all employees of small firms were in services, while about 8 per cent were engaged in construction.[23]

As had been the case during the war, those small- and medium-sized manufacturing enterprises that were or became closely associated with large firms as subcontractors and suppliers tended to become more productive and technologically advanced over time than those operating largely on their own. Even for those smaller firms in this fortunate position, however, lags in productivity, wage levels, and working conditions compared with the larger firms on which they depended persisted during the first quarter-century after the end of the war. This was because large firms tended to treat 'their subcontractors ... as supplementary suppliers and as a buffer mechanism'.[24]

In other words, during the two to three decades following the end of the war, small subcontractors were usually dispensable, and they could be – and were – routinely squeezed in terms of prices and conditions of delivery, especially when demand fell for the products of the companies they supplied. Not surprisingly, then, the much-vaunted Japanese industrial

> practice of permanent employment is least applicable in the small-scale private sector, where working conditions are poor, bankruptcy rates high, product demand unstable, and capital funds often in short supply. It is here that a large percentage of the Japanese labor force is concentrated. Workers in establishments of less than forty-nine employees accounted for more than 40 percent of all Japanese employees in 1968.[25]

The challenges posed through the persistence of industrial dualism were singled out explicitly in a 1957 Japanese government White Paper on the Economy, which presented a 'theory of dual structure'. '[T]he modern sector and the pre-modern sector exist side by side in one country,' it contended, and the only way to 'reduce the dual structure' was through a strong and sustained commitment to promotion of economic growth. In a nod to the heralded 'permanent employment' policy that was becoming a salient feature of Japanese big business by this time, the scholar summarising the 1957 White Paper highlights the conviction in government that such economic growth would 'eliminate the seemingly permanent unemployment in the Japanese economy'.[26] In any event, the officials who penned the White Paper were correct in some ways, and at least for a time. High-speed growth in Japan eventually did get rid of permanent unemployment, even in many smaller firms, something that lasted until the recession of the 1990s.

* * *

Regardless of what has happened since, the environment for SMEs in Japan in the quarter-century following the end of the war was generally favourable for growth and development, just as in West Germany. And a huge variety of firms from all over Japan took advantage of this fortunate situation, although, as in Germany, some regions were more conducive to positive SME performance than others. The central Chūbu region (which, to a large degree, overlaps with the regions designated as Tokai and Shoryudo) of the Japanese main island features many localities and firms with long craft traditions, not unlike parts of Baden-Württemberg and Bavaria. And, like those two German states, the homes to emerging auto giants Mercedes-Benz (Stuttgart) and BMW (Munich), Chūbu's Aichi prefecture features what quickly became a world-class automaking cluster around Toyota after the war.

In 2021, about half of Toyota's over 200 domestic tier-one suppliers were located in the region, mostly concentrated in Aichi prefecture near the car company's headquarters. Most were founded not long after the war to supply specialist parts to the automaker as it made its way from bit player to global leader in the industry. They include, for instance, Aichi Hikaku Industry, Ltd, a leather goods company founded in 1957, which currently employs about 140 and is a specialist supplier of leather-covered steering wheels and interior knobs and handles. Another, also based near Toyota, is Aisin Chemical Company, Ltd. Founded in 1952, the company now has just over 1,000 employees and supplies paints and adhesives to the automobile giant.[27]

A third Toyota supplier located close to the carmaker's headquarters in Toyota City is Tokai Rika Co., Ltd. Unlike Aichi Hikaku and Aisin Chemical, however, which have focused on relatively narrow, medium-technology manufacturing operations, Tokai Rika developed highly specialised technological capabilities on the coat-tails of Toyota in demanding segments of the automobile parts industry. Consequently, in 2021, it employed nearly 20,000.[28]

Still, Tokai Rika started off small, just like the two other Toyota suppliers described above. The firm was established in 1948 to supply switches to Toyota. According to company folklore, its founder, Yoshio Kato, visited a Toyota warehouse three years after the end of the war and found

> an automobile part abandoned in a corner. He asked, 'What is this' and got the reply, 'It's a switch.' It was explained to Kato

that manufacturing switches took a lot of trouble and nobody wanted to do it. He thought, 'Even if nobody wants to do it, somebody has to. This is just the field that we should expand into.' He decided to produce switches and established 'Tokai Rika Co., Ltd'...

Starting production of these switches in a small subsection of a candy-manufacturing facility, the firm quickly branched out into designing and making a wide variety of switches, locks, keys, and other related parts for the auto industry, and for Toyota in particular. The strategy was to manufacture a large variety of related parts in small production runs, something that in turn required development of several interrelated technological capabilities. These included resin moulding, metal stamping, and forging. The company's focus and specialised set of interdisciplinary capabilities allowed Tokai Rika to become the major supplier of parts in this specialist area by the early 1950s, eventually expanding through related diversification and innovation into electro-mechanical automotive controls as well as security and safety devices.[29]

However, many of the companies involved in this post-war success story in the Chūbu region are not connected to Toyota. Indeed, their fortunes are not directly tied to any single large-scale enterprise. And some of them have origin myths not all that dissimilar to Herrenknecht's cuckoo clock story, narratives that are often also deeply rooted in the region in which the firms are located and in what has become known as *mono-tsukuri*, the Japanese 'thing-making', or manufacturing, tradition. For example, Nabeya Bi-tech Kaisha (NBK), located in Gifu in the central Japanese Chūbu region, is one of a number of regional firms that emphasises its craft heritage, stretching back in NBK's case to the sixteenth century. In the words on the NBK website:

> Our tradition of creating high-quality products dates back to 1560, the year Oda Nobunaga won the battle of Okehazama and was heralded as a new hero in Japanese history.
>
> Our founders acquired advanced knowledge and skills to create cast metal products such as pots, pans, lanterns, and temple bells, and received the title of 'Licensed Foundry Craftsmen' from the Imperial Court. Thus, our company name, 'Nabeya', literally meaning 'pan shop', indicates that the abilities of our craftsmen have been officially recognized as being associated with quality.[30]

In fact, though, NBK as it currently exists harks back to a much more recent date: 1940. Not surprisingly, then, the firm also characterises itself (perhaps more accurately) as 'an old, yet new, company'. Associated initially with the war economy, Nabeya Kogyo Kaisha corporation (as it was known until 2001, when it changed its name to Nabeya Bi-tech Kaisha) was set up to make power-transmission equipment, in particular specialist pulleys and couplings for industrial machinery. However, its products were also in demand for civilian applications, and the company thrived in the decades immediately following the end of the war, gradually developing its product lines, using new materials and designs. By 1980, it had a strategic partnership with a Swiss firm and had negotiated a trade contract with China Metallurgical Export Import Corporation. Four years later, NBK established a dedicated Power Transmission Research Centre for further product development. In the decades that followed, it has continued this strategy of highly specialised, high-value-added, precision manufacturing for B2B sales based on technological innovation, and it remains a medium-sized company with about 400 employees. A senior manager in the company described its aspiration 'to do business like a sushi bar: the customer is right in front of you, orders different things, and a highly skilled artisan makes it right away'.[31]

However, another firm in the Chūbu region, Nousaku, has perhaps a better claim to being the direct heir of a long craft tradition associated with metal casting and manufacture in particular of religious objects, although the company was founded only in 1916. Still, Toyama prefecture's city of Takaoka, where Nousaku is located, boasts copperworking traditions extending back to the city's founding in 1609. The firm specialised in casting copper and tin vases along with accessories for household Buddhist altars, work for which it mostly was subcontracted by wholesalers. Demand for its products remained steady throughout most of the twentieth century, even during the war and for much of the post-war period. And it could meet that demand regardless of levels of turmoil in economy, politics, and society because its workforce remained tiny. In fact, just eight people worked at the firm in 1984. It has since grown by virtue of its careful cultivation of tradition, innovative designs, and embrace of industrial tourism and the global market to 150 employees. And it continues to specialise in its original product line.[32]

* * *

The extent to which small- and medium-sized enterprises, known in Germany as the *Mittelstand*, have formed 'the backbone of the German *Wirtschaftswunder*, or economic miracle, and subsequent rise to economic power'[33] is an open question. And the degree to which this applies also to the post-war Japanese miracle is perhaps even more debatable. But there is no doubt that SMEs engaged in manufacturing in the two countries have served as buffers, providing larger firms with flexibility and stability. They have, however, also functioned as drivers in German and Japanese post-war economic development, complementing – and this is the crucial term here – the performance of larger and more well-known firms. The recovery and resurgence of the two nations' economies in the quarter-century following the Second World War cannot be understood without reference to the synergies between the two types of companies.

But SMEs in post-war Germany and Japan have served another crucial function, one more social than economic. After all, continued industrial dualism from the pre-1945 period, which had caused considerable social unrest, was likely to impede the realisation of the vision of many 'miracle makers' in Germany and Japan of a more equal society of citizens who would sustain economic growth and democracy. The extent of the problem differed between Germany and Japan. Consequently, so did the ways in which it was addressed. And industrial dualism was also far from completely overcome by the 1970s, when industrial structures and traditions were buffeted by a variety of developments, including stagflation and two oil crises, which had particularly deleterious effects on SMEs.

However, regardless of what happened afterwards, there is no question that the period from around 1950 to about 1970 was an economic and social Golden Age, with Germany and Japan among the most fortunate of the beneficiaries. And they did not accrue their gains just through more effective and efficient manufacturing in large firms and SMEs. Making things was only half the battle. The other half involved selling the wares they made, first at home and then abroad.

5 CONSUMING MIRACLES

'Three Sacred Treasures'

On 1 May 2019, Emperor Naruhito ascended to the Chrysanthemum Throne. In keeping with centuries-old Japanese tradition, the new monarch received as his imperial birth right the Three Sacred Treasures – a jewel, a mirror, and a sword. The Treasures, never seen by anyone other than the emperor and selected high priests, are the material embodiment of the Japanese Imperial family's origin myth. In 1945, Emperor Hirohito thought them so important that he ordered their protection at any cost during the chaos and destruction his country had brought down on itself at the end of the Second World War.

A few short years after 1945, a hefty proportion of the emperor's subjects dreamed of owning a new, completely different, and much more mundane set of Three Sacred Treasures as they began to enjoy the fruits of Japanese post-war economic recovery. They urgently desired, and soon acquired, a refrigerator, a washing machine, and a black-and-white television set, the consumer durables that formed the material embodiment of the Japanese economic miracle in the 1950s. Acquisition of these Three Sacred Treasures, of course, represented a highly visible act, which was not restricted to the Japanese. When West Germany came into existence after the war, for instance, Imperial Germany and all of its accoutrements – including the Kaiser himself – had long been banished. But 1950s West Germans, too, hankered after these three particular treasures, which represented objects of keen desire. And, after a large proportion of the population in both countries had acquired them by the late 1950s, the treasures were soon replaced in the 1960s by new objects of consumer desire: an automobile, a colour television, and, for the Japanese, an air conditioner.[1]

Widespread ownership of these consumer durables symbolised the success of the economic miracles in both countries. However, such consumption simultaneously constituted one of the key drivers propelling the post-war German and Japanese economic miracles forwards. In other words, although exports constituted a significant part of the explanation as to why the two countries became major players on the world stage after the Second World War, as we will come to in the next chapter, that was only one side of the coin. And export of goods furthermore played its most important role only from the 1960s, especially for Japan.[2] In the earliest years of the German and Japanese miracles, it was instead domestic consumption of big-ticket consumer items – which were, not incidentally, usually designed and manufactured domestically – that was instrumental in bringing about and sustaining economic growth.

Poverty and Progress

From the late nineteenth century, Germany was already one of the world's premier powers in science, technology, and industry. Its scientists dominated the Nobel Prize awards from their establishment in 1901 into the 1940s. And German companies such as Siemens, MAN, Mercedes-Benz, and AEG were world-beaters on international markets, not least because their products were renowned for high quality and technological excellence. The country's widely acknowledged talents were put to nefarious uses in the two world wars of the first half of the twentieth century, but that did nothing to stop much of the world – and certainly those on the other side – from marvelling at some of the stupendous achievements of German science, technology, and manufacturing during that conflict, including V-2 ballistic missiles and jet aircraft. Yet, in spite of these accomplishments, Germany ranked well behind its notional peers – the United States and Great Britain – in per capita gross domestic product (GDP) as late as the 1950s. The simple fact was that most Germans were very poor. War and defeat served only to exacerbate the dire situation.

Because Japan was a later developer, its science, technology, and industry lagged well behind Germany's throughout the first half of the twentieth century. Nevertheless, Japanese scientists were by then already working at the cutting edge of global knowledge production. As early as the 1880s and 1890s, for instance, Kitasato Shibasaburo collaborated with Robert Koch as well as Emil von Behring in Berlin in developing serum therapies and vaccines. Shibasaburo went back to Japan in 1891 and founded the Institute for Infectious Diseases, which later became part of the University of Tokyo. He was the first Japanese person to be nominated for the newly created Nobel Prize in Physiology or Medicine in 1901, although it was not he, but instead von Behring, who received the award. In 1921, Kitasato Shibasaburo also established the Termumo corporation, a global leader in medical technologies and therapeutics to the present day.[3] Japan's scientific and technological achievements reached new peaks in the years just before and during the Second World War. Again, the end products – including, for example, the sophisticated Zero aircraft – were put to nefarious purposes, but they were also products that attained globally respectable levels of technology. Yet, in spite of these indubitable achievements, poverty levels in Japan throughout the first half of the twentieth century were far worse than in Germany, to say nothing of the United States or Great Britain. And war and defeat served only to make life even more grim for the bulk of the Japanese population.

The extent of this relative poverty – as well as the speed and degree of catch-up – is evident from Chart 5.1, which portrays changes in per capita GDP in Germany, Japan, the United Kingdom, and the United States between 1920 and 1980 in constant 2011 dollars.[4] The United States outpaced its nearest competitor throughout this period, generally by a margin of about 25–30 per cent, although there was a considerable narrowing of that gap during the 1930s in the depths of the Great Depression. The United Kingdom was the 'nearest competitor' to the United States for most of the period.

The overall trend lines in Chart 5.1 indicate clearly that, for most of the time between 1920 and the 1950s, per capita GDP in Germany and Japan trailed behind that in the United Kingdom by a fair margin. The gap with Britain decreased substantially, if briefly, for Germany in 1940, no doubt owing to the Nazi regime's earlier commitment to massive wartime expenditure. Still, throughout the 1950s, Germany's per capita GDP was generally only about 40–50 per cent that of the United States, while Japan's stood at around 20 per cent of America's. In other words, while destruction from the war and ongoing economic disruption

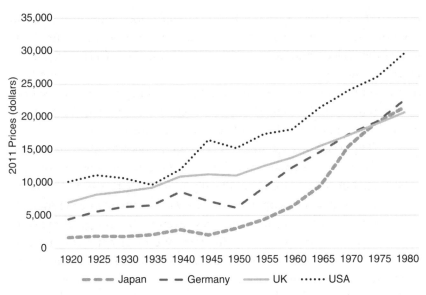

Chart 5.1 Per capita GDP in Germany, Japan, the United Kingdom, and the United States, 1920–1980.

in the immediate post-war period had some effect on the lag in per capita GDP in Germany and Japan compared with the United States, the relative situation of the two countries in 1955 was not all that different from what it had been in 1920. The same held true for the United Kingdom.

However, the extent and impact of the German and Japanese post-war economic miracles – and the relative lag of the United Kingdom – are evident from the trends from the mid-1950s onwards. By 1965, German per capita GDP approached that of the United Kingdom. Five years later, Germany had overtaken the world's first industrialised country. It had displaced the United Kingdom as the 'nearest competitor' to the United States by this measure. And Japan's progress was even more stunning. Starting at a much lower level than Germany relative to Britain, Japan overtook the United Kingdom's per capita GDP by 1975. By 1980, Germany's GDP per capita stood at 76 per cent that of the USA, Japan's at 72 per cent, and the United Kingdom's at just under 70 per cent.[5]

***

Germany, then, moved, within the first few decades following the end of the Second World War, from a country of middling wealth on a per capita basis to one of the wealthiest countries in the world. In the meantime, the Japanese, who had been very poor indeed in 1945 in spite of a strong showing in terms of industrialisation and technology, joined that select club only about a decade after the Germans. But, as is well known, GDP per capita is a very rough and imprecise measure of economic well-being, because it tells us nothing about how that per capita share of national income is distributed. In other words, it tells us virtually nothing about levels of economic equality.

There is, however, no doubt that in the decades after the Second World War both Germans and Japanese became in general not only wealthier, but also more economically equal. There were, of course, exceptions, and some people in both countries remained economically and socially disadvantaged, sometimes severely. But the great majority shared in the growing prosperity. In 1960s West Germany, for instance, about half of all of those employed worked in industry.[6] A significant proportion of them, moreover, worked for firms where codetermination, which legally mandated trade-union representation on the supervisory boards of joint-stock companies, meant that workers shared in productivity gains through higher wages. They also enjoyed steadily improving conditions of employment.

In Japan, many aspects of industrial employment differed from those in Germany, but there was a similar trajectory towards wider inclusion of the working population in reaping the fruits of prosperity. The permanent employment system characteristic of many large firms applied to broad swaths of the workforce; here, many industrial workers shared in productivity gains through higher wages. What is more, land reforms undertaken during the occupation period immediately after the war combined with political commitment to the well-being of those in the countryside to ensure that those engaged in agriculture also benefited from increased prosperity.

Put another way, both countries underwent substantial economic growth accompanied by a revolution in equality: in West Germany and Japan, there was a strong and sustained commitment to the realisation of some measure of economic democracy.

Consumption: From Needs to Wants to Desires

At a certain – and fairly early – point in the process of becoming wealthier, people start to spend a smaller proportion of their income on the bare necessities of food, shelter, and fuel, and instead allocate a larger proportion to other things. As they become wealthier still, the amount of 'disposable income' that can be spent on consuming these 'other things' can become quite substantial. When exactly these turning points – from barely covering basic needs through fulfilling some additional wants to consuming some segment at least of what is desired – were reached is a matter of some conjecture. Some find evidence of a 'consumer revolution' in the eighteenth century, or even before, in the late seventeenth century. A small but growing middle class at that time in northwestern Europe and, above all, Great Britain, began purchasing fancy clothing, deluxe bedding, and some luxury items to an increasing extent, apeing the aristocracy. Others highlight increased expenditure by the middle and also the working classes in the nineteenth and early twentieth centuries on leisure activities and other elective goods and services, as a small portion of the vast wealth generated by the industrial revolution and the first globalisation trickled down to more and more of the population, especially in Britain, northern Europe, and the United States.[7]

There is no question that consumerism flourished as more and more economies moved from scarcity to abundance during the first half of the twentieth century, and as that abundance extended, at least in part and even if only in a highly select group of countries, from the few to the many. There were glimmers of a consumer society, for instance, in no less a place than Nazi Germany, even as it devoted an ever-increasing share of the economy to preparation for, and conduct of, war.[8]

There is, however, also no question that the transition to an economy in which it became possible for large swaths of the population to fulfil not only their needs and wants for goods and services, but also many of their material desires, represented a step change in this overall trend. In terms of the sheer range and quantity of consumer goods and services on offer – and also in terms of the breadth of the population who could access them – mass consumption was therefore something entirely new and different. Through the end of the 1940s and into the 1950s, neither the Germans nor the Japanese had made that transition. By the 1970s, they had.

As in many areas, including not least the mass-production regime that enabled it, the United States pioneered the realisation of a mass-consumption society. Its foray into the glistening era of mass consumption began in the 1920s, although the path was disrupted by the Great Depression and the Second World War. After the war's end,

though, Americans made up for lost time with a vengeance, enjoying sustained widespread real growth in incomes and corresponding
increases in expenditure through the entire Golden Age into the 1970s.
In fact, spending on consumption actually exceeded income growth for
many households owing to easier access to consumer credit, including,
by the late 1960s, credit cards.[9]

During this period from the 1920s through the early 1970s,
Americans purchased a wide range of goods and services, often in large
quantities. But, in addition to the increasingly ubiquitous automobile,
some of the most visible and concrete expenditure was devoted to electrical home appliances designed to entertain or to alleviate housework.
These in turn, of course, required the infrastructure essential for these
consumer durables: an electrified, or wired, household. About three-
quarters of US households had access to electrical power in 1946, and
that figure grew to about 98 per cent of all households by 1970.[10]

Even before this nearly universal access to electrical power in
the home, however, Americans living in wired households became avid
consumers of electrical appliances. About 75 per cent of wired households in the United States in 1931, for instance, owned a radio; the
corresponding figure for 1970 was 99.8 per cent.[11] As it turns out,
the 'diffusion rate' for radio ownership in the United States was, surprisingly, not that unusual: regular radio broadcasts started across the
industrialised world in the early 1920s, and by the 1930s British and,
even more so, German households were almost as likely as American
ones to own receivers. What is more, during the Great Depression, diffusion of radio ownership actually increased practically everywhere.
As David Landes has pointed out, prices for radio sets decreased substantially over time, and, as that happened, investing in one became an
even more important source of entertainment in poor households than
in rich ones.[12]

In Japan, on the other hand, radio ownership did not become
widespread until later, with diffusion in rural areas in particular hampered by the fact that electrical power was often not available except
at night, and then only for lighting. Only about 18 per cent of Japanese
households had a radio in 1936, although the post-war take-up of radio
receivers was rapid. Consequently, around 90 per cent of Japanese
households owned a radio by 1957.[13]

For electrical appliances other than radios, though, US
Americans were the earliest and most enthusiastic adopters by a

considerable stretch. Over half of US wired households had clothes-washing machines already by 1936, for example, while 41 per cent had a refrigerator. Diffusion really took off, though, in the post-war boom years. Even as the percentage of households with electricity grew apace, the proportion owning clothes washers grew to three-quarters by 1950, 85 per cent by 1960, and 92 per cent by 1970. And the uptake of refrigerators by wired households in the United States during this period was even more striking. The proportion of wired households owning a refrigerator was over 86 per cent in 1950, 98.2 per cent in 1960, and 99.8 per cent in 1970. Television broadcasting, moreover, had started with a trickle before the end of the war, but it grew exponentially beginning immediately after 1945. American wired households snapped up TV sets voraciously to watch the new shows. Ownership rose from just under 3 per cent in 1948 to over a third of all households by 1951. By 1960, nearly 90 per cent of wired households in the United States had a black-and-white TV, a figure that had risen to 98.7 per cent by 1970. Meanwhile, colour televisions had come onto the horizon, and Americans bought them with similar alacrity. Colour TV ownership by wired households in America (by this time very nearly all households) rose tenfold between 1964 and 1970, from 5.1 to 51.1 per cent.[14]

Appliance adoption rates (with the exception of that for radios) in other countries lagged well behind those of the United States, and they did so well into the post-war period. This was not due to lack of infrastructure. The United Kingdom, for instance, approximately paralleled the United States in extending the proportion of wired households to very nearly 100 per cent by 1970. And, surprisingly perhaps, a 1950 census in West Germany indicated that about 98 per cent of households had access to electricity, a much higher proportion than in either of the two wealthier Anglo-Saxon countries at the time and about the level reached by the United States and the United Kingdom by 1970. Japanese households, too, appear to have been electrified earlier than their Anglo-Saxon counterparts. Already in the 1930s, about nine out of ten Japanese households had access to electricity, although, again, connections and conditions of supply there were generally unfavourable for anything other than lighting. Until post-war legislation changed the situation in the 1950s, wiring and outlets in Japanese households were installed and owned by the power company, even inside the home, and electricity was generally supplied on fixed-price contracts rather than on a usage-based, metered basis. Prior to that change, there were only limited and inadequate power outlets and light fixtures – often just one or two to a dwelling. The power company had no incentive to increase the number because of fixed-price contracts, which in turn induced users to try to circumvent the system through jury-rigged 'octopus' extension leads.[15]

Infrastructure, then, was not the major impediment to adoption of electrical appliances by consumers in the post-war period in the United Kingdom or Germany, although it did have more of an impact in Japan. Instead, three major factors shaped consumer behaviour in the latter two countries: levels of wealth compared with the United States; the cost of electricity supply; and space within dwellings. Importantly, too, cultural preferences, such as differing attitudes towards debt and priorities about how to spend disposable income, militated in favour of a more gradual adoption of 'labour-saving' devices outside the United States in the post-war period. After all, as many historians of consumption tell us, the US consumer's path to modernity may well have been the first one forged; but it was most certainly not the only one taken.[16]

* * *

West German and Japanese consumers, along with those in the United Kingdom, did, however, eventually catch up with their US counterparts as their wealth grew apace in the Golden Age from about 1950 through the early 1970s. They just did so gradually; and differently. In 1957, for instance, when about 97 per cent of all households in the United States had a refrigerator, only about 10 per cent had one in Britain. For West Germany in that year, the figure was 14 per cent, while in Japan it was below 5 per cent. The waning years of the 1950s, however, corresponded to rapid growth in refrigerator ownership across the board. Already in 1959, for instance, refrigerator ownership had risen to about a quarter of all households in Germany, outpacing the richer British, among whom about a fifth of all households had a fridge. And, in the meantime, refrigerator ownership in Japan had more than doubled, to about 10 per cent of households.[17]

Washing machine ownership grew even more spectacularly in the late 1950s, particularly in Japan. In 1957, about 20 per cent of Japanese households had an electric washing machine, a figure that nearly doubled by 1959. By 1962, more than half of all households in Japan had one. And the Japanese had by then overtaken the richer British in this regard, in spite of rapid growth in the United Kingdom, too, to just under 45 per cent by 1962. For West Germany, growth was strong during the late 1950s and early 1960s, but slower than in the United Kingdom. About a quarter of all West German households had purchased a washing machine by 1957, while about a third had done so by 1962.[18]

As West German and Japanese GDP per capita approached and then exceeded UK levels in the 1970s, their catch-up with the United States in ownership of consumer durables was largely complete, although some discrepancies remained. In fact, in the mid-1970s, a West German householder was actually slightly more likely to own a refrigerator (99 per cent) than an American one (98.1 per cent), while the difference between the two in automobile ownership had narrowed substantially. About three-quarters of West German households had a car in the mid-1970s, compared with 83.8 per cent of households in the United States. West Germans also lagged behind the United States somewhat in washing machines (58 vs. 72 per cent) and televisions (82 vs. 96.6 per cent), and the lag was particularly noticeable in colour TV ownership: in the mid-1970s, 61.3 per cent of US households had one, but only 29 per cent of German households did. Meanwhile, although Japan continued to be just a bit poorer than Germany in per capita GDP in the mid-1970s, Japanese consumers were almost as likely as their German counterparts to own a refrigerator (96.7 per cent), and far more likely than either the Germans (or even the Americans) to own a colour television (90.3 per cent). Car ownership in Japan, though, lagged considerably behind both West Germany and the United States: just 41.2 per cent of Japanese households had an automobile in 1975.[19]

* * *

Consumer durables changed in status in Germany and Japan during the three decades following the end of the Second World War. Refrigerators, washing machines, and televisions moved from luxuries beyond the grasp of most households towards being more or less easily attainable items that most people came to perceive as necessities. In part, this was a completely understandable transformation. In aggregate, at least, the trend does not require much explanation: many if not

Figure 5.1 Bosch refrigerator advertisement, 1955. Interfoto/Alamy

most people who became wealthier wanted goods that would – they thought, at least – make their lives easier and better. And their rising affluence tended to ratchet desirable items up into essentials.

However, there is no question that advertising and marketing, more than anything else, shaped specific decisions about which brand and model of consumer durable to buy and how much to spend on it. Advertising developed differently in different countries. But what was common in ads for consumer durables both in Germany and in Japan in the 1950s and 1960s was their emphasis on elegance, abundance, modernity, and savings in terms of work and time. They also tended to be highly gendered, directed primarily at women. A 1955 German advertisement for a Bosch refrigerator (Figure 5.1), for instance, showed a stylishly clad housewife and her daughter happily examining their carefully stocked fridge, which was stuffed to the brim. Two years before, in 1953, an ad in Japan for a Matsushita Electrical Company washing machine depicted a similarly well-dressed and elegantly coiffed housewife smilingly drawing her clean laundry out of the washing machine. In the background is a stove well stocked with cooking implements, and, inset at the side, is a smaller ad for the same company's electric rice-cooker, also designed to make life easier and more pleasant. The fact that such appliances resulted, as Ruth Schwartz Cowan has shown for the United States, not in less, but, as her book's title puts it, *More Work for Mother*, went entirely unrecognised.[20]

* * *

All in all, then, as German and Japanese people grew richer, they spent considerable and ever-increasing amounts of money on acquiring consumer durables, including automobiles, although there were many differences in detail owing to differing habits, size of dwellings, population density, and so on. They also expended ever-larger amounts (although decreasing percentages of overall household expenditure)[21] on other consumer goods such as clothing and higher-quality food and drink, which contributed to one of the characteristic dynamics of mass consumption: greater expenditure on clothing, food, and drink, for example, was directly correlated to an increased uptake of washing machines and refrigerators (Figure 5.2).[22] In all of this, advertising contributed to the specific decisions of German and Japanese consumers

Figure 5.2 Consumers in Tokyo shopping for white goods, c. 1956. The Asahi Shimbun/Getty Images

about what to buy. And it is worth underscoring that, although a substantial number of German and Japanese households still did not possess these consumer durables by the mid-1970s, the proportion of households that did have them reflected broad dispersion throughout society. Both countries thus became both richer and more equitable in the distribution of wealth than they had been previously.

One other key trait unites the experience of the emergence of mass consumer society in Germany and Japan and simultaneously distinguishes both from the United States. Consumer credit emerged as a driving force behind mass consumption everywhere, but, in Germany and Japan, consumers were much more reluctant to go into debt than their American counterparts. This same coin had another side, which was significant: German and Japanese consumers also tended to save to a much larger extent than did Americans.[23]

The unfolding of the era of mass consumption in both countries was in many ways both striking and remarkably similar. Dramatically rising real incomes in the quarter-century after the end of the Second World War enabled Germany and Japan to join the United States and the United Kingdom in the age of mass consumption by the 1970s. Purchases by German and Japanese consumers in turn provided an impetus for the countries' economic miracles, and the growing domestic demand for many of the most important products was met for the most part domestically rather than through imports. Significantly, though, consumers in both countries were not just buying. High rates of savings in Germany and Japan also played a major role in the dynamic by providing domestic companies with investment capital to finance domestic industrial expansion. The resulting capacity increases met not only higher domestic demand, but also that from foreign markets.

Producing for the Age of Mass Consumption

As the 1950s drew to a close, with countries such as Germany and Japan entering the age of mass consumption, international trends in the production and acquisition of consumer durables attracted the attention of officials at the US Commerce Department's Business and Defense Services Administration. Ownership of items such as refrigerators and washing machines in the United States was approaching full coverage of households, in other words 'saturation'. Selling abroad would therefore be a potential avenue for growth for US

manufacturers. Indeed, this would be essential. The report that the officials commissioned and compiled, which appeared in autumn 1960,
therefore surveyed the state of the industry across the capitalist world,
with 'emphasis ... given to competitive factors, market potential, trade
opportunities, and other factors of interest to U.S. industry'.[24]

Intended to prod US producers to think about ways they might
exploit the situation to their own benefit, the report perhaps understandably focused more on the weaknesses of, and threats to, US
international competitiveness in consumer durables than on strengths
and opportunities for the sector. In spite of the persistence of controls
on foreign trade and foreign exchange in some countries, there were
clear market opportunities abroad for US firms. However, in order to
take advantage of them, those running the companies needed to take
on board the fact that they could not simply export what they were
producing for the US domestic market. In most countries outside the
United States, smaller appliances were preferred, and manufacturers
were reminded that electric current was different elsewhere, both in
voltage and in frequency. The latter could not be addressed by a simple transformer; it would require differences in design of motors and
other electrical parts. Moreover, 'traders in major exporting countries'
often offered 'attractive credit terms ... [which] are a decisive factor
in taking away business from U.S. exporters'. On top of that, US producers who wished to exploit international markets needed to bear in
mind repair and maintenance issues, which were not just technical, but
also might require some changes to prevailing norms in US business.
Austrian dealers, for example, were singled out as being 'reluctant to
invest in spare parts, which are soon made obsolete by rapid changes
of models'.[25]

Some of the statistics presented in the Commerce Department
report reinforced this sense of weakness and threat. It must also have
made for sobering reading for the target audience, US manufacturers.
On the eve of the Second World War, for instance, the United States
produced about 90 per cent of all refrigerators made in the entire
world. That share had dropped to 37 per cent by 1958. The countries
that had gained substantially in share of production at the expense
of the United States were, perhaps, the ones that might be expected
from today's perspective. But they must also have sent a chill down the
spines of contemporaries in the US industry who were seriously assess-
ing the prospects for sustained growth through export.

For instance, in 1958, the last year for which complete figures were available for the report, West German producers accounted for 18.5 per cent of all refrigerators made in the world, compared with the US share of 37 per cent. West Germany's output of refrigerators, moreover, had grown threefold between 1955 and 1958, while US output had actually declined by about 25 per cent in the same period. The next three largest producers of refrigerators in 1958 were also western European. France was responsible for about 8 per cent of world output of compressor- and absorption-type fridges in that year, the United Kingdom for 6.5 per cent, and Italy for 5.8 per cent. The next largest producer of such refrigerators globally in 1958, remarkably, was none other than Japan. Japanese manufacturers accounted for 4.8 per cent of world output in that year.

What is more, the increase in Japanese output in absolute terms from 1955 to 1958 was nothing short of breathtaking: the number of units manufactured rose more than thirteen-fold during those three short years. In the meantime, Japan's world ranking in output of refrigerators rocketed from worldwide rank eighteen in 1955 – well behind such countries as Argentina and Brazil, slightly behind Chile, Mexico, and Uruguay – to sixth globally in 1958.[26]

Those US consumer-goods manufacturers on the lookout in 1960 for even more depressing news about their prospects for growth in exports and the stiff competition from the emerging industrial power-houses Germany and Japan could find disturbing details in the report's brief accounts of developments by country. West Germany, for instance, had increased its output of refrigerators during the 1950s from 118,300 units at the start of the decade to 1.9 million in 1959. They were produced by companies such as Bosch, Siemens, and AEG, as well as some smaller firms. Significantly, the growth in output was accompanied by enhanced quality. And about 80 per cent of refrigerators produced in West Germany were purchased domestically, with the remaining fifth exported, indicating both the importance of the domestic market for growth and the stiffening of competition for the United States and others in third-party markets. During the first ten months of 1959 (the only figures available in the report), about 19 per cent of the total value of refrigerator exports from Germany went to Austria, followed by Belgium–Luxembourg and the United Kingdom (13 per cent each).

At the same time, West Germany started 'to ship to the United States substantial numbers of 1½–2½-cubic-foot absorption refrigerators, which are not manufactured by U.S. firms', although the total value of those exports was still quite modest. If, however, overall refrigerator exports from West Germany in general were substantial, corresponding imports were negligible, amounting to a grand total of 1,700 units for the first ten months of 1959 (the only figures available in the report). About two-thirds of them came from Italy, with imports of refrigerators from the United States particularly feeble, just seventy-seven units in all.[27]

Again, we are dealing mostly with dry numbers here. The most hair-raising information for US manufacturers came in the final section on West Germany on 'Market Potential'. Germans, it seems, placed considerable emphasis on quality, but price was also important. Sales of American appliances in this context 'might increase if prices were more attractive'. Regardless, though, one of the exhibitors of a new American washing machine using the latest technology at the autumn Cologne trade fair reported

> that prospects for continued success were limited. German manufacturers are reportedly quick to recognize the advantages offered by imported models and are able to produce comparable items at lower costs, *being less constrained by mass-production techniques and therefore able to retool faster.*[28]

Rapid learning and being free of the handcuffs (and sometimes higher costs) of the US mass-production regime seemed to give a competitive edge to German appliance producers.

* * *

For Japan, there was no question that developments there seemed less threatening to US producers than those in Germany, at least from the perspective of 1960. But some aspects of the report presaged a few of the storm clouds that eventually came onto the horizon for US producers. The detailed section on Japan began by noting that 'Japanese production of household electrical appliances has grown phenomenally since 1951'. Moreover, this growth had come together with a pronounced increase in technological capability, much of which was supplied through technical assistance and licensing arrangements from US firms and had been facilitated and paid for by the US government. Indeed, the report noted, 'introduction of overseas modern technology [primarily from the US] has caused domestic [Japanese] manufacturers to claim a level of technical competence equal to that of foreign producers'. The result was that technical assistance and licensing 'have recently been severely curtailed'.[29] Nothing made it more clear that the Japanese were catching up, and quickly.

Strong domestic demand was even more important for this growth in Japan than it was in Germany.[30] Indeed, only about 1 per cent of Japanese domestic production of washing machines and refrigerators was exported in 1958. About 300 Japanese firms supplied the domestic market, 10 of them 'major'. The latter included Toshiba, Matsushita (later Panasonic), Sanyo, and Hitachi. But, regardless of the impressive performance both in quantity of output and in technological level, the report was sanguine that Japanese competition posed little danger to US manufacturers. Japanese consumer durables, after all, were too small for US households, while the motors that powered them were not approved by Underwriters Laboratories (the US safety certification authority, which operated on behalf of American insurance companies), further inhibiting export sales.

Cheap Japanese manual labour, moreover, would not significantly affect costs of production here because labour was a relatively unimportant component of overall costs of production. In fact, it was estimated that motors for Japanese washing machines accounted for nearly half their production cost, and these motors were actually 25–30 per cent higher in price than in the United States. The result was that only three(!) Japanese washing machines were exported to the United States in 1957 and 1958, two in the former year and one in the latter. On the other hand, US exports to Japan were pretty paltry too. Japan purchased 735 US refrigerators in 1958 (a figure which included commercial purchases), along with 112 washing machines, 140 electric ranges, and 22 vacuum cleaners.[31]

* * *

By the late 1950s, 'Made in Germany' had reinstated itself as a watchword for quality around much of the world. 'Made in Japan' remained a label that invited suspicion, if not derision. Still, increasingly affluent consumers in each country showed no hesitation whatsoever in purchasing domestically manufactured white goods and many other products. In doing so, they helped power the countries' respective economic miracles. And their purchases and savings also stimulated the companies that produced the goods financially and enabled increasing levels of technological capability. All of this provided a sound basis for those firms to move ever more aggressively into export markets by the end of the first quarter-century after the war's end. West Germany forged into these export markets earlier than the Japanese. Eventually, and astonishingly, by the 1980s, Germany sold goods valued at nearly a third of its gross national product (GNP) abroad, in the process becoming for some time the world's largest exporter. Earlier in the post-war period, however, export as a proportion of GNP was much lower, more like 10 per cent in the early 1950s. From there, it crept up slowly and steadily to around 15 per cent from the late 1950s to the mid-1960s, and 20 per cent in the early 1970s.[32] In other words, the German economic miracle was fuelled to a large degree into the 1960s by domestic consumption.

For Japan, on the other hand, export has never been as important as a proportion of GNP as in Germany. In 1966, for instance, Japanese exports stood at just 11.5 per cent of GNP,[33] a figure typical for much of the first decades of the post-war period. The Japanese economy, of course, was growing at a furious rate during this time, and the value of exports also increased substantially to maintain its steady proportion of GNP. Nevertheless, for Japan, even more so than for Germany, domestic consumption played a vital role in the unfolding and sustaining of the economic miracle.

6 EXPORTING WONDERS

A Tale of Two Objects

1959, New York City, USA

In 1959, Carl Hahn, the New York City-based head of Volkswagen of America, was doing the rounds of the advertising agencies around Madison Avenue. His task was to cement VW's growing presence on the US market (having sold just under 100,000 cars there the previous year) in the face of the imminent entry of the large American automakers into the small-car market. Hahn's budget for accomplishing his objective was minuscule. But he was nevertheless choosy. He rejected one big, well-established, and conservative agency after another before finally settling on Doyle Dane Bernbach (DDB). DBB's partner Bill Bernbach 'was the most innovative ad man of his time, being a key player in what is today known as the Creative Revolution'.[1]

The Mad Men in Bernbach's agency – some of whom were of German descent and/or Jewish, and therefore more than slightly uncomfortable at the prospect of creating the advertising campaign for the Führer's automobile – came up with what many regard as the greatest print ad of all time (Figure 6.1). In black-and-white (because VW could not afford colour), the full-page advert appeared in *Life* magazine and elsewhere. The lower fifth of the page featured minimal (and highly ironic) text, festooned with a small VW logo. Fully

Figure 6.1 Volkswagen's legendary 'Think Small' advertisement, 1959.
Retro AdArchives/Alamy

four-fifths of the page was consumed by a vast blank white space, populated only with a tiny photo of a Beetle. The legend underneath read,
simply, 'Think small.'

The self-effacing ad and its successors in the DDB campaign
in the years that followed – one of which featured a picture of a Beetle
hovering above the headline 'Lemon' and another, later, one portray-
ing the Apollo lunar landing vehicle with the caption 'It's ugly, but
it gets you there'[2] – are credited with stimulating sales of the Beetle,
along with the firm's other iconic vehicle, the Volkswagen Bus, in the
United States in the first half of the 1960s. Indeed, by 1962, about a
third of VW's exports of worldwide exports of over 600,000 vehicles
went to the United States. And the firm also sold substantial numbers
of its wares elsewhere across the world. Production of all vehicles at
VW (90 per cent or more of which were Beetles) grew more than tenfold between 1950 and 1962. But global exports as a percentage of

production grew even faster, from about a third of production in 1950 to nearly two-thirds in 1962.[3]

Of course, the product that DDB's adverts promoted made the agency's task immeasurably easier. The Beetle may have been small, ugly, and noisy. But it was also relatively inexpensive to buy and very economical to run. It got more than thirty miles per gallon of gasoline at a time when most cars on American roads were averaging in the teens. And it provided a sense of freedom and independence for many who would otherwise have been priced out of the car market in the 1960s. Small wonder, then, that the first English-language popular history of the Beetle was called just that: *Small Wonder*.[4]

Spring 1966, Pittsburgh, Pennsylvania, USA

As a ten-year-old, I excitedly unwrapped a birthday present from my parents. I was delighted to find a pocket-sized transistor radio! Now I could listen to every single Pittsburgh Pirates baseball game, even (if only surreptitiously) the ones on the West coast that started after my bedtime. And the Top-40 countdown would now be on tap for hours each week, at home or on the go. Here, too, was a small wonder, and it was within the reach of a young child.

I was unaware of this at the time, but as recently as a decade earlier, the gift would have been impossible for my parents to afford. The first portable transistor radio – a Regency TR1 designed by an Indiana-based electrical engineering firm in close collaboration with Texas Instruments (TI), which fabricated the transistors – came to market in October 1954, priced at $49.95. The price barely covered the costs of making it, not least because transistors were extraordinarily expensive, in no small part because initial manufacturing processes produced so many duds. Nonetheless, the firm did its level best to price it as cheaply as possible. But at the equivalent of over $550 in 2022 prices, it understandably reached only a limited market. About 100,000 were sold in the first few years of production, far fewer than the 20 million plus forecast by TI's marketing team (a figure based in large part on expected demand from Americans equipping their bomb shelters in the mid-1950s).[5]

My 1966 transistor radio was not much improved over the 1954 version in terms of audio fidelity. Broadcasts were tinny, as though they emanated from a telephone rather than a stereo. And, although capable only of receiving AM stations, the pocket radio nevertheless often had

Figure 6.2 Sony transistor radio advertisement, 1960. Hera Vintage Ads/Alamy

trouble maintaining a clear signal, even with its retractable antenna fully extended. But, priced at about $5 (about $47 in 2022), it was inexpensive enough in the mid-1960s for hundreds of thousands of US American parents to afford it as a gift for their child or teenager. The radio was appreciated, not least because it ushered in an unprecedented sense of freedom and independence for youngsters coming of age at the time.

One more thing: by the mid-1960s, it was also frequently made in Japan, often by what was then a still relatively unknown company, Sony (Figure 6.2).

* * *

The VW Beetle and the Sony transistor radio were just two – although also two of the most prominent – embodiments of the miracles in miniature that spearheaded surging export sales for Germany and Japan during the quarter-century or so following the end of the war. The total value of West German exports in 1970 was a whopping 17.4 times what it had been two decades earlier. The increase for Japan was even more impressive, although admittedly from a much lower base: in 1970, the value of Japanese goods sold abroad was 23.5 times what it had been in 1950. What is more, by 1970, Japan had drawn even with the United Kingdom in value of exports, which at the time stood at just under half of the value of goods and services sold abroad by the world leader, the United States. Meanwhile, the value of German exports stood at a highly impressive 80 per cent of that of the United States in 1970 and soon surpassed it. In other words, selling abroad became vitally important to both economies. The measure known as the export quota – the value of exports divided by the total gross national product (GNP) – indicates just how important: by the late 1960s, Japan's export quota stood at 9 per cent of its GNP, and, for Germany, sales abroad accounted for nearly a fifth of GNP.[6] Both were growing.

What lurks behind these impressive statistics on exports, however, is just as significant as the numbers themselves. And, if we return briefly to the VW Beetle and the Sony transistor radio, we can gain a glimpse behind the curtain. Both objects, for instance, point to the centrality of the US market for the growth in sales abroad up to 1970 both for Germany and for Japan. But they also help us uncover stark differences between the two countries. For, although the Beetle represented a striking and highly visible symbol both of the post-war German economic miracle and of the country's related export success, it was the exception rather than the rule among the goods that Germany sold abroad during the quarter-century after the end of the Second World War. In contrast, the Sony transistor radio, although playing in and of itself a minor role in the overall increase in Japanese exports through 1970, was highly representative of some of the key developments that explain the timing, character, and sustainability of that increase. The radio and high-visibility products like it also contributed to the backlash against imports of Japanese goods from the 1970s onwards, especially in the United States.

Selling the World the Things That Make the Things; or, the Wonders of Invisibility

Nowadays, the most visible objects sold abroad by German manufacturers are, without question, automobiles. It is therefore unsurprising that cars and car parts constitute the single largest product category among the country's exports: 17.5 per cent of the total in 2018. A further 4.6 per cent of German exports in that year were 'other vehicles'. Selling mobility, then, accounted for more than 22 per cent of all overseas sales, earning Germany a lot of money, and guaranteeing a lot of jobs.

If we look at it from the other end of the telescope, however, about 78 per cent of German goods sold abroad were *not* vehicles. If we exclude from this nearly four-fifths of exports that were not cars and products from other categories that, like autos, have high levels of visibility and consumer recognition – electrical appliances and (less likely) food and feed – what is striking about those that remain is that they are virtually all producer or capital goods, that is items sold by German manufacturers to businesses in other countries, which are therefore invisible to all but specialists in a particular sector.[7] What is more, although the precise mix has varied, the heavy focus on producer and capital goods exports has been a persistent characteristic of German foreign trade since the 1950s.[8]

Aside from vehicles, three groups of producer goods stood out from the rest in terms of Germany's export volume in 2018, just as they have for the entire post-war period: machines, chemicals, and (often closely related to chemicals) pharmaceuticals. These three categories alone comprise nearly one-third of all exports and belong to a group of goods that some have called 'the things that make things'.

* * *

'Machines' represent a broad category of things that make things, which is worth breaking down a bit. Let's start with machine tools, machines that cut, shape, and form metal. These, then, are the things that make the machines (or parts of machines) that make things. By any conventional measure – proportion of value added by manufacture or percentage of industrial employment, for instance – it is a tiny industrial sector with a few large players and many smaller ones. By the late 1970s, for instance, machine tools accounted for only about 0.3 per cent of the value of manufactures produced in the United States. In West Germany, moreover, the sector provided only 1.5 per cent of total industrial employment. While average employment in the United States was 62 per machine-tool establishment, firms in Germany were larger, but still employed only 225 on average. Twelve German machine-tool companies employed more than 1,000, whereas there were just 10 such large employers in the machine-tool sector in the United States in the late 1970s.[9]

Machine tools, however, deliver an outsized impact on manufacturing industry as a whole. Their significance for the broader economy and competitiveness therefore vastly outweighs their relatively modest nominal economic contribution and employment figures. On the one hand, they are essential to the production process for about half of all other manufacturing, including, for example, such demanding sectors as automobiles and airplanes. But, perhaps even more importantly, they shape the organisation of work and production, as well as enabling precision manufacturing, and thus have a profound and direct impact on productivity and competitiveness.[10]

German firms have counted among the leaders in production and technology in the global machine tool industry since the late nineteenth century, and they resumed that position shortly after the end of the Second World War. Significantly, this traditional strength was maintained not just in the Federal Republic, but also in the German Democratic Republic, communist East Germany. East German machine-tool producers continued to manufacture quite respectable conventional metalworking machines during the early post-war period. And East German factories also made decent transfer machines, which combined a number of machining operations such as drilling, milling, and cutting into a single integrated, mechanically automated machine. The machine also transferred the workpiece (such as an engine block) from one operation to another. The machine tools produced in East Germany, though, were inferior in quality to those made in West Germany, and exports were accordingly restricted for the most part to other countries in the Soviet bloc.[11]

For West German machine-tool producers, however, the accent by the 1950s was once again on the global. For instance, by 1964, Germany produced just under 16 per cent of the world's machine tools, but was responsible for just under 29 per cent of all machine-tool exports. Not surprisingly, given the prevalence of manufacturing in general in Germany, the country also imported a lot of machine tools. But it sold three times as many abroad as it imported. In other words, Germany had an export/import ratio in machine tools of 3:1. The corresponding figures in 1964 for the post-war leader in virtually all areas of manufacturing, the United States, were as follows: a quarter of world production of machine tools; just over 21 per cent of exports; and an export/import ratio of 8:1. Germany, however, was able to maintain – and even extend – its share of world production, its exports, and its export/import ratio up to 1980. By then, the United States continued to enjoy a slightly larger share of world production than Germany, but its export share had shrunk to 6.6 per cent, and the American industry's export/import ratio was reduced to just 0.6 per cent, meaning that the United States was now importing many more machine tools than it was exporting.[12]

West Germany's maintenance of its world market share is all the more impressive when we consider that it occurred during a period of rapid and profound technological change in the machine-tool industry. Numerical control (NC) of machine tools – initially using rudimentary programmes punched into paper tape to guide boring machines to produce aluminium aircraft wings – was first developed in the United States in the late 1940s and early 1950s with the support of the US Air Force in a series of projects undertaken at MIT. On the basis of this generously funded military-related research, initial commercialisation of NC technology took place in the United States already in 1952. By the late 1950s, it had been applied to complex, multi-function machines that were highly automated. NC technology was taken up, albeit slowly at first, by conventional machine-tool producers, who could now offer a path to automate even small- and medium-sized production runs, thus offering a complement and an alternative to mass production.[13]

By the 1970s, both the conventional and the transfer-station sectors of the machine-tool industry – as well as NC itself – were revolutionised still further when increasingly sophisticated and powerful computer technology enabled computerised numerical control (CNC) machine tools. Eventually, these technologies were applied more broadly in manufacturing, in computer-aided manufacturing (CAM), computer-aided design (CAD), and the combination of the two (CAD/CAM). The extensive overlay of computing technologies onto machine-tool technology dramatically changed the character of the industry, requiring old, established players to acquire new capabilities, while also providing an opportunity for companies involved in computing to use their capabilities to enter the machine-tool market.

US machine-tool producers did not fare well in this technological transition. By and large, they failed to invest in R&D (research and development), or in much of anything else for that matter. The problems were exacerbated by takeovers of machine-tool producers through mergers and conglomeratisation. As one MIT study put it in the 1980s, conglomerate managers who took over machine-tool firms 'thought that they could make money by selling the same old designs and building them on depreciated equipment'.[14] Incidentally, the East Germans did not do too well in this technological transition either, although for different reasons. Perhaps most importantly, the economic planning system there discouraged innovation, in particular through hindering cooperation across traditional industry lines that would foster technological development through the overlay of different technologies.[15]

In stark contrast both to their near neighbours in East Germany and to their capitalist competitors in the United States, West German machine-tool producers navigated through the NC revolution (and subsequent CNC and CAD/CAM revolutions) largely successfully, although not without encountering some crosscurrents and bumps along the way. (Japanese producers did the same, although in often very different ways, as we will see shortly.) One of the biggest challenges for conventional machine-tool builders in Germany lay in acquiring the required expertise in computing technology, an issue that became more pressing as the latter became more sophisticated. However – and this was crucial – the German producers *knew* about this challenge early on owing to their emphases on, first, fostering close contacts with their domestic and foreign customers and, second, keeping a close eye on competitors, especially abroad. And, just as crucially, they were able to act on that knowledge quickly owing to support from private foundations and state-level governments, especially the training and apprenticeship programmes they provided.[16]

* * *

Beyond the machines that make other (or parts of other) machines, there is another group of things that make things: just plain machines. Again, it is a broad category, ranging in the immediate post-war period from mechanical adding machines and cash registers to electricity generators and turbines. Moreover, clusters of related machines and apparatus also count as machines in the statistics. These conglomerations are called 'turnkey plants', involving ready-made factories for the petrochemical industry, for example. Again, the Germans were not only past masters in the sector; they were also able to regain and retain their strong global position in the decades after 1945.

In some areas of the machine branch, German firms are not merely important in world markets, but have dominated during most of the period since the end of the war. Printing presses represent an admittedly extreme example of this. As late as 2021, for instance, three German manufacturers – Heidelberger Druckmaschinen, Koening & Bauer (KBA), and Manroland – controlled nearly two-thirds of the global market in the sector.[17]

Other companies in different branches of the machine industry in Germany have more modest global market shares, but they have nonetheless been or become key players in international markets. A good example is Krones, located in Neutraubling, near Regensburg, in Bavaria. Hermann Kronseder, a young master mechanic and electrician, founded the firm in 1951. Kronseder spotted a market opportunity in labelling machines, primarily for the expanding drinks industry, and, for that reason, it is unsurprising that the new company's first advertising leaflets were sent to Germany's hundreds of local breweries. Initially the machines were fairly basic and only semi-automated. By the late 1950s, however, Kronseder and his company had developed fully automatic labellers capable of handling thousands of bottles per hour. And the firm soon expanded into packaging, packing, unpacking, and filling machines as it implemented a strategy of selling integrated systems. In the process, the company gained a strong presence in Germany and other parts of Europe. Targeting other overseas growth markets starting in the early 1960s, Krones worked hard to capture US juggernaut Coca-Cola as a client, as the American drinks producer moved in 1966 from burned-in applied ceramic to paper labelling of its distinctive glass bottles. Export growth has been essential to the company's success from the outset, and sales abroad have become increasingly important. Exports of its products regularly account for about 90 per cent of all sales.[18]

Other German engineering companies have taken the strategy of integration of machines and related apparatus still further. Two of the most prominent examples, Uhde GmbH and Linde, have a history stretching back long before 1945. Friedrich Uhde founded a limited engineering company in Dortmund in 1921, soon specialising in design and construction of apparatus for ammonia synthesis, which was used in the production of fertiliser, a major growth area worldwide in the

1920s. Uhde expanded into design and construction of other apparatus deploying high-pressure chemical technologies in the course of the 1930s. After the war, the company became a subsidiary of Hoechst AG, in a move by the large chemical firm in 1952 to embrace related diversification by integrating plant-building into its product palette. Uhde GmbH remained a distinct and largely independent entity under Hoechst, however, with much of its growth in sales volume occurring beyond Germany's borders.[19]

Linde's history started even earlier, in 1879, when theoretically trained engineer and inventor Carl Linde, backed by investors, established a factory to produce refrigeration machines based on patents he developed at the University of Munich. The primary customers at first were German breweries, and the company soon began to sell abroad as well. By the late nineteenth century, having removed himself from day-to-day management and returned to his beloved applied research, Carl Linde had patented machines and apparatus for air separation and rectification, which by the early twentieth century serviced a burgeoning market in producing gases – especially purified oxygen – for welding and cutting. The air-gases market expanded markedly thereafter, including, for instance, producing gases for medical applications, neon lighting, and steel production, but also large quantities of nitrogen for ammonia synthesis. Linde's company produced and sold the gases themselves. But it remained primarily an engineering company, and one of the few in the world capable of producing high-quality, large-scale, and expensive air-separation units (ASUs) and related apparatus. After 1945, the firm, now based in Wiesbaden, near Frankfurt, regained and reinforced its position as a high-quality specialist engineering company. It did so by making integrated air-gas manufacturing facilities, both for industrial gases companies, such as Swedish-based AGA, and for on-site ASUs to service large oxygen steel plants, oil refineries, and food-processing plants. The lion's share of Linde's sales was outside of Germany.[20]

What unites all of these otherwise highly varied stories from the post-war German machine industry is this: the intertwined rise of mass production *and* of mass consumption in the so-called 'Golden Age' from the early 1950s through the early 1970s created a space for highly specialised engineering firms.[21] These companies, many of which were already in existence before 1945, found willing customers among firms in the publishing, drinks, and automobile industries, among others. Companies in these industries in turn were directly engaged in producing *en masse* for increasingly wealthy and apparently insatiable consumers, many of them located abroad.

* * *

The same dynamic was at work behind the scenes in the development of the German post-war chemical industry, which also built on previous achievements to enter new areas, with a heavy focus on exports. True, its performance after 1945 was nothing like it had been during the heyday of German organic chemicals prior to the First World War, when German firms controlled nearly 90 per cent of world trade in the area. After all, from the 1920s, companies in a number of other countries – especially in the United States, but also in Britain and elsewhere – had developed substantial domestic capability to rival that of the Germans, not only in production, but also in research and development for new products and processes. In fact, in one area – producing organic chemicals from petroleum rather than coal, employing the relatively new field of chemical engineering – the Germans had fallen well behind the emerging world leader, the United States. And the association of IG Farben, the largest chemical company between its founding in 1925 and the end of the war, with the wartime criminal behaviour of the Nazi regime played a part in poisoning the international brand of German chemicals. This was especially true because the major post-war players (BASF, Bayer, and Hoechst, among others) were all formed out of IG Farben. In addressing these significant technological and reputational issues, however, the IG successor firms brought considerable experience and scientific and engineering capability to the table, qualities essential to participation in this industry, which was already highly globalised in terms of trade in, and use of, intellectual property.[22]

Thus, although two chemists from BASF's paint and plastics division embarked with some trepidation in 1953 on an extended visit to forty US chemical firms, they 'soon perceived that the "Badische" [BASF] has a good name and has, even over there, friends who are happy to stand helpfully by our side'.[23] Their visits laid the groundwork for more intensive international cooperation that resulted in the purchase – but also, crucially, the sale – of intellectual property that propelled BASF and the two other major successors of the IG into the top ten chemical firms in the world by 1964; a decade later, BASF was the largest corporation in this highly competitive global industry, and the other two IG successors were also in the top five worldwide.[24]

That growth of the international chemical industry from the 1950s into the 1970s was most pronounced in three areas: plastics, pesticides, and pharmaceuticals. The three IG successors played a major role in developing and refining processes to produce plastic and pesticide intermediates for other producers, both in Germany and, increasingly, abroad. Hoechst and, particularly, Bayer were also key players in the ever more sophisticated and lucrative pharmaceuticals market. The drugs produced were often highly visible to consumers, although more so to the physicians who prescribed them. The German chemical giants, however, more often than not supplied the constituent ingredients – for instance, polyethylene pellets for making plastic products, or the active agents for pesticides or cleaning products – of what consumers purchased from other, more visible companies, at home and abroad. BASF tried desperately to counter that lack of consumer awareness when it kicked off a fourteen-year campaign in the 1980s in North America with the slogan 'We don't make a lot of the products you buy. We make a lot of the products you buy better.'[25]

Technologies for Conspicuous Consumption: Japan and Its Export Markets from the 1950s to 1970

The Economist, that barometer of emerging global trends in political economy, ran a brief notice in July 1952 about Japan's attempt to return to the world's trading stage when it made a request to join discussions on the General Agreement on Tariffs and Trade (GATT).[26] Other than that, the weekly magazine piped up only occasionally during most of the 1950s on the subject of Japanese exports, for instance to note the country's threat to the British apparel and textile industries or its balance-of-trade deficit with the Sterling Area.[27]

The spell, however, was broken in March 1958, in an article tellingly entitled 'Heartbreak of a Salesman'. The subtitle, though, told the news magazine's pitying story still better – 'Where Are the Japanese to Sell Their Goods? So Many Doors Are Shut to Them':

> Where the boots of the Imperial Army tramped 16 years ago, the shoes of the salesmen now pad on their soft inquiring way.

Their destinations are Manila and Jakarta, Peking, Rangoon and Saigon; and, beyond that, the other capitals that the soldiers aspired to but never reached. The briefcases that their wearers carry contain some awesome requirements. Last year the value of the goods that Japan sold abroad, though well above the previous year's total, fell short of the cost of things it bought by some ... 30 per cent.

The *Economist*'s reporter went on to note that, despite falling commodity prices that would translate into lower bills for imports, Japanese manufactured goods remained relatively expensive, preventing them from reaching lucrative potential markets in Europe, and especially the United States.[28]

Fast forward just a dozen years, to 1970. *Fortune* magazine used similar military imagery to tell a very different story:

To hard-pressed competitors around the world, Japan's export drive is taking on the overtones of a relentless conspiracy to invade and dominate every vital international market. Almost everywhere, from North America to Southeast Asia, the Japanese are steadily increasing their enormous share of sales. The very rhetoric of Japanese businessmen reinforces the image of a hyperaggressive trading power – with talk of 'advancing' into a new area, 'forming a united front' against foreign rivals, and 'capturing' a market.

By then, the United States purchased about a third of all the goods Japan sold abroad, and it was the largest of its many foreign customers. Japan, however, did not reciprocate with the United States or any other country, carefully 'shield[ing] its own market'. Its trading partners abroad were thus 'doubly provoked and are now threatening economic warfare'.[29]

Exactly twenty-five years after the end of the military conflict that Japan and Germany had started, then, *Fortune* warned that Japan was fomenting war by other means. And this was even before the Japanese auto industry demonstrated, in the decade that followed, just how effectively they could challenge traditional producers in Europe and North America in markets around the world. In any event, though, the juxtaposition of the 1970 *Fortune* article with the one that appeared in *The Economist* in 1958 suggests some striking conclusions. It is clear that Japan's emergence as a major exporter after 1945 happened later, faster, and for the most part in different sectors from that of Germany.

* * *

Of course, from the 1980s, Japan, like Germany, exported a lot of automobiles. There was one other area of significant export presence that Japan and West Germany had in common, especially after the late 1950s: machine tools. Unlike Germany, however, Japan's presence in the global machine-tool industry before 1945 was virtually non-existent. And it was very limited even domestically, despite efforts by the Riken Institute for Physical and Chemical Research to develop such a capability in the 1930s, and in spite of the establishment of several subcontractors in the sector to supply state-owned military arsenals. As a result, the country was heavily dependent on foreign suppliers, mainly Germany and the United States, a dependence that proved devastating in the lead-up to, and during, the war: imports from Germany were blockaded, and those from the United States dried up owing to sanctions even before America entered the conflict.[30]

Nevertheless, the urgent necessity of developing and enhancing capability in the machine-tool industry during the war, especially in conjunction with airplane and vehicle production, provided a basis for post-war development. Crucially, however, emergent Japanese machine-tool producers were also able to take advantage of their very backwardness by being willing and able to leapfrog conventional machine tools and machine-tool manufacture. In other words, Japan's fledgling machine-tool companies had little experience, but at the same time were keen to learn from industry leaders and unencumbered by ingrained traditions that they needed to unlearn. They could therefore get in on the ground floor in the early 1950s when the first NC machine tools were first developed and then produced in the United States.

Prompted by a detailed report on the MIT research delivered to Japan by Professor Yasuhito Takahashi, a Japanese academic working in the University of California system, trade associations in Japan pushed successfully, and almost immediately, for publicly funded research on the new technology at universities and government labs. Not long afterwards, the idea – and the extensive public-sector R&D activity in developing it – soon attracted the private sector. By 1956,

Fujitsu had produced the first Japanese NC machine. Its unreliability, however, prompted the firm, with its expertise primarily in electronics, to team up with Makino, an innovative machine company that specialised in milling machines. The two demonstrated the first fruits of their labours at an exhibition in Osaka in 1958, although their NC milling machine did not work for long: it had to be taken away for repairs partway through the initial demonstration. But, despite this embarrassing public setback, Fujitsu developed the promising technology to commercial application, in cooperation with Hitachi and Mitsubishi Heavy Industries.[31]

Interest and experience in applying the new technology snowballed in Japanese firms thereafter. On the one hand, it proved well suited to the industrial structure and domestic market of Japan, which involved a large number of small firms producing small runs of goods in relatively small quantities primarily for the home market.[32] Meanwhile, however, the new technology continued to stimulate cross-industry cooperation; its further development deployed the complementary talents and expertise of companies in electronics and machines. By 1966, then, the Japanese firm Fanuc had pioneered the design and building of machine tools that incorporate integrated circuits, which had been produced for the first time in the United States in 1959. The commercialisation that followed saw steady technological improvement through internal research, purchase of licences and patents from domestic and foreign companies, and acquisitions abroad, along with substantial and rapid cost reductions. Other Japanese companies, moreover, soon joined in on the bonanza and were therefore well positioned to take the lead in the next major technological wave, CNC machine tools, which led eventually to pioneering work in robotics and fully automated factories.[33]

The newfound competitive edge of Japanese machine-tool producers was soon apparent in international export markets. In fact, Japan pretty much displaced the United States as world leader in the sector between the mid-1960s and mid-1980s, a period during which, as we have seen, Germany maintained or slightly improved its position. The statistics are jaw-dropping, as is the speed at which the change occurred. In 1964, the United States was responsible for about a quarter of global production, while the fraction produced by Japan's machine-tool sector stood at 6.4 per cent. The United States accounted for about a fifth of all exports in that year, the Japanese for just 1.3

per cent. By 1985, though, Japanese firms produced nearly a quarter of all machine tools by value and were responsible for fully 23 per cent of world exports. The corresponding figures for the United States in 1985 were 12.6 per cent of world production and under 5 per cent of exports.[34]

As its presence on global markets grew, the Japanese machine-tool industry imported less technology. Instead, to an ever-increasing degree, it developed and improved new products domestically. An additional factor enabling Japanese firms to catch up with, and then decisively overtake, their US competitors was that Japanese producers oriented themselves towards commercial applications, with clients and customers of Japanese firms for the most part in the private sector. In contrast, US machine-tool producers, highly dependent on military contracts that called for often needlessly complicated designs and design changes, showed 'little concern with cost effectiveness and [had] absolutely no incentive to produce less expensive machinery for the commercial market'.[35]

* * *

Bell Labs, the research arm of the American Telephone and Telegraph Corporation (AT&T) US telephone monopoly, was a storied place. Lavishly kitted out and luxuriously resourced, Bell Labs featured some of the most talented researchers on the planet. Shortly after the end of the Second World War, a small team of those scientists, led by John Bardeen, Walter Brattain, and William Shockley, set to work on finding a replacement technology for the vacuum tubes used in electrical devices such as radios. The task was one that occupied researchers in many other parts of the developed world, as they sought alternative materials that would conduct electricity more efficiently than tubes, allowing devices to operate at cooler temperatures and use less power. The devices would also be much more compact.[36] Unlike their competitors, however, the Bell Labs team was successful. Just before Christmas 1947, they produced a prototype of the world's first semiconductor device, the transistor. Their successful research earned the three team leaders the 1956 Nobel Prize in Physics.[37]

Like any other breakthrough technology, transistors had to undergo considerably more development work to be translated into a commercial product. Much of it was carried out at another AT&T

subsidiary, Western Electric, which held the main patents, and at Radio Corporation of America (RCA), which was linked to AT&T through cross-licensing agreements. The new, high-profile technology promised the American telecommunications giant fabulous additional riches.

AT&T's top managers, though, knew all too well the danger that yet another highly visible and profitable monopoly – that is, after all, what a patent entails – might pose to its main monopoly, the US telephone system. They therefore decided they would bring other firms into the fold. At least thirty-five other US electronics firms got on the bandwagon by 1952, by which time the first hearing aids using the new technology were being manufactured. During the year that followed, French, German, and British companies joined the American ones. And, in summer 1953, so did one little-known Japanese company, Tokyo Tsushin Kogyo Ltd (Totsuko, or Tokyo Telecommunications Engineering Corporation).[38] Within a few years, that firm was marketing its products under its new name: 'Sony'.

**

The company later known as Sony was established in early May 1946 by Masaru Ibuka and Akio Morita, two engineers who had previously worked together in the Japanese Wartime Research Committee. The new company's start-up capital was minuscule. It possessed practically no equipment. And the firm could afford to employ only a handful of staff. At first, the founders and their fellow workers developed niche products such as heated seat cushions and pickups for record players using reclaimed materials and their own ingenuity. Quickly, though, they branched out into radio receivers and related equipment, primarily supplying NHK, Japan's national broadcaster. The firm's managers, moreover, clearly recognised that friends in high places were essential, and they therefore also cultivated a close relationship with officials from the US military government in Japan, many of whom were located in the main NHK building in Tokyo. One day, on one of their frequent visits to SCAP's Civil Information and Education section, Ibuka and Morita were treated to a demonstration of a new type of recording device, which used magnetic tape instead of stainless-steel wires as a recording medium and featured far better sound quality than wire recorders. Already committed to sound recording devices as a new line of business to complement radios, where there was stiff competition from established companies, the managing directors of Totsuko decided to focus their efforts on developing this new technology.[39]

It is worth reminding ourselves that, at the time, this was no small matter. Magnetic tape had been developed only in the mid-1930s in the laboratories and factories of Germany's mighty IG Farben for use on recorders built by the country's AEG electrical concern. Making the tape in particular posed massive challenges for even these firms, which were among the world's most technologically advanced. After all, they had to ferret out the optimal magnetic materials, the ideal adhesives, and the best tape for the job. Small wonder, then, that the technology counted as prize booty when Allied investigators in Germany interviewed the developers and carried away technical documents for use in US and British industry, which is why the SCAP authorities in Japan could demonstrate the technology in the NHK Building. Meanwhile, Ampex, an American firm founded only in 1944, benefited substantially from the information gleaned in Germany. Backed also by its own development work, Ampex subsequently secured a leading commercial position in the latest recording technologies.[40]

Engineers at Totsuko in the late 1940s worked at a distinct disadvantage to those at companies such as AEG and Ampex. Not only did they not have the resources and personnel enjoyed by firms in more technologically advanced countries; they also were not privy to the information seized in Germany. Instead, they had to feel their way forward by trial and error.

They did so, and with aplomb. Already in 1950, they had produced protypes of two tape recorders that used the magnetic tape they had developed and sold under the trade name 'Soni-Tape'. One of the prototype recorders was for institutional use. The other, crucially, was intended for the consumer market. Even in this early stage of its existence, the company that would soon be known as Sony oriented itself towards – and was constantly on the lookout for – new and challenging technologies for consumer electronics. It was therefore no accident that Ibuka, on one of his many and often extended trips to the United States, stumbled across transistor technology and, by dint of dogged persistence, managed to obtain a licence from Western Electric in 1953. The Japanese company then cajoled, humoured, and humbly begged reluctant officials at the Ministry of International Trade and Industry (MITI) to supply it eventually with the required foreign exchange to complete the transaction.[41]

Sony's immediate focus for applying the transistor was on a radio. Again, the technical challenges were immense. Transistors, for example, were extremely difficult to make, requiring a level of cleanliness unparalleled in most other manufacturing processes. Early transistors were also unable to convey the human voice; in other words, they had to be tweaked substantially to make them suitable for radio applications. The licence from Western Electric, moreover, did not help with either of these issues, because it did not include any provision for the supply of know-how, the additional information needed to turn a patent into a product. And, added to this, while working feverishly on the transistor radio with a commercial product in sight, Sony engineers encountered a discouraging setback in 1954, when Regency, working closely with Texas Instruments, introduced the TR1 model, the world's first transistor radio available to consumers. We have already heard about the small pocket radio's $49.95 price tag, more than $550 in today's money, with an optional 'earpiece for convenient listening' available for $7.50 more, around $83 now.[42]

Sony therefore did not just have to learn how to manufacture transistors. Its engineers also had to figure out how to make their radios much more cheaply, while at the same time ensuring they were of high enough quality to satisfy consumers, especially abroad. The company did so, eventually dominating world markets for the tiny electronic gadgets together with their Japanese colleagues and competitors, such as Toshiba. Sony continued its laser focus on emerging technologies in consumer electronics in the years that followed, with a special interest in miniaturisation. It pioneered, for instance, the application of the transistor to television, producing a highly portable (if also quite rudimentary) model by the early 1960s. Later in the decade, it also invested heavily – and ultimately successfully – in a new concept for sharper and more reliable colour television pictures. The firm's Trinitron, based on patents from 1966 and available to consumers for purchase from 1968, dominated the high end of colour television markets worldwide until the patents expired in 1996. Most of its sales were abroad.[43]

* * *

Sony's performance in the quarter-century following the end of the Second World War was dazzling, a potent combination of technological sophistication, commercial acumen, and export success. And it was not alone among Japanese electronics producers, which included such successful firms as Toshiba, Sanyo, NEC, Fujitsu, and Kobe Kogyo Corporation (which merged with Fujitsu in 1963).[44] This suggests that context was extremely important for the success of Sony and other Japanese electronics firms, as indeed it was.

The first thing to emphasise here is the breakup of *zaibatsu* during the American occupation after the war, which opened up a space for some new domestic players in a variety of industries to enter and thrive in the Japanese market. Sony was the most prominent in electronics. But we have encountered others in other industries, including, for instance, Honda Motor Corporation, which produced its first automobile well after the end of the war.

A second contextual factor also had roots in post-war American policy: by the late 1940s, the United States had come to regard Japan not as an enemy to be tamed, but instead as a crucial ally to be fostered. As it became increasingly evident in January 1949 that the Chinese communists led by Mao Zedong would be victorious in China, the administration of US President Harry S. Truman decided to open US technological information to developing countries. Japan, although far poorer and much less developed than the United States at the time, clearly did not count among them. But, given the destruction wrought in the country during the Second World War and the need to bolster it as tensions rose in the Asia–Pacific region, the US government placed it in that category anyhow. The Korean War, which started in 1950, then gave even greater impetus to this US willingness to help Japanese firms develop their technology.[45]

A third contextual factor was also linked to Japan's perceived technological backwardness. American companies viewed Japanese firms as no threat whatsoever technologically or commercially, and they therefore proved willing to provide licences, know-how, and other intellectual property at cut-rate prices and without any reservation.

The final contextual factor in the rapid success worldwide of the Japanese electronics industry after 1945 relates to another, lesser known consideration. There is, of course, no doubt that the emergence in particular of the electronics industry in Japan (as elsewhere) required high levels of scientific and engineering capability and skilled work of

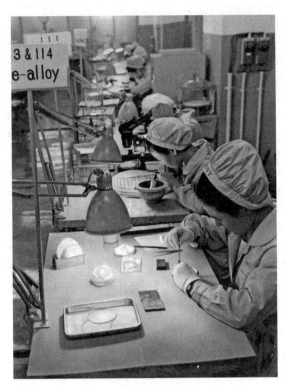

Figure 6.3 Sony workers assembling transistor radios, 1961. The Asahi Shimbun/Getty Images

all sorts, most of which is attributed (sometimes wrongly) to males. But what is often overlooked is the crucial role of semi-skilled and unskilled – mostly female – labour. Making transistor radios and other electronic gadgets was a labour-intensive process, requiring nimble fingers, endless repetition, and long hours. And, of course, low wages, and wages were invariably, if unfairly, lower among women. Cheap labour was abundant in post-war Japan, especially in the female workforce. Many Japanese women were already working in the textiles sector, and the rapid rise of the consumer electronics industry in Japan starting in the late 1950s provided alternative – if still far too poorly paid – employment opportunities for them (Figure 6.3).[46]

The Political Consequences of Making and Selling

One key distinction that is made in measuring world trade is between 'visibles' and 'invisibles'. The former are tangible goods, including raw materials, food, and manufactures; the latter are services, most prominently insurance, shipping and other logistical services, and intellectual property, such as patents and licences. The West Germans and the Japanese became increasingly proficient during the first quarter-century after the end of the Second World War at making things and then selling them abroad, which translated into growing balance-of-trade surpluses with much of the rest of the world. The two countries were net importers of invisibles, but that only slightly dented the massive surpluses accrued through trade in visibles. In contrast, the United States and the United Kingdom exported services to an ever-increasing degree in the post-war period, even as they abandoned their previously dominant and apparently unassailable positions in the sale of manufactured goods abroad. These trends led by the 1970s to persistent and growing balance-of-trade problems for the United States and the United Kingdom, especially with Germany and Japan.[47]

But there was a puzzle in terms of perceptions, in the United States in particular, insofar as Germany and Japan were not placed on the same footing, in spite of the fact that the trade deficits with these two countries posed a similar level of political and economic risk to America. In fact, there were some ways in which Germany's threat was larger. For instance, the total value of Germany's manufacturing exports exceeded that of the United States by the 1970s, in no small part because German manufacturers were able to displace US competitors in third countries. What is more, at the time, both Germany and the United States exported far more than Japan in absolute terms.[48]

Yet, it was the Japanese who became the primary target of the wrath of US politicians by the 1970s. The question is: why? Part of it had to do with the fact that the US trade deficit with Japan by that time was larger than that with Germany, which directed attention away from what was arguably a much more important problem, the loss of US manufacturing markets to German competition in third countries. Second, the Japanese domestic market was viewed – correctly – as far less open than Germany's. But a third, extremely important, and frequently overlooked reason had to do with the relative level of visibility of the manufactured goods imported into the United States from each of the two countries. Goods from Germany, including machine tools, machines, and chemicals, tended to flow directly to manufacturers of other things, thus rendering them largely invisible. Some Japanese exports to the United States also went to other manufacturers, but the growing presence of Japanese products and names in highly visible sectors such as consumer electronics and motorcycles led to the inescapable conclusion that the Japanese were quickly eroding American industrial dominance.

The verdict was reinforced with the initial arrival of large quantities of fuel-efficient and inexpensive Japanese automobiles in the United States. This coincided almost exactly with the start of the first oil crisis of 1973–1974, which in turn sent American car buyers scurrying away from US-made gas guzzlers. The VW Beetle also benefited from this trend, but its German manufacturer was already in the process of pivoting away from producing the long-selling icon, at least in Germany, where the last Beetle rolled off the line in 1978. Instead, Volkswagen embarked on a new strategy of offering multiple models for sale, including many more up-market, higher-value-added cars. The output of other German automakers such as Mercedes and BMW was far less visible on US roads and highways. They were relatively few in number. Just as importantly, however, they constituted symbols of affluence and refined taste that, unlike Japanese automobile imports at the time, did not represent an existential threat to American manufacturing jobs. US carmakers at the time focused primarily on the mass market, where Japanese producers were becoming increasingly competitive.

Part III
SUSTAINING MIRACLES, 1973–1989

7 THE WAGES OF CONSTRUCTION

Years of sabre-rattling and intensive girding up for war in Germany and Japan during the 1930s culminated in one of the most wide-ranging and cataclysmic armed conflicts in recorded history. The two countries then reaped what Adam Tooze has called *The Wages of Destruction*: soundly vanquished in 1945, both faced the monumental task of rebuilding cities, factories, housing, and infrastructure in the years that followed. Both, moreover, underwent extensive reform at the behest of Allied military occupation authorities, while at the same time, as in the title of John Dower's book, *Embracing Defeat* as an opportunity for long overdue reform of politics, society, and the economy. Their fundamental reorientation – from bellicose national-security states with large military–industrial complexes that attempted to operate independently from world markets to commercially oriented civilian economies working within a US-dominated capitalist economic and security system – was spectacularly successful.[1]

During the quarter-century that followed their defeat, goods made and designed in Germany and Japan gradually conquered world markets. Even before that, German and Japanese households were becoming steadily more affluent, directing a considerable amount of their newfound wealth into savings, but also using it to purchase their way into mass consumer society. The two countries also availed themselves of military protection from the United States, which enabled full attention to commerce. All of these factors taken together drove their economies onwards and upwards. It was a virtuous circle, which propelled Germany and Japan into the highly select club of the very richest nations by the 1970s.

After just a few revolutions of the virtuous circle, however, as Germany and Japan started to pay back the wages of destruction, it became clear that they would also have to confront new and very different challenges as they began to reap the wages of construction.

'The Smell of Prosperity'

If rapidly industrialising regions and countries throughout time and around the globe have something in common, it is the experience – and apparent widespread toleration – of environmental degradation. As late as the 1960s, this was true even in parts of the United States, the richest and most heavily industrialised country in the world.

Alabama in the US south is a case in point. Governor George C. Wallace, best known for his robust confrontations with the nascent Civil Rights Movement starting with his 1963 promise of 'segregation now, segregation tomorrow, segregation forever', was also committed to 'low-grade industrial development, low taxes, and trade schools as keys to the state's future'. Part of his industrial development strategy involved attracting investment in new pulp and paper mills in order to pivot away from agriculture and textiles towards high-value-added, high-wage manufacturing in the state. Inevitably, complaints about the obnoxious odours emanating from the plants soon followed. Wallace countered the critics by saying that this was just 'the smell of prosperity'.[2]

There is no question that, regardless of the level of economic development, making things is a dirty business. And, if economic growth and high profits are the goals, as they are in capitalist countries in particular, a balance must therefore be struck between industrial expansion and environmental protection. The German legal framework, its civil code, has long since attempted to define the parameters within which that balance can be found through its 'toleration clause'. It requires individuals to accept considerable vexation – for example, for property owners in the most recent version of the code, from 'gases, steam, smells, smoke, soot, warmth, noise, vibrations and similar influences' – in the interest of 'the common good'.[3]

Wallace's words reflected an especially broad – one might even say exceptionally liberal – conception of 'the common good', one that would have found favour among many in Germany and Japan during the initial decades of the post-war period. Wallace managed to express pithily and memorably the acceptance – indeed, the insistence – that industrial growth must take precedence over environmental protection in order to facilitate economic development. It is a sentiment that has prevailed in many countries during the course of industrialisation, not least, most recently and prominently, in China.

Post-war Germany and Japan, then, were not that unusual in privileging industrial expansion over the environment in the pursuit of rapid economic growth. What set them apart from other countries while simultaneously unifying them in this experience, however, was the speed of growth within a highly compressed timeframe. And the West Germans and the Japanese also shared a single-minded dedication to GDP growth and increased standards of living to the exclusion of virtually everything else. As Harold James has argued convincingly, West Germany achieved political legitimation from its inception into the late 1970s by defining its identity through its economic performance. And, already in the 1960s, Ezra Vogel's carefully researched book *Japan's New Middle Class* demonstrated persuasively the identity formation that came from being part of the growing and increasingly affluent Japanese white-collar workforce.[4]

An identity based on economic performance was certainly strong and compelling for the citizens of both countries. After all, previously deeply held identities based on bellicose nationalism had been thoroughly discredited through the provocation of a disastrous war that ended in ignominious defeat. Nevertheless, widespread consensus about prioritising industrial expansion over the physical environment soon showed signs of erosion in the face of repeated and sometimes horrifying environmental disasters during the post-war period. The cracks appeared already in the 1950s.

Shattering Revelations and Realisations

The mighty Rhine River flows northwards from Switzerland to the Netherlands, where it empties into the North Sea. It marks about half of the French–German border and winds its way through heavily populated stretches of Germany and Holland, cutting a path through some of the most picturesque landscape of northwestern Europe. Yet, in 1970, a couple of decades into the West German economic miracle, the *New York Times* reported that the Dutch called the river "'het

Figure 7.1 Smog in the West German Ruhr district, 1985. Ullstein bild/ Getty Images

riool van Europe" – the sewer of Europe'. That was a pretty accurate description. By the time the Rhine arrived at the North Sea, it consisted of only about 80 per cent water. The remaining 20 per cent was a toxic cesspool of human and, especially, industrial waste. In fact, the river was so dirty that BASF chemical corporation, with main plants on the Rhine that themselves counted among its biggest polluters, had to develop specialist water purification technologies by the early 1970s to ensure undisturbed production.[5]

Meanwhile, in Japan in 1971, the Tokyo metropolitan government presented a report on pollution in the much less grand, but still highly important, Sumida River that ran through the Japanese capital. Especially after 1955, the Tokyo authorities reported, the river 'was contaminated with factory effluents and domestic water [sic] to such an extent that it had turned into an open sewer, not only prohibitive for fish and other aquatic life but also giving off unpleasant and obnoxious odors'.[6]

It was not just the water. By the end of the 1950s, more than 300,000 tons of dust rained down annually on the inhabitants of Germany's highly industrialised Ruhr District (Figure 7.1). And things were worse by 1961, when the region's citizens 'suffered from 1.5 million

Figure 7.2 Smog in Tokyo, 1977. The Asahi Shimbun/Getty Images

tons of dust, ashes, and soot, and four million tons of sulphur dioxide'. Most places within the region experienced more than 5 kg of dust per 100 square metres in a month, with some burdened by up to 20 kg. Experts at the time agreed 'that up to three kilograms were tolerable'.[7] But the situation seems to have deteriorated still further by June 1970, when Cologne's main newspaper, the *Kölner Stadt-Anzeiger*, 'warned that residents of West German cities would soon be wearing gas masks'.[8]

Industrialised and heavily populated areas of Japan did not fare any better. In 1960, Osaka residents choked in heavy smog for nearly half the year. Those living in Tokyo in 1969 could see Mount Fuji, about 60 miles away, for only 38 days during that year, down from the previous and longstanding norm of over 100 days.[9] And, in July 1970, a Japanese correspondent for the *New York Times* echoed the *Kölner Stadt-Anzeiger*'s dire prediction from a month earlier, reporting that 'Tokyo's top pollution expert warned today that gas masks would become a necessity for the city's residents if effective measures against air pollution were not taken immediately' (Figure 7.2).[10]

* * *

Air and water pollution had been widespread in Germany and Japan since they began to industrialise in the nineteenth century. The same was true in other industrialising countries. In all cases, complaints and, sometimes, popular outrage ensued, although almost invariably they had little effect on the pace of industrialisation. Pollution levels, moreover, no doubt worsened during the Second World War, when the primary objective was output in service of the war effort regardless of cost to workers' health or the environment.

However, air and water pollution became still more troublesome and ubiquitous in the post-war period in all industrialised countries, in the face of untrammelled, pell-mell industrial and economic growth, especially in rapidly expanding Germany and Japan. And vastly increased quantities of soot, dust, and filthy water were not the only issues. After all, regardless of the nuisance and dislocation these pollutants caused, they were at the very least highly visible and/or malodorous, so they could be easily detected by the senses of the individuals affected. The same could not be said, however, for some of the new pollutants spewed out by recently built factories, especially those that manufactured or used the products of modern organic chemistry and, to a lesser degree (at least in the industry's formative years), electronics.

***

In the mid-1950s, residents around Minamata Bay in Kumamoto Prefecture, located about 570 miles southwest of Tokyo, noticed something strange about the local cat population. Many of them had started dancing. The odd and comical effect of the cats' behaviour soon dissipated, however, when the poor creatures suffered seizures, many of them dying soon thereafter. Yet worse tidings were to befall the residents themselves. Starting in 1956, local hospitals found themselves deluged with an unusual number of patients with unexplained illnesses ranging from severe brain and neurological disorders to impaired sense of smell and hearing. What is more, an alarming spike in birth defects accompanied the tragic outbreak. Minamata City Government immediately formed a Committee on Unknown Disease, commissioning scientists at Kumamoto University to undertake intensive investigations into the causes of the appalling developments. By November, they had determined that heavy-metal contamination of fish and seafood was to blame, although they were as yet unsure about which heavy metal was at fault and where it came from.[11]

The cause of the misfortune, however, was obvious to many: Chisso Company, Ltd, which had started producing nitrogen at its factory in the area in the 1930s before branching out into the production of acetaldehyde and other organic chemicals. It had been dumping tons of waste mercury compounds left over from its manufacturing processes into the bay. Although the company initially denied any responsibility whatsoever, a 1968 Japanese government report assigned sole blame for the tragedy to effluent flowing from Chisso's plant. It also conclusively identified the mechanism by which humans were affected as the concentration of methylmercury in the fish and shellfish that they ate. The report, moreover, identified a separate incident involving severe methylmercury poisoning of the surrounding population from 1964 emanating from effluent dumped in the Agano River in Niigata Prefecture by Showa Denko Company's petrochemical factory there.[12]

The case of Minamata disease 'was one of the most serious incidents in the history of industrial pollution' anywhere in the world. Unfortunately replicated since then in other countries and regions, if generally on a smaller scale, the Japanese case from the 1950s is so infamous that it is the formal name for a United Nations-sponsored Minamata Convention on protecting human health and the environment from mercury contamination, which came into force in August 2017.[13]

* * *

Minamata disease is one of the most notorious examples of industrial pollution and its impact, but it is unfortunately far from unique. In Germany and in other industrialised and industrial countries, a range of 'industrial diseases' has emerged since the 1950s. They include cancers attributable to polyvinyl monomer production and handling, as well as industrial illness and land contamination from polychlorinated biphenyls (PCBs).[14]

What is common to all of them is not just their industrial genesis. They also share the very significant characteristic of being undetectable by human senses. They thus usually come onto the radar after the initial, and often devastating, damage has already been done, and then only with the aid of more or less sophisticated scientific instruments and testing. What is more, and partly for this reason, establishing causality – between the substance and the illnesses or environmental damage that it induces – is notoriously difficult.[15]

Through her highly influential 1962 bestseller, *Silent Spring*, Rachel Carson pioneered the identification of this new phenomenon. Carson tackled the invisible, odourless, yet devastating impact of increasingly widespread use of the insecticide dichlorodiphenyltrichloroethane (DDT), which, if unchecked, would eventually result in a spring without insects, and, consequently, without much wildlife, birdsong, or vegetation.[16] Carson's book appeared in German translation later in 1962, and two years later in Japanese. A broader indictment of chronic industrial pollution in Japan, *Osorubeki kōgai* (*Fearsome Pollution*), was published in 1964 by an economist, Kenichi Miyamoto, and an engineer, Hikaru Shoji. It, too, sold widely.[17]

By the 1960s, West Germany and Japan were becoming vastly more affluent than they had been previously. But, with most of this affluence stemming from their status as emergent manufacturing juggernauts, they paid a high price for joining the elite club of the world's wealthiest nations. The two countries were therefore surprisingly quick in following the lead of the world's richest industrial country, the United States, where, starting in the mid-1950s, the novel concept of 'environmentalism' gradually bubbled into popular consciousness. Nascent environmentalism was fuelled by increasing levels of pollution and emboldened by a much more comfortable standard of living than ever before, which itself provided increasing leeway within which to confront the problem.[18]

Consuming's Miseries

Mass production in the post-war period, especially when it involved new products and processes in the chemical and electronics industries, represented not just a quantitative change, but also a qualitative one. What is more, it was one that was particularly pernicious when the pace of increase was as torrid as that experienced in West Germany and, even more so, in Japan. But the concomitant of mass industrial production – mass consumption – did substantial damage as well. Eventually, rising levels of automobile ownership in both countries led to much higher levels of air and noise pollution as well as dependence on overseas sources of petroleum for fuel. But the problems associated with cars emerged more gradually in Germany and

Japan than they did in the United States, indeed for the most part after the 1970s. Before that, though, people in both countries had already begun to enjoy the first fruits of their newfound affluence through increased consumption. First, there was more and higher-quality food and drink, and then more and more varied clothing and household goods, often made of synthetic fibres and plastics. Then came a wide range of consumer durables. Mass production enabled mass consumption. The inevitable and invariable consequence of both was the output of masses of household rubbish. And this, in turn, and quite predictably, posed the question of where to put it all.

There are really only four possible answers to that question: bury it; burn it; send it off somewhere else to become someone else's problem; or find some way to reuse or repurpose it. There are downsides to all of them, not least cost, which tended to rise with each successive option. And all four are even more expensive if they are done safely and more or less permanently. Not surprisingly, then, Germany and Japan, like other wealthy, industrialised countries in the post-war period, tried the first two before moving on more recently towards the third and, ultimately, fourth option. The most recent moves have also been in the direction of safer and more sustainable implementation of all four measures.

* * *

Perhaps the most ancient disposal method for solid household waste involves simply digging a hole, depositing whatever has been discarded, and covering the hole over again. Up to a point, the method works reasonably satisfactorily. It can do the trick if the land available fairly locally is extensive enough, the population is low enough, and the rubbish produced is both limited in total amount and inert. When those conditions cease to exist, however, things can get tricky. And when they change rapidly and in tandem, the situation can get very ropey quite quickly.

That is what happened in Germany, Japan, and other industrialised or industrialising countries in the post-war period. Long-term trends towards urbanisation and population growth led to unprecedented levels of population density in some cities. Affluence amplified the resulting increases in volumes of rubbish produced. And, on top of all that, there were profound changes in the composition of municipal

solid waste. It tended to become lighter, less inert, and more volumi-
nous, because of increased levels of food waste (which had previously
been used for animal feed or compost), decreased levels of cinder and
ash from household fires (owing to widespread adoption of central
heating in Germany, although far less so in Japan), and elevated usage
of single-use plastics and other packaging. At the same time, however,
tradition, regulation, and legislation guaranteed that the task of getting
rid of this waste remained highly localised in the first decades after the
end of the Second World War. It is therefore unsurprising that many
local authorities in Germany, Japan, and elsewhere found themselves
on an apparently endless search for what environmental historian Joel
Tarr has called 'the ultimate sink'.[19]

What this meant in practical terms can be graphically illustrated by the post-war experience of the city of Frankfurt am Main.
The city opened a landfill facility in its nearby city woods in 1925, to
which it transported household waste by truck. It had seemed adequate
into the 1950s, but that all changed in the course of the decade. Instead
of a hole, it became a fairly decent-sized – and rapidly growing – hill,
dubbed 'Monte Scherbelino' because of the many shards of broken
glass littering the small mountain. The dump eventually became over-
stuffed with around 20 million cubic metres of household and industrial waste. By the early 1960s, moreover, Monte Scherbelino was not
only overfull, but often on fire, as a result of the highly flammable
methane gas arising from food waste deposited there. The fire service,
called to the site repeatedly, decided to make the most of a bad and
then worse situation by creating a fire pond on the site. But water seep-
ing from the pond and the dump leached out toxic materials, which
flowed into a nearby stream.

The site was closed as a municipal waste dump in 1968. Four
years later, having been covered with fresh topsoil and planted with
grass, wildflowers, bushes, and trees, it reopened as a park and recre-
ational facility. But its newfound purpose was short-lived. It gradually
emerged that the site, although it appeared bucolic, was so severely
contaminated as to be a grave danger to public health. It was duly
closed in 1992. Now known as Scherbelino-Weiher, the old dump is
currently in the process of being thoroughly detoxified and cleaned up.
When that is completed, however, there are no plans for it to be used
as a leisure park again. Instead, it will become a place for 'quiet relax-
ation' ('*stille Erholung*'), whatever that may mean.[20]

In post-war Tokyo, its population larger, more densely packed, and more recently rich than Frankfurt's, things were no better, and became if anything worse. Household waste was collected on carts, which were loaded from Tokyo's streets into trucks or barges. Significant spillage resulted from the process, posing public health risks. The rubbish was then transported to the ironically named Dream Island (Yumenoshima) in Tokyo Bay, an artificial island originally built in the 1930s for a new airport for the Japanese capital. The war interfered with the development of the airfield, and, after 1945, the site was repurposed as a landfill facility. The waste transported there included considerable amounts of foodstuffs and other organic material, which was not properly buried or treated in any way. Not surprisingly, the site was subject to 'spontaneous combustion caused by garbage fermentation gases, foul odors and plagues of flies'. By 1957, things had become so bad that a major clean-up effort ensued. 'The waste was covered, and a park was established with trees, sports facilities and even a large spa.'[21] That certainly has a familiar ring to it!

* * *

Getting rid of rubbish by setting it on fire is almost as old a practice as burying it. In fact, the two are often complementary in that incinerating rubbish simultaneously decreases its volume and (generally) makes it inert, making more efficient use of landfill space. But, unless carried out under controlled conditions, the drawbacks of burning rubbish are obvious, especially for those living in the immediate vicinity. Depending on what is being burned, the smoke that results can range from merely annoying to acrid and choking, all the way to toxic and deadly. The severe downsides of highly localised burning of rubbish thus became apparent very quickly, especially in urban areas. Therefore, already in the late nineteenth century, as waste streams grew in early industrialising and rapidly urbanising Britain and, later, Germany, experiments began with incinerators – initially called 'destructors'. But these more centralised – although still local – incinerators, too, produced smoke and gases ranging from the noxious to the highly toxic.[22]

There were, though, also real benefits to be reaped from incineration, not only by rendering waste more compact and inert, but also by using it to generate electricity or heat. And, as waste streams burgeoned in Germany, Japan, and other countries as post-war economic recovery and resurgence began in the 1950s, the search was on to design cleaner and more efficient – in a word, more modern – waste incinerators. Portrayed in publicity photos as glistening and pristine, with sweeping, curved access roads, the new facilities featured extensive internal highways of conveyor belts to automate delivery of trash to, and ash from, the incinerator. In 1958, they made their appearance in cities as diverse as Glasgow, Düsseldorf, and Tokyo.[23]

The new plants were yet another sign that Germany and Japan were rapidly catching up with the first industrialiser, Britain, not only in industrial production and affluence, but also in their confrontation with an inevitable consequence of both. Yet the spanking new facilities did not solve the problem either. They were perhaps much more efficient in turning trash into ash. Yet they still belched out a lot of smoke and stench. And two even more serious – and closely related – problems soon emerged. First, as Rachel Carson and others forcefully brought to the fore in the early 1960s, the invisible threats of pollution were likely to be particularly devasting. And, sure enough, when effluent into the water, air, and soil from incineration plants was put to the test by scientists and engineers, the new facilities failed miserably. Part of the reason for this was the second emergent issue: profound changes in the composition of the household waste stream, in particular the torrent of waste from new, single-use thermoplastics.

Here again, the crisis caused by the rapid upsurge in plastic waste was common to all industrialised countries. But plastics consumption was particularly high in West Germany, with Japan not far behind. It all started out differently, however. In the 1950s, per capita consumption of plastics was 6.4 kg in the United States, 2.5 kg in Britain, 1.9 kg in Germany, and a paltry 0.2 kg in Japan. Growth in consumption was very rapid in all four countries during the rest of the decade, and, by 1962, when Silent Spring appeared, US consumption of plastics per capita hovered near 20 kg. By then, however, West Germany had caught up (and in fact slightly surpassed) the United States. Plastics consumption in the United Kingdom, on the other hand, had grown substantially, but was still only about 10 kg per person. Remarkably, though, Japan had by then caught up with the UK. By 1969, British consumption levels had more than doubled to just over 20 kg per capita, while the US rate had risen to just under 35 kg. Consumption of plastics per capita in Japan, however, had surged to 32.8 kg, far outstripping the UK and approaching the level reached in the United States. In fact, Japanese production of plastics (not the same as, but closely correlated with, consumption) increased nearly tenfold during the 1960s. However, at 49.9 kg of plastics consumed per capita at the end of that decade, West Germany reigned as plastics champion by a wide margin.[24] Here was yet another indicator of the extent to which the former laggards had caught up with, and in some measures even surpassed, former world leaders.

Naturally, vastly increased levels of production and consumption of plastics translated into ever-larger quantities of plastic waste, especially because much of the plastic was single-use packaging. And when that waste was burned in incinerators, the resulting chemical transformations poisoned the air. Moreover, the ash buried after burning adulterated adjacent soil and groundwater. The combination of still-rising output of household waste and diminishing landfill capacity, however, meant that incineration continued to be used in the decades that followed. The problems were especially chronic in Germany and Japan, both dense in population and therefore short of suitable land. Even there, though, substantial research and development funds went into finding technologies to maximise efficiency and minimise pollution while at the same time ensuring significant output of power and/or hot water. Optimising all these objectives was expensive, which was one reason why some referred to them not as trash-burning, but instead as *cash*-burning, power plants.

* * *

As practised from the late nineteenth century into the post-Second World War period, landfill and incineration were primarily matters of local responsibility. Still, as indicated already, the sites where these activities took place involved some degree of centralisation. And this in turn meant that some sort of transportation was necessary, generally trucks or barges. In this context – and given the severity of the waste crisis as it threatened to spiral out of control by the 1960s – it is hardly surprising that the thoughts of waste professionals turned towards another solution. Why not just collect the municipal solid waste as usual and transport it not to the local dump or incinerator, but instead somewhere far away?

The first steps in this direction took place early on and involved taking waste from larger cities to less populated areas in the

German and Japanese countryside. But these sites were limited, and in the 1970s and 1980s, as the flood of municipal garbage overwhelmed landfill and began to overtax increasingly unpopular incinerators, the search for alternative places to put the trash became intensive. As in so many cases, growing and ever more challenging waste streams combined with increasingly stringent regulations and legal requirements to push rich countries to offshore their problem into poorer ones.

West Germany – or, more precisely, West Berlin, the still-occupied western sectors of united Germany's capital city that were notionally attached to the Federal Republic – was the first to move. A landlocked island surrounded by the East German Democratic Republic (GDR), West Berlin ran out of landfill and incineration capacity early on. And so, in 1972, city officials negotiated an agreement whereby, on the basis of ongoing and substantial payments of hard-currency Deutschmarks, garbage trucks from West Berlin dumped their contents in landfill sites on the other side of the Berlin Wall, in East Germany. The East Germans, ever on the lookout to maximise hard-currency returns, set up fast-food stands for the bin lorry drivers for their breaks. Drivers could purchase a curry wurst and a coffee at typical West Berlin prices in Deutschmarks, which were of course worth many times the local eastern-Mark currency. West German cities such as Düsseldorf and Frankfurt, moreover, soon followed West Berlin's lead. By the 1980s, substantial quantities of household and toxic wastes were being transported daily to the GDR. The situation reached a high – or low – point in Frankfurt in 1989–1990. The city's incinerator had to be closed for refurbishment for a year, and a nearby landfill facility reached capacity, prompting a 'garbage emergency'. The head of the city's environmental department – a representative of the Green Party, no less – therefore had no choice but to take the embarrassing step of sending virtually all of the city's waste to the neighbouring GDR, albeit with the feeble excuse that at least it would be transported by environmentally friendly barge rather than by truck.[25]

East Germany, of course, ceased to exist in October 1990, and the former country's waste-handling facilities became subject to West German law, which immediately removed a convenient option for beleaguered West German cities. They responded in two ways. First, they substantially increased incineration during the 1990s in spite of all of its drawbacks. And second, in tandem with the federal government, German cities and towns began to export their waste further afield.[26]

The Germans formed part of a group of rich countries that did likewise, starting with a trickle in the late 1980s and intensifying until 2018, when China abruptly decided to curtail its imports of waste. The main waste export from rich countries was plastics. The UK, France, the Netherlands, and Canada were among the rich countries sending their plastic waste abroad. However, nearly a third of all plastic waste exports between 1988 and 2020 came, in rank order, from the United States, Japan, and Germany. The UK was a distant fourth, with the United States exporting nearly three times as much as Britain during that period. Japan's exports were double those of the UK, and Germany's just under twice the British rate. The main importers included Malaysia, Indonesia, India, Turkey, and Vietnam, but the lion's share was absorbed by China after it opened to the West in 1978. In all, China absorbed nearly two-thirds of the rest of the world's legally traded plastic waste between 2010 and 2020. Its drastic and sudden change of tack through its 2018 'National Sword' policy has thus thrown the global plastic waste trade into disarray, a situation that, not surprisingly, has led to an increase in illegal exports and imports.[27]

* * *

The fourth major option for dealing with the waste stream involves recycling, which is often bundled together with reduction and reuse as the 'three Rs' of contemporary waste-management policy. Like the other methods of waste disposal, there is a long history of collecting worn-out or broken material and using it again, although, significantly, it was not called recycling, but described as salvage. Both involve using discarded material as an ingredient to produce something new, but the two differ fundamentally in terms of the motivations behind them, the economics, the location of markets, and the people carrying them out. Salvage was motivated by poverty and want; dictated entirely by the free market, which was usually highly localised; and carried out by marginal figures in society. Most recycling, in contrast, is motivated by concern for the environment; dictated by law, regulation, and a market skewed by subsidy and frequently operating at the national or international level; and usually carried out by established, and often quite large, firms in the private sector. Recycling in this sense is therefore a concept of much more recent vintage than salvage.[28]

Beginning in the 1970s and 1980s, Germany and Japan proved relatively early and enthusiastic adopters of recycling, mainly as the result of citizen pressure and activism along with the government mandates that came in their wake. And, because recycling involved competences and familiarity with markets that exceeded the capabilities of local authorities, realising the targets set by government required, perhaps ironically, involvement of the private sector, although third-sector organisations also played a part. But so did everyday people. Recycling systems for municipal solid waste have tended to work best when different types of household waste are segregated from one another, and when the waste to be recycled is as clean as possible. A high level of buy-in from householders is essential to both, just as it is for the related objective of waste reduction. Germans and Japanese have been particularly willing – and sometimes downright enthusiastic – separators and reducers, as often highlighted in media reports. In fact, keen embrace of recycling and reduction has had the unintended consequence in both countries of shortages of trash to fuel newly built energy-generating incinerators, which are capital-intensive and therefore very expensive when kept idle.[29]

The interaction between citizen buy-in and governmental activism in Germany and Japan has led to development of unified waste-handling systems. The systems are anchored in the so-called 'polluter pays principle' (PPP) defined initially in 1972 by the Organisation for Economic Co-operation and Development (OECD). In addition, they are based on the doctrine of 'extended producer responsibility', which transfers liability from the consumer to the producer for disposal not only of packaging of products, but also of the products themselves when they are discarded. The systems therefore involve high levels of public–private cooperation.[30] Germany's dual system and the related Packaging Law, enacted in 1990 and 1991, respectively, represent excellent examples. The Duales-System-Deutschland AG joint-stock company formed as a result has been plagued with capacity issues and occasional fraud. But its ubiquitous 'Green Point' logo for packaging, sold to producers around the world, has helped finance its operations to recover and recycle cardboard, plastic, and other materials. In Japan, on the other hand, a series of laws on recycling of various materials enacted in the 1990s has led, for instance, to a thriving trade in household appliances that have outlived their usefulness. In the process, it has prompted development of new technologies and resulted in substantial business opportunities.[31]

From Heresy to Dogma[32]

Were Germany and Japan more polluted than other industrialised countries by the 1970s? That is an extraordinarily difficult question to answer. If we could reliably count not just the number of incidents in these and other countries, but also their severity and longevity, it might be possible. But it would also be necessary to take into account sometimes extreme regional variation as well as differences between rural and urban areas within a country. And we would have to include consideration of the fact that pollution, especially of the air and water, does not recognise national borders.

So, it is a question that is perhaps nearly impossible to answer, certainly with any precision. And it is possibly also the wrong question. It is perhaps better to ask instead this question: did Germans and Japanese *believe* their countries were more polluted than others by the 1970s?

In 1972, in a written submission to the first ever United Nations Conference on the Human Environment (UNCHE), held in Stockholm in June of that year, prominent Japanese environmental activist and engineer Jun Ui laid claim to that dubious distinction. Ui asserted boldly that 'Japan probably had "the worst environmental pollution of any country in the world"'. And, to back up his claim, he could point not only to severe smog in Tokyo and other major cities, but also to the 'Big Four' pollution incidents of the mid to late 1950s. The notorious foursome included methylmercury poisoning at Minamata; 'Yokkaichi asthma' caused by a petrochemical plant; cadmium poisoning known as Itai Itai ('It Hurts, It Hurts') disease; and another outbreak of methylmercury poisoning on the Agano River. These incidents of severe industrial pollution led to public health emergencies and had, moreover, been preceded by another incident involving radiation poisoning. On 1 March 1954, crew members of the Japanese fishing boat *Lucky Dragon V* were unlucky enough to be downwind of a US atomic bomb test at Bikini Atoll. The exposure led to several cases of radiation sickness, and one of those affected died seven months later. It was a small episode, but it attracted worldwide attention in 'a peak of transnational environmentalism during the 1950s', as 'fears about radiation and nuclear war inspired a transnational protest movement'.[33]

Some West Germans also believed that their country occupied a special place in the problematic pantheon of the most polluted countries. But, unlike the Japanese, they could not make the case for this in June 1972 in Stockholm. Part of the reason for this lay in the simple fact that neither West nor East Germany held a seat in the United Nations until more than a year later, when they finally recognised each other's existence in conjunction with Chancellor Willy Brandt's opening to the east (*Ostpolitik*), which started around the time of the Stockholm Conference in 1972.[34] It is, however, in any case unlikely that there would have been as prominent and forceful a spokesperson as Jun Ui making the case that Germany led the world in pollution. There had, after all, been plenty of environmental problems in Germany throughout the 1970s, but no equivalent to Japan's Big Four incidents of the 1950s. It was not until the 1980s, in the context of widespread concerns about the environmental impacts of nuclear weapons and power as well as 'death of the forest' (*Waldsterben*) through air pollution, that West Germans began to stake a claim to being particularly hard-hit environmentally. The January 1980 establishment of the German Green Party, which soon became a potent force first in local and eventually in national government, provided a strong indication of this emerging change in consciousness. In the process, Germany became – possibly – 'the greenest nation'.[35]

From that point forwards, two aspects of German and Japanese environmentalism unite the experience of the two countries. First, the environmental movement in each case was both grounded in the local, where pollution occurred and people were most immediately affected, and at the same time closely connected to international and transnational partners and movements. Environmental groups in Germany and Japan made common cause with compatriots abroad, both in other developed countries and in developing countries.[36]

Second, it was not only environmental activists – and eventually politicians – in both countries who saw the emergent crisis as an opportunity for action. Businesspeople did so as well. After all, attacking environmental degradation not only requires modification of individual and collective behaviour; it is also an engineering problem. And, as both countries are leading manufacturing powerhouses, many German and Japanese companies, encouraged by their home governments, have seized the opportunity to innovate through environmental remediation.

World-beating German chemical firms such as BASF and Bayer, for instance, have carefully repositioned themselves through innovation and advertising. They now present themselves not as a large part of the problem for industrial pollution and household waste but rather as purveyors of sound solutions to these problems. German automakers have also begun designing cars with eventual complete recycling in mind. Meanwhile, relatively small Japanese companies such as EcoValley Utashinai have pioneered the development of plasma-arc technology to generate electric power from trash more efficiently than ever before. And at the same time, larger firms such as Hitachi Zosen and Mitsubishi Heavy Industries have joined other companies and local authorities to develop complete waste-management packages designed to provide integrated solutions for disposal and recycling of, and power generation from, waste.[37] The managers of all of these firms, moreover, have their eyes focused not just on the domestic market, but also on lucrative exports.

Harrowing experiences of heavy industrial pollution and consumer waste crises associated with extremely rapid industrialisation and growth of consumerism have therefore stimulated social and political change both in Germany and in Japan. And, more recently, they have also prompted innovation as many German and Japanese companies embrace green technology for growth, especially in foreign markets. The other side of the coin, however, is that industrial pollution and waste continue to plague both countries, with the added realisation of the challenges of climate change coming to the fore since the 1990s. Environmental scandals and legacy, moreover, have formed just one dimension of the recurring need to deal with the unmastered past both for Germany and for Japan.

8 THE HAUNTINGS OF THE PAST

Sado Island, in the Sea of Japan off the country's west coast, was once one of the world's largest producers of precious-metal ores. Following the closure of its gold and silver mines in 1989 after more than 400 years of operation, many leading Japanese figures believed the site and its history deserved recognition and commemoration. They therefore worked hard to get the mine complex on the tentative list of UNESCO world heritage sites in 2010. Years of further lobbying, including an intervention by former prime minister Shinzo Abe, finally bore fruit in 2022. In January, Prime Minister Fumio Kishida nominated the mine complex for full UNESCO world heritage status. If the application succeeds, it will stimulate tourism and unlock substantial grant income for preservation and further development.[1]

The apparently good news for Japan precipitated outrage in South Korea. Sado Island's mines, after all, operated for decades during the first half of the twentieth century on the backs of a substantial Korean workforce labouring under abominable conditions. During the Second World War, many of them effectively became slave labourers. The provocation was felt all the more intensely because it came on the back of court rulings in South Korea awarding compensation from Japanese firms, including Mitsubishi Heavy Industries and Nippon Steel & Sumitomo Metal, to Koreans forced to work for them during the war. The Japanese government, however, intervened to insist that the companies should not pay, claiming that a 1965 intergovernmental agreement settled the claims once and for all.[2]

The discord between the two countries in the wake of the court rulings has therefore been palpable, the atmosphere fraught, and the stakes high. Reporting on one of the South Korean court decisions from 2019, the *New York Times* claimed that 'The $89,000 Verdict [Was] Tearing Japan and South Korea Apart.' This has worried the American government. Wading in following the furore over Japan's UNESCO application in 2022, US officials appealed to the two countries to settle all remaining disputes as a matter of urgency, given the security threats from North Korea and China.[3]

***

Meanwhile, in 2000, Germany took a different tack. Many large German firms faced a renewed barrage of lawsuits from Second World War-era forced and slave labourers at home and abroad. They consequently teamed up with the German government to form the foundation 'Remembrance, Responsibility, and Future'. As many as 6,500 German firms are now among the contributing members of the foundation, which took political and moral – and some financial – responsibility for what German government, business, and society, acting in combination, inflicted on National Socialist-era forced workers and concentration camp inmates. At the same time, this did not stop several Italian former forced workers from seeking – and being awarded – compensation from Germany in Italian (and also Greek) courts between 2004 and 2008. Germany responded by instituting formal proceedings against Italy in the International Court of Justice (ICJ), accusing the Italian government of having failed to respect its immunity from such lawsuits.[4]

In this particular case, the judges of the ICJ found in favour of Germany in 2012.[5] But that does little to change two fundamental facts applying to both countries. First, the interconnection between state and military actions on the one hand and those of private firms on the other crops up repeatedly. And, second, related to this, even decades after the end of the Second World War and in a new century, the issue of German and Japanese use of forced and slave labour and mistreatment and imprisonment of others during the conflict refuses to go away.

Perhaps it never will, and perhaps it never should. In moral terms, at least, German and Japanese culpability for the crimes and maltreatment visited upon foreign workers and occupied peoples during the war forms a central and undeniable part of each nation's history, just as contemporary Britain is being held accountable in many ways for its empire, and the United States, among many other things, for its shameful record of treatment of native Americans. But there are also important differences here. Unlike for the British and the US Americans, where demands for acceptance of responsibility and liability have emerged gradually and for the most part relatively recently, attempts to hold the Germans and Japanese to account for their actions during the war came even before it ended.

Perhaps the fact that this continued after 1945 was mostly because they had lost. In any event, though, in spite of some admirable if scattered instances of acceptance of responsibility and contrition, the overall response by German and Japanese government and industry since 1945 has been underwhelming, to say the least. It may be virtually impossible to set a price for causing human suffering and death, but there is also no doubt that virtually all attempts to do so by Germany and Japan in the last half of the twentieth century and, to a large degree, into the twenty-first, have been grudging, late, and entirely inadequate.

Resisting the Past

But let's remember – there was never any real expectation that the Germans and Japanese would bring themselves to justice. That task was supposed to fall to the Allies, with criminal prosecutions of individuals the mechanism. The highest Allied leadership, meeting in Yalta and Potsdam in the spring and summer of 1945, decided that they would stage unprecedented trials of German and Japanese war criminals before international tribunals following the end of the war. The novelty lay not only in the convening of international military tribunals to hear the cases: many of those brought before the tribunals were accused of entirely new categories of criminal behaviour, including 'genocide' and 'crimes against humanity'.[6]

The first of the trials of major war criminals before an International Military Tribunal (IMT) began in November 1945 in Nuremberg, the city that had previously hosted the annual meetings of the Nazi Party. It lasted nearly a year. Of the twenty-four defendants from the upper echelons of the Nazi Party, the German state, and the military named in the indictment, twelve were sentenced to death, three to life imprisonment, and four to long spells of incarceration. One had committed suicide well before judgement was rendered, and one was declared medically unfit for trial. Only three were acquitted.

The IMT for the Far East was similar in scope, charges, and outcome to the IMT held in Nuremberg, although it started later in Japan than in Germany – in April 1946 – and lasted longer – until November 1948. Twenty-eight former leaders from Japanese politics and the military were charged. When the trial ended, the twenty-five remaining defendants were found guilty of at least one charge. Two of those indicted had died already, and one had been deemed mentally unfit to stand trial. Seven of those found guilty were sentenced to death, and sixteen to life imprisonment, with just two given shorter prison sentences.[7]

There were other trials as well, conducted by the Americans, British, Soviets, French, Poles, and Australians, among others. They featured conviction rates broadly similar to those reached at the IMTs.[8] Still, though, and regardless of conviction rates, the absolute numbers of those tried for war crimes in Europe and Asia after the Second World War are minuscule in comparison with what many seeking justice expected and desired. Shortages of prosecutorial personnel and money placed curbs on expectations in the short term, which was coupled with the desire by the former Allies to put the military occupation completely behind them. And on top of that, the growing conviction – especially on the part of US policymakers and security experts – that West Germany and Japan would be essential allies in the Cold War helped bring this attempt at justice – unprecedented in scale and scope though it had been in the first post-war years – to an end by 1952.

* * *

That outcome rankled many. And they included not only those feeling aggrieved at the incomplete course of justice, but also those who had survived maltreatment and malnourishment as concentration camp inmates and forced or slave labourers. The situation was exacerbated by the fact that responsibility for bringing war criminals to justice and

Figure 8.1 German chemical industrialist Otto Ambros on trial at Nuremberg, August 1947. Keystone/Hulton Archive/Getty Images

compensating their victims had passed from the Allies to the Germans and Japanese themselves by the early 1950s.

For its part, German law made it extremely difficult to obtain justice by means of a criminal trial, since, until the 1980s, there was a strict statute of limitations on alleged crimes. Moreover, the law required incontrovertible evidence that a particular individual had assaulted or killed another specific individual. Being proven to have been a guard at the Auschwitz death camp, where millions were severely maltreated and murdered, was not enough, not even for a guilty verdict of the lesser crime of being an accessory to murder or assault. What is more, corporations that had deployed forced or slave labour, generally by voluntarily utilising the SS or other Nazi organisations as intermediaries, proved even more difficult to prosecute (Figure 8.1).[9]

Japanese law has made bringing a case against alleged war criminals before the courts even more difficult. Although the government accepted the verdicts of the IMT (Figure 8.2) as part of the price for a peace treaty in 1952, it did not recognise them in legal terms – a fine distinction that has continued to the present day. For that reason, successive Japanese prime ministers and other prominent politicians from the country's Liberal Democratic Party (LDP), who have been in

Figure 8.2 Allied legal delegates to the Tokyo War Crimes Trials, March 1946. AFP/Getty Images

power for most of the post-war period, have seen nothing wrong with visiting the Yasukuni war shrine, where fourteen of those convicted as Class A war criminals are enshrined. One of those interred there even received a First-Class Award from a post-war government. As Prime Minister Shinzo Abe told the Japanese Lower House of Parliament in an address in autumn 2006, 'They are not war criminals under domestic law.'[10]

Only one potential avenue for recourse remained for survivors of the concentration camps and forced- and slave-labour regimes during the war: civil courts.

***

On 1 August 1950, former concentration camp inmate and slave labourer Norbert Wollheim saw a newspaper advertisement inviting creditors to lodge claims against the former German chemical giant IG Farbenindustrie AG and its successors. Just over a year later, the former inmate's lawyer filed a civil suit on Wollheim's behalf against IG Farben in Liquidation (IGFiL), the firm's legal successor. It sought

DM 10,000 in compensation, a pittance, and wholly inadequate, but the maximum allowed under the court's regulations. Wollheim won.[11]

Lawyers for IGFiL appealed against the decision, and at the same time tried unsuccessfully to reach an out-of-court settlement. In the meantime, though, a number of other former slave labourers from IG-Auschwitz also filed suit, making IGFiL officials increasingly alarmed at the prospect – however unlikely – of being forced to pay out substantial sums to hundreds or even thousands of survivors.

A *deus ex machina* was urgently needed to break the dead-lock between the firm and the workers it had abused so shamefully. It came in the form of a settlement brokered by the West German state. The government set a deadline of 1 January 1958 for all claims to be registered, after which they would be invalid. In return, IGFiL, while not admitting any liability, agreed to 'donate' DM 27 million to the Conference on Jewish Material Claims against Germany, a charity established in 1951 and known simply as the Claims Conference. Each of the successful claimants received about DM 5,000 (just under $14,000 in 2022), or half that if they had been forced to work for less than six months, even if that work was sometimes slave labour.[12]

The government-brokered settlement drew a line under the matter not only for IGFiL, but also for many other companies for many years afterwards. In the meantime, firms and trade associations busied themselves with an effective public relations operation that recast themselves as victims of National Socialism rather than enablers at best, and at worst often co-perpetrators.[13]

Distasteful and unacceptable though this rear-guard action was, most would concede that West Germany has actively engaged with, and taken a great measure of moral responsibility for, the Nazi past, in a process known as *Vergangenheitsbewältigung* (overcoming the past).[14] Even so, many remained deeply dissatisfied for many years.

By the 1990s, however, several developments converged to move things along. An upsurge of interest in human rights and in punishing those who infringed upon them led to the United Nations creating the International Criminal Court (ICC) in the Hague, which was agreed under the Rome Statute in 1998. The ICC began regular activity in 2002. What is more, the expiration of thirty-year rules blocking access to official governmental historical records led to their release for research. And another crucial factor was the widespread use of class-action suits in civil courts in the United States, especially in New Jersey, New York, and California. Many of the legal actions were directed at German companies and their managers, who became anxious to resolve them once and for all, not least because of the importance of the US market. One main result, as mentioned already, was the foundation 'Remembrance, Responsibility, and Future', which was set up in 2000.[15]

* * *

The quest for justice in the civil courts was more difficult in Japan. Civil courts there frequently accepted the state's argument that it enjoyed sovereign immunity from prosecution, which meant that potential cases never started in the first place. And even if they did, Japanese civil procedure also specified that the defendant could dispute the basic facts of the case, which then had to be proven by the plaintiff. When sued, the state frequently did dispute the facts, and it did so successfully. What is more, courts routinely summarily dismissed civil claims against Japanese companies.[16]

Nevertheless, persistent calls for some form of restitution came from outside Japan, for instance from the Republic of South Korea. The Japanese government responded – on its own behalf and on that of the companies headquartered in Japan – with negotiations for a treaty with the South Korean dictator Park Chung-hee. These bore fruit on 22 June 1965 with two official agreements. The first centred solely on matters of foreign policy, among other things establishing full diplomatic and consular relations between the two countries. The second was designed to draw a line under economic disputes arising from the past. Japan, by far the richer of the two at the time, agreed to supply products and services to South Korea equivalent to a total of $300 million over the next ten years. This would be a grant, not subject to repayment. In addition, Japan agreed to provide long-term, low-interest loans amounting to $200 million for the purchase of Japanese goods over the same period. The total amounted to about 1.5 times South Korea's overall national budget at the time. The agreement specified explicitly that the 'problem [sic] concerning property, rights and interest *of the two Contracting Parties and their nationals (including juridicial persons)* and concerning claims between the Contracting Parties and their nationals ... is settled completely and finally'.[17]

However, in spite of the Japanese government's insistence since 1965 that all was settled once and for all, there has been mounting pressure for further settlements not only from South Korea, but also from other countries. Again, we have to keep in mind the context of the 1990s already mentioned in relation to Germany – the growing international concern with human rights and their infringement that culminated in the establishment of the ICC; the increasing availability of historical records; pressure from trading partners; and so on. Particular international outrage arose out of the realisation of the scale, scope, and organisation of the Japanese military's routinised use of 'comfort women' from other countries, who became the unwilling sexual victims of army personnel. In 1995, the Japanese government, under intense pressure, contributed the equivalent of $3.5 million to the establishment of an Asian Women's Fund, and it also issued an unprecedented apology to those harmed. The agreement settled disputes with five Asian countries, excluding South Korea.

In 2015, South Korea and Japan then reached a 'final and irreversible deal to settle the issue' with a one-off payment by the Japanese government of $9 million to establish a charitable foundation to provide compensation to former Korean 'comfort women'. Again, the financial contribution came with a rare and explicit apology directly from Japanese Prime Minister Shinzo Abe. However, the administration of South Korea's next president, Moon Jae-in, elected in May 2017, dissolved the foundation, saying that it had been set up without sufficient consultation with the survivors of the abuse. That set the stage for the Korean court verdicts mentioned at the start of this chapter ordering compensation from Japanese companies, and for the subsequent confrontation between the two governments.[18]

The Perils of Palocracy and the Coordinated Market Economies

The ongoing and apparently endless attempts to force or cajole the Germans and Japanese into paying for their crimes during the Second World War, both morally and financially, provide potent illustrations of the entanglement of the interests of government and industry. In both cases, the intertwining applied both to wartime misdeeds and to trying to dodge responsibility for them afterwards.

But the very same confluence of business and state interests that has hindered German and Japanese firms and governments from assuming sufficient responsibility for committing or facilitating war crimes is a special instance of a more general problem for Deutschland AG and Japan, Inc. A consultant specialising in Japanese firms' activities in the UK put it this way in 2018: 'While corporate governance scandals are not unique to Japan, there are certainly unique cultural factors that mean bad business behaviour is allowed to fester in Japan.'[19] What might be added is that Germany's 'unique cultural factors' also contribute to corporate governance misconduct. Or, put another way: the very act of coordination of these two coordinated market economies (CMEs)[20] requires actors and business practices that themselves enable and easily accommodate sustained corporate misbehaviour and corruption.

Dealing in Deutschland AG's Dark Shadows

It started out as a sordid, but seemingly simple, affair.

In autumn 1975, Peter Müllenbach, managing director of the business arm of the West German Christian Democratic Union (CDU) party, filed a lawsuit in Bonn. The prominent businessman alleged that his investment advisor had swindled him out of DM 110,000. The sum involved was relatively modest, and the dispute was not that unusual. Nevertheless, it set off a chain of events that culminated in the biggest political and economic scandal in West German history up to that point, what some have called the 'German Watergate'.[21]

As it transpired, the apparently workaday case landed on the desk of a lawyer from the Bonn prosecuting attorney's office, who mentioned it while playing a regular game of cards with tax investigator Klaus Förster. Förster's curiosity was immediately piqued, and he joined in on official inquiries into the allegations. He came at it, however, from an unexpected direction. Instead of looking into whether the investment adviser had swindled Müllenbach out of DM 110,000, Förster asked instead where the money came from in the first place and why no taxes had been paid on the income. Müllenbach was unable to give satisfactory answers, and his prevarications were enough to convince a judge to grant a search warrant. The subsequent raid on Müllenbach's apartment on 20 November 1975 yielded a file box labelled 'EU'. Förster's team of investigators soon ascertained that EU was an abbreviation for the German name for a company called the European Business Consultancy Institute, headquartered in Vaduz, in tax-haven Liechtenstein.

Members of the investigation team soon realised that they had struck gold. Invoices and payment records in the EU file documented a wheeze through which firms including Mannesmann, Deutsche Babcock, Siemens, Volkswagen, and others paid generous sums as 'honoraria' for 'worthless' consultancy reports, which the companies could then write off their tax bill. The fees they paid, however, eventually found their way into the coffers of the CDU. The total for the years 1972–1974 alone amounted to DM 1.6 million.

And it turns out that the CDU was not alone: companies had also paid the left-leaning Social Democratic Party of Germany (SPD) generously – although far less in total than had been paid to the CDU – for bogus consultancy reports and also for ads in the party's newspaper that never appeared. All of the transactions were clearly illegal according to a 1958 German constitutional court ruling, which outlawed such secret 'donations' to political parties.

However, the best was still to come. Not long after the discovery of illegal party donations, chance developments led investigators to tug further at the complex threads of the elaborate subterfuge. A woman scorned started things off. Unceremoniously fired from her longstanding position as secretary in the office of the treasurer of the liberal Free Democratic Party (FDP) in North Rhine Westphalia, Gertrud Rech decided to get even. She told investigators about how she had arranged arms export licences and other favours for companies, which the FDP, as part of the coalition running West Germany's federal government, could deliver on. The fees paid by companies for these 'arrangements', which were essentially bribes, were again – illegally – funnelled into party coffers.

It was excellent information, but Frau Rech had miscalculated in one important respect. She, too, had received a small proportion of the arrangement fees, which amounted in total to more than six figures. But investigators soon discovered that she had also not paid taxes on the income. Like Müllenbach, she had been hoist by her own petard. The investigation team, though, did not dally long on Frau Rech's affairs before continuing their work untangling the FDP's money-laundering operation, which brought them to the former FDP treasurer for North Rhine Westphalia, Otto Graf Lambsdorff, who had in the meantime become West Germany's Minister of Economics: a very big fish indeed.

Suspecting that there were still bigger ones to catch, Förster's team cast its net even wider. But the investigators, who by now had worked on the case for years, had little inkling of the extraordinarily large haul that still awaited them.

* * *

In the scenic hills along the River Rhine, across from the then West German capital of Bonn, lies the small city of Sankt Augustin, home to the German branch of the Catholic missionary order Steyler. By the late 1970s, Förster's investigatory team had become suspicious about some of the donations paid into the mission's house bank. The largest of them involved the Flick Group, a massive Düsseldorf-based holding company that was Germany's largest family firm by far at the time. There was also more than a hint of notoriety to the Flick Group, which was wholly owned by a family that was presided over by Friedrich Karl Flick, the son of a convicted Nazi-era war criminal.[22]

Team members paid a visit to Steyler's Father Josef Schröder to follow up. Among other things, they came away with the telephone number for Flick's accountant, Rudolf Diehl. Deciding it might be better not to phone ahead, the tax investigators turned up unannounced at Diehl's office in January 1980, surprising the accountant just as he was poring over his files on Steyler. It was not the last visit, nor the last evidence they would collect. Nearly two years later, on 4 November 1981, they discovered a key to a safe-deposit box in a briefcase leaning against Diehl's desk. When they opened it in the bank's vault, they discovered lightly coded information that unlocked the secrets of the deeply entangled, far-flung scheme that later became known as the Flick Affair.

This was the motherlode.

* * *

For years, it had worked fabulously. Overseen by Flick's in-house fixer, Eberhard von Brauchitsch, the company 'donated' millions of Deutschmarks to the mission. For every million transferred to Steyler's accounts, the missionaries got to keep DM 100,000, and the 'intermediary' – in other words, the money launderer – received the same amount as a service fee. The remaining DM 800,000 was then returned to Flick in cash, and the group was also able to write off DM 500,000 for its 'donation'. In other words, every million in donations turned into DM 1.3 million in ready money for use by the Flick firm. And they say there is no such thing as a magic money tree!

That much was clear from Diehl's Steyler files. The material in the safe-deposit box documented the recipients of the ready loot. The initials used for each transaction were easily deciphered. FKF stood for the company's *pater familias*, Friedrich Karl Flick, and v.B. for its fixer, von Brauchitsch, the main donors. As for those on the receiving end, FJS meant Franz Josef Strauss, the main force in the Bavarian-based Christian Social Union (CSU) party, always part of any CDU-led coalition government. Strauss personally pocketed a total of DM 925,000. And some of the other recipients of the largesse were named explicitly. Helmut Kohl, designated simply Kohl and at the time the shadow chancellor, trousered a total of DM 565,000 between 1974 and 1980, as well as some 'Russian marmalade', which turned out to be caviar for Kohl's wife, Hannelore. Graf Lambsdorff, named as such in the documents, and his predecessor as Economic Minister, Hans Friderichs ('Dr. Friderichs', also from the FDP), had benefited to the tune of several hundred thousand each.

All in all, between 1969 and 1980, Flick had distributed DM 25.5 million to West Germany's three main parties and the powerful politicians leading them. About DM 15 million went to the CDU and CSU parties or their leading politicians, DM 6.5 million to the FDP, and DM 4.3 million to the SPD. This complemented the even larger sum of DM 214 million dispensed to these parties by other German firms whose underhanded activities were exposed by the investigators. Only the Greens had been left out of the bonanza and emerged with their hands clean.

Just like the journalists who exposed the American Watergate scandal by following the money, the West German investigators laid bare the mechanisms of a gigantic money-laundering operation as well as its beneficiaries. But what benefits accrued to the donors such as the Flick concern who were seeking to 'cultivate the Bonn landscape', as Eberhard von Brauchitsch put it? Frau Rech, the disgruntled former secretary in the office of the FDP treasurer for the state of North Rhine Westphalia, had indicated some of the types of favours companies received in return for their generosity. In Flick's case, there was a much bigger and more brazen example.

In 1975, Friedrich Karl Flick had sold his substantial shareholding in Daimler Benz, at a profit of DM 1.9 billion. He did not, however, want to pay any capital-gains taxes on his windfall, which, if taxed at full rate, would amount to DM 989 million, and therefore was nothing to sneeze at. Under German tax law at the time, however, there was a nifty way out: if, within three years, he invested his profits in something demonstrably beneficial to the German economy, he would not have to pay the taxes. So Flick reinvested part of the money in German firms – which meant that those funds were clearly exempt from taxation.

But more than half of that sum flowed into US-based firms, including a large stake in W. R. Grace, a chemicals producer. The precise mechanism by which this may have benefited the German economy in any way was impossible to discern. Nevertheless, FDP Economic Minister of the time Hans Friderichs began to certify most of the US investments as tax-exempt under the provisions of the tax code, and his successor, Graf Lambsdorff, certified full and final tax exemption for the rest. Förster's investigative team thought it a reasonable leap to conclude that the decision on tax relief for Flick's US investments was connected to entries in Diehl's notebooks from the safe-deposit box, which indicated that Dr Friderichs had received a series of payments from Flick's secret fund totalling DM 315,000 between 1 April 1976 and 31 May 1977.

The trickle, and then torrent, of revelations prompted an attempted cover-up, and, when that did not work, an amnesty that would protect Friderichs, Lambsdorff, and von Brauchitsch, the three most exposed in the affair. But that didn't work either, and a parliamentary commission that was convened only made things worse. The whole affair threatened to topple Helmut Kohl's still relatively new coalition government, which he had formed in 1982 as head of the CDU with the CSU and FDP.

Lambsdorff, Friderichs, and von Brauchitsch were then charged with corruption and tax evasion. Lambsdorff, the first serving West German government minister to face criminal charges, resigned. Friderichs also resigned from his position as CEO of the Dresdner Bank, which he had assumed after leaving the government. All three defendants were exonerated in 1987 from the corruption charge, but they were found guilty of tax evasion or facilitating tax evasion. Friderichs was fined DM 61,500, Lambsdorff DM 180,000. Von Brauchitsch (Figure 8.3) got a jail sentence, which was suspended in return for paying a fine of DM 550,000. Two other CDU officials were

Figure 8.3 Eberhard von Brauchitsch on his way to trial for his role in the 'Flick Affair', August 1985. United Archives/Getty Images

subsequently charged with aiding and abetting tax evasion, but the cases against them were later dropped. The companies involved were merely required to pay back taxes.

There were no further repercussions, not even for Helmut Kohl, who had demonstrably lied to an official inquiry about his knowledge of what had been going on over the past decade or more. He continued as German Chancellor until 1998, after which he became honorary chairman of the CDU. He was, however, forced to resign that post in 2000 in the wake of yet another scandal involving secret and illegal donations to the party he led. Many were not at all surprised.

***

Had a Hollywood scriptwriter sought a vehicle for depicting the seamy underside of the West German economy and society at its high tide in the 1970s and 1980s, the Flick Affair would have been a godsend. At the heart of the drama, there was a very large and cosy network of powerful politicians and businessmen, connected by dint of personality, interests, and ambition, one hand washing the other using money laundered out of the untold wealth generated by the Economic Miracle. There is a solitary female supporting character in the role of a mistreated secretary, whose plans for revenge backfire spectacularly, but who provides crucial information to the authorities. A shady priest has an important walk-on part. And, central to it all, and working in the shadows, stands Eberhard von Brauchitsch, a suave aristocrat and charming string-puller, working on behalf of his fabulously rich and highly secretive boss, the son of a convicted war criminal. His work is enabled by the obligatory crooked accountant funnelling money through the back channels of foreign banks in luxurious tax havens, which comes back as stacks of ready cash.

It is the stuff of a blockbuster thriller; a flick based on a true story; and, as the result of inward-looking and tightly knit business–government networks, in many ways quintessentially West German.

Operating in the Nether Worlds of Japan, Inc.

Eberhard von Brauchitsch cut a colourful figure as the behind-the-scenes fixer in the Hollywood-style drama that was the Flick Affair. In comparison with Yoshio Kodama, the wire puller in Japan's contemporaneous Lockheed scandal, though, von Brauchitsch fades to black and white. Kodama, older, richer, and far more colourful than von Brauchitsch, was the lynchpin in post-war Japan's version of Watergate, which exposed the dark and seamy underside of the Japanese economic miracle.[23]

Kodama was born in 1911 to a family 'of the *samurai* rank', which made him, like von Brauchitsch, a minor aristocrat. Already at the tender age of eighteen, he entered the murky world of ultra-right-wing nationalist Japanese politics, which culminated in his first arrest, for presenting an unpopular petition to the emperor. He was imprisoned for about a year, until late 1930. The period of incarceration did not dissuade him, however. Instead, it whetted his appetite for confrontational political action: in 1932, Kodama joined an even more extreme ultranationalist group, where he helped develop plans to assassinate a number of high-level politicians.[24]

His efforts got him jailed again, this time for much longer, from late 1932 until 1937. By the time he was released, his political persuasions were much more to the taste of the Japanese authorities, who leaned increasingly far to the right. Already in October 1937, Kodama was travelling to China as a 'special staff official' of the Japanese Foreign Ministry. He subsequently headed a purchasing agency in Shanghai on behalf of the Japanese Naval Air Force. Later known as the 'Kodama *Kikan* (Kodama Organ)', the organisation engaged in black-market activities – including trafficking everything from precious metals and industrial diamonds to heroin – and intelligence operations, which 'enable[d] Kodama to amass a huge personal fortune through wartime trade with both the Nationalists and the Communists'. He also managed a right-wing newspaper and headed several mining companies. And, just as the war was ending in August 1945, Kodama was appointed to the Japanese government's Cabinet Advisory Council.[25]

His ascendancy to great personal fortune and the heights of Japanese business and politics also earned him yet another arrest, this time by the American occupation authorities in December 1945, when he was 'detained in Sugamo Prison as a Class A war criminal suspect'. As post-war Japanese war crimes prosecutions sputtered and finally ground to a halt, however, Kodama emerged from prison three years later as a free man, although 'he remained in purge status until the end of the occupation in 1952'.[26]

He had used his jail time wisely, though. Barred from direct participation in politics, Kodama nevertheless cultivated close connections with politicians and members of the business community. The former included Ichiro Hatoyama, head of the Liberal Party (which, in spite of its name, was conservative, and later became the Liberal Democratic Party, the dominant force in Japanese politics to the present day). Hatoyama became Japanese Prime Minister in 1954. Kodama could apparently always be quite persuasive, but his influence was bolstered immeasurably by his ability to raise funds for Hatoyama's party and various conservative causes. Kodama's personal fortune – according to one source, he may well have been the richest man in Japan at the end of the war – does not seem to have been impaired much by Japanese defeat and personal jail time either. Indeed, it probably grew through 'commissions' from his fundraising activities, and, even more so, from 'his access to top government officials and his inside information on government policy in various profitable financial transactions'.[27]

By spring 1953, Kodama was able to bounce back entirely from the (surprisingly elastic) confines of his post-war purge status, although he remained very much behind the scenes as a fixer, or *kuro-maku*. He also added substantially to his shady palette. For one thing, he allegedly began working as an agent for the US intelligence services, and eventually the Central Intelligence Agency (CIA). More certainly, though, according to information gathered by the CIA itself, 'he reportedly has numerous underworld connections and has been closely associated with gambling and gangster groups [i.e. *yakuza*].... He reportedly has been attempting to bring ... gangster groups under the control of *Toa Doshikai*, which he personally heads.'[28]

Slightly more legitimate activities provided the final string to Kodama's post-war bow. One of them, starting in 1958, involved acting 'on and off' 'as a secret agent for Lockheed in Japan'. Lockheed was one of the five largest airplane producers in the United States at the time, along with Grumman, Boeing, McDonnell, and Douglas (the latter two merged in 1967 into McDonnell Douglas). In 1958, Kodama managed to close a deal that led the Japanese government to purchase Lockheed's F-104 Starfighter combat planes (later known as 'flying coffins' because more than eighty pilots perished in crashes) for its Self-Defence Air Force instead of Grumman's F11F-1F Super Tiger jets. It was a coup: Grumman's airplanes had been the preferred option until just before Japan's ministers made their final decision. In this and other activity on behalf of Lockheed through the 1960s, Kodama was successful not just in delivering the goods for the American firm, but also in attracting practically zero public attention or comment.[29]

That happy situation – from the perspective of Kodama, Lockheed, and many others involved – changed dramatically by the mid-1970s, however. The proximate cause of the unravelling came in summer 1972. Lockheed was in a bit of trouble, having lost out to Boeing on a US government contract for developing a supersonic airplane and having had another government contract for a combat helicopter cancelled after a prototype crashed during testing. But the firm was even more exposed financially through heavy investment and significant delays in developing a wide-bodied passenger plane, the TriStar. The long-delayed plane was now finally ready for sale. Lockheed identified Japan's All Nippon Airways (ANA) as a major customer after a deal with the country's Japan Airlines (JAL) had inexplicably fallen through. In August 1972, CEO A. Carl Kotchian was on one of ten trips to Japan he took in conjunction with this particular sales campaign. This was the most important of the ten, and he had therefore ensconced himself for a marathon eleven-week stint in a luxury suite in Tokyo's Hotel Okura (whose most recent tenants included US Secretary of State Henry Kissinger) to oversee the complex negotiations. For, in addition to the usual barrage of political and commercial details to be ironed out in any sale of high-end aircraft, ANA had a pre-existing commitment to buy DC-10 planes from Lockheed's closest rival, McDonnell Douglas.[30]

To help solve the problem, Kotchian enlisted the services of Marubeni Corporation, the fourth-largest trading company in Japan. Such trading companies played a crucial role in facilitating the difficult task of navigating through Japan's complicated bureaucracy and business culture, and their work was explicitly encouraged by the government. McDonnell Douglas, too, had availed itself of such services, in its case through one of the top three trading companies, Mitsui Bussan. But, because of the many hurdles standing in the way of achieving a deal, Kotchian and his fellow top managers decided that Lockheed needed more firepower. So, without Marubeni's knowledge, they also brought Kodama on board as a well-connected, effective, and long serving 'secret agent'. In all, Lockheed paid him over $7 million between 1958 and 1972 to keep or dispense as he saw fit to help secure sales. A large proportion of the payments – $2.24 million in all – came in conjunction with Kodama's work in 1972 to secure the ANA sale.[31]

When the scandal erupted in Japan in the aftermath of Kotchian's testimony before a US Senate subcommittee in February 1976, Kodama was one of those charged with criminal offences, in his case one count of tax evasion and two of violation of regulations on foreign-currency exchange. The former strong man, now having reached the ripe old age of sixty-five, did not appear before the courts for very long, however, neither as defendant nor as a witness in the other cases, and his own trial was never brought to a conclusion. One very good reason was what a contemporary academic analyst, Hans Baerwald, called 'a mysterious illness that was affecting his brain' – it later transpired that Kodama had suffered a cerebral thrombosis. But one of the other factors advanced by Baerwald – 'a kamikaze-style light airplane attack by a presumably deranged pornographic film actor' – stands out as a particularly apt, if bizarre, coda to the fixer's lurid past. Baerwald's prediction 'that his career as a wire-puller (*kuromaku*) in Japanese politics has ended' was spot on, not least because Kodama's

Figure 8.4 Yoshio Kodama at the Lockheed Trial in Tokyo, June 1977.
The Asahi Shimbun/Getty Images

ill health worsened. He died of a stroke in January 1984, aged seventy-two. If it can be said of anyone, though, Yoshio Kodama (Figure 8.4) had certainly led a full life, one that puts von Brauchitsch's role in the Flick Affair well in the shade.[32]

***

The second half of the 1970s represented a traumatic era for the United States in the wake of the Watergate Affair and its aftermath, which resulted in a constitutional crisis averted by the resignation in 1974 of President Richard Nixon. It was a time of profound reflection and attempts to reform what was clearly a deeply flawed political system. It was also a time when reputations could be made. Senator Frank Church, Democrat of Idaho, was determined to make the most of it as he prepared for an ultimately unsuccessful bid to run for the US presidency in 1976 (he lost out to the relatively unknown former Georgia Governor Jimmy Carter). Starting in 1975, Church chaired a highly influential Senate Select Committee on covert foreign and domestic US intelligence operations that, among other things, exposed programmes to infiltrate American civil rights organisations and to assassinate leaders of foreign countries. He built on that success in his role – held at the same time as he chaired the Select Committee – as chair of a prominent subcommittee of the Senate Foreign Relations Committee investigating the activities of multinational corporations and their impact on US foreign policy.[33]

Among those ensnared in the inquiries of Church's Senate subcommittee were telecommunications conglomerate ITT, in particular regarding its activities in Chile; oil multinationals including Gulf Oil and Exxon; and Lockheed. Dubious overseas dealings on the part of ITT and the oil firms had long been known or suspected. In contrast, Church stumbled upon Lockheed largely by accident. The subcommittee's initial investigations of suspicious payments abroad in the aviation industry focused on another firm, Northrop Corporation, whose 'president testified that they used Lockheed as a model'. Records of several government agencies provided basic information to the committee. They included those of the Emergency Loan Guarantee Board (ELGB), which had guaranteed loans to Lockheed to help it through its financial crisis in the early 1970s. ELGB staff were angry at the possibility that some of the money had been used to fund bribes in foreign countries.[34]

ELGB staff members collected further information on the bribery allegations in a visit to Lockheed headquarters in California in late August 1975. It caused considerable anxiety among management, which became so severe that the company's treasurer and vice president committed suicide. Subcommittee investigators, following up on the leads that had been turned up in the Netherlands and West Germany, soon discovered in Germany that the 'really important payoffs were in Japan. Before that, nobody understood what those documents were, because many of them were written in Japanese.' Congressional Research Service translators took care rendering them into English for use by the subcommittee.[35]

Kotchian was invited to testify to the subcommittee over two days in early February 1976. He had decided that the best strategy was full cooperation, not least, crucially, *because he believed he and his firm had done nothing wrong.* As he said in an interview with the *New York Times* in July 1977, just a few months after the Lockheed board had dismissed him for his role in the scandal, 'My experience has some of the elements of Watergate … I can compare it because some of the things that came out in Watergate were things that were going on previously – and all of a sudden, there's a different set of standards.'[36]

Subcommittee members, led by Church and based on what investigators had uncovered, focused their questioning of Kotchian on Japan. Kodama's role figured prominently. The subcommittee chair put it to Lockheed's CEO: 'You paid him $7 million [from the late 1950s to the early 1970s]. You must have been paying him for something valuable.' 'Well, yes, very much valuable,' Kotchian replied. The exchange went on, soon revealing that Kotchian had miscalculated very badly by thinking the subcommittee would view his testimony benignly. Church stated baldly what his understanding of the situation was:

> Now, the truth of this is, isn't it, that Mr. Kodama was known as a fixer; you paid him seven million dollars to accomplish certain objectives and the real objective was to try to get that sale.... And you didn't ask him how he would use the money or what he would do with it, or anything else. You just didn't ask him any further questions about it.

Church then concluded this particular round of testimony with a question: 'Was there ever a time afterwards or during this connection with Mr. Kodama that you ever asked him for an accounting of what the money had been spent for?' 'No sir,' Kotchian replied.[37]

* * *

Kodama was far from the only Japanese figure implicated in the scandal. Kakuei Tanaka had been newly anointed as Japanese Prime Minister in July 1972, six weeks before the series of intensive meetings in late August about the potential sale of Lockheed aircraft to ANA. Marubeni Trading Company executives Hiro Hiyama and Toshiharu Okubo paid him a visit early in the morning of 23 August 1972 to discuss the sale. Okubo having been sent out of the room, Hiyama offered the new PM, who was already very wealthy, half a billion yen – about $1.6 million at the time – on behalf of Lockheed to facilitate the deal. It was expensive, but potentially worth it. Tanaka had a summit meeting with US President Richard Nixon in Hawai'i later in the month, primarily to discuss America's yawning trade deficit with Japan, and Kotchian hoped the purchase of Lockheed planes for ANA might be one of the Japanese prime minister's peace offerings. Tanaka was no longer the head of the Japanese government when later indicted on criminal charges of bribery, but he was the first ever former Japanese minister to be charged with crimes committed while holding high office.[38]

Marubeni managing directors Toshiharu Okubo and Hiroshi Ito were also indicted, in their cases for perjury in testimony to the Japanese Diet (Parliament). Among other things, they had lied about liberally doling out some $2 million to the government bureaucracy to grease the wheels of approval for the Lockheed–ANA deal. They had recovered their outlays by presenting receipts to Lockheed that were as scrupulously recorded as they were nonsensical, seeking reimbursement for 'peanuts', 'pieces', or 'units'. The mystery had been solved in the Church subcommittee through testimony from a representative of Lockheed's accounting firm Arthur Young and Company. Subcommittee counsel sought clarification for one such chit that Ito had submitted for '100 peanuts'. He asked whether this was a code for ¥100,000 or $100,000. Neither, replied the accountant. After helpfully pointing out that '100,000 yen at a 300 to 1 exchange isn't a large sum of money', he indicated that the sum involved was actually ¥100 million, or about $333,333 at the time. That, of course, *was* a rather tidy sum.[39]

***

As it unfolded in Japan, the Lockheed scandal and its fallout occasioned an admixture of sardonic commentary (not least about the peanuts), embarrassment, and soul-searching. The arduously negotiated sale of the American company's planes to ANA was cancelled. Kodama was charged, but never tried and convicted, owing to ill health. Some other major players, including the Marubeni managing directors Okubo and Ito and former Prime Minister Tanaka's private secretary, were sentenced to two years in jail each, although Ito's jail sentence was suspended on appeal. Several others were never charged, although in total seventeen officials were arrested. The biggest individual 'casualty' of the affair in Japan, however, was Tanaka, who was found guilty at the end of a long trial in October 1983 and sentenced to four years in jail and a fine of roughly $2.1 million, nearly a third more than the total amount he had been bribed. The jail sentence and fine were confirmed by a higher court in 1987, although Tanaka appealed against the verdict in Japan's Supreme Court. Tanaka also retained his seat in the Japanese Diet even after the convictions, being repeatedly re-elected as an LDP MP from his home Nagaoka constituency until his retirement due to ill health in 1990. He died in 1993 while the Supreme Court decision was still pending.[40]

In other words, the Lockheed scandal laid bare the sleazy inner workings of post-war Japanese coordinated capitalism without causing much damage to those whose misdeeds were exposed. Neither did it cause any fundamental reform in Japan, not unlike the Flick Affair in West Germany, although it did cause collateral damage in the form of the ousting of A. Carl Kotchian as CEO of Lockheed. And it formed a major impetus behind the passage of the US Foreign Corrupt Practices Act (FCPA) in 1977.[41]

In large part due to the minimal reform to the Japanese political economy in the wake of Lockheed, other corporate scandals have emerged, just as the lack of full engagement with the Flick Affair led to similar scandals in twenty-first-century Germany. Since 2011, for instance, Japan has experienced a flurry of corporate governance scandals, including dodgy accounting practices at Olympus, massive over-reporting of operating profits by Toshiba, falsification of data by Kobe Steel, and a cover-up of deadly airbags manufactured by the Takata corporation. There was also the infamous 'Nissan crisis' beginning in 2018, which involved the arrest of then CEO Carlos Ghosn for alleged non-reporting of substantial income over several years. In Germany, the early 2000s also saw the unfolding of a major scandal involving Siemens, with roots in no small part in German corporate law, which until 1999 permitted companies tax write-offs for bribes dispensed abroad.[42]

It is, of course, important that such scandals come to light in the first place, and this is due, in part, as in the case of Siemens, to a relatively recent phenomenon in both countries: whistle blowers. However, unlike the case of Siemens in Germany, where exposure led not only to substantial fines, but also to major reform, fundamental recasting of corporate governance has been far less common in Japan. In mid-2021, for instance, Toshiba was at it again, this time accused of colluding to suppress investors' interests with the full knowledge of the Prime Minister and the Ministry of Economy, Trade, and Industry. And, a month later, an inquiry found that Mitsubishi Electric had falsified data on inspections of railway equipment for the past thirty years.[43]

Analysts suggest that the problem lies with longstanding cultures of management and corporate governance in Japan involving cosy relationships among top managers who have worked at the same corporations – and therefore with each other – for decades. They tend to be insiders, who are reluctant to challenge more senior figures or to think differently from the rest of the in-group. And even in those rare cases where major Japanese companies have turned to foreign CEOs, it does not seem to have helped. When Michael Woodford became the first non-Japanese CEO of Olympus Corporation, he immediately blew the whistle on accounting fraud at his firm. For his efforts, he was fired within two weeks of being appointed. The case of Carlos Ghosn's alleged financial misconduct as head of Nissan appears to be more complex. Regardless, it appears to be yet another indictment of the Japanese corporate governance system.[44]

A Verdict: Hauntings through Space and Time

Watergate has come up several times in this chapter. It is in many ways an excellent benchmark for situating the Flick Affair in West Germany and the Lockheed scandal in Japan. All of them erupted as scandals at about the same time (although they have often involved events from the more or less distant past). And each exposed unsavoury practices at the heart of business and politics in the country involved. The Watergate analogy, moreover, is also a powerful reminder that West Germany and Japan are far from the only rich, highly industrialised countries where such shady dealings take place.

There are also at least two other ways in which Watergate serves as a heuristic, a helpful tool for thinking about post-war scandals in Germany and Japan. For one thing, Watergate, the Flick Affair, and the Lockheed scandal may or may not be representative of the rot in each country's political economy at the time the scandal emerged, not least because we have no idea of what other shenanigans were going on. White-collar crime – even if done on a large scale – is notoriously difficult to detect, and it usually comes to light through a series of accidental discoveries, which are amplified and unpicked by investigative journalists, avid tax investigators, and/or eager-beaver prosecutors. Or the alleged crimes may be initially revealed by whistle blowers. In any case, though, they usually need to be followed up on by some combination of these other groups. The other way in which Watergate can be a useful starting point for thinking about the scandals in West Germany and Japan in the 1970s involved something that disgraced

Lockheed ex-CEO A. Carl Kotchian pointed out in a 1977 interview. The Lockheed scandal, he said, was like Watergate in that both, arguably, involved something that 'everyone' was doing. In other words, Nixon, Kotchian, Kodama, Tanaka, Flick, and von Brauchitsch were all, to their minds, just following the rules of the game. No wonder they all felt aggrieved at being at the sharp end of a criminal justice probe, as well as at how things turned out.[45]

All the same, there were ways in which crime and justice in post-war Germany and Japan were different from in the United States and many other developed countries. Chief among them was the fact that a large number of individual Germans and Japanese had been called to account for their crimes before and during the Second World War. True, there were certainly atrocities on the side of the Allies, but there were very sound reasons for the development of new legal concepts such as crimes against the peace, crimes against humanity, and genocide specifically for use in the unprecedented international tribunals set up after 1945. Justice may have been regrettably incomplete. But there was at least *some* attempt at it early in the Allied occupation. And, although enthusiasm for pursuing war criminals and gaining compensation for survivors waned considerably and unforgivably in the context of the Cold War and the partial restoration of pre-war elite networks, repeated reminders of the injustices carried out during the war in the press and in the courts during the decades that followed finally bore some fruit from the 1990s onwards.

The other way in which Germany and Japan differed from other countries involved long-term continuities in business–government networks in their coordinated economies. It is therefore not surprising that some of those who had been charged with war crimes – and/or those whose wealth derived at least in part from activities conducted during the war, and often on behalf of the war effort – should figure so prominently in the scandals that took place during the post-war period. However, at the same time, and in spite of the speculations of some, these cases did not constitute evidence that Nazism remained rampant in West Germany, nor were they proof that extreme right-wing ultranationalism prevailed in post-1945 Japan. Both countries changed profoundly, and in essential ways, as a result of their defeat and its aftermath. Their militarily oriented national security states were discredited and replaced by commercially oriented states with limited armed forces and armaments industries. Trade unions, hitherto entirely excluded from political and economic power and decision-making, gained a sometimes booming voice. And societies previously characterised by inequality and often extreme poverty became more egalitarian and affluent.

Yet, there is no denying that strong vestiges of the old established networks remained in place well into the post-war era. Over time, however, not only did those directly tainted with pre-1945 crimes and practices begin to retire and die off, but also the export orientation of both countries, combined with other aspects of the globalisation of business, finance, and markets, changed the composition and dynamics of the networks.

This happened more rapidly and thoroughly in Germany than in Japan, in part owing to Germany's greater dependence on exports, its central role in the European Union, and its greater openness to foreign imports and investment. As a result, German corporate governance has experienced more far-reaching reform than its Japanese counterpart. And, for many of the same reasons, Germany has made greater strides towards coming to terms with its pre-1945 past than Japan.[46]

9 FRAGILE STRENGTH
Coping with Currency and Oil Crises

Sombre and staring straight into the camera, US President Richard M. Nixon addressed his fellow Americans on 15 August 1971 on national television. Blaming foreign 'speculators' who insisted on converting the US-dollar reserves they held into their equivalent in gold for alleged sustained attacks on the currency, he announced an immediate suspension of the dollar's convertibility into the precious metal. Furthermore, to tame the scourge of rising inflation, the US President announced an immediate freeze on wages and prices. His third weapon of choice to combat the severe problems dogging the American economy was the imposition of a 'temporary' 10 per cent additional tariff on imported goods.

The president insisted that these actions were not directed at any specific country; they were instead meant to ensure that American workers and firms were not disadvantaged by 'unfair' competition from abroad. He also explicitly denied that the dollar was losing its value through his decision:

> Let me lay to rest the bugaboo of what is called devaluation.
>
> If you want to buy a foreign car or take a trip abroad, market conditions may cause your dollar to buy slightly less. But if you are among the overwhelming majority of Americans who buy American-made products in America, your dollar will be worth just as much tomorrow as it is today.[1]

The US President was being more than a bit disingenuous in his surprise announcement, yet another example of why Nixon was often referred to as 'Tricky Dicky'. In fact, his suspension of the convertibility of the world's leading currency into gold, which had been fixed since 1944 at $35 per ounce, caused an immediate and permanent devaluation.[2] And, although Nixon's televised address was directed at the American public, policymakers and analysts around the world understood immediately who these actions were targeted at, and who would be hurt by them. The 'speculators' Nixon referred to, for instance, included such august culprits as the government of the UK and the Bank of England, which had recently sought to convert a substantial portion of Britain's substantial US dollar reserves amassed since the 1950s into gold.

But it was not so much the British whom Nixon targeted with the effective and immediate devaluation of the dollar, combined with a 10 per cent import-tariff surcharge. Ostensibly not directed at any country in particular, the actions unmistakably targeted America's biggest trading partners, which included those running the largest foreign-trade surpluses with the United States. Most prominent among them were West Germany and, even more so by the early 1970s, Japan. It is little wonder Japanese government officials and media immediately dubbed the measures announced by the president 'the Nixon shock'.[3]

* * *

In fact, for the Japanese and for many other contemporary observers of geopolitics, the US President's 15 August surprise announcement was the second 'Nixon shock' in as many months. On 9 July, Henry A. Kissinger, Nixon's National Security Advisor, travelled to the People's Republic of China (PRC) to meet secretly with Chinese Prime Minister Zhou Enlai, an encounter revealed in global media later the same month. Kissinger's mission was twofold: to kick off the process of diplomatic recognition of the PRC, which the United States had officially ignored since its founding in 1949; and, related to that, to pave the way for an official state visit by Nixon himself in 1972.

According to an internal White House assessment of the 9 July talks written by Winston Lord, one of Kissinger's aides, the Chinese premier and his government prioritised three key issues. First, of course, there was the perennial conundrum of Taiwan. Second, there was 'Indochina' (i.e. Vietnam). Here, Zhou's 'language was relatively restrained, but he gave firm support to his friends and a hands-off attitude, even while recognizing the link you [Kissinger] were establishing between this issue and Taiwan'. And the third main takeaway from the talks that Lord identified was Zhou's 'pre-occupation with Japan'.[4] Given that Japan was one of the main targets of Nixon's August announcement, this was clearly one fixation the two estranged countries had in common. The Japanese were therefore quite understandably in a state of shock after the unexpected double body-blow from their erstwhile protectors in summer 1971.

* * *

As it turned out, this was just the rocky start to a turbulent decade. The two Nixon shocks of summer 1971 formed a harbinger of the definitive end of the Golden Age of growth and prosperity that had followed the end of the Second World War. This in turn involved fundamental changes to the geopolitical and economic order that had prevailed since the late 1940s. From 1969, for instance, slightly before the United States began opening diplomatic channels with the PRC and forming the basis for future economic relationships, Chancellor Willy Brandt's West German government embarked on its *Ostpolitik*. Formal recognition of what had previously been known as 'the so-called German Democratic Republic' in East Germany formed a vital part of West Germany's political and economic rapprochement with the Soviet bloc and, together with the US initiative in China, something of a thaw in the Cold War. It paved the way for full UN membership for both Germanies in September 1973, undergirding Germany's relationship with its neighbour to the east over the subsequent period. As it developed since the late 1960s, *Ostpolitik* is credited among other things with ensuring Soviet assent to German unification in 1990 following the fall of the Berlin Wall in November 1989. It laid the foundations of German policy towards Russia since unification and the collapse of the Soviet Union as successive German governments pursued close and cordial economic relations with Germany's large neighbour to the east. The path is captured in the slogan *Wandel durch Handel* (change [in Russian governance] through trade), although the policy has also been criticised from the outset for its prominent role in Germany's growing energy dependence on Russian gas and oil, which the invasion of Ukraine in early 2022 laid bare.[5]

As the 1970s progressed, however, additional and, for a time, quite jarring shocks arrived on the scene. The oil crises of 1973–1974 and 1978–1979 exposed the vulnerability of rich developed countries to dependence on energy supplies from abroad. Rises in the price of fuel fed through to virtually all areas of the economy, resulting in unprecedented levels of inflation in most wealthy nations. At the same time, most economies were stuck in the doldrums, with very low levels of growth. The 'stagflation' that followed baffled economists and policymakers as much as it troubled householders around the world.

Out of the Bretton Woods

Nixon's announcement of 15 August 1971 of 'temporary' inconvertibility of dollars to gold heralded the end of the US-led Bretton Woods System, which ended officially in 1973, and from which Germany and Japan benefited magnificently as they enacted their postwar economic miracles. The system's name comes from a resort hotel located in New Hampshire in the United States, where delegates from forty-four nations met during the first three weeks of July 1944 to discuss the shape – and to establish the institutions that would be the pillars – of the post-war international monetary system. Delegates to the meeting, officially known as the United Nations Monetary and Financial Conference, were anxious above all to avoid the extreme economic fluctuations that had followed the First World War, which led eventually to the Great Depression and, by implication, the Second World War. The way forward, however, depended heavily on their analysis of the causes of that economic chaos.

They identified three culprits. The first, they thought, was extreme economic inequality and, related to that, limited financing for economic development. To help address these particular problems, they created the International Bank for Reconstruction and Development (IBRD), which eventually became the lending arm of the World Bank.[6]

A second set of major economic problems during the interwar period, delegates agreed, stemmed from currency instability. Many looked back fondly and longingly to the fixed-exchange-rate regime of the gold standard that had existed until the outbreak of the First World War in 1914. Yet others recalled more recent, often disastrous, attempts during the early 1930s to reinstate the gold standard, which highlighted the fact that such a fixed regime was inflexible and ultimately unworkable, constituting, in the words of a later economic historian, 'golden fetters'.[7] The consensus that emerged from discussions favoured a fixed yet flexible regime and led the delegates to create the International Monetary Fund (IMF), which, among other things, tied the US dollar to gold, which in turn was fixed at a price of $35 per ounce. Other countries' currencies were then set at a fixed exchange rate in relation to the dollar, although their exchange rates could also be changed in the event of persistent imbalances in trade, albeit only in the case of 'fundamental disequilibrium' and only with the permission of the IMF. The intention, however, was that US dollar reserves would always be freely convertible into gold at the fixed rate.

The third villain of the piece, according to the delegates, was the erosion and then widespread suspension of free trade. Tariffs imposed wantonly by many countries during the 1920s – and especially after 1929 in response to trade deficits – had led to beggar-thy-neighbour policies, which had been good for no one. The delegates consequently agreed to meet on a regular basis to hammer out a General Agreement on Tariffs and Trade (GATT), which became an ongoing set of talks and international agreements to reduce trade barriers. Eventually, the GATT process formed the foundations for the World Trade Organization (WTO).

The three-legged stool underpinning the Bretton Woods System worked reasonably well for a short time, but its long-term viability depended crucially on the discipline of the American government as well as the stability of the US dollar. By the mid-1960s, both were wobbling seriously. Spending on defence, including a large US military presence abroad in West Germany and Japan, among other places, represented substantial and on-going outlay for the government. The duration of the Vietnam War and its escalation during the administration of President Lyndon Johnson, however, increased overseas military spending dramatically. And substantial outlays continued during the first Nixon administration. In addition to its growing spending on guns, the US government also began spending heavily on butter through expansion of the welfare state under Johnson's Great Society programme.

The profligacy of the US government, furthermore, was matched or bettered by vastly increased consumer spending, much of which was spent on imported goods. The big-ticket item funnelling dollars abroad, however, stemmed from America's ever-increasing thirst for imported oil. The lion's share of this vastly increased over-seas spending by the US government and American consumers – both directly, and indirectly through imports – was covered by the simple expedient of resorting to the printing press.

But American purchases abroad were not the only factor at work here. After 1945, the US dollar was also the preferred currency worldwide for buying and selling commodities – not least oil; it was the currency vehicle of choice in international banking and invest-ment transactions; and US Treasury bonds (obviously denominated in dollars) represented a safe and stable haven for people and countries around the world. For all of these reasons, the overseas dollar holdings of foreign nationals and nations soared in the years following the end of the war, and pressure on the dollar as a reserve currency convertible to gold grew precipitously.

* * *

Germany and Japan (as well as their Axis alliance affiliates) were of course still deep in the throes of war with the Allies in summer 1944. Consequently, they were not invited to send delegates to the Bretton Woods Conference. But the two countries benefited enormously from the US-led monetary system during the twenty-five years after their defeat. The IBRD played a role, initially by facilitating reconstruction financing, including for the defeated nations, and then by providing financing for developing countries, which soon became customers for German and Japanese products. In the medium to long term, however, the steady removal of barriers to international trade provided substan-tial benefits to both economies, not only because this made their exports less expensive, but also because it had the same effect on their imports (especially of raw material and energy inputs for manufacturing).

The impact of the other leg of the stool – the dollar as the world's reserve currency, the only one fixed to gold – was also impor-tant. But it had more ambiguous effects, benefiting Germany and Japan in many ways, but also causing significant problems. The upsides and the downsides resulted from two related issues. First of all, the economic and political conditions prevailing at the initial setting of exchange rates under the new system were important. Because of the devastation to their economies resulting from the war and the need for rapid and extensive reconstruction, the exchange rates for the West

German Deutschmark and the Japanese yen by 1950 were set quite low in relation to the dollar. Rapid recovery and quick conquest of export markets in the decades that followed (in part owing to this favourable initial exchange rate, which made German and Japanese goods relatively cheap) entailed swift boosts to their balance-of-trade surpluses.

The second issue involved the sticky nature of the system itself: remember that within the Bretton Woods System it was possible to alter exchange rates in relation to the US dollar, but only after a 'fundamental disequilibrium' had been ascertained. Even then, this could happen only after IMF agreement. Essentially, this meant that there were significant ramifications arising from ever more impressive German and Japanese export successes, which turned quickly into large current account surpluses – and simultaneously into substantial deficits for their customers, most prominently the United States. And they affected not only the international trading partners of the two countries, but also the domestic economies of Germany and Japan. However, the problems that emerged and how they were dealt with differed for the two countries.

In and Out of the Bretton Woods: The German Path

When the Deutschmark (DM) was introduced in June 1948, the new currency was pegged at DM 3.33 to the US dollar. However, it soon became clear that this was optimistic. Like many of the other initial exchange rates set under the new Bretton Woods regime, the DM needed devaluation. Accordingly, in September 1949, not long after the official establishment of the Federal Republic of Germany in May, the new currency was devalued substantially, to DM 4.20 to the dollar. Even so, the DM devaluation was considerably lower than the drop experienced at the same time by other European currencies, including the British pound sterling. And the rate for the DM remained in place when the IMF officially set the still new West German currency to gold parity in relation to the dollar shortly thereafter. That exchange rate then remained in place into the early 1960s, by which time the DM was well on its way to becoming one of the most successful and stable currencies in the world, and by far the most stable in twentieth-century German history.[8]

As the West German economy recovered from the conflict and surged forward in the 1950s, however, the country's exports grew substantially, and at a much faster pace than domestic consumption.

Heightened exports and relatively slower growth in domestic consumption (and imports) were both aided in part by the favourable (from the perspective of German exporters, at least) exchange rate. They also translated into galloping increases in balance-of-trade surpluses. It thus soon became clear to many that the DM was undervalued. As early as 1956, Economics Minister Ludwig Erhard, for instance, advocated a revaluation. He and others came to this conviction partly in response to pressure from trading partners such as France, the United Kingdom, and, eventually and most importantly, the United States. But it was also partly to address growing domestic concerns about 'imported inflation'. Erhard and others worried that ever-increasing demand for German manufactured goods from abroad, especially in places like France and Britain, which were themselves experiencing considerable inflation, would combine with increases in domestic money supply stemming in large part from growing current account surpluses to drive up prices in West Germany.[9]

Short of going to war – the danger of which had become non-existent for 1950s Germany – there was no bigger bugbear than inflation for the country's policymakers and the public. Erhard was certainly not alone in his bitter personal recollections of the hyperinflation of the early years of the Weimar Republic. And, if balancing foreign trade through revaluation of the currency was a promising path towards defusing the threat of dreaded inflation, he was all for it. But Erhard and those who shared his views were not the only ones with a strong opinion on the matter. The vast army of successful German exporter-manufacturers and the trade unions representing the workers those companies employed counted among the numerous and vigorous opponents of revaluation. Besides, there were other ways of throttling inflationary threats. There was consensus in West Germany that one of the most obvious ones – wage, price, and other controls imposed by the state – should be avoided, not least because of painful recent experiences of them during the Nazi and early post-war periods. Excluding that, however, still left a raft of useful tools, which Germany made good use of. They included restrictions on growth of money supply; relatively high interest rates; maintaining balanced government budgets through fiscal discipline; and keeping rates of wage increases below those of rises in productivity.[10] The latter has formed a prominent feature of the German political economy since the advent of codetermination gave many workers a strong say – and stake – in the companies they work for.

The measures adopted did indeed curb inflation. Between 1950 and 1972, price increases were far lower for German households than for those in Germany's European neighbours. German consumer prices went up by a factor of 1.7 during that period; in France, on the other hand, the increase was by a factor of 2.9, and in Britain 2.6. But the measures did nothing to plug the influx of foreign exchange into the country. Indeed, they almost certainly made things worse. Relatively low prices in Germany, for instance, served to lower costs for German manufacturers, rendering their goods even more attractive in international markets. Germany's current account surplus therefore continued to rise, driving France, Britain, and other trading partners to anger and distraction while at the same time attracting unwelcome currency speculators betting repeatedly on an imminent revaluation.[11]

The deadlock in Germany continued until 1961, when a revaluation was finally agreed. The outcome was underwhelming. After years of domestic wrangling and external pressure from trading partners, the DM was revalued, resulting in an appreciation of just under 5 per cent. The new exchange rate was fixed at DM 4 to the US dollar instead of DM 4.20, simultaneously disappointing speculators (which may well have been a German objective) and infuriating trading partners. The modesty of the revaluation may have had something to do with appearing to comply with the agreements signed in London in 1953 to settle German pre-war external debts. But, more importantly, it served a domestic political purpose, bringing fractious division and debate over the issue to a close. As one commentator put it, 'The ... reason for the silence probably lies in the smallness [of the revaluation] itself.'[12]

There is no doubt, however, that the revaluation did nothing to solve the structural problem of German trade imbalance, which worsened during the 1960s. Again, some argued that there were ways of addressing it short of revaluing the DM. The guest workers who flooded into Germany in the 1960s and beyond – first from Spain and Italy, and later from Yugoslavia and Turkey – sent huge swaths of their earnings home as DM 'remittances'. For its part, the US government negotiated a series of 'offset' agreements whereby the West Germans purchased armaments and invested in Treasury bonds to ensure a flow of dollars back into the United States to compensate for American military outlays in Germany. The Grand Coalition government that came into power in Germany in late 1966, not least as a result of the country's first economic downturn of the post-war period, included not only the Christian Democratic Union (CDU) and its partners from the Bavarian Christian Socialist Union (CSU), who had led the German government since 1949, but also the left-wing Social Democratic Party of Germany (SPD), who argued successfully for more government spending. Nothing, however, was enough to stem the incoming tide of foreign exchange into Germany, which continued, not incidentally, to enjoy relatively low rates of inflation. So, by the end of the decade, speculators were again hard at play, betting heavily on another, more substantial revaluation. And Germany's trading partners, who included an increasingly vocal and angry United States, clamoured for the same.[13]

Again, though, there was a deadlock in Germany, most prominently within the Grand Coalition itself. Both Karl Schiller, the SPD Economics Minister, and Franz Josef Strauss, the CSU Finance Minister, were strongly in favour of a 'strong Mark'. But the same phrase had diametrically opposed meanings. The 'Schiller-Mark' would be one that would be revalued, which would translate into lower prices for imported goods and cheaper vacations abroad, while at the same time eliminating most inflationary pressure. The 'Strauss-Mark', on the other hand, would be strong by virtue of maintaining its parity in the face of adversity. When new elections took place in 1969, the Grand Coalition was ousted in favour of a new coalition between the SPD and the liberal Free Democratic Party (FDP). Schiller remained in his post as economics minister. Strauss was out. So, the Schiller-Mark was bound to triumph, although not immediately, and not without some sleight of hand: Strauss and outgoing Chancellor Kurt Kiesinger (of the CDU) refused to approve formal revaluation at the last meeting of the outgoing cabinet in late September. Schiller, unruffled, conspired with the West German central bank, the Bundesbank, to allow the exchange rate to float through the simple expedient of not intervening in exchange markets to maintain existing parity. The DM appreciated almost immediately by 6 per cent. And, in late October, with a new government led by Chancellor Willy Brandt (of the SPD) now fully in charge and the DM's appreciation against the dollar now 9 per cent in total, Schiller fixed the new rate.[14]

Although this, too, proved inadequate for easing Germany's chronic balance-of-trade surplus, the country had now demonstrated a willingness to make changes that went some way towards the demands of its trading partners. What is more, through flirting briefly with a 'floating' exchange rate, the Bundesbank and the German government had developed some facility and experience, which would prove useful after Nixon announced a 'temporary' suspension of Bretton Woods in August 1971. The experience, moreover, was doubly important when Bretton Woods and dollar convertibility into gold ended formally and permanently in March 1973.

In and Out of the Bretton Woods: The Japanese Path

When Nixon announced the 'temporary' suspension of the Bretton Woods System in the middle of August 1971, Germany's current account surplus (export income minus import outlays) was 2.1 per cent of its GDP; Japan's was 4.4 per cent.[15] So, although neither country was named, both were well aware of who the US President had in mind when he spoke of punishing those engaged in 'unfair' trade practices. Japan, with its much larger trade surplus, was a source of particular irritation. The suspension of the US dollar's convertibility into gold and the imposition of punitive 10 per cent tariffs did nothing to fix the problem in the short term. The American fixation on Japan's large and growing trade surpluses and stocks of dollars consequently continued, prompting Nixon to arrange a summit with Japanese Prime Minister Kakuei Tanaka in Hawai'i in August 1972. Among the many concrete measures on the agenda for the talks was the possible purchase of a large fleet of Lockheed airplanes by Japan's ANA airline.

Japan figured more prominently than Germany among America's top economic concerns at the time in part because of the speed with which the Asian country's current account surpluses had grown. During the mid-1960s, remember, Japan concentrated heavily on rebuilding and growing its domestic market and struggled to gain a foothold in export markets, resulting in a chronic foreign trade deficit. By 1969, however, an OECD report commented on the recent 'radical change of Japan's external position'. The reason for this dramatic change, and the OECD's forecast for the immediate future, was that 'The current external surplus, after 3½ years of fast growth of activity, is running at record levels and ... seems likely to remain substantial.'[16] The issue of Japanese current account surpluses became pressing and chronic much later than for Germany. But when they arrived, they did so with a vengeance. They rapidly became larger, more intractable, and much more highly visible than Germany's.

The source of these differences between Japan and Germany lay in the Asian country's later industrial development, which required that it take an alternative path towards realising its own economic miracle. With much further to go than Germany to catch up with the United States and Britain, Japanese government and business focused on rapid industrialisation and technological development. They drew, of course, on expertise, knowledge, and ideas from abroad. But the process was carried out, initially at least, primarily on the domestic front and based on industrial financing, which constituted the main source of high-powered money – the currency and central bank reserves that form the basis for economic growth and development. This led, by the late 1960s, to Japanese success in manufacturing exports. But export growth was neither the main impetus for nor the most important outcome of the country's economic trajectory. When all was said and done, after all, Japan in the post-war period has been, and remains, far less reliant on foreign trade than Germany.[17]

As Mark Metzler has put it, Germany's export-led financing model and Japan's industrial-financing one 'overlap but are far from identical'. It is also striking that Japan's focus on industrial rather than export financing entails a far greater acceptance – and even an embrace – of inflation than was the case in Germany. Leading economists in Japan in the decades after the end of the Second World War were, like their German counterparts, keenly aware – sometimes through personal experience while living and studying in Germany at the time – of the German inflation that took place after the First World War, but they drew quite different lessons from it.[18]

Still, however, if export was far less important in Japan than it was in Germany, it was nevertheless a vital component of Japanese economic and business strategy in the post-war period. To promote and protect potential export industries, a number of controls over imports came into force in the aftermath of the war, placing curbs on goods from abroad, on the use of foreign exchange, and on overseas investment. What is more, the Japanese government proved extremely reluctant to lift such controls when the situation altered by the mid-1960s.

On the other hand, like Germany, Japan benefited enormously from the initial setting of its exchange rate in dollars and thereafter from the stickiness of the Bretton Woods System, which slowed down adjustments owing to changes in flows of goods and money. In 1949, as the Japanese yen joined the system, its value was set at ¥360 to the US dollar. As the speed in growth in Japan's exports and dollar reserves accelerated from the mid-1960s, however, the exchange rate moved only haltingly to compensate. It was a glacial pace that helped the Japanese promote sales of their manufactures abroad.

There was minor liberalization in 1959 and 1963, when the yen was allowed to float within prescribed limits in relation to the dollar. It was, however, only in December 1971, in the aftermath of Nixon's suspension of dollar convertibility, that the Smithsonian Agreement set a new rate of ¥308 to the US dollar, again with fluctuation set fairly narrowly within a band of plus or minus ¥7. The formal end to the Bretton Woods System in 1973, combined with pressure from the US government, caused Japanese authorities – reluctantly – to allow the yen to float freely. It appreciated almost immediately to ¥263 to the dollar. Yet, the new rate did nothing to stop rising Japanese sales abroad, especially in the United States, even though, by 1978, the yen had appreciated to as much as ¥173 to the dollar.[19]

In spite of the strength of these rapid (and probably belated) adjustments, Japanese export success continued unabated into the 1980s and beyond. In the meantime, however, a separate set of challenges emerged in the form of worldwide energy crises. They sent shockwaves through the German and Japanese economies, which had become particularly heavily dependent on overseas sources of fossil fuels.

Elements of Exposure: Navigating the Energy Crises

Still sombre in demeanour even after gaining re-election in 1972, President Richard M. Nixon had some more bad news when he once again addressed the American public in his televised address on the evening of 7 November 1973.

'I want to talk to you tonight about a serious national problem', Nixon began, before rapidly getting to the point:

> As America has grown and prospered in recent years, our energy demands have begun to exceed available supplies. In recent months, we have taken many actions to increase supplies and to reduce consumption. But even with our best efforts, we knew that a period of temporary shortages was inevitable.
>
> Unfortunately, our expectations for this winter have now been sharply altered by the recent conflict in the Middle East. Because of that war, most of the Middle Eastern oil producers

have reduced overall production and cut off their shipments of oil to the United States. By the end of this month, more than 2 million barrels a day of oil we expected to import into the United States will no longer be available.

We must, therefore, face up to a very stark fact: We are heading toward the most acute shortages of energy since World War II. Our supply of petroleum this winter will be at least 10 percent short of our anticipated demands, and it could fall short by as much as 17 percent.

Nixon's plan to deal with the projected shortages centred on increased generation of non-petroleum energy, especially coal and nuclear; rationing of petroleum-based heating oil, airplane fuel, and gasoline; and decreasing consumption of oil, especially through lowering speed limits on federal highways. The president admitted that '[g]as rationing, oil shortages, reduced speed limits – they all sound like a way of life we left behind with Glenn Miller and the war of the forties'. Yet, if Americans could pull together and deploy their unbounded ingenuity as they had in developing the atomic bomb and putting a man on the moon, Nixon continued, they could solve this problem as well.

In closing, Nixon reassured his fellow Americans that he was not planning to bail out of this challenge just because of 'the deplorable Watergate matter'. 'I have no intention whatsoever of walking away from the job I was elected to do,' he stated unequivocally.[20]

* * *

At the end of the Second World War, the United States had taken unprecedented levels of responsibility for leadership of the capitalist world economy, offering the dollar as the anchor for world currencies and championing free trade. It had also set the standard for the consumer society, to which most other countries aspired. Related to that, through mass motorisation and climate-controlled comfort at home, at work, and while shopping, it had been a pacesetter in the adoption of petroleum-based fuels. And, for three decades, the system championed by America seemed to work well for many, not least the West Germans and the Japanese. Suddenly, however, they must have felt that, instead of entering a US-style Garden of Eden of earthly delights and high comfort, they had instead been led down the garden path. Everything seemed to be falling apart. And the situation was soon to reach a nadir because of the president's direct involvement in 'the deplorable Watergate matter'.

* * *

As the first country to undergo mass motorisation during the first decades of the twentieth century, the United States was also by far the earliest – and largest – user of petroleum in the world. And until 1977, when it was overtaken by Saudi Arabia, the United States produced more crude oil than any other country. By then, however, oil consumption in the United States far outstripped production as motor vehicle usage soared and petroleum was used increasingly for heating and for firing electrical generators. As late as 1945, the country had been a net exporter of crude oil and petroleum products. By 1950, however, it had become a net importer. The trend continued in the decades that followed. And, by the time Richard Nixon gave his 1973 address, the United States imported fully a third of its demand for petroleum.[21]

The leader of the post-1945 capitalist world forged a clear path towards intensive energy usage, including heavy use of oil products. Germany and Japan, like many other countries, followed that path, although, at the same time, each also diverged from it and from one another. One important way in which Germany and Japan (like virtually every other country) differed substantially from the United States, for instance, was in per capita consumption of energy. As Richard Nixon reminded Americans in his November 1973 address:

> the average American will consume as much energy in the next 7 days as most other people in the world will consume in an entire year. We have only 6 percent of the world's people in America, but we consume over 30 percent of all the energy in the world.[22]

Germans and Japanese used far less energy on average than did Americans. But, during the initial post-war decades, both Germans and Japanese began to use much more than ever before. Increases in the use of petroleum products accounted for a large part of this new consumption. The pace and extent of the embrace of oil differed in the two cases, however, in part owing to availability and cost of domestic energy resources, and in part owing to geography and policy choices.

* * *

Germany had plentiful, high-quality coal available domestically, one of the country's few abundant resources. On the other hand, it had virtually no domestic oil reserves, as had been ascertained by the 1940s, expensively and conclusively. For that reason, solid fuels accounted for the lion's share of energy consumption by far into the 1950s. In 1925, for instance, coal was the basis for nearly 99 per cent of all primary energy (energy used directly for heat or to produce electricity) consumed, and, as late as 1950, that figure stood at nearly 95 per cent. Petroleum usage in 1950, on the other hand, stood at a mere 4.4 per cent of total West German energy consumption.

Enhanced demand owing to motorisation and the adoption of oil-fired central heating on the one hand, and greater and cheaper supplies of petroleum, mostly from the Middle East, on the other entailed a decrease in coal's share to just under 90 per cent by 1955, while oil's share had increased to nearly 9 per cent. The Suez Crisis of 1956–1957, which demonstrated the vulnerability of reliance on oil from the Middle East, might well have been expected to curb this trend, all other things being equal.[23] But Suez did not have this effect, mainly owing to a deliberate decision by the West German government, backed in particular by free marketeer Ludwig Erhard and his economics ministry, not to use tax policies, rationing, or other levers to channel demand away from oil and back towards coal. Indeed, Germany's reaction to Suez consciously modelled itself on the American one, and involved a heavy reliance on the private sector, the free market, and, above all else, the international oil companies. As one ministry official put it in December 1956:

> The American government does not intend to use bureaucratic regulations to control supply of petroleum and oil products to Europe. The American government will instead 'proceed on a grand scale in the same way as the Federal Republic does on a small one', namely through making use of the available oil companies.[24]

As a result of such decisions and the decreasing costs and rising availability of petroleum from abroad, coal consumption decreased precipitously as a source of primary energy through the following decades, displaced above all by petroleum. By 1963, coal accounted for only about two-thirds of energy consumption in West Germany, while oil stood at about a third. However, the tables had turned entirely by

1970, with coal at 38.8 per cent of total primary energy consumption and oil at 54.6 per cent. And, in 1973, coal dropped to less than one-third of total energy consumption, while oil stood at well over half: 56.2 per cent. By then, however, and starting in the mid-1960s, a newcomer had entered the energy mix, with a major impact: in 1973, natural gas accounted for nearly 10 per cent of all energy used in West Germany, up from less than 1 per cent a decade earlier. Again, most of it came from abroad.[25]

The profound change in West Germany's energy sources entailed a switch from domestic to imported supplies, most of which had to be paid for in US dollars. This obviously posed no problem, given the country's perennial trade surpluses, growing dollar reserves, and the fact that oil and gas were relatively cheap, with much of the former coming from the Middle East and North Africa and the latter from the Netherlands and, eventually and increasingly, from the Soviet Union/Russia. However, the energy crises of 1973–1974 and 1978–1979, which constrained supplies and, at the same time, led to much higher costs proved a major challenge. After all, crude oil prices tripled from 1972 to 1973 to unprecedented levels, and then nearly doubled again between 1973 and 1980. In other words, the cost of petroleum had now reached nearly six times its 'normal' level. Therefore, not only were many more dollars flowing out of the country to pay for it than ever before,[26] but also the practically simultaneous appreciation of the West German DM and widespread economic slowdown (coinciding in most countries with inflation, a phenomenon known as 'stagflation') meant that it became more difficult to sell German manufactures abroad.

The German response to these crises was in broad contours similar to that of the United States, although the emphases were different. Incentivised by the government, Germans started to use much less energy due to better insulation in homes. Manufacturing firms also paid much greater attention to energy efficiency in the design and use of appliances and automobiles that Germans – as well as many others around the world – bought. And, partly as a result of this, they also used less oil. By the 1980s, petroleum usage had fallen to about 40 per cent of total primary energy consumption, where it remained into the twenty-first century. Total energy usage, moreover, also declined somewhat and then stabilised during the same time period, despite highly respectable economic growth and the substantial enlargement of the country's geographical area and population as a result of unification with the former East Germany in October 1990. The decline in oil consumption within this generally stable level of overall energy consumption has been accompanied by rises in the use of natural gas – supplied mostly from the Russian Federation – and of nuclear power, combined with substantial and accelerating commitment since the 1990s to generating electricity through renewables.[27]

Germany, though, differed considerably from the United States in another important way. To gain the foreign exchange – mostly dollars – needed to pay for continued imports of ever more expensive oil, German industry, supported by the country's federal and state governments, mounted a concerted export drive, focusing on the oil-producing states, especially those in the Middle East and North Africa. What German firms had to offer was extremely attractive, and, not incidentally, also very expensive. The oil-rich states were, after all, interested not only in exploiting their mineral resources by selling them directly to countries like Germany, but also in developing higher-value domestic industry, such as petrochemical plants. German firms were, of course, world leaders in designing, building, and supplying these, and countries such as Saudi Arabia were keen customers. More visibly, German manufacturers also found a large, lucrative, and growing market for expensive, high-quality automobiles and other high-end goods.

In the short term, the overall impact of the energy crises of the 1970s on Germany's current account was to throw it unaccustomedly into deficit by the late 1970s and early 1980s, with a nadir of −1.87 per cent of the country's GDP in 1980. However, the combination of reductions in the use of energy, changes in the energy mix, and a highly successful export drive led to a pronounced recovery soon thereafter. Germany's current account returned to deficit in the 1990s, largely as a result of the costs of unification. But, since 2002, it has reached unprecedented and sustained surpluses of between 5 and 8 per cent of GDP, primarily owing to the country's manufacturing exports.[28]

* * *

Japan, like Germany, had very little oil beneath the soil of its home islands. And, to add to its fossil-fuel woes, the East Asian country also had limited coal deposits. Nevertheless, Japan used solid fuels – mostly coal – for more than four-fifths of its total energy consumption in

1950, although it must also be emphasised that Japan's far less developed economy at that time used no more than just over a third as much energy overall as West Germany, despite having a larger population. Japan also differed from Germany and the United States in the scale of its reliance on hydropower, which amounted to more than a tenth of its overall energy usage in 1950.[29]

Japan's limited domestic sources of energy combined with ever cheaper and easily available coal, and then, increasingly, oil, to change the mix. The development was facilitated by American leadership of the capitalist world economy, which led to freer trade and a privileging of petroleum. Oil accounted for a mere 6.1 per cent of total Japanese energy consumption in 1950, but it had risen to more than 22 per cent by 1955, all at the expense of coal, despite an increase in total energy consumption during the same period of nearly 50 per cent. This trend continued apace during the rest of the 1950s, the 1960s, and into the 1970s. By 1973, overall Japanese energy consumption lay at tenfold what it had been in 1950. Solid fuels accounted for just under a fifth of that, while oil usage stood at nearly four-fifths (77.8 per cent) of total consumption. Natural gas remained of minor significance (1.6 per cent), and hydropower's share had dropped to 1.9 per cent, indicating an increase in absolute terms, but at a pace far lower than the growth in overall energy usage.[30] Japan's rapid embrace of petroleum, moreover, accounted in part for the country's balance-of-trade deficits during the mid-1960s, although thereafter it was easily able to pay for cheap and apparently abundant oil – from the Middle East, but also Indonesia and other countries – with its export earnings, mostly from manufacturing.

Japan was therefore even more exposed than the United States and Germany as a result of the energy crises of the 1970s and the massive price increases that accompanied them. Dealing with the crises in Japan again showed similarities to the other two countries in government-assisted or -mandated conservation measures in the short term and the diversification of energy sources. The changes in Japan in the aftermath of the crises, however, differed from those in Germany in three key respects. First of all, although oil usage declined in Japan as elsewhere in the wake of the oil crises, petroleum continued to supply over half of Japan's consumption of primary energy until the turn of the twenty-first century, when the proportion finally dropped below 50 per cent. Second, unlike Germany, but like the United States, overall energy usage in Japan resumed its upward trajectory after a short hiatus during the crises, rising by a factor of nearly 1.5 between 1973 and 2004. Third, the Japanese embraced nuclear power to a much greater extent than either Germany or the United States. On the other hand, Japan, like the others, used natural gas to meet a growing proportion of its energy needs after the oil crises. However, unlike the United States or Germany, where delivery was mostly by pipeline, Japan as an island nation received its gas in the form of liquefied petroleum gas (LPG), and the LPG was regasified and distributed in Japan after being offloaded from ships.[31]

Just as for Germany, the crises posed a short-term challenge for Japan owing to the massive increase in foreign-exchange outgoings to meet vastly higher oil prices. As a result, there was a brief return to negative current account balances for Japan in 1974–1975 and 1979–1980. But, as was the case with Germany, a renewed, and again highly successful, export drive led to a resumption of surpluses in spite of heavy outlays for imported energy and the appreciation of the yen. These surpluses have remained positive ever since, although generally at far more modest levels than has been the case since the beginning of the twenty-first century in Germany.[32]

Part IV
NAVIGATING WAVES OF GLOBALIZATION, 1990 TO THE PRESENT

10 MANAGING IN MAJOR MARKETS
Selling and Making in the United States and China

With its neatly laid-out streets, well-kept single-family homes, and tidy town centre, Columbus, Indiana, population around 50,000, is in many ways the archetypal small midwestern US city. Not unusually for such a locale, about four out of five residents of the sprawling, landlocked city are white according to the latest American Community Survey of the US Census Bureau, with just over half of the remaining residents Asian.[1] They live and work about an hour's drive away from the nearest large urban conurbations, Indianapolis, Indiana, and Louisville, Kentucky.

On the basis of these barebones facts alone, Columbus, Indiana, is a completely unremarkable place. Yet, initial impressions are deceptive, as a quick look around the city would confirm. One of the city's fire stations was designed by the renowned modernist architect Robert Venturi. Irish-born award-winning architect Kevin Roche created the plans for the main post office, among other buildings. And Finnish-American architect and industrial designer Eero Saarinen designed a conference centre and a soaring, spectacular church for the town. In all, internationally acclaimed architects have been responsible for around seventy buildings and other structures built in the city since the late 1950s, their fees paid by the Cummins Foundation. The foundation was established by the Miller family, the owners of Columbus-based Cummins Diesel, a designer and manufacturer of engines and their components. It continues its work to the present day, although the company has long since become a joint-stock corporation, Cummins Inc. Unusually for a Fortune-500 multinational, Cummins remains headquartered in small-town, midwestern Columbus.[2]

Cummins Inc. is by far 'the biggest company in town and the key player in its push for internationalization', a campaign it has been waging for some time as an extension of its earlier and successful efforts to make the city highly liveable and extremely attractive. Already in the mid-1960s, the First Lady of the United States, Lady Bird Johnson, dubbed it 'The Athens of the Prairie'.[3] The long-term proactive stance of the firm, which has worked closely with the city's Economic Development Board, has combined with the city's demographic make-up, its isolated and insulated location, and its treasure trove of architectural gems to enable its astonishing success in attracting substantial overseas foreign direct investment (OFDI). An astonishing thirteen subsidiaries of foreign companies count among the city's top forty-three employers. A total of eight of these foreign firms were Japanese; the others came from five different other countries. They include a German firm, powdered-metal component manufacturer PMG Indiana Corporation, employing 308. All in all, a grand total of more than two dozen Japanese firms up to 2020 have located manufacturing, North American headquarters, and/or R&D operations in Columbus. Five of the town's top eleven employers are subsidiaries of Japanese firms. These firms employ just over 4,400 in total.[4]

The factors affecting these and other firms' decisions to locate operations abroad – including where, and which specific operations – are many and varied. But a highly significant one is often omitted, and it is brought into sharp focus by the case of Columbus, Indiana: the home country headquarters of the firm can have a decisive impact, and not just on deciding whether – but also where and how – to locate operations in the United States. There has been a recognisably Japanese pattern to OFDI in the post-war period, one with its roots in culture and in the history of Japan's relationship with the target country for the firms' investments. And there is a distinctly German one, too.

Playing Ball in the World's Richest Market

From the beginning of its existence, the United States has been a lucrative market for overseas products and a highly remunerative playground for overseas investors. Both exports to and investment in America have grown markedly through time, with the pace and scale of increases in OFDI in the United States particularly striking. By 2015, about 6.8 million US workers were employees of affiliates of companies headquartered outside the country's borders, and they were paid on average nearly 25 per cent more than those employed by domestic companies. A clear majority – 58 per cent – of this employment was by affiliates of firms headquartered (in rank order) in the UK, Japan, France, Germany, and Canada. With about 1.1 million employees in the United States, UK companies were the largest among this group, but Japanese firms were not far behind, with about 856,000 employees. Firms headquartered in France, Germany, and Canada were very closely clustered in terms of US employees, with over 600,000 workers for each national grouping.[5]

If the overseas investors in the United States are ranked by OFDI 'stocks' – that is, the cumulative investment through 2019 by companies based in other countries in shares, buildings, equipment, and other assets located in the United States – a somewhat different picture emerges. Again, five countries accounted for a clear majority – 57 per cent – of investment. Using this measure, though, Japan is the clear leader, with 15 per cent of the OFDI total, followed by Canada (12.9 per cent), Germany (11.6 per cent), the UK (9.9 per cent), and Ireland (7.6 per cent). France (6.9 per cent) comes in sixth place using this metric. Over 40 per cent of this cumulative foreign investment is in manufacturing, while financial and insurance (12.1 per cent) and wholesale trade (10.3 per cent) are the other key foci of foreign ownership. Together, these three sectors have accounted for nearly two-thirds of all OFDI in the United States up to 2019.[6]

In many ways, this statistical picture, whether drawn on the basis of employment or capital invested, is entirely unsurprising: the countries that stand out from the crowd are for the most part the usual suspects. All of them – with the exception of Ireland, a relative latecomer to the club – are wealthy and highly industrialised. OFDI generally flows most freely between such relative equals, and US-based firms have reciprocated with OFDI in all of these countries. The UK and France have long had avid business interests in North America, which pre-date the founding of the United States. Canada, moreover, is geographically adjacent and economically complementary in various ways. And the UK, Canada, and Ireland share a common language with the United States as well as extensive shared kinship (and business) networks.

As the third- and fourth-largest economies in the world, respectively, Japan and Germany are distinguished members of this elite club of rich and developed countries that trade with and invest heavily in one another. Predictably, therefore, firms from those two countries have a major presence in the United States. But the two are also outliers among the biggest investors in the world's richest nation, not only because of their different languages, but also because their interests and those of the United States clashed so strongly in the first half of the twentieth century. Germany went to war twice with America. Japan went to war with the United States only once during the period, but the combat between them was severe and bloody, representing as it did the culmination of escalating and irreconcilable tensions dating back to the 1920s.

However, although the two countries share a status as outliers among large post-war foreign investors in the United States, there are also significant differences between them. Japan, for instance, diverged from Germany in that its companies had no real track record of industrial investment in the United States until the 1970s, the result of the Asian country's relative economic and technological backwardness and more limited kinship ties. Most Japanese foreign investment during the 1970s was in developing countries. The Japanese government, moreover, also imposed significant controls on – along with other measures to hinder – imports of goods and services and foreign investment for much of the post-war period.[7] Indeed, the country's relatively closed economy combined with its extraordinary, rapid, and highly visible success in selling its manufactures in the United States and other countries resulted in howls of protest over 'unfair' trade practices. Consequently, the US government, especially under President Richard Nixon in the early 1970s, began to exert massive pressure on Japan. Nixon urged the Japanese not only to buy more US goods and services – for instance airplanes produced by Lockheed and Boeing – but also to make substantial investments in the United States to provide good jobs there and to ameliorate the yawning US trade deficit.

In contrast, despite its different language and the deep and at times violent conflicts with the United States during the first half of the twentieth century, Germany has a lengthy record of trade with, and investment in, the United States, in part owing to its complementary economy, and partly due to deep ties of kinship and commerce. The distinguished historian Volker Berghahn has even gone so far as to characterise the German–US relationship as a second 'special relationship', co-equal with the much more widely acknowledged one between Britain and the United States.[8]

In line with this view, West German firms arrived on the American scene after the Second World War much earlier than their Japanese counterparts, first of all to sell. Highly successful sales there then led by the 1970s to vast German balance-of-trade surpluses with the United States, just as it did for Japan. This naturally provoked a backlash in US government circles, but it was much more muted than the adverse reaction elicited by Japan. After all, German imports were either higher-end luxury goods or far less visible (because they were purchased by American companies rather than consumers) than Japanese ones. Just as importantly, though, the West German economy was far more open than Japan's, with the result that US firms were able to sell goods without impediment there (although also without sufficient success to overcome the manufacturing trade deficit with Germany). US multinationals were also able to invest at will in West Germany, as many of them did – including big oil companies such as Esso and Texaco and technology firms such as IBM.[9]

In any event, though, the ballooning balance-of-trade surpluses of both Germany and Japan in the United States led to pressures on both countries to invest heavily there. Given the differing historical links, experiences, and motivations affecting the development of business and commercial relationships after 1945, however, the forays of corporations from the two countries into owning and operating factories in the United States were bound to be different as well. But the paths chosen – and their outcomes – were also a function of divergent national styles and cultures of OFDI.

Investing in America, Japanese Style

In late 1972, soon-to-be-disgraced Japanese Prime Minister Kakuei Tanaka flew to Hawai'i for a summit meeting with soon-to-be-disgraced US President Richard M. Nixon. The main item on the agenda was the widening American trade deficit with Japan. Among Nixon's proposals for solving the problem was the sale of a large number of passenger airplanes made by soon-to-be-disgraced Lockheed to Japanese airline ANA.[10] The discussions were the first in an increasingly acrimonious diplomatic wrangle about the nature and sustainability of the economic relationship between what had by then become the two largest economies in the capitalist world.[11]

The main solutions embraced initially, however – diplomacy, bilateral sales agreements (including contracts for Japan to buy military hardware to help 'offset' the costs of the US military presence there), and voluntary limitations on exports from Japan – could only go so far towards addressing the fundamental issues at stake. A more long-term fix for the chronic structural imbalance in trade had to be found, one which also counteracted what was becoming a serious shortage of manufacturing jobs in the United States. And, for that, the private sector had to come on board.

* * *

Five years after the Hawai'ian summit, in October 1977, Japanese entrepreneur Soichiro Honda shook hands with Ohio Governor James Rhodes on an agreement for Honda to invest $25 million in a motorcycle production plant to be constructed near Marysville, Ohio. Honda had chosen the greenfield site, Rhodes recalled later, while on a fly-over in a state-owned airplane. The only structure of any significance among the cornfields and woods was an Ohio Transportation Research Center. Honda was delighted, both by the site and by the generous tax and other incentives offered by Governor Rhodes and his state government. Shortly after the Honda–Rhodes handshake sealed the deal, Honda's company created a wholly owned subsidiary, Honda America Manufacturing, Inc., to oversee construction of the facility, which commenced production in 1979 (Figure 10.1).[12]

It was by no means Honda's first foray into the United States. Two decades earlier, already in 1959, Honda had taken the unusual step of setting up shop in North America independently rather than through a trading company, the usual route for prospective Japanese exporters. American Honda Motor Company, Inc. opened its doors at 4077 West Pico Boulevard in Los Angeles, California. It had just six employees.[13]

Initially, American Honda did not sell many motorcycles. Not only were the product and its manufacturer unknown quantities in the United States, but also the bikes were diminutive and not very powerful. However, sales grew apace on the back of a growing reputation for quality and excellent value for money; new and more powerful

Figure 10.1 Billboard outside Honda plant in Marysville, Ohio, March 1983. Bettmann/Getty Images

models; and a slick advertising campaign under the slogan 'You meet the nicest people on a Honda.' By 1970, Honda had sold half a million Japanese-made motorcycles in the United States.[14]

The motorcycle plant that started production in Marysville, Ohio, at the end of the decade represented the classic next step for a budding multinational enterprise: Honda moved from investment in relatively inexpensive overseas sales operations to investing in much more capital-intensive manufacturing. It was a major move, but also characteristically cautious. The Ohio factory was fitted out with Japanese tools, machines, and production lines, and it was staffed with Japanese managers. In other words, it was primarily an assembly plant, with little more potential for facilitating technology transfer than a sales subsidiary. Many of its suppliers, moreover, were also transplants to Ohio from Japan, at least initially, as Honda sought to replicate its just-in-time system in the American context through trusted Japanese manufacturers. And all of these typical assembly plant characteristics remained when, in 1980, Honda announced plans to expand the Marysville factory to produce automobiles alongside motorcycles. The first Japanese car, a four-door Accord, came off the new assembly line in November 1982.[15]

Honda's ambitions for its North American operations were still unfulfilled, however, not least because the continued weakening of the US dollar against the Japanese yen led to unsustainable price increases for the firm's imported cars. So, it soon set up an engine factory in nearby Anna, Ohio. And its supplier network grew as well, again mostly in the Buckeye State. Headlights were manufactured in London, Ohio, for example, and exhaust pipes in Russells Point. As a 1984 article in the *New York Times* pointed out, 'all the facilities, aside from a distribution center in Dayton, are being built away from heavily unionized urban centers'. Honda denied that the presence or absence of trade unions had anything to do with its choice of locations; instead, the 'company cites cheap land costs, a pleasant work environment and an absence of traffic jams as reasons for choosing rural areas'.[16]

Honda's next step doubled down on its previous choices and investments; it also marked a quantum leap in the nature of the subsidiary. In 1987, the Japanese firm announced a five-part strategy for establishing 'a self-reliant motor vehicle company in the U.S.', which entailed a fundamental shift in orientation towards considerable technology transfer and development of localised, subsidiary-based technological capability. The strategy comprised the following elements: expansion of the Anna engine plant; establishment of a new auto factory in East Liberty, Ohio; an increase in purchases of parts from domestic North American suppliers; establishment of production engineering and R&D operations; and export of cars manufactured in Ohio. The first US-produced Accord sedan was exported to Taiwan the same year. By 1997, Honda's initial investment of $25 million in its Marysville site had ballooned to nearly $2 billion.[17]

* * *

Honda was not alone. By 2021, 860 Japanese companies had invested in operations in Ohio, accounting for 27.2 per cent of all foreign-company employment in the state, by far the largest contingent. The UK, for instance, was a distant second with 14.1 per cent, and Germany third, with 12.2 per cent, while all other foreign countries' companies had employment shares of well under 10 per cent. Honda was the largest Japanese employer by a considerable distance, but there were several other large Japanese firms, many of them suppliers to the auto giant, and many of them were located in rural parts of the state.[18]

The same pattern held for other Japanese transplants. In 1983, shortly after Honda, for example, Nissan established an assembly plant for cars, trucks, and engines in rural Smyrna, Tennessee. Honda's rival, too, was responding to US pressure to locate production in country, a move made far easier by financial and tax incentives, relatively low wages, and the rural setting. Again, the plant was small at the start, and it focused on assembly rather than other, more demanding functions. But, like Marysville, the Smyrna factory has grown by leaps and bounds over the years. By 2022, it employed more than 7,000 directly, and employment by the plant's suppliers, both Japanese and American, is even greater. To that point, Nissan had invested a total of $7.1 billion in a plant with a capacity for producing 640,000 vehicles per year. And hundreds of other Japanese firms have chosen to locate in Tennessee, Kentucky, and other parts of the American South as well.[19]

Each of these cases has several distinctive features. Honda, for instance, was unusual among Japanese firms at the time in choosing not to engage the services of a trading firm for its forays into the US market as well as in the scale of its investment and the speed with which it took place once the decision to locate in Marysville, Ohio, was made. Japanese firms in Columbus, Indiana, on the other hand, have been drawn into the city, in large part, owing to the efforts of Cummins Inc.

There are nevertheless enough common features to identify a Japanese style of investment in the United States. As epitomised by Honda, investment in manufacturing followed investment in sales (directly or through a trading company) and the pace of investment was gradual. The extent to which Japanese-headquartered firms gave their subsidiaries functions beyond assembly was limited at first, although this gradually increased. Factories, moreover, tended to be situated in rural or small-town locations on greenfield sites. And regardless of Honda's claim that its decision on location had nothing to do with the absence of trade unions, it is certainly striking that the sites chosen by Honda and other Japanese firms almost invariably had no traditions or presence of organised labour. Two additional characteristics stand out: the overseas ventures tended to be undertaken without much fanfare; and they have also generally been successful over a long period of time.

Investing in America, German Style

When Volkswagen's sole CEO during the post-war period, Heinz Nordhoff, died in April 1968, the limits of his strategy of intensive focus on a single model, the Beetle, had already been reached. Nordhoff's incremental improvements to the iconic car to enhance its quality and reliability, containment of costs to enable low prices, an instantly recognisable and arresting design, and clever advertising had translated into booming sales across the world, with the company particularly successful in the US market. In 1968, it sold a staggering 40 per cent of its output from the VW factory in Wolfsburg to customers in the United States, where the German firm enjoyed a market share of 5 per cent of the total automobile market by the early 1970s.[20]

But the company was in crisis by that time owing to chronic underinvestment in new plant, neglect of new model and design development, and rising costs. Addressing these issues, Nordhoff's short-serving successors Kurt Lotz (to 1971), Rudolf Leiding (to 1975), and Toni Schmücker (to 1982) set in motion a series of projects to develop competitive water-cooled, front-wheel-drive models to follow in the Beetle's footsteps. With the company teetering for a time on the brink of bankruptcy, Leiding oversaw the development and introduction of the Golf by the mid-1970s, a new platform that served as the basis for the company's wildly successful Polo–Golf–Passat range, which proved an immediate hit in Europe. Under Schmücker, VW began exporting the Golf to the United States under the Rabbit marque (Figure 10.2). And he was so confident of the viability of the new model that he decided to shut down German production of the Beetle entirely in 1978 (although production continued in Mexico until 2019).[21]

Initially, though, the Rabbit was markedly less successful in the United States than it was in Europe, and much less so than the Beetle had been in its prime. Sales of VW cars in America had peaked at over 570,000 in 1970 before dropping by almost half to just under 268,000 in 1975, with VW's share of the US market falling from about 5 to 2 per cent. The tumble was the result of increased prices owing to the dollar's weakness against the Deutschmark (the price of VW's cheapest models increased by nearly 50 per cent in the United States between 1970 and 1976); the waning appeal of the Beetle; and slow sales of the new Rabbit. Added to that, there was pressure from the US government for Germany to do something about its trade surplus

Figure 10.2 Volkswagen Rabbit advertisement 1980. Retro AdArchives/ Alamy

with the United States, although the pressure was more muted than with Japan.[22]

Schmücker and other top officials at Volkswagen therefore decided in 1976, just two years after he had become CEO, to invest heavily in manufacturing operations in the United States. Purchasing everything except the engine and drive train from US suppliers, and having the cars assembled by American workers, would contain costs for the German auto giant. VW's executives also reckoned that the move would allow them to regain market share in the lucrative American market.[23]

The motivations behind VW's investment in US manufacturing were clear, and not all that different from those behind later decisions by Honda and Nissan to follow the same strategy. However, the way the German company entered the US market diverged from that of later Japanese (and other non-American) investors. Instead of undertaking a greenfield investment in a previously undeveloped location, it instead acquired an existing factory, a brownfield investment. As *Time* reported in May 1976:

> Three sites are leading contenders for the VW plant: a former Westinghouse appliance factory in Columbus, Ohio, a federal tank plant in the Cleveland suburb of Brook Park and a partially completed Chrysler Corp. assembly plant at New Stanton, Pa. Whichever site Volkswagen chooses, it will soon have company. Now that it is moving into U.S. manufacturing, Japanese car makers are almost certain to follow.[24]

* * *

Japanese carmakers were certainly watching the actions of VW's Volkswagen Manufacturing Corp. of America subsidiary very closely indeed. Perhaps the most salient lesson centred on the fact that overseas automakers were knocking on an open door in considering manufacturing in America. The US federal government was exerting pressure on the governments in Germany and Japan to decrease the countries' trade surpluses. Private German and Japanese firms rather than their respective governments would be most effective in accommodating the wishes of the US federal government. But it was American state and local governments that had the biggest incentive to entice those companies to take the plunge.

The prospect of lots of lucrative manufacturing jobs – and the votes that would go with them – to offset deindustrialisation in many parts of the United States, or to create employment opportunities in manufacturing where few had existed before, unleashed a frenzied competition among states and localities to land the foreign investment. They avidly courted the firms considering the move towards American production sites, vying to outdo one another with loosened purse strings and a smorgasbord of incentives and emoluments. In the end, Pennsylvania and its Westmoreland County bested their Ohio counterparts in that state's two biggest cities, Cleveland and Columbus. Pennsylvania's total bill for subsidies amounted to $75 million. Volkswagen ponied up more than $250 million.[25]

Top managers at the German firm thought they had made an excellent – and historic – deal. Chairman Toni Schmücker went so far

in his speech at the New Stanton factory's inauguration as to para-
phrase Neil Armstrong, who had become the first person to walk on
the moon just under a decade earlier: 'This may be one small step for
America, but it is one giant step [sic] for Volkswagen.'[26]

* * *

New Stanton, Pennsylvania, was truly a giant leap for VW, but not
quite the one the German carmaker expected. The company's brave
plunge into the promised land proved more to be a giant lunge into an
abyss. Volkswagen withdrew from its ambitious American venture in
summer 1988, less than ten years after it had begun.

There were many reasons for this, but two sets of factors stand
out. For one thing, VW's decision to locate operations in America was
predicated on wages remaining considerably lower than those paid
by the American Big Three automakers in Detroit, whose workers
were members of the United Auto Workers (UAW) trade union. They
earned $7.50 an hour in 1978; the initial pay rate for VW workers was
about three-quarters of that, $5.60. As James McLernon, head of VW
America, put it when the New Stanton plant opened, 'This plant could
not exist if it started out at parity with UAW wages scales.' The choice
of a semi-rural location was meant to guarantee this differential, at
least for a certain amount of time, because workers who were not part
of the union tradition could be drawn from the local area.

In the event, VW's workforce tended to come from the nearby
Pittsburgh area, which was heavily unionised, and they soon joined the
UAW, achieving parity with their counterparts in Detroit. Nevertheless,
higher than expected labour costs did nothing to prevent the factory
exceeding its original production targets within two years of opening.
In 1980, working on two shifts, New Stanton manufactured nearly a
quarter of a million cars, and it employed 5,700. Still, by 1987, 2,500
workers operating on a single shift produced fewer than 80,000 automobiles.[27] High labour costs, however, did not bring about the plant's
demise, at least not on their own.

Instead, a combination of factors accounted for the eventual
failure of the plant. First was the fact that VW targeted the low-end,
high-volume market in the United States, where profitability was also
low. Then there was the Rabbit itself, which proved deeply unpopular, ensuring it would never enjoy high sales. The third factor lay in

the technological obsolescence of the Westmoreland plant. VW management favoured traditional assembly line manufacturing at the very same time that robotics and other technologies were coming onto the scene. These innovations were embraced by the Japanese, both at home and, before long, also in their American transplants.[28]

In other words, just as Volkswagen had aped earlier developments at Ford in its pursuit of a highly successful single-model strategy, it joined its ailing American counterparts in the early 1980s in misjudging the market and persevering with an outmoded production regime. VW management, moreover, did so brashly and brimming with confidence, which lent particularly high prominence to the plant's eventual closure in 1988.

* * *

VW's initial attempt at making things in America contrasted sharply with the success of German firms in other industries that were more in keeping with traditional German strengths in less highly visible producer-goods industries. German chemical firm Bayer, for instance, built back manufacturing operations in the post-war period that they had started already in the early twentieth century, but which had been disrupted by wars and property seizures associated with them.

Bayer set up a production plant in the United States in 1903, mainly to evade tariff barriers by mixing chemical intermediates imported from Germany. In other words, this was a simple assembly plant with limited technology transfer. Regardless, Bayer's American operations were seized during the First World War, along with its patents, trade names, and trademarks, including the Bayer cross. After the Second World War, it gained a foothold in American production operations early on in spite of having limited capital for investment. In fact, by 1956 Bayer was able to parlay its technology and know-how into a 50 per cent ownership stake in Chemagro Corporation. In the years that followed, it added to the production portfolio steadily – but gradually, in keeping with the growing but still limited capital available to the firm and the caution of its management.

By the early 1970s, it had six American manufacturing subsidiaries, and the German firm decided that consolidation was its next step. It could not use the Bayer name in the United States, however, because this had been transferred following the seizure in the First World War to Sterling, an American drug company. For this reason, Bayer founded its US headquarters in Pittsburgh, Pennsylvania, in 1974 under the name of the Mobay Corporation. Mobay not only manufactured in numerous different American locations, but also invested heavily in US-based research and development involving significant technology transfer. Subsumed under the name of another Bayer subsidiary in the United States in 1991, Mobay became Miles Inc. After the German firm had reacquired the rights to its name and trademark in the United States through its purchase of Sterling Winthrop's 'self medication [sic] business' in 1994, Miles was duly renamed Bayer Corporation the following year. The headquarters remained in Pittsburgh.[29]

* * *

Large German firms from other industrial sectors where Germany has longstanding strength also invested heavily in manufacturing operations in the United States, especially from the 1970s onwards. In the electrical industry, for instance, Siemens became a major player in America. The firm had set up its first manufacturing operation in the United States in 1892, although, like Bayer, it was forced to withdraw from making things in America because of the wars of the first half of the twentieth century. From the 1970s, Siemens returned to the United States in earnest. By the twenty-first century, the United States was the company's 'biggest single market in the world', 'account[ing] for some 20 percent of total Siemens revenues' in 2006.[30]

It was not just large German firms that invested heavily in sales and manufacturing in the United States. Complementing them, just as in the German domestic economy, are Germany's 'hidden champions': smaller, usually family-owned, and often tightly focused companies from the so-called *Mittelstand*. In fact, among the nearly 5,000 subsidiaries of German-headquartered companies operating in the United States by 2018, the vast majority were affiliates of small- and medium-sized enterprises. They contributed strongly to making Germany the fourth-largest foreign employer in the United States, accounting for about 10 per cent of total US employment by overseas enterprises and about the same share of overall US OFDI.[31]

Like their Japan-headquartered counterparts, some of these smaller German firms manufacturing in the United States are key suppliers of the larger firms that have transplanted some operations to

America and have simply followed their main customers overseas. But, to a much greater extent than for smaller Japanese firms, companies from the German *Mittelstand* locating operations in the United States are independent. Such 'pocket multinationals' tend not only to be family-owned and highly specialised, with a very high global market share in their special market segment, but also mostly have headquarters in small towns in southern and southwestern Germany, for the most part in Baden-Württemberg and Bavaria.

The companies are supported by their state governments in Germany with market intelligence about opportunities overseas. What is more, crucial applied research and development capacity for the *Mittelstand* firms comes from Germany's Fraunhofer Institutes. These innovative institutions do high-quality, applied contract work on behalf of smaller companies that would otherwise not be able to afford their own research. All of these support measures have given *Mittelstand* firms some of the advantages that only larger firms would otherwise be able to afford, allowing them in turn to embark on a number of substantial investments in the United States.[32]

* * *

Eventually, success in establishing manufacturing operations in the United States came to German automobile producers, too. Automaker BMW, for instance, had considerable success after deciding in 1992 to invest heavily in its first manufacturing operation outside of Germany, in Spartanburg, South Carolina. Already in autumn 1994, the factory was producing cars for the US market, and it has since expanded several times, producing over 5 million vehicles by 2020. BMW, like VW in New Stanton, engaged in a strategy of partnering with American-based suppliers. It had about 300 of them by 2020. But the Bavarian luxury auto producer learned from VW New Stanton's failures, and also from Japanese successes, in locating in the American south on a greenfield site with considerable scope for expansion and with a ready and willing local non-unionised workforce. By 2020, there were more than 11,000 employees on site.[33]

Encouraged by the success of BMW, keenly aware of the need to have a manufacturing as well as a sales presence in the United States, and buoyed by the reception there of its retro New Beetle (produced in Puebla, Mexico), Volkswagen also summoned up the courage to take its second crack at manufacturing in America. The German auto giant, too, had clearly learned a thing or two from its previous disappointment and from its Japanese competitors. It decided in 2008 to reboot manufacturing operations in the United States, choosing to locate in Chattanooga, Tennessee, in the American south. The factory started production of the Passat model in 2011, and it has since gone on to produce the Atlas, a mid-sized SUV designed for the American market. By mid-2020, the factory had assembled its millionth car in America, again relying heavily on US-based suppliers. And a year earlier, in 2019, Volkswagen of America announced plans to expand the plant considerably to produce electric vehicles for the US market.[34]

There is at least one ironic postscript to this story. In 1990, Japanese electronics giant Sony took about $40 million in incentives to locate a factory in none other than New Stanton, Pennsylvania, the former site acquired and then abandoned by Chrysler and subsequently by Volkswagen. Sony lasted longer than the previous two tenants, but by 2007 laid off most of its workforce in favour of a new manufacturing site in Mexico.[35]

Doing Business in the Middle Kingdom

In autumn 1977, Chinese planners developed a first blueprint for constructing the Baoshan steel works, a substantial dedicated port and iron-smelting facility meant to supply existing steel mills in Shanghai. Over the following year, however, the plans ballooned. Five design changes through September 1978 expanded the scale and scope of the original project to mammoth proportions:

> From an ordinary large investment, the project had been pyramided into a completely integrated state-of-the-art steel mill, with virtually all technology and equipment to be imported from Japan. Foreign exchange requirements more than tripled from about $1.8 billion in the original version, to $5.7 billion in the September 1978 version.[36]

The story of the Baoshan steel works underscores the fact that the 'opening up' of China, conventionally dated to the Third Plenum of the Eleventh Chinese Communist Party Central Committee under Deng Xiaoping in December 1978, actually started before the official reforms made to the Chinese economy.[37] In fact, there were initial significant cracks in Chinese economic and political isolation much earlier in the decade in the wake of US Secretary of State Henry Kissinger's secret visit to Beijing in summer 1971 and the subsequent state visit of President Richard Nixon in 1972.

For Japan as America's closest Asian ally, Kissinger's visit represented the first of two 'Nixon shocks' in summer 1971, the second being the American President's decision to withdraw from the Bretton Woods Agreement, which had underpinned currency stability and favourable exchange rates for the Japanese since the late 1940s. However, as the Baoshan story also shows, the Japanese were quick to recover from their sense of shock to take advantage of the dramatically changing situation. Japan was in fact again hard on the heels of the Americans following Kissinger's visit to the People's Republic of China (PRC) in July 1971, establishing formal diplomatic relations with the PRC in 1972. And Japan, as China's most economically developed and technologically sophisticated Asian neighbour, also had clear attractions for the awakening giant.

'Opening up' China proved a far from straightforward process in the decades following Deng Xiaoping's reforms. But one thing was clear from the outset to everyone associated with international business: companies in developed countries would have to do all they could as soon as possible to gain access to China's vast pool of cheap labour as well as to its gigantic market, which eventually assumed global importance rivalling that of the United States. The Japanese and the Germans were early and important movers on both fronts. However, their strategies, experiences, and levels of success in making and selling in China differed from parallel efforts in the United States because they were investing in a developing rather than highly developed country. Furthermore, just as was the case for their investment in the United States, their experiences also differed from one another as the consequence of several factors, including the history of relations between the countries as well as variations in national styles of OFDI.

Investing in China, Japanese Style

In his search for ideas and resources to implement the 1978 economic reforms that would 'open up' China, Deng Xiaoping visited Osaka early that same year. Touring an electronics factory of the Matsushita Electric Industrial company – as Panasonic was then

Figure 10.3 Konosuke Matsushita of Matsushita Electric (later Panasonic) departing for the People's Republic of China, October 1980. The Asahi Shimbun/Getty Images

known – Deng turned to his host, the firm's founder, Konosuke Matsushita (Figure 10.3), and asked him for help. 'You are called the god of management,' Deng said. 'Will you help us modernise our economy?'[38]

Matsushita agreed, and he visited China the following year to kick off the process. Addressing workers at a Beijing electronics factory, Matsushita made what at the time would have seemed a utopian observation, although in retrospect it was prophetic: 'You are working very hard to learn to make TVs. If you keep up the effort, you'll catch up with Japan in several years and start developing new technologies.'

Matsushita's vision of a future dominated technologically by Asian countries was, however, somewhat premature. 'Several years', for instance, have in fact turned into decades. Even as late as 2021, the president of Murata Manufacturing, the global leader in capacitor manufacturing, observed that his and other leading Japanese corporations 'are probably three to four years ahead of the Chinese'. He added, though, that 'their pace of catch-up is getting faster'. It would be only a matter of time before parity was reached, with China moving on to a position of one of the world leaders in high-technology industry.[39]

Matsushita's prediction was also oversimplified. 'Working very hard' was no doubt a prerequisite for technological development in China, but hard work on its own could never translate into acquisition of high levels of technological competence. Instead, like any other developing country – including nineteenth-century America and Germany and late nineteenth/early twentieth-century Japan – China used a variety of mechanisms to acquire technology and transfer best practice. Some of these involved reverse engineering: buying machines and devices from the world leaders and then producing large numbers of copies of them. Again, this was something that the United States, Germany, and Japan had also engaged in when they were in the early stages of economic development. That had certain advantages in saving development costs and in speed of acquisition, but it was often extraordinarily difficult to copy non-mechanical (for instance, chemical and/or electronic) technologies. And it was in any case impossible to sell the copied product on world markets; or to avoid the wrath of those whose technologies had essentially been pilfered.[40]

As part of its reform and development policy, China also engaged in the tried-and-true tactic of sending its citizens abroad to acquire cutting-edge knowledge, which could then be applied – or taught in domestic colleges and universities – when they returned home. As always, the strategy has led to some success, but that has generally been piecemeal and over the long term. In another typical gambit, China also focused resources, including some of the people trained in cutting-edge technologies overseas, to design and make things on its own. It was a strategy that was particularly effective (and viewed as necessary) in key defence and security-related technologies, and one that was generally associated with the Chinese Academy of Sciences. It has had some notable successes, including, for instance, what eventually became Lenovo, now a leading producer of computers and laptops. But, again, the successes have been patchy, frequently restricted to specific areas, and not translated into more generalised technological capability.

There is little doubt, though, that the most effective and predominant source of technology inflows into China occurred in association with OFDI, in particular when the trickle starting around 1978 turned into a flood after 1992. Japanese firms and their subsidiaries were among the pioneers of making things in China, and of making China a global technological force to contend with by the second decade of the twenty-first century.

***

Panasonic predecessor Matsushita Electric Industrial made good on its founder's 1978 promise to Deng Xiaoping in 1987 when it launched a joint venture with a Chinese firm in Beijing. It was the first such investment by a Japanese company. As part of this venture, 250 Chinese workers went to Japan for 6 months to learn onsite about the company's production processes and management structures. They returned to China after their training, starting manufacturing operations at the new joint venture in 1989.[41]

Panasonic has since become a major player in China, with sales there accounting for nearly 25 per cent of the Japanese consumer electronics giant's global business. Most of this involved manufacturing in China for the Chinese market, as well as for export, primarily to Japan. It has led, eventually, to the parent company learning from its once fledgling operations in China, so much so that in 2019 Panasonic founded a new and largely independent Chinese subsidiary, China & Northeast Asia Company, with capabilities not only in manufacturing, marketing, and sales, but also in R&D and design of consumer electronics. The new company is well on the way to realising the instructions of Panasonic president and CEO Kazuhiro Tsuga in mid-2018 to 'Make another Panasonic in China.'[42]

What prompted Panasonic's pioneering push into China in the 1980s and its steady doubling down since then was of course not altruism, but rather enlightened self-interest. And, as is the case for the large number of Japanese firms that followed the leader in the decades that followed, it was accomplished primarily by trading technology for access to markets and inexpensive labour. On the back of this Japanese (often non-financial, immaterial) investment, technological capabilities accrued to their Chinese partners. This happened not least because, invariably, the organisational form of inward investment was a joint venture owing to Chinese government policies, which limited foreign ownership and control as China moved cautiously down the road of reform of business and the economy. It was the price paid – reluctantly, but also deliberately – for a ticket to participate in one of the most spectacular examples of rapid and sustained economic growth ever witnessed.[43]

As a result of efforts in China since the 1980s by Panasonic and many of its Japanese counterparts, both larger and smaller, Japan became the third-largest source of OFDI there by 2000, behind only Hong Kong and the United States. And it remains one of the largest investors in China in spite of the Japanese economic doldrums since 1990.[44]

Nevertheless, for profound historical reasons, business relationships between the two Asian economic superpowers since China opened up economically have been accompanied by recurring, and sometimes quite serious, difficulties. Not to put too fine a point on it: Japan's behaviour before and during the Second World War towards China – as well as its other neighbours in Asia, including Indonesia and Japan's colonies at the time, Taiwan and Korea – was abominable. It included widespread economic exploitation; frequent use of slave and forced labour; chronic abuse of women as 'comfort women' for Japanese soldiers; mass torture and executions; use of biological weapons; and some experimentation on human subjects for testing poison and nerve gases and medicines. These deeply felt bases for resentment, moreover, have been exacerbated since 1945 by ongoing territorial and other disputes that have flared up on a regular basis, for instance over Taiwan as well as the uninhabited but potentially oil-rich Diaoyu/Senkaku Islands.[45]

The coexistence of episodes of intense tension on the one hand – the result in no small part of the behaviour of Japan before and during the Second World War – and extensive underlying cooperation with the other Asian countries subjected to Japanese aggression and exploitation through 1945 on the other has been characterised as 'cold politics, hot economics'. In the case of Japan and China, business and economic interrelationships started even before 1978. And, after China opened up, both countries participated actively in the globalisation process that unfolded in the last decades of the twentieth century and beyond, in no small part by widening and deepening these interrelationships.

But, for China, the process of globalisation involved not only closer relationships with firms from highly developed countries seeking to take advantage of cheap labour to make things for export, but also making and selling to its vast, underdeveloped, and increasingly affluent domestic market. Globalisation also entailed increased realisation – and assertion – of Chinese foreign political power. Not surprisingly, heightened Chinese nationalism was therefore a function of the country's participation in globalisation. And, unlike South Korea, which was much more highly dependent on foreign trade than on its domestic market for growth and therefore tended to separate political disputes from ongoing business relationships, China's government and the Chinese public have often linked the two. Boycotts and other economic action against Japanese companies or products have been the result, with the owners of potent symbols of Japanese culture such as Toyota vehicles sometimes subjected to abuse or vandalism.[46]

Investing in China, German Style

Sharp-featured and quick-witted Carl Hahn became Volkswagen AG's CEO in 1982, the fourth successor in fourteen years to Heinz Nordhoff, who had ruled the roost on his own for over twenty years. Hahn took over not long after VW began making cars in America in 1978 at its big and brash – if ultimately ill-fated – New Stanton factory. Keenly aware that things had already started to go awry for the company in the United States, he began to pivot the German firm's internationalisation strategy towards a new and largely untested market, with massive potential: China. The upshot was a new initiative to internationalise manufacturing in a joint venture with the Shanghai Automotive Industry Corporation (SIAC), which was agreed in 1984. The Shanghai-Volkswagen Automotive Company (SVAC) began production of the Volkswagen Santana the following year. Along with Panasonic, Volkswagen was therefore one of the pioneers in doing business in China. It was the first overseas automaker to establish a manufacturing presence in China, and its investment was one of the largest.[47]

But Hahn was far from a newcomer to the automaker. In fact, he had arrived at the firm, which was still a state-owned limited company, as Nordhoff's assistant in 1954, just twenty-eight years old. The managing director's trust in him grew rapidly, so much so that he dispatched him to the United States in 1959 to head Volkswagen of America. There, Hahn commissioned the US subsidiary's famous advertising campaign that played an important role in burgeoning sales of the Beetle and, to a lesser extent, the VW bus, as they made their way towards achieving iconic status (and a starring role in the counterculture) in America and elsewhere. Having proven his worth in the world's biggest market, Hahn then returned to VW's headquarters in Wolfsburg in 1964. Just thirty-eight years old at that point, he was named to the managing board of Volkswagen AG, now a mostly privatised joint-stock company. Nordhoff groomed the young man as his successor. However, other board members, backed by stockholders, had other ideas. Following the long-term CEO's death just short of retirement in 1968, the firm named Kurt Lotz as his successor instead. Lotz departed after just three years, but again Hahn was passed over in favour of Rudolf Leiding. Shortly thereafter, and ostensibly because of a dispute with the rest of the board over firm strategy in relation to divisionalisation and market segmentation, Hahn left VW to head Continental tyre company in 1972.

It was, in many ways, a good time for him to leave. The trio of CEOs who succeeded Nordhoff between 1968 and 1982 undertook the daunting task of turning the ailing carmaker around. They introduced a range of new models even while embarking on an ambitious programme of internationalisation of manufacturing. The latter included not only the large investment in New Stanton in the United States, but also a significant one in Puebla, Mexico, where production of the original version of the Beetle continued until 2003 after stopping in Germany in 1978. Not incidentally, talks also started in the late 1970s with China about manufacturing investment there.

By the time Hahn returned to Wolfsburg as CEO in 1982, then, much of the heavy lifting had been done. But, during more than a decade at the helm of the firm through 1993, Hahn propelled its transformation into a truly global player. Part of that transformation, of course, involved pulling out of manufacturing in the United States in 1988, although efforts were redoubled to export to the lucrative American market, which met with some success. But, for Hahn, China was where the action was. The SVAC joint venture expanded its factory rapidly after it started production in 1985. And the business was so successful that VW set up a second Chinese joint venture in 1991 – FAW-Volkswagen, in Changchun – with First Automobile Works.[48]

In the course of the decades that followed the end of Hahn's tenure as CEO of VW in 1993, the German company became the world's second-largest producer of automobiles, not least because of its sales in China (Figure 10.4). Its Santana model was the country's

Figure 10.4 Ferdinand Piëch of Volkswagen AG and German Chancellor Gerhard Schröder at VW's Shanghai plant, November 1999. Ullstein bild/Getty Images

number-one seller for a decade, and the firm's success has prompted it to invest in a third joint venture (JV), Volkswagen Anhui. This time around, the German firm has a majority stake in the JV, a palpable sign of the trust placed in it by Chinese authorities. In fact, by 2022, more than half of Volkswagen profits came from China. The headquarters of the firm remains in Wolfsburg, Germany. 'But beneath the hood, in terms of revenues and profits, VW is more Chinese than German.'[49]

* * *

Volkswagen has been a highly visible pioneer among German firms investing in the Chinese market since it opened in the late 1970s, but its followers have been legion. Exports to and imports from China have made it Germany's largest trading partner, and some 5,000 German firms have deepened that relationship through direct investment, mostly in manufacturing. In 2018, in fact, total German OFDI in China was narrowly behind that of Japan, and slightly ahead of that of the United States. All the German multinationals are there, including, besides VW, Mercedes, BMW, Siemens, and Germany's chemical giants. Bayer, for instance, was also an early investor, in a joint venture with Shanghai Dental Materials Factory that was agreed in 1986 and began operating in 1988. But, as in the United States, the usual suspects among the German multinationals have been joined by a large number of *Mittelstand* firms, also keen to gain access to the massive Chinese market and also, of course, to take advantage of relatively low labour costs.[50]

* * *

Like Japanese companies investing in China, German firms have had to pay a price to enter that massive market, and not only in cash, but also in terms of knowledge transfer, whether willing or unwilling, and wittingly or unwittingly. As a result, their Chinese partners and suppliers have increasingly developed capabilities that have made them independent innovators – and, more recently, competitors. And one thing that competitors do is to engage in OFDI in other developed countries through mergers and acquisitions or through greenfield investment. After all, the stories of OFDI by German and Japanese firms in the United States from the first part of this chapter indicate clearly that advanced economies are often highly attractive investment targets. And, as China develops and many Chinese firms become much more adept technologically, those companies are starting to invest in Europe and America.

Growing competition, however, is not the only issue affecting relationships in business and technology between China on the one hand and Japan and Germany on the other. Starting in early 2020, for instance, there was massive disruption to global supply chains owing to the coronavirus pandemic. This has called into question long-held assumptions about globalisation, global division of labour, and the virtues of just-in-time production systems. But, even before that, many top managers from developed countries began to question the wisdom of locating production in China. Some of this questioning has arisen from purely business concerns related to management, organisation, monitoring, and control. For example, the managing director of a *Mittelstand* company located in Upper Bavaria that makes specialist electrical connectors for the nuclear power industry decided to withdraw from his company's Chinese investment in favour of establishing a branch factory in Romania. Operating in the eastern European country offered similar savings in labour costs while at the same time being easily accessible by air, and even by car: it was well within a day's drive of the firm's headquarters.[51]

Such decisions are almost invariably made at firm level. There are, though, other trends that portend more systemic and long-term changes in the investment behaviour of German and Japanese companies in China. A 2019 survey of German firms with operations in China indicated that difficulties in getting licences for investment and production along with increased concerns over the Chinese government's economic and political policies were hindering investment. The same hesitancies cropped up with other foreign-owned enterprises. The Chinese government's policies in relation to COVID-19 and the uncertainties about business and trade that have accompanied the Russian invasion of Ukraine in February 2022 – as well as the fear of a parallel move by China on Taiwan – have only added to the morass of unpredictability.[52]

Such fears in and of themselves are inchoate and amorphous. But they have gained specific shape for German and Japanese business through repeated threats and realities of trade and technology wars between China – the valued OFDI partner – and the United States – valued OFDI partner of both and, perhaps even more importantly, their close political – and military – ally. For many German firms (although not, apparently, Volkswagen), the vagaries of Chinese–American foreign relations have not only curbed enthusiasm for extending their already quite deep involvement in China, but also hindered trade through restrictions imposed on the use of US technology. The same has held true for many of their Japanese counterparts. But, on top of this, several Japanese firms have actively sought to redirect OFDI to other destinations, including Vietnam, as a result of Japanese government policy, which has been backed up by substantial subsidies. Indeed, government encouragement and cash have also led at times to relocation of manufacturing back to Japan itself.

In spite of these recent developments, however, there is no indication that, short of a war or a similar catastrophe, Japanese and German firms will withdraw *en masse* from the Chinese market. Like America, the scale and scope of that market, as well as its key functions as a hub for innovation and vantage point for monitoring competition, ensure that it will remain extremely attractive to globally engaged enterprises.

11 COPING WITH THE CLOSE OF THE COLD WAR

During what we now know were the last throes of the Cold War in the late 1980s, anxiety and apprehension hovered in taut tension with hope and optimism throughout the Soviet-dominated bloc. The cauldron of conflicting emotions and uncertain outcomes had its epicentre in the archconservative East German Democratic Republic (GDR). The regime looked on anxiously as Hungary dismantled its border fence with Austria in June 1989. High anxiety turned into panic when streams of East German 'tourists' took advantage of Hungary's loosening of its borders, travelling there via neighbouring Czechoslovakia before moving on to the West. East German pressure on the Czechs hampered some of those who were fleeing, but at the cost of a diplomatic incident when the would-be emigrants holed up in Prague's West German embassy. Dangerously for the regime, demands for the right to travel to – and crucially also return from – the West without penalty and persecution found expression in massive weekly Monday demonstrations in Leipzig. As tensions rose, the GDR's leaders debated a range of measures to alleviate them, including a 'Chinese solution' along the lines of the recent violent crackdown on unrest in June 1989 in Tiananmen Square in Beijing.

Almost incredibly, however, the tensions dissipated, literally from one minute to the next, the result of a gaffe. In the last eight minutes of another in what had become a long series of hour-long news conferences at East Berlin's International Press Centre on 9 November 1989, haggard East German government spokesperson Günter Schabowski

Figure 11.1 East German Trabant automobile arriving in West Berlin,
November 1989. DPA picture alliance/Alamy

made a now famous blunder. He had been handed a hastily prepared set
of liberalised travel regulations just before going in front of the assembled
press corps and understandably put off dealing with them until the very
end of the briefing. When Schabowski finally read out extracts of the new
regulations to his audience, he was visibly shocked by just how liberal the
new regulations were. An Italian reporter followed up, asking him when
they would go into effect. Shuffling through the papers in front of him in
a desperate attempt to find the answer, Schabowski overlooked a clear
statement that the new regulations would come into effect the following
day so that they could be implemented in an orderly fashion. Instead,
Schabowski answered, mistakenly: 'immediately, without delay'.[1]

Schabowski rounded off the 9 November press conference at
7.01 pm. In the minutes and hours that followed, East Berliners headed
in droves to checkpoints to take advantage of the unexpected announcement, which was amplified by the West German media watched and
listened to by many East Germans. GDR border guards, also taken by
surprise, at first tried to stem the flow. But, overwhelmed and vastly out-
numbered, they quickly lifted previously impenetrable barriers, allowing
untrammelled access to West Berlin. Television images circulated across
the world in real time: Trabants full of happy people (Figure 11.1); East

German citizens smiling broadly as they sampled the delights of capitalist West Berlin for the first time; and people from both sides of the previously divided city dancing and partying in front and on top of the Berlin Wall.

Schabowski's error set a train of events in motion that led to German monetary union in March 1990, which then culminated in full political unification in October. But the fall of the Berlin Wall resonated far beyond Germany's new borders. After all, the Wall had been a symbol, literally in concrete, of the Cold War division that had deeply affected the entire world. When it was breached in late autumn 1989, its fall symbolised the end of the Cold War. And the global reach of that decades-old conflict meant that its conclusion was celebrated not just by Germans, but also by many others, including the Americans and the Japanese.

* * *

Celebration is too mild a word. There was in fact global *euphoria* as a new age dawned, shimmering with possibilities. The threat of nuclear war seemed to disappear, practically overnight. Debates ensued on how best to spend the 'peace dividend' that would accrue from the cessation of the Cold War arms race. Perhaps a good choice would be replacing the military–industrial complex with an environmental–industrial one to implement some of the recommendations of the recently formed Intergovernmental Panel on Climate Change? But, more immediately, genuine globalisation of international trade could now be realised as the 'transition states' of the former Soviet bloc joined China as new participants in the capitalist international order. For Germany and Japan in particular, with their track record of success as powerful trading nations, the prospects seemed mouth-watering.

Yet, within the next decade, both countries suffered from (at best) anaemic economic growth, structural unemployment, ageing populations, and other endemic problems. By the dawn of the twenty-first century, Germany had become for many 'the sick man of Europe', while Japan looked back mournfully on its 'lost decade'.[2] Ironically, then, for both countries, the opportunities that presented themselves when virtually the entire world opened up for the first time since 1914 were overshadowed by fevered preoccupation with internal issues. Naturally, not all of these developments stemmed directly from the end of the Cold

War. But, as had been the case from at least 1945, evolving relationships with the United States still loomed large for both countries, and not just because of the fundamental recasting of defence and security arrangements in the post-Cold War world. Bill Clinton's America, like Tony Blair and Gordon Brown's 'Cool Britannia', appeared to offer a highly flexible, deregulated, and, crucially, phenomenally prosperous neo-liberal and financial-capitalist alternative to the old-fashioned coordinated manufacturing capitalism that prevailed in Germany and Japan.

Picking Up the Pieces after the Fall of the Wall

Nobody expected a more direct and tangible share of the post-Cold War 'peace dividend' in 1990 than the 16 million former East Germans. Gerhard Lauter, one of the architects of the reforms to GDR travel regulations that had been spectacularly misinterpreted by Günter Schabowski on 9 November 1989, insisted quite correctly in a later interview that those who streamed into West Berlin in the aftermath of his announcement were not economic refugees. For the most part, they had furnished apartments, full refrigerators, and decent jobs. They certainly wanted to visit West Berlin and to travel freely to other places in western Europe and beyond, but they also fully expected to return afterwards to their moderately prosperous and comfortable homeland.[3] But even as the so-called 'Ossies' embraced the powerful Deutschmark and their new West German passports, they remained confident that the sale of the GDR's vaunted People's Owned Enterprises through the *Treuhand* privatisation agency would yield tidy sums, shares of which would ultimately flow into their own pockets.

That didn't happen. The vast majority of People's Owned Enterprises produced goods that were technologically backward and often of poor quality. Moreover, their previously keen yet captive markets in the former Soviet bloc countries of eastern Europe – which were also ones that might have continued to be serviced by factories located in the former GDR, at least in the medium term – evaporated immediately after the Deutschmark was introduced. The products of the former East German factories were suddenly priced in a strong, hard currency and were therefore out of the reach of the transition economies.

Just as importantly, though, efforts to privatise the state-owned enterprises of the former GDR met seemingly insuperable difficulties.

Not only were plant and equipment often outdated and dilapidated; there were also severe environmental problems, against which any potential buyer wanted to be indemnified. And it soon emerged that there was a profound discrepancy not only between the socialist and capitalist systems in the abstract, but also between the concrete definitions of what *actually* constituted a 'firm' or 'enterprise' under each system. What potential capitalist investor, for instance, could possibly wish to purchase a manufacturing company in former East Germany that included as part of its operations vacation homes, extensive housing estates, and even department stores?[4]

The answer was, of course, that investors did indeed prove willing to purchase some – but not all – such firms, but only under certain strict conditions. High on the list was that operations deemed non-essential, such as vacation homes, would be hived off into separate companies. Moreover, prospective buyers generally insisted on indemnification against environmental risk and the right to slim down employee numbers severely. And, not incidentally, the buyers also demanded – and got – a variety of subsidies, for instance to underwrite purchase of new technologies and equipment. In sum, former East German companies were usually 'purchased' for less than nothing. Even so, the *Treuhand* found it difficult – and sometimes impossible – to sell off all the properties that had been entrusted to it. But 'selling' even those 'assets' that found a 'buyer' cost hundreds of billions of Deutschmarks, which was ultimately covered by the German federal government.[5]

* * *

The costs directly incurred through privatisation of former East German enterprises were just the tip of the iceberg. Devastatingly rapid deindustrialisation followed in the wake of closure of plants that the *Treuhand* privatisation agency could not sell, and burgeoning rates of unemployment invariably followed, even when factories attracted a buyer. A policy decision to equalise wages across industry throughout Germany, in spite of the fact that productivity in the old East was just one-third that of West Germany, exacerbated rates of joblessness, especially in the former East Germany.

Social costs consequently skyrocketed, and the federal government covered them. As a matter of policy and equity, moreover, pension payments to former employees of East German enterprises were set at a level that, admittedly, was lower than in West Germany, but at the same time was in real terms quite high because there were effectively no prior pension contributions to fund them. The federal government again covered them. And that was not all: the German government also paid for much-needed upgrades of existing buildings, housing, and infrastructure, for instance to renew and expand railways and roads built during the Third Reich (and sometimes barely touched since then) and to replace outmoded telecommunications equipment.

And still that was not all. As part of the price for the Soviet Union's somewhat surprising assent to unification, Germany paid it and its successor, the Russian Federation, substantial sums, for instance for relocation of the troops who had been stationed in East Germany. What is more, the Soviets were not the only ones who lined up for payments from the German government to help make unification happen. Not only did the French demand – and receive – first dibs on some of the few lucrative companies privatised, for instance a major oil refinery at the former Leuna chemical works, but also French President François Mitterand made his country's consent to German unification contingent upon further progress on European integration. In concrete terms, this entailed German agreement to a currency union, which would ultimately replace the beloved Deutschmark with the euro, and the trusted central Bundesbank with an unknown quantity, the European Central Bank.[6]

Taken together, the costs of unification were sky high, amounting to an estimated $2 trillion in all. That bordered on the unaffordable even for fabulously wealthy Germany. As a paper from the Centre for European Reform put it in 2003, fully fourteen years after the raucous celebrations at the Wall took place:

> Germany's main problem is that it is still nursing a severe hangover from its reunification party in 1990. The shock of absorbing an economy with 16 million people, thousands of outdated smokestack factories and a 50-year legacy of central planning would have brought any economy to its knees.[7]

Indeed, as the new century dawned, in large part a consequence of unification, Germany was underperforming significantly in comparison with its peers. Unemployment was stubbornly high, even in the former West German states, where it approached 10 per cent of the working population in 1998. But it was devastatingly high in the 'new German states' of the former East Germany, where official rates of joblessness in 2003–2004 averaged about 20 per cent, with some regions and localities having even higher rates. What is more, those rates applied to those who remained after a massive outflow of population from the new federal states towards the old ones. And those who departed were often young and female, while those who remained tended to be older and male, thus skewing demography.[8]

On top of all this, Germany also broke with longstanding traditions of fiscal discipline by borrowing heavily to finance unification. In fact, in 2004, its budget deficit of 3.9 per cent of gross domestic product (GDP) significantly breached the limit of 3 per cent set out in the Maastricht Treaty that established the European Union (EU) in 1992. And economic growth was also weak, with German GDP rising only 1.6 per cent per year in the second half of the 1990s, a full percentage point lower than average growth in the rest of the EU. Things looked bleak, as newspapers in Blair's Cool Britannia gleefully pointed out: 'Germany, quips the British press, is Britain in the 1970s. Germany is heading for a Japan-style quagmire. Germany is the sick man of Europe. Some even pronounce the patient dead.'[9]

After the Bubble, the Quagmire

Like most Germans in 1990, the Japanese were generally delighted that the Cold War was ending, although many of them also worried about some of the implications. And, as one commentator wrote in that year, 'Japanese anxiety about the post-Cold War era is not hard to understand, since Japan has benefited more than any other country from the Cold War.' Protected by the United States military, Japan was spared major spending on defence even as the United States promoted its economy, not least through generous and extensive technology transfer and military procurement, especially in the Korean and Vietnam wars. And, at least as importantly, US interests both in security and in lowering barriers to trade dovetailed nicely with those of Japanese business: America proved willing to open its borders to Japanese goods without demanding that Japan do the same. 'As Japan's economic capabilities grew, Washington approached Tokyo to liberalize its foreign economic policies, but was constrained by a broader interest in promoting good bilateral security relations.' Would this all change with the end of the Cold War? There was much uncertainty, but also considerable clarity over the fact that potential danger loomed.[10]

In the event, though, the threat to the Japanese economy and society came from an entirely different direction. Indeed, it grew primarily out of the very system that had led to domestic and international success during the period since 1945.

GDP growth in Japan had already begun to slow down in the 1980s, although it was still a healthy 4–5 per cent per year. At the same time, large Japanese corporations – the motors of employment, the economy, international trade, and, not incidentally, domestic banking – became so cash-rich that they could finance investments at home and abroad from profits rather than borrowing from banks. Much of that investment, moreover, was going abroad, which placed a drag on productivity growth at home. In the meantime, Japanese banks, deprived of their blue-chip clients, feverishly sought other borrowers from sectors apart from those in the 'real' economy. Many of them were far less creditworthy. Land and housing became the main engine of growth, and the primary source of collateral. Valuations soared, and credit was extended accordingly. In Tokyo in particular, any price demanded from a seller was deemed worth paying since it would only keep rising. At the same time, the Japanese stock market was skyrocketing. This was occurring, however, at a time when Japan as a society was ageing dramatically even as the normal age of retirement remained at just sixty. Older people not only consumed less, but also had to be supported financially by a diminishing working population.[11]

Something was bound to give. It did. The stock market began to deflate in 1990, and the property bubble burst in 1991. Combined with all the other factors hampering economic performance, the end of the bubble ushered in a decade marred by recession and deflation. Unlike virtually everywhere else in the developed world, prices in Japan in the 1990s therefore actually fell. The previously urgent need to purchase – especially real estate – before prices rose (in the confidence that they would keep on rising) was replaced by reluctance to buy much of anything (in the confidence and expectation that prices would keep on falling). In this context, the usual tools to stimulate the economy through fiscal policy, generally by dropping interest rates, did not work. Neither did increasing government spending. In Paul Krugman's analysis, Japan became enmeshed in a 'liquidity trap' from which there was no obvious escape. Meanwhile, GDP growth lagged.

Between 1995 and 2003, Japan's economy grew by an average of 1.2 per cent per year, an even more paltry performance than Germany's during the same time, and the lowest rate of growth among the G-7 countries. It was also lower by far than the rates in many other OECD countries.[12]

Recession and deflation invariably entail rising joblessness, just as rising unemployment accompanies deindustrialisation. Both post-unification Germany and post-bubble Japan therefore experienced a rapid increase in numbers of those out of work. Unlike 1990s Germany, however, where extraordinarily high levels of joblessness prevailed in the new federal states of the former East Germany, Japanese unemployment was high throughout the country, particularly among young people. And it remained stubbornly so for a considerable period of time.

* * *

When the Japanese economy began to slow down in the 1980s, followed by a precipitous drop in growth after the property bubble burst, the job market became increasingly dismal, especially for permanent posts. A significant number of young people therefore decided to use the lemons they faced to make lemonade, making the best out of a grim situation. Members of the 'freeters' (which could be loosely translated from Japanese as 'slackers') movement rejected the set career path of the salaryman and instead embraced a less structured life, supporting themselves financially at the minimal level possible through part-time, short-term employment.[13]

Unfortunately for all of them, and for many other young people, the options available for getting out of this 'slacker trap' were limited. And the situation did not improve substantially as the 1990s gave way to the new millennium. Companies responded to the economic crisis by slashing outlays, with labour costs a main target. Permanent posts in particular fell victim to cost-cutting in industry, which relied more and more heavily on part-time, temporary workers to take up the slack. Add to that the fact that a considerable and growing level of industrial investment was directed abroad, and the outcome was predictable. Freeters in early 1990s Japan pioneered the gig economy that is now ubiquitous in much of the developed world. As they entered their thirties and forties in the first decades of the twenty-first century, nearly a third of them still did not hold a regular job, and many have yet to land one. A large number live in poverty, and about a fifth of them still live with their parents. No wonder mental health has been severely affected: ageing freeters file 60 per cent of claims for mental-health insurance, while the suicide rate has risen sharply and steadily from the 1990s into the first decades of the new century, especially among those in their thirties.[14]

The problem did not improve substantially even after the end of the 'lost decade'. Reliance on part-time, temporary workers by Japanese firms remained high, and young people continued to be affected disproportionately. The practice by companies may be understandable in the light of the need to contain costs, but it also has its price. There is a plausible connection between labour precarity owing to unstable employment – and the lack of training and commitment that invariably goes with that – and Japan's poor recent performance in raising productivity.

Plus ça Change...

Paltry growth rates both in Germany and in Japan in the 1990s, along with persistently high unemployment and rising social problems associated with it, led in turn to fevered speculation about what had gone wrong and who was to blame. Perhaps the German and Japanese models, so successful in the four decades from 1950, had run their course?

Certainly, some of the basic conditions that had enabled those models to perform so admirably for such a long time had changed radically. Competitors in other countries now posed significant challenges, manufacturing high value-added goods at ever higher levels of quality and with increasing technological sophistication. Chinese economic opening transformed global markets, and the Chinese newcomers were now joined by the transition economies of the former Soviet bloc entering into the capitalist system, along with rapidly growing economies such as India, Vietnam, and Brazil. Financial capitalism, featuring most prominently US and UK banks as trailblazers, appeared to pose existential questions for the old-fashioned manufacturing capitalism epitomised by Germany and Japan.

One other trend became apparent around the same time: business and banking in the global economy were finally starting to resolve the so-called 'Solow paradox', identified by Nobel Prize-winning economist Robert Solow. In 1987, Solow had famously observed that 'You can see the computer age everywhere but in the productivity statistics.' A decade later, however, the needle had started to move decisively, especially in the United States. This trend only accelerated in the years that followed, with major implications not only for business, but also for daily life.[15] Japan counted among the frontrunners in producing computers and the chips that drive them, but Germany did not. But would business and banking in either country, so conservative in their practices, be able to apply the new technologies fully and successfully?

Yet, in spite of this raft of challenges, cooler heads had already started wondering just why the alarm bells were so shrill. Sick and lost though they may have been, the German and Japanese economies had not fallen off a cliff. Far from it.

What is more, as the twenty-first century commenced, both countries had begun serious work to address some of the structural issues that hindered efforts to compete more effectively still in the evolving landscape of global business, economy, and innovation.

* * *

As the joy of gaining the right to travel freely and to enjoy the fruits of West German prosperity that most East Germans had only experienced on television faded away in the wake of the steep rises in unemployment and corresponding decline in standards of living that followed unification, former Ossies soon discovered yet another drawback to their new status. Town and city centres previously well supplied with shops (if not always with stock to fill them up or to suit all tastes) were quickly hollowed out. As had happened decades earlier in much of the United States because of rising car ownership and economies of scale accruing to increasingly big-footprint big-box stores, retail shopping in the new federal states of Germany migrated to malls and large shopping centres with plenty of parking, which were located in open spaces on the urban fringe or in the countryside beyond. But the transformation, with its enormous impact on urban economy and society, in no small part through the effective privatisation of shopping spaces and the areas surrounding them, occurred much more quickly in the former East Germany than it had in America.[16]

Remarkably, these developments had not occurred to anywhere near the same extent in the old federal states of West Germany.

There, zoning and other regulations placed a brake on untrammelled development of out-of-town retail, helping to preserve small businesses and town and city centres, but also causing some inefficiencies. During the initial post-unification period, however, these regulations did not apply in the former East German states. The consequence in the new federal states was rapid development of malls and shopping centres on the periphery of towns and cities.[17]

The sudden liberalisation of land-use restrictions for retail in the former East Germany had a parallel in the breakneck speed with which state-owned enterprise was privatised there. Both were perhaps understandable given the need for radical restructuring of the state that had failed so miserably in 1989–1990. But they also represented a first stab at developing models and policies for fundamental reform of the old West German economy in the context of globalisation and the apparent success of Anglo-Saxon neo-liberalism.

Take the development of shopping centres, for instance, which are defined as a large building or buildings devoted to retail, service, and hospitality that have been planned and financed together, and featuring extensive parking. There were only two of them in all of West Germany in 1965, a number that grew steadily, but also quite slowly, over the next quarter-century, to ninety-three in 1990. Five years later, that number had nearly doubled, to some extent because of retail development in the new federal states, but also because of loosening of restrictions in the old federal states. A decade later, in 2005, the number of shopping centres in Germany had more than doubled again, with most of the growth in the old states. By then, a considerable amount of the growth resulted from an increase in city- and town-centre malls and shopping centres. It was a trend that now applied both to the new and to the old federal states, caused by new urbanism, the desire to limit use of automobiles and preserve green space, and, importantly, the growing availability of large tracts of urban land, which had been put up for sale in the wake of 'restructuring by post, railway, military, and industry'.[18]

The very 'restructuring' that freed up the urban land for shopping centres and malls was to a large degree the result of deliberate decisions by the conservative (West) German government to privatise large swaths of the economy. Already in 1989, for instance, it separated the sprawling Bundespost into three companies, one devoted to handling mail, one to postal banking, and the third to telecommunications.

The postal bank and the Telekom businesses were then fully privatised in the mid-1990s, with the postal service partially privatised thereafter. German railway operations, in contrast, have remained largely in public hands, but here, too, there has been considerable restructuring and reform. Following guidelines enacted by the EU in 1991, which directed EU governments to 'make railways more independent of government, create a healthy financial structure and separate accounting for infrastructure and transport', the German government accordingly passed legislation in 1994. The law converted 'the Bundesbahn and the [former East German] Reichsbahn into a **joint stock company with a strict entrepreneurial approach to business**. This limited the influence of the government on the company's corporate governance.'[19]

In other words, key aspects of the agenda to restructure business and society in the new federal states had been under consideration in West Germany before reunification occurred, in fact before unification seemed even a remote possibility. Deregulation and privatisation were, however, far from the only steps taken in the direction of addressing perceived structural problems in the German economy starting in the 1990s. During that decade, too, a trend towards greater dispersion of share ownership began. For many observers, this represented a move towards the principle of shareholder value along Anglo-Saxon lines, as opposed to that of stakeholder value, which had hitherto been predominant in Germany (and Japan). Some have argued, however, that Germany was not so much converging with Anglo-Saxon norms of corporate governance as developing a hybrid form of 'negotiated shareholder value'. Regardless of the terminology used, though, there is no doubt that major changes in corporate governance occurred, which were accompanied by alterations in traditional management practice and in widespread adoption of outsourcing, both domestically and abroad.[20]

The concept of 'negotiated shareholder value' hinges to a significant degree on the notion that there have been relatively limited changes in the power of organised labour in (especially large) German firms by virtue of works councils and guaranteed board representation. Again, there is no question that there has been some diminution of organised labour's clout, not least through the so-called Hartz IV reforms undertaken early in the twenty-first century under Chancellor Gerhard Schröder's SPD-led government. Hartz IV shook up the labour market, among other things by placing strict limits on unemployment benefits and early retirement and by providing more effective state support for job searches and training opportunities. The reforms were motivated by a perceived need for greater labour-market flexibility, and they were enacted at great political cost amidst accusations of social injustice. It is likely, though, that Hartz IV had less impact on resurrecting Germany's economic competitiveness than organised labour's agreement with employers in the mid-1990s to rein in wage demands to preserve jobs, this in order to provide breathing room for German industry to restructure so as to become more competitive globally. In other words, although there have been significant changes in the German labour relations system that had dominated since the 1950s, reform and restructuring were in fact crucially enabled by the longstanding cooperation between labour and management at the heart of that system.[21]

The slow but steady recalibration of German business and management practices in the 1990s was accompanied by extensive German investment in the transition economies of eastern and central Europe. Again, progress was very slow at first, but the development of these links, in particular through creation of new supply chains, lowered costs, and, not incidentally, expanded markets. It also consequently increased the competitiveness of German business, especially in manufacturing. As a result of all of these changes, Germany was poised to take full advantage of the worldwide economic boom starting in 2004, which involved rapid growth in emerging markets in particular. Already in 2003, the country became the world's largest exporter, a position it maintained for several years. Europe's 'sick man' had once again regained its former status as the continent's 'slick man'.[22]

* * *

Japan's Large-Scale Retail Store Law (LSRSL), enacted in 1974, aimed to protect smaller retailers in cities and towns from larger competitors. As was the case with similar regulation and legislation in West Germany, it achieved its objectives, albeit at the cost of higher prices to consumers. As in West Germany, this drew increasing levels of criticism and calls for reform, demands echoed by foreign suppliers, especially in agriculture, who complained about non-tariff barriers to trade. Unlike West Germany, however, Japan did not benefit from a dry run in this direction undertaken in the new German states of the former East Germany. Nevertheless, already in 1992, Japan began to deregulate its retail sector, a move that culminated early in the twenty-first century in the abolition of the LSRSL and its replacement with the far less draconian and bureaucratic Large-Scale Retail Store Location Law.[23]

The reforms formed part of a general wave of deregulation and reform that swept through Japan during the 1990s as the country sought to 'modernise' its economy and society. The Japanese, like the Germans, began jettisoning key aspects of the system that had brought so much success in the decades following the end of the Second World War, but seemed to have run its course by the 1990s when it 'switched from market-conforming "accelerationism" to market-defying "preservatism"'. To do so, they adapted Anglo-Saxon models forged in the neo-liberalism that took hold in the United States and the UK starting in the 1970s. Awarding of public contracts became more transparent, for instance; trade restrictions were liberalised; and previously strict regulations on the financial system were loosened. Japanese corporate governance, too, was transformed, with more emphasis on profitability, more flexibility in the permanent employment system, and more openness to foreign ownership through mergers and acquisitions. The changes to corporate governance practices resulted in the previously inconceivable phenomenon of foreign managers taking posts at the very top of major Japanese corporations.[24]

Japan joined Germany in riding the Anglo-Saxon wave towards privatisation of state-owned enterprise, although the initial forays in this direction under Prime Minister Yasuhiro Nakasone from the mid-1980s also resulted from a desire to address concerns about national debt. First on the auction block were three publicly owned 'special corporations', including the privatisations of Nippon Telegraph and Telephone (NTT) beginning in 1985, followed in 1987 by Japan National Railways (JNR) and Japan Airlines (JAL). Another major wave of privatisations started under Prime Minister Junichiro Koizumi in 2005 when the Post Bank was hived off from Japan Post and sold to the private sector. The effectiveness of the transfer to the private sector is, in general, well regarded. According to a recent study of the performance of JNR and postal bank successors, had they not been privatised, with the 'resultant diversification and transformation of business models, they would have not been profitable and dynamic as today [sic]'.[25]

However effective the privatisations may have been, the general pace and extent of reform in Japan were relatively slow compared with Germany. Possibly this was due to the existence of more entrenched interests favouring the status quo in Japan; possibly it turned out thus owing to the effects of an even more aged and more rapidly ageing population. It is, however, likely that the urgent need to address persistent deflation also played a part, perhaps not in constraining reform efforts per se, but in preventing them from having a larger impact.

After all, although extricating an economy from an inflationary spiral is extraordinarily difficult, recovering from deflation seems nigh on impossible. There are proven and effective tools for reining in inflation, for instance through curbing the money supply, raising interest rates, and/or cutting government spending. It can take a while, especially when expectations about perennial wage, price, and profit increases become entrenched over several years, but the tools can eventually work. In contrast, for a deflationary spiral, in which prices of many goods remain steady or go down rather than up and economic growth is sluggish or even non-existent, the tools at the disposal of the government and the central bank are far more limited. The money supply can, of course, be increased, and so can government spending, although both actions are often hampered by prevailing public opinion and perceptions. Cutting interest rates, however, can only go so far, with zero as the limit. The Japanese central bank made decisive moves in the direction of that limit in the mid-1990s and embraced it fully in 1999 as an explicit policy.[26]

As the twenty-first century began, the combination of (sometimes tentative) reforms to the economy, finance, and corporate governance with the central bank's macroeconomic and the government's fiscal policies seemed finally to bear fruit, although, as a Brookings study from 2000 put it, 'Japan's "transition to a market economy" is [still] far from complete.' Nevertheless, by 2006, the Bank of Japan's governors felt confident that the worst of the deflation lay in the past and that the economy was poised for a full recovery on the basis of reforms undertaken. They therefore raised interest rates by 0.25 per cent, ending the era of free money. Like most, however, the governors did not suspect what lay just around the corner in the form of the 'Great Recession' that began in 2008. In fact, partly because of this worldwide shock, deflation and recession persisted in Japan into 2013.[27]

Do Something, Even if It Is Wrong...

Already in the mid-1980s, Mercedes Benz's Chief Financial Officer, Edzard Reuter, recognised the challenge posed by maturing markets and increased global competition. Something had to be done to globalise German firms such as his to make them more competitive. Reuter's solution, implemented over the course of his stint as CEO of the luxury carmaker during the decade until April 1994, was to redefine his firm as a global technology group. He persuaded the board to invest heavily in specialist turbine manufacturing, aerospace, and household appliances, which led to the creation of four separate divisions within the group in 1989. Vehicle producer Mercedes-Benz AG, by far the most prominent member of the group, was reduced to a junior status, just one of the four divisions. Its profits also paid for the investments in the other three groups, and also offset some of their losses.[28]

Thinking globally and in terms of high-value-added technology and innovation: these measures seemed a fool-proof recipe for success. But technology-led diversification at Mercedes was a disaster. Reuter was ousted in April 1994 after racking up losses of DM 5.7 billion. His successor, Jürgen Schrempp, had a completely different idea. Motivated by some of the same trends as those Reuter had detected that necessitated fundamental change in his company, Schrempp was also inspired by direct competitors such as Toyota as well as other globalised or globalising vehicle manufacturers. Mercedes under Schrempp would be global. It would be innovative. But, in stark contrast to Reuter's vision, Schrempp's company would focus entirely on vehicles. Among his very first moves was to get rid of the non-core investments that had been at the heart of his predecessor's technology group strategy.

As for vehicles: a thoroughgoing recasting of internal management processes and outsourcing practices was already under way at the automaking division of Reuter's technology group from 1992 onwards. Schrempp wanted to build on that, identifying three additional elements that would be required to enhance and sustain his firm's competitiveness. First, he wanted to develop a product line that would appeal to multiple market segments, not just the luxury market. Second, Schrempp sought to minimise product development costs and at the same time achieve economies of scale by means of a 'platform strategy', whereby different product lines shared parts and systems. And finally, as a fundamental means of realising these first two objectives, he wanted to manufacture vehicles in and increase outsourcing from different locations worldwide. But his global ambitions extended well beyond this: he was also determined to seek out strategic partners abroad. Schrempp called his overall strategy *Welt AG*, 'World Incorporated', underscoring his determination to distance his firm from Deutschland AG.

Figure 11.2 Robert Eaton and Jürgen Schrempp, co-CEOs of DaimlerChrysler, December 1998. Ullstein bild/Getty Images

An initial step to realising this vision, taken as Schrempp assumed his position in 1995, came in the form of a manufacturing plant in the United States. Located in Tuscaloosa, Alabama, in the American south, it was the first Mercedes manufacturing operation outside of Germany. The Tuscaloosa factory focused on producing new M-series vehicles, part of a suite of new model lines providing a wider range of choice for customers in all possible markets. A partnership with the Swiss-based SMH corporation to develop the Smart car range formed an additional strand of the same strategy.

But Schrempp was not content to stop there. Indeed, his next move demonstrated clear blue water between his Welt AG vision and previous practice anywhere else in Deutschland AG. On 7 May 1998, Schrempp signed a merger deal with Bob Eaton, the CEO of Chrysler Corporation, creating DaimlerChrysler AG. Schrempp and Eaton (Figure 11.2) were to be joint CEOs. Costing $35 billion, the 'merger of equals' and 'marriage made in heaven' was the costliest ever to that date. What is more, it rapidly became clear that the 'merger' was in fact a takeover, not least because Mercedes had paid the entirety of the eyewatering costs to arrange the marriage in the first place. Nor was there much equality in the fusion. The new DaimlerChrysler firm was a German-based AG, not a US-headquartered Corporation. Eaton therefore no longer had much influence and decided to leave the firm, and Schrempp was left in sole charge. But, instead of making sure that DaimlerChrysler realised the synergies and economies of scale that provided the rationale for the new firm's very existence, Schrempp did little to encourage integration, and the North American (Chrysler) operations were plagued by quality-control issues and substantial losses.

One reason for this neglect was that Schrempp was busy elsewhere. Even as DaimlerChrysler was coming into being, extending Mercedes decisively into North America, its CEO was deep in talks to acquire a controlling stake in Japan's Nissan, aimed at extending the Mercedes sphere of influence decisively into East Asia. That initiative did not materialise, largely owing to dissatisfaction about Nissan's plans to address its heavy debt load. Schrempp broke off negotiations in March 1999, saying in his statement about it that 'We have emphasized that the integration of Daimler and Chrysler has utmost priority in our current business activities.' That was most certainly not true, however, because within a year Schrempp, continuing to neglect the integration of Mercedes and Chrysler, instead led the charge in pursuit of his East Asia strategy, this time acquiring a 33.4 per cent controlling stake in Mitsubishi.[29]

In the end, Schrempp's Welt AG strategy proved no less disastrous than his predecessor's. Shareholder wrath, not least owing to the fact that Schrempp had paid far too much for Chrysler, forced him into retirement in 2005. Two years later, the Chrysler operations were sold to Cerberus, a private equity firm, for $7.4 billion, about a fifth of the original purchase price. As one analyst has pointed out, the fact that the American firm could be sold 'as a more-or-less intact unit' speaks volumes about the limits of integration within DaimlerChrysler. Holdings in Mitsubishi (along with a smaller one in Suzuki) were wound down as well. Some 99 per cent of shareholders agreed to change the German firm's name once again: to Daimler AG.[30]

* * *

By the late 1990s, Japan's second-largest carmaker, Nissan, was in dire straits. The firm had saddled itself with at least $20 billion in debt and had lost money for six years on the trot. Its sales were declining in two of its three main markets, and it had failed to master its cost structure, which was very high even by Japanese standards. It was being bailed out effectively by the Japanese government, but that could not continue forever, even though the failure of the firm could mean job losses on such a scale as to push the country's already high unemployment rate up by fully 0.1 per cent. That was why Nissan had been casting about with increasing desperation for a white knight to save it, even – because Toyota and Honda were not interested – at the cost of foreign ownership and control. Possible foreign suitors, however, were also in short supply. Ford, for example, already controlled Mazda. Volkswagen, on the other hand, was interested only in acquiring additional luxury brands to complement its recent purchase of Rolls-Royce Motor Cars. When advanced talks with DaimlerChrysler failed in March 1999, a *New York Times* business correspondent drew the only possible conclusion: 'the outlook is grim'.[31]

There was, though, one glimmer of hope on the horizon. French automaker Renault had managed to pull itself out of extremely high losses in 1996 through the introduction of new, popular models such as the Scenic minivan. But its market was overwhelmingly focused on Europe, and in particular France. And its offerings in that relatively small market were limited to the mid- and low-price range, where the competition was most intense and potential profits therefore severely constrained. It needed to become more international, and also bigger, in order to compete effectively with rivals such as DaimlerChrysler and Volkswagen. Not surprisingly, then, Renault's CEO Leo Schweizer expressed interest in pursuing a tie-up with Nissan when the news of the failure of the DaimlerChrysler deal reached him at a Geneva auto show in March 1999. Schweizer cautioned, though, that there would be some way to go before he might be in a position to submit a formal offer.[32]

It actually went much more swiftly than anticipated. In fact, it was done and dusted later that month. The speed with which the deal was concluded was in part a function of the desperation of the two companies involved. There were also clearly recognised complementarities: Renault had cash as well as experience in the European market; Nissan had debt that needed to be paid down and had long and lucrative experience in the United States.[33]

Figure 11.3 Carlos Ghosn of Renault–Nissan, at Tokyo Motor Show, 1999. Kurita KAKU/Getty Images

But the main reason it happened so fast was that the two firms decided not to merge, but instead to enter into a strategic alliance, a much simpler arrangement. In return for Renault assuming $5.4 billion of Nissan's debt, the French automaker would get a 36.6 per cent equity stake in Nissan. By 2001, Renault's holding in the Japanese carmaker climbed to 43 per cent, while at the same time, Nissan, now profitable again, took a 15 per cent stake in Renault. The difference, however, lay not just in the size of the holdings, but, more importantly, in the fact that Renault's stake in Nissan had voting rights from the outset. Nissan's eventual holdings in Renault did not.

In any event, from the start of the alliance, the level and nature of Renault's shareholding in Nissan meant that, although the firms remained nominally independent, this was not a strategic alliance of equals. The French-based company's large share in Nissan's ownership gave Renault the right to intervene in its partner's affairs. And CEO Louis Schweizer wasted no time. Just after the deal was concluded in March 1999, he put in a phone call to one of his trusted deputies, Carlos Ghosn (Figure 11.3), who had extensive international experience and had been a senior member of the team tasked with facilitating

Renault's recovery from a failed takeover of Volvo. Schweizer asked Ghosn if he would be willing to go to Tokyo to take the lead in Nissan's turnaround. Ghosn agreed.

In a 2002 article in the *Harvard Business Review*, Ghosn described his arrival in Tokyo, where he found that the situation was even more fraught than anyone had realised. Costs were up to a quarter higher at Nissan than at Renault, and its vehicle production capacity vastly exceeded sales. This meant that capital was tied up unproductively. And the dire situation was exacerbated by splintered holdings amounting to more than $4 billion in hundreds of other companies, as a result of *keiretsu* partnerships undertaken in conjunction with other companies associated with Nissan's house bank. Vast additional sums were therefore tied up unproductively. Taken together, all of these factors meant that Nissan was haemorrhaging cash, which in turn severely curtailed its ability to undertake the expensive work involved in developing new models. One of Nissan's flagship cars, the March (or Micra in Europe), for instance, was already nine years old in 1999 when Ghosn arrived, and there was as yet no replacement. Competitors such as Toyota and Honda, in contrast, introduced new models every five years.[34]

Ghosn took enormous pride in (and full credit for) the speed of the turnaround at Nissan. Within three years of his arrival, the carmaker was again profitable, at the same time enjoying a considerably lower debt burden. As a non-Japanese who was installed at Nissan by Renault, the senior partner in the alliance, he emphasised the extent to which he had to be cautious in his relationships with Nissan management and rank-and-file workers. But he also acted decisively to address the issues the company faced. There were many changes, including measures to slash costs. But one immediate alteration to Nissan's business as usual to that point stands out. Ghosn insisted on a dismantling of *keiretsu* relationships, thus freeing up capital to invest in new model development and increasing brand power. There were changes in management, labour, and sales practices at Nissan as well, to bring it more into line with global best practice in the automobile industry. However, disentangling the firm from these *keiretsu* relationships, hitherto taken for granted in the Japanese business ecosystem, marked a sea change.[35]

* * *

DaimlerChrysler and the Renault–Nissan alliance represented responses of German and Japanese industry to the challenges of globalisation of the systems that had enabled the two countries to compete so effectively for so long. Renault–Nissan has lasted far longer than DaimlerChrysler did, but neither has been without its problems. Most of them stem from the inequality inherent in the relationship between the two component companies. Just as the 'the mid-market cowboys of Detroit and the high-end knights of Stuttgart' did not get along particularly well because the Stuttgarters had the upper hand in terms of ownership and prestige,[36] Nissan's managers and workforce have chafed under the clear ascendancy of their French partners.

On top of that, for Renault–Nissan, there have been issues about authority and coordination that are particularly acute in the case of a strategic alliance in comparison with the more straightforward case of a single firm. For a considerable amount of time, all of this was kept in check by a clear and longstanding leader and linker, Carlos Ghosn, who eventually became CEO of Renault and chairman of Nissan (as well as of the additional junior partner Mitsubishi, which joined the alliance in 2016).[37]

In 2018, after nearly a decade in charge and under pressure from the French government, which part-owned Renault, Ghosn decided to try to find a long-term solution to the issues plaguing the alliance. Central to those plans was the creation of a holding company that would own Renault and Nissan, although they would retain their identities as brands.

We still do not know exactly *how* what happened next took place. But we know it did, and also that it may have resulted in part from the anxiety of Nissan executives about further incursions by the French. In any event, in November 2018, Ghosn was arrested on his return to Tokyo from a business trip and charged with understating his salary and misuse of Nissan company funds. Held at first in prison and then, after posting a substantial bail, under house arrest, Ghosn made a daring escape, first by bullet train from Tokyo to Osaka, and then transported in a private plane packed in a large box meant for musical instruments. He eventually ended up in Lebanon: he holds a Lebanese passport and is immune there from the threat of extradition back to Japan.[38]

Since then, the alliance has laboured under continued strains of Japanese resentment as well as sometimes lacklustre performance, all exacerbated from spring 2020 by the COVID-19 pandemic, and all without the previously (mostly) unifying presence of Ghosn.[39]

* * *

Obviously, there were crucial differences between the DaimlerChrysler 'merger' and the Renault–Nissan alliance. Yet, they happened at about the same time and for similar reasons. Both of them, moreover, stemmed from globalisation and its attendant competitive pressures. And they constituted prominent indications of the extent to which top managers at German and Japanese companies felt compelled to jettison aspects of the corporate governance systems that had prevailed since the late 1940s and instead to ape Anglo-Saxon practices. At the same time, both indicated – admittedly in different ways – the persistence of previous practice. And, indeed, they arguably illustrated that what was required was not jettisoning, but simply adjusting previously prevailing practice. Daimler AG, after all, has been by any measure extremely successful since its divorce from Chrysler. And Nissan has retained key aspects of its identity while thriving for the most part within its alliance.

The same might be said for the German and Japanese economic and business systems as a whole. It is easy to forget when contemplating the low growth rates, high unemployment, and general doldrums faced by both countries in the 1990s that they continued to perform at levels that were envied around much of the world. Indeed, as the new century dawned, they retained their places firmly among the top five economies in the world. Their export performance remained stellar, especially that of Germany, which, starting in 2003 and continuing for some years thereafter, became the world's largest exporter overall. Moreover, German and Japanese business performed well by any standard in terms of productivity and innovation. And even in the depths of their doldrums, Germany's deserved reputation for quality remained intact, while Japanese technology continued to be world-leading in many fields.

12 THE SHOCK OF THE NEW CENTURY
Three Crises (and a Near Miss)

At the end of 1999, as the clocks ticked inexorably towards the dawn of a new millennium on New Year's Eve, with attendant celebrations, trepidation dampened the occasion for many: anxiety abounded about what *seemed likely* to happen when clocks struck one minute past midnight: chaos arising from a global computer glitch.

In the early days of computing, programmers coded dates – for instance, a date of birth, the day when a loan was taken out, use-by dates for food – with up to six digits, two each for the day and month, and just two rather than four for the year. This was to save data storage in IT's early days, when space for memory was at a premium. The practice seemed unproblematic at first. In the late 1980s, however, the first indications of the unexpected consequences of ambiguity became apparent. A supermarket chain's computers, for instance, ordered that cans of meat with an expiry date of 01/00 (January 2000) be withdrawn from shelves for being nearly ninety years past their sell-by date. And shortly afterwards, in the early 1990s, a 104-year-old Minnesota woman was invited to sign up for kindergarten because her year of birth, coded as 88, was mistakenly read as 1988 rather than 1888 by the computer generating the invitations.

Hilarity soon gave way to consternation, however. The havoc that might ensue when 2000 became indistinguishable from 1900 for computers controlling nuclear reactors and missile systems was anyone's guess. So, experts took the potential fallout from the so-called 'millennium bug' extremely seriously.[1]

Expensive moves towards what became known as Y2K compliance, especially for things such as nuclear power stations, therefore began in earnest in the mid-1990s. The United Nations Y2K Compliance Centre estimated that the total cost of the work was between $300 billion and $500 billion internationally. Computer scientists and programmers had never been in such demand, especially those trained in the early machine languages that controlled many power plants and defence and security installations. And government officials, engineers, and scientists around the world held their breath as New Year's Day 2000 arrived. When it did, though, there were only very minor disruptions, although it is likely that careful preparation for this known unknown staved off worse.

In the short term, the bullet dodged, there was a collective sigh of relief, followed by one of two reactions: collective amnesia, on the one hand; or dismissal of the alleged threat from the bug as a damp squib on the other. But the surprisingly auspicious start to the new century proved deceptive, a point made most clearly two decades later when Germany and Japan, in tandem with the rest of the world, confronted the first cases of a mysterious new 'bug', a previously unknown disease known as COVID-19.

The two 'bugs' – one a human-made known unknown that was nipped in the bud, and the other an unknown unknown that definitely was not – framed a series of crises, some global and some more localised, which stress-tested the German and Japanese brands of capitalism.

Globalisation, Financialisation, and the Great Recession

For Germany and Japan, the arrival of the new millennium brought some hope of revival. Germany's outlook, in fact, could even be characterised as auspicious. The 'sick man of Europe' in the 1990s was emerging as the 'slick man of Europe'[2] as exports soared, the economy boomed, and unemployment rates sank. Japan, for its part, was still very much in the doldrums until about 2003, although it was making up ground on its 'lost decade' as the dangers of longstanding recession and deflation receded, albeit slowly. Still, even as some promising economic news poured in, even more trouble was brewing.

At first, however, the renewed dangers seemed distant because the dark clouds were gathering far away.

* * *

Nowadays, most of us have heard of collateralised debt obligation (CDOs) and other sophisticated financial instruments, however vaguely we might understand exactly what they are and how they work. Knowledge of these securities among the general public, however, was not at all widespread in the initial years of the twenty-first century, when they were increasingly applied to the mortgage market, especially in the United States, and, in the process, became ubiquitous and highly significant. And the public understood even less about the instruments involved. Truth be told, though, even those in the financial services community who were using them often had little understanding of how they functioned.

But what they did understand, and what the broader public took advantage of, was that they constituted a licence to lend – and borrow – more and more money, especially for housing. And as the pool of solvent borrowers was gradually exhausted by financial services firms anxious to lend, they soon turned to those less able to repay their loans: the so-called 'subprime' market. The lenders then sold the questionable loans almost immediately to other financial companies, where they were bundled into allegedly risk-free 'securities'.[3]

The gathering storm clouds marked the culmination of a trend that had started in the United States after the Second World War. Known as 'financialisation', the phenomenon involved the spectacular growth of the financial services sector by means of increasing levels of consumer debt, government borrowing, and higher corporate debt-to-equity ratios, all fuelled by deregulation. Between 1950 and 1970, the financial sector (including insurance) grew by a factor of 1.5, rising from 2.8 per cent of US GDP in 1950 to 4.2 per cent in 1970. By 2007–2008, that share was more than three-quarters higher, having risen to over 7.5 per cent of total US GDP. And it had, in addition, become by far the most profitable sector, accounting for nearly a quarter of the profits of *all* industrial sectors in 1970 and well over a third by the start of the first decade of the twenty-first century. What is more, these staggering figures actually *undercount* the financial sector's clout. By the start of the 2000s, the financial divisions of major manufacturing firms such as Ford and General Electric – which were not included in the statistical reporting for the financial sector – were among their largest and by far their most profitable.[4]

A substantial part of this growth came through 'securitisation', the repackaging of debt into tradeable financial instruments. And this practice, along with the other accoutrements of financialisation, was not limited to the United States. Japan was an exception in this regard by virtue of its limited embrace of the newfangled securities, but the UK and many other countries joined the party with gusto.

One of them was Germany. In part, this was related to the country's efforts in the 1990s to 'modernise', to become more like the United States and UK in terms of shareholder value, deregulation, and privatisation. But there had been a trend towards investing abroad from the 1970s, as the *Landesbanken* (LBs, banks owned wholly or in part by the German federal state governments, which accounted for about a fifth of the German banking sector) sought higher returns. By 2000, those holdings increasingly consisted of bundled securities such as CDOs. It has since become clear that few in charge of the LBs possessed the financial literacy to understand these instruments. As a result, a number of them were early casualties of the US subprime crisis that began in 2007: WestLB, IKB Deutsche Industriebank, Sachsen LB, and Bayern LB.[5]

But it was not only the LBs that had engaged in risky behaviour. Large and established private banks, including Dresdner and Deutsche Bank, were also heavily exposed. Dresdner had to be part-nationalised; eventually its former competitor Commerzbank had to take it over. *Newsweek*'s Stefan Theil was therefore exaggerating only slightly when he claimed in 2009 that:

> German banks weren't just victims of Anglo-Saxon cowboy banking, but were among its most aggressive players from the start, pouring the country's capital surplus (second only to China's over the past five years) into high-risk areas like U.S. toxic assets, Spanish real estate and Irish hedge funds.

As a consequence of this reckless behaviour, and almost incredibly given their reputation for probity and conservatism, German banks were on average more heavily leveraged as the financial crisis began than those in the United States, with an estimated debt to net worth ratio of 52:1 compared with 12:1 in the United States.[6]

The apparent paradox was therefore this: the epicentre of the financial eruptions emerged in the United States in 2007 through subprime mortgage lending; the crisis then spread by 2009 to Greece, Ireland, Iceland, Spain, and Italy, the peripheral countries of the eurozone, because they had taken on debt far beyond their ability to pay. But, because German banks were among the biggest investors fuelling the frenzy of mortgage and debt in all of those countries, it was German taxpayers who had to foot one of the highest bills for bailing out their banks. Financial journalist Michael Lewis put it succinctly, and in the earthiest way possible in 2011: 'Germans longed to be near the shit, but not in it. This, as it turns out, is an excellent description of their role in the current financial crisis.'[7]

* * *

Just to be clear: German banks and the German banking system were by no means solely – or even primarily – responsible for the subprime and eurozone crises from 2007 onwards. But, at the same time, Germany provided a link between them. On the one hand, German government deregulation and lack of effective oversight of banks enabled irresponsible levels of investment in shaky securities and other ropy financial instruments in the United States and the eurozone. On the other, when the euro was agreed upon as a common currency for most of the members of the European Union, overseen by the European Central Bank (ECB), there was a fudge that allowed countries such as Greece and Ireland to borrow in massive amounts under favourable conditions, as if their economies were as strong as Germany's.

There are therefore many twists to the sorry tale of the part played by Germany in the financial crises that started at the end of the first decade of the new millennium. But one of the biggest impacts came from what followed: Germany exerted an outsized influence within the ranks of two of the three major players shaping the response to the crisis, the ECB and the European Commission, which, together with the International Monetary Fund (IMF), imposed a regime of austerity on the (much poorer) countries of the eurozone at the centre of the crisis.[8]

* * *

The deep implication of German banking and government in the financial crises that started in 2007 caused financial pain in Germany and, to an even greater extent, elsewhere in the eurozone. Yet German manufacturing, although affected at the outset of the downturn, recovered swiftly and strongly. And, as German manufacturing went, so did the German economy.

The rapid recovery stemmed in large part from the fact that China's economy was largely unaffected by the Great Recession. It quickly resumed growth at breakneck speed. This translated in turn into high demand for German-made cars, auto parts, machinery, and chemicals, the high-value-added manufactured goods that have perennially comprised the lion's share of German exports and maintained Germany's position as one of the top three exporters in the world since the early 1950s. Those goods were supplied not just by Germany's large and well-known firms, but also by the lesser known, smaller, and often family-controlled companies of the country's *Mittelstand*. Both types of enterprise had undergone sometimes painful reform and restructuring, with *Mittelstand* firms orienting themselves more and more towards global markets.

German companies, large and small, were thus well poised to take advantage of the upsurge in demand led by China, a position reinforced by the very German reaction by business and government to the economic downturn that started in 2007. Instead of laying off large numbers of workers to contain costs in the face of declining demand and economic contraction, German firms, aided by the German state, tended to keep their – often highly skilled – workers in post, albeit frequently with reduced hours and pay. This left companies and their workers in a prime position to ramp up hours, pay, and, therefore, output immediately when demand from China (and subsequently elsewhere) kicked in.[9]

* * *

The fact that Japanese financial institutions had by and large shied away from investment in the toxic securities associated with subprime loans did not shield the country from the full force of the impact of the global financial crisis that started in 2007–2008. In other words, and ironically, Japan was far less directly involved in the causes of the crisis than Germany, but it suffered far more and for much longer. And it did so even though it, like Germany, was a major trading partner of China and was and remained one of the world's leading exporters of manufactured goods.

Part of this had to do with long-term trends in overall Japanese export performance. After the end of the Second World War, Japan had taken much longer to enter the top flight of exporting nations than West Germany had, largely because, unlike Germany, it had never been a major exporter. But, with its economy growing exponentially during the decades that followed, mostly through greatly enhanced capabilities in sophisticated and high-value-added manufacturing, it became the world's third-largest exporter in 1970, displacing the UK. Japan then retained that position, behind the United States and Germany, for more than thirty years. By 2003, however, still in the doldrums of the 'lost decade', it fell to fourth place worldwide, behind surging sales abroad by China.[10]

Japan remained in that position until 2017, when it fell to fifth place behind the Netherlands. The downward spiral started in earnest in 2007, as Japanese exports fell faster and further than German exports in the wake of the global economic crisis. What is more, its recovery was much slower than Germany's and America's, and it lagged far behind the Chinese juggernaut. Indeed, its sales abroad latterly were often less than half the value in US dollars of the world's number three exporter, Germany.

Sub-par Japanese export performance over the course of many years was both cause and effect of the ingrained recession that had plagued Japan's domestic economy since the beginning of the 1990s. Fragile recovery as the twenty-first century began was then choked off as the global economic crisis once again stoked up deflationary expectations. But there were other persistent underlying issues at work as well. Japan's heavy reliance on the US market for sales abroad made it more susceptible to the severe American downturn than Germany. What is more, Japanese companies were, on the whole, otherwise much less globally oriented than their German counterparts, and, related to that, they had not restructured or reformed to the degree required to meet the challenges of the globalised economy. In fact, Japan's economy continued to be much more closed and protected than Germany's, and its domestic economy remained more important than foreign trade.

This brings us back to the rapid resurrection of deflationary expectations lurking just beneath the surface when the world went into its economic tailspin in 2007. Consumer spending in Japan once again collapsed, and the consequent recession and deflation were exacerbated by a population that was growing on average much older than else-where. Government and Bank of Japan fiscal policies also did not help, choking off recovery instead of promoting it.

* * *

Enter – or, more accurately, re-enter – Prime Minister (PM) Shinzo Abe (1954–2022). The son and grandson of prominent Japanese pol-iticians from the party that governed Japan for most of the post-war period, the Liberal Democratic Party (LDP), Abe had himself long been a prominent member – and president – of the party. He led the LDP to electoral victory in 2006, becoming Japan's PM, but he left office within a year owing to a chronic illness. During this short first ten-ure at the top, Abe advocated a number of conservative – as well as many controversial – positions. He pushed, for instance, for Japan to take more responsibility for its own defence rather than relying on the United States. He was, however, unsuccessful in this endeavour, as it required an unpopular major change to the Japanese constitution, which limited Japan's army to self-defence only.

Despite the illness that caused his first resignation, though, Abe stormed back to electoral victory in 2012 on the basis of a set of pol-icies that he called 'Abenomics', which was designed to tackle Japan's persistent deflation and low growth. On this occasion, he had ample time to implement much of his programme. Although his plans for extending the Japanese military were again not fully realised, he was able in 2015 to push through changes to allow it to be deployed abroad for purposes of collective security. Thereafter, Abe stayed in office until summer 2020, becoming Japan's longest-serving PM. His second resig-nation was again due to ill health, but it also came in the wake of sev-eral scandals. Even after he left office, though, he remained an active and central figure in the ruling LDP until his death at the hands of an assassin in summer 2022.[11]

His 'Abenomics' policy targeted Japan's chronic deflation and low economic growth with 'three arrows': increased government spending, looser monetary policy, and structural reforms. The target was to *increase* inflation to 2 per cent, a remarkably different strat-egy from the inflation-containing policies pursued by central banks and their governments in other major industrial nations. And, indeed, the initial impact of massive asset purchases by the Bank of Japan in

2013 had a pronounced positive impact, with the stock market booming and unemployment falling, although, crucially, average wages did
not increase much at all. But Abenomics stumbled when the government implemented a hike in the country's consumption tax in spring
2014 that had been planned by Abe's predecessor. The move plunged
Japan back into recession, which further stimulus measures failed to
shift. Looking back on the accomplishments of Abenomics after Abe
stepped down, Ken Shibusawa, former Goldman Sachs banker and
adviser to Fumio Kishida, one of Abe's successors as PM, characterised Abenomics in graphic terms: 'I didn't see three arrows,' Shibusawa
said. 'I saw one big bazooka.' The big bazooka, furthermore, show-
ered money on those who already had it. It therefore did not have the
desired effect of ramping up consumer spending by shaking broadly
and deeply held deflationary expectations.[12]

* * *

At the closing ceremony for the Summer Olympics held in Brazil in
2016, Japanese PM Shinzo Abe emerged dramatically dressed as Super
Mario to promote the next Olympic summer games, scheduled to be
held in Japan in 2020. A few months later, in November 2016, he
hightailed it to Trump Tower in New York City. Abe risked violating
protocol, by-passing still sitting President Barack Obama, to ensure he
was the first foreign leader to congratulate newly elected US President
Donald Trump in person. (And Trump, of course, also ignored staff
entreaties to stick to protocol.) Abe presented the president-elect with
a gold golf club valued at $3,800, which Trump used at the first official
meeting of the two heads of government at Mar-a-Lago in February.
Previously, Abe had raised eyebrows in Japan and abroad when he
expressed his fondness for the heavy metal rock band Metallica. He
was therefore not only the longest-serving Japanese PM since 1945, but
also stood out from his predecessors (and successors) as PM in becoming a celebrity of sorts, a globally recognised brand. As political analysts commented shortly after his untimely death in July 2022, Abe's
'was an outsized incumbency ... for an outsized political figure'.[13]

   Combined with his flamboyant bid to wrest Japan from years
of deflation through his signature Abenomics policies, Abe's unusually
assertive global persona may give the impression that he was somehow
un-Japanese. That would be a mistake, however. After all, his haste

to get an audience with President-elect Trump in November 2016, even at the cost of violating protocol, stemmed from a highly conventional desire to minimise diplomatic and security risk. On the basis of an astute assessment of Trump's personality, Abe gambled that flattery, accompanied by an expensive gift, would help avert the new US President's threats during his campaign to cut military aid to Japan severely, and potentially even to force it to develop nuclear weapons.

Following up on that ninety-minute visit to Trump Tower in November with a round of golf on his first official visit to the newly inaugurated President in February 2017 – and again in November of the same year, when Trump continued without noticing to the next hole when Abe fell backwards into a sand trap[14] – was also far less unconventional than it sounds. In fact, it built on a family tradition: during an official visit to the United States in 1957, US President Dwight D. Eisenhower and then Japanese PM Nobusuke Kishi (who was also Abe's grandfather) used time spent together on the golf course to cement the close relations between their two countries.[15]

Abe was, then, simultaneously highly unusual in the Japanese context and deeply entwined in the Japanese establishment. And his unconventional posturing at times belied his strong desire to resurrect and reinvigorate Japanese traditions. This was perhaps best evidenced in his relationship with the infamous Yasukuni Shrine, which enshrines the spirits of several war criminals. He visited Yasukuni in December 2013, just a year after becoming PM for the second time, the first visit by a serving PM since that of Junichiro Koizumi in 2006. Decried by the Chinese and South Koreans and upbraided by the US Embassy in Tokyo, Abe did not revisit it during the rest of his long incumbency. However, within days of resigning his office in September 2020, he was back. By April 2022, moreover, still a prominent and powerful LDP politician, Abe had paid no fewer than six visits after his second and final resignation.[16]

The circumstances surrounding Abe's murder in July 2022 seem to encapsulate the complex admixture of at once breaking loose from the past and being engulfed by it that had epitomised his life – and also perhaps suggest something about the state of current-day Japan. The country has some of the strictest gun control laws anywhere in the world and, not surprisingly, deaths from firearms are correspondingly small, with political assassination practically non-existent since 1945. Yet the former prime minister was shot to death while on the campaign trail, admittedly by a crude handmade weapon.[17]

Initial assumptions were that the assassin's motivation was terrorism, but it has since become clear that it was entirely different. The forty-one-year-old perpetrator, Tetsuya Yamagami, targeted Abe because of the former PM's association with the Unification Church led by Reverend Sun Myung Moon until Moon's death in 2012. Abe's father and grandfather, both prominent politicians in their day (his grandfather had even been PM of Japan), had cultivated ties with the church. This was not just because of Moon's hard-line stance against communism during the Cold War, but also because the reverend consistently delivered votes for their beloved LDP. Yamagami, on the other hand, detested Moon's church because he believed it had destroyed his family: once relatively well-off, his mother had impoverished the family by donating more than ¥100 million (nearly $700,000) to the church after joining it in 1998. Yamagami's grudge against the Unification Church translated into violence, which he initially planned against members of the church and their facilities, and then finally and fatally enacted against Abe.

Japan has a reputation as one of the most secular nations in the world. Yet a significant minority in Japan has been attracted to so-called 'new religions' since the Meiji Restoration of the late nineteenth century, and especially since 1945. The outcome has been disproportionately unfortunate at times: the Unification Church has been the target of successful legal action because of its fundraising, for instance from Yamagami's mother. But, as this suggests, the Yamagami family saga is far from unique. More worryingly still, the Aum Shinrikyo cult carried out a sarin nerve-gas attack on Japanese subways in 1995. Abe's assassination – and, indeed, Abe himself – thus highlight links between the fringe groups that have arisen among those disaffected by Japan's rapid and sometimes painful modernisation and westernisation on the one hand and the continuing ascendancy of traditional Japanese social and political elites on the other.

Like many Germans, it seems, many Japanese like to flirt with the offbeat and the alternative, but they also like to keep a respectable distance. Sometimes, though, the barriers are transgressed, with dire repercussions.

Energy Choices and Their Consequences

On 11 March 2011 at 2.46 pm local time, the Great East Japan Earthquake struck in the ocean just east of the city of Sendai.

It registered 9 on the Richter scale (about as high as you can get on the logarithmic scale of 10). The most powerful quake to hit Japan in recorded history, it actually shifted the earth off its axis, in the process triggering a giant tsunami. Gigantic waves, some as high as 40 metres (131 feet) battered surrounding coastal areas. Residents in the area had just ten minutes' warning of the seawater onslaught. Nearly 20,000 perished, with 2,500 still missing as of December 2021, over a decade after the disaster. Nearly half a million were made homeless.

After the tsunami struck, it became clear immediately that the abject misery of those living and working in the region had only just begun. Earthquake-protection measures ensured an automatic shut-down at the Fukushima Daiichi Nuclear Power Plant south of Sendai. However, the tsunami's waves breached the seawall designed to protect it. Back-up generators available to keep the still red-hot fuel of the plant's reactors cool in the aftermath of a shutdown failed, and battery-powered additional back-ups soon ran out of power. The disastrous result involved explosions, a major nuclear meltdown, and the release of substantial quantities of radiation.[18]

After the 1998 Chernobyl disaster in the Soviet Union (Chornobyl in current-day Ukraine), Fukushima was the worst nuclear accident in history. The direct cause of the accident was the tsunami – the earthquake itself did not damage the plant. Moreover, the plant's private-sector owner and operator, Tokyo Electric Power Company (TEPCO), claimed that no one could have predicted the unprecedented severity of this particular pair of natural disasters, and the lack of anticipation of what might – and did in fact – happen had shaped the decisions that determined the height of the seawall and the design of other back-up systems meant to protect the facility.

But there were also undoubtedly human factors that contributed to the accident, its severity, and its fallout. For instance, TEPCO engaged in deceptive reporting, systematic neglect, and safety compliance breaches. As a result, in July 2022, a court found four executives of the company liable for a whopping ¥13 trillion (about $88 billion) in damages. And there were also clear regulatory failures by the Japanese government, which led already in 2017 to a court judgement that it was partially liable for the accident and required the government to join the company in paying compensation to survivors.[19]

Questions of causation and culpability are notoriously difficult to answer conclusively, as illustrated by the length of time it has taken to find some measure of justice for survivors of the Fukushima nuclear accident. But perhaps the key question is one that is posed far less frequently: why on earth was the plant there in the first place?

***

Japan is unique among the world's very largest economies in its paucity of domestic deposits of all forms of fossil-fuel energy. Admittedly, Japan's coal resources were sufficient not only to supply its (limited) needs during early industrialisation, but also to export elsewhere in East Asia until the very early twentieth century. Still, domestic supplies of coal were insufficient for further industrialisation, and they were completely exhausted by the 1960s. This is significant because petroleum, natural gas, and even coal still constitute the most important sources of primary energy by far, since they are essential for transport, home heating, and electricity generation. As a result, in 2021, as in most of the preceding decades, Japan imported about 90 per cent of its energy needs. This placed the country in an extremely vulnerable position, which involved extraordinary expense at all times, coupled at others with unexpected and sometimes enormous price fluctuations. This was grudgingly accepted as the price of membership in the elite club of the globe's richest nations.[20] But there was also a strong desire in Japan to do something to offset this eyewateringly high level of dependence on imported energy. To this end, the country had long had a substantial hydropower industry, but its output barely dented its growing appetite for energy as Japan developed economically. More recently, solar energy and other renewables came online to provide some additional energy independence and security. But, well before that happened, Japanese policymakers and industrialists had placed their greatest hopes in atomic energy, despite the fact that the country was the only one to have ever fallen victim to military attacks using nuclear weapons.

From a slow start in the 1960s, Japan's electricity generation from nuclear power increased more than tenfold between 1972 and 1982. This output more than doubled again in the decade that followed, only to rise by more than 50 per cent additionally by 2002. Until 2011, nuclear power plants generated nearly one-third of all of Japan's electricity. At the time, the nation was the third-largest consumer of nuclear power globally, behind only the United States and

France. In 2010, nuclear power accounted for about 13 per cent of the country's total primary energy consumption.[21]

These were fateful decisions. Japan is not only poor in energy resources; it is also situated on geological fault lines that are notoriously prone to earthquakes. Aside from the universally recognised issues related to disposal of nuclear waste and decommissioning of nuclear plants, this made heavy reliance on atomic energy a risky proposition. After the Fukushima accident, nuclear power's share in total primary energy consumption dropped to just 3 per cent, with increased consumption of renewables and fossil fuels making up the difference. The government's plan, however, is to expand production of nuclear power once again 'by 2030 to reduce hydrocarbon fuel imports and to enhance the country's energy security'.[22]

* * *

Although far richer in coal than Japan, Germany is similarly poorly endowed with the 'modern' fossil fuels, namely petroleum and natural gas. It therefore faced difficult and expensive accommodation similar to Japan to become and remain one of the top members of the global economic elite. And its leaders also sought some respite from that dependence through a combination of continued reliance on coal and nuclear power, supplemented in recent decades by considerable investment in renewables.

Yet, in Germany, nuclear power was never embraced to the extent it was in Japan. Although Germany's atomic power plants eventually generated about a quarter of the country's electricity, public opposition to nuclear energy grew from the early 1980s, and especially after Chornobyl in 1986. It was an antipathy that the increasingly popular Green Party and some segments of the SPD championed. The strength of that sentiment and the political clout behind it translated into an undertaking by the coalition government elected in 1998 to phase out nuclear power altogether. Although a subsequent government, elected in 2009, cancelled that policy, it was reinstated with a vengeance two years later in the wake of the Fukushima disaster. Eight of Germany's seventeen reactors were shut down immediately, and others followed over the course of the next several years, with all remaining reactors phased out by the end of 2022. In October 2022, however, the government gave a stay of execution until the middle of

April 2023 to three of the remaining nuclear power plants as part of its policy of weaning itself off imports of Russian natural gas.[23]

As early as the 1990s, the German government planned to make up considerable ground in ensuring its energy security by investing heavily in domestic production using renewables, especially wind power. And that commitment was strengthened in the new millennium. As part of the strategy, dirty domestic (and imported) coal was to be phased out. However, in the short to medium term, much of Germany's energy demand would have to be met through recourse to a much cleaner-burning fossil fuel, natural gas. And that gas would be supplied by pipeline from Russia, which had already begun to do so through its predecessor state, the Soviet Union. The start of the move towards natural gas was slow, but, by the first decades of the twenty-first century, the extent of the dependence on Russia had become crystal clear. By 2020, about half of Germany's natural gas came from Russia. And that was not all: approximately a third of its petroleum and around half of its coal imports also came from its large eastern neighbour.[24]

The central figure in the development was, like Shinzo Abe, an uncustomary, yet at the same time supremely conventional politician, Gerhard (Gerd) Schröder. Schröder took charge as Chancellor in the centre-left, SPD-led, German government in 1998. One of his signature accomplishments in office was the distinctly un-SPD reform of German labour law and relations known as Hartz IV. This contributed to him ceding the Chancellorship to Angela Merkel of the centre-right CDU in 2005. He had maintained, and strengthened, German–Russian relations during his incumbency, not least through his growing friendship with Vladimir Putin, and in particular through putting the government's muscle behind the Nord Stream gas pipeline project that would provide natural gas to Germany and other nearby western European countries. The friendship with Putin paid off handsomely only seventeen days after he left office. The Russian President called him on his mobile phone, urging him to accept the post of head of the shareholder committee for Nord Stream. Schröder intimated that this might not be ideal optically, but he took the position anyhow. He has since also served on the supervisory board of Russian fossil-fuel giant Rosneft.[25]

To be fair, Schröder's post-chancellor antics were hardly noticed, not least because his stance vis-à-vis Russia and Russian gas was firmly supported by the governments that succeeded his, led between 2005 and 2021 by Angela Merkel (of the CDU). That support lasted until February 2022, when the Russian invasion of Ukraine exposed the wishful thinking behind *Wandel durch Handel*, the notion at the heart of longstanding German foreign policy that trade with Russia would lead to positive political change there.

After the Russian invasion of Ukraine in February 2022, the recently constituted SPD-led German government declared, along with the rest of the European Union, that it would wean itself off Russian gas. To make up the shortfall, Germany has had to embrace a number of measures, including putting previously mothballed coal-fired power plants back into operation, rationing natural gas, and finding alternative sources for natural gas imports. But, since alternative sources of gas are not available via pipeline, the country has scurried to embrace liquefied natural gas (LPG), long used in Japan, but hitherto rejected as too expensive by the Germans, given the largely unchallenged assumption that plentiful supply from Russia was guaranteed by pipeline (through Nord Stream 1 and the additional pipeline capacity available through Nord Stream 2, which was due to come online in 2022). Aside from the issue of building infrastructure for regasifying the liquefied gas, the fuel has become even more expensive in any form as Germany competes with other countries for limited non-Russian supplies.[26]

The dilemmas inherent in choosing the optimal mix of energy – how best to balance trade-offs among environmental concerns, economic growth, social equity, and security of supply – are legion. Burdened more than most other highly developed countries with a deficit of viable options, both Japan and Germany wagered heavily on risky ones. Neither nuclear nor natural gas, however, has panned out very well in the new millennium, underscoring rather than resolving both countries' fragility in energy security.

Even as they placed their bets on nuclear, natural gas, or some combination of the two, however, Japan and Germany have also led the global charge towards investing in renewables. The idea here is that, eventually, renewables will minimise the impact of electricity generation on the environment, while at the same time making it possible for the two countries to become largely independent in supply of energy needs. Both nations have made great strides in this direction. But it is worth bearing in mind that renewables are reliant on rare earths. The mining of these minerals entails severe environmental damage, as does the disposal of worn-out or outdated renewables equipment and storage batteries. What is more, the rare earths essential to renewables production are available in quantity only as imports into Japan and Germany, primarily from China and some African and South American countries. In other words, investment in renewables will never enable complete energy independence, but will instead *transfer* dependence to different parts of the world, still well beyond their borders.

Tackling COVID-19

In late November or early December 2019, the first cases of a new, pneumonia-like disease were reported in China. By 12 January 2020, Thailand had identified its first case, which was traced back to China. Japan followed with its first laboratory-confirmed case three days later. And Europe did not have long to wait before it experienced its first confirmed cases, on 24 January in France and 28 January in Germany. In the meantime, the first deaths were reported. The World Health Organization (WHO) officially named the disease COVID-19 on 11 February. Exactly one month later, WHO declared the outbreak a pandemic.[27]

* * *

In Germany, the response to the emerging crisis was swift, but calm. With one of the highest levels of hospital beds per capita in Europe, extensive availability of intensive-care units, more than adequate testing capacity, and strong buy-in from government officials at federal and state levels and the public, the country was confident it could cope well with the virus. German efforts intensified as the severity and contagiousness of the disease became apparent, but, by the summer, Germany, like almost all other developed countries, was in lockdown, although it managed to minimise deaths from the disease. Its effectiveness was routinely singled out for praise and emulation.[28]

Germany's efforts were certainly not perfect: under the leadership of the European Commission, the country rolled out its vaccine programme slowly; there were shortages of protective gear for medical staff at times; there was strong resistance among a substantial minority of the population to vaccination; and, related to that, there was a worryingly deadly spike in infections in autumn 2021. Nevertheless, as of March 2023, the country's overall estimated number of deaths per

100,000 population – 203.16 – was substantially lower than that of virtually all of its European neighbours. At that point, Germany's mortality rate from coronavirus was about 60 per cent of that of the United States and just under two-thirds that of the UK.[29]

It is not entirely clear what factors best account for these differentials in countries' mortality rates from the virus, not least because, in their haste to counter the cascade of cases and deaths, they all introduced a wide variety of policies, guidelines, and legally binding rules.[30] Yet there are some explanations that are particularly plausible for Germany's relative success compared with many other countries in dealing with the COVID-19 pandemic. For one thing, the country's track-and-trace and testing systems were exemplary, and they are themselves a function of its highly developed network of laboratory facilities and medical monitoring systems. Then, too, Germany had more than adequate hospital facilities, with relatively high numbers of intensive-care beds for its population, so much so that it was able to accommodate cases from France, Italy, and other neighbouring countries when their own hospital services were overwhelmed. Furthermore, although extensive parts of hospital and medical provision were in the private sector, there was coordination of public and private provision through state and federal bureaucracies and subsidies. And, finally, the country's well-established and highly regarded pharmaceutical industry should be mentioned, with one of the leading players in development of a key vaccine, BioNTech SE, based in Mainz.

At least some of Germany's relative success in countering the medical and social impact of COVID-19, therefore, appears to have stemmed from its highly advanced biochemical and biomedical industries and its related testing infrastructure, this combined with its elaborate social and medical welfare systems, an effective bureaucracy, and a mixture of centralised and local/public and private policies and practices. In other words, key features of the German form of capitalism that had emerged after the Second World War may well have been at play.

* * *

However, before we get too carried away with some parts of this explanation for Germany's relative COVID-19 success, let us compare some of the main features with Japan's experience in the pandemic. Unlike Germany's, Japan's medical system is highly fragmented. And, unlike

Germany, Japan also does not have anywhere near the number of intensive-care beds needed to treat patients suffering the worst effects of a disease such as COVID-19. What is more, Japan's highly central-ised government has no legal authority to order nationwide lockdowns or vaccinations. Yet Japan's mortality rate from coronavirus as of summer 2022 is one of the lowest in the world's wealthiest countries, indeed just 15 per cent that of Germany. Related to that, its testing and track-and-trace regimes have been exemplary, and its vaccination rate is one of the highest globally, despite an initially slow rollout.[31]

Again, no one knows for certain, but it appears as if the secret to Japan's extraordinary success in containing the worst effects of the coronavirus lies in large part in the behaviour of its population. From the outset, and to the present, this has featured a mixture of self-restraint, peer pressure, and a general conformity to the advice of public health officials at national, regional, and local level. Other key factors at work were an efficient and effective bureaucracy; and, incentivised by government grants, widespread business compliance with guidelines about opening hours, ventilation, and other measures to prevent the spread of the virus.

In other words, although the precise dimensions of the Japanese response to the coronavirus pandemic differed from those in Germany, it appears that in Japan, too, key features of the form of capitalism that emerged there after the Second World War had a positive impact. In both countries, however, the pride in the way the pandemic has been navigated so far needs to be mixed with a good measure of humility. As one academic virologist who advises the Japanese government has remarked: 'The response [to each new twist in the virus's behaviour] is like an Othello game.... All of a sudden, the most successful countries can become the worst country [sic] in the world.'[32]

CONCLUSION
Deutschland AG and Japan, Inc. – Lessons and Limits

Financial meltdown, a nuclear disaster, and a pandemic. Japan and Germany, like the rest of the world, emerged bruised and battered by the first and last of these calamities during the first two decades of the new millennium. Japan suffered the middle one largely on its own, although Fukushima also galvanised Germany's opposition to nuclear power. This in turn reinforced the European country's overreliance on Russian gas, a folly laid bare when Russia invaded Ukraine in spring 2022. Taken together, the crises exposed some of the vulnerabilities and deficiencies of Japanese and German capitalisms as they have evolved since the Second World War. But they also highlighted key sources of strength, not least resilience and adaptability in the face of extreme adversity. On balance, the two countries therefore weathered the crises better than most.

From the perspective of early 2023, however, there is understandable trepidation that the Japanese and Germans should not be so much congratulating themselves on 'mission accomplished' as gearing themselves up for a confrontation with a fresh set of nearly insuperable trials. Record-breaking heatwaves and droughts remind us of the unrelenting onward march of human-induced climate change. Soaring prices for food and energy, combined with the likelihood of widespread economic recession, are probably more transient phenomena, but this does not make them any less painful. And populist leaders in many countries in recent years, not least in the United States, have campaigned for higher levels of national self-sufficiency, undermining longstanding trends towards greater globalisation of trade, finance, and manufacturing on which Japanese and German capitalisms have relied heavily for growth. The coronavirus pandemic, moreover, has quite possibly hastened this trend towards deglobalisation through disruption of global value chains and the demise of widespread industrial practices such as the just-in-time production systems that the Japanese developed before they were replicated throughout the world.

As if all this were not enough, the Russian invasion of Ukraine in February 2022 may eventually result in a widening of the war into other parts of Europe, which has the potential, however unlikely and unwanted, of bringing other members of the North Atlantic Treaty Organization (NATO) – including, most worryingly, the United States – into the conflict. The Middle East, too, remains an unstable region, with yet another war (with certainly broad, yet entirely unpredictable, consequences) breaking out in October 2023. And, on the other side of the world, tensions between the United States and another authoritarian superpower, China, have been running high for years, more recently threatening to boil over into direct and dangerous confrontation over Taiwan. Then there is the icing on this dreary and depressing East Asian cake: the perennial problem of that loosest of cannons, North Korea.

How these dangers play out in the months and years ahead will have an impact on every country in the world, not least poor and less developed ones. But, among highly developed nations, Germany and Japan are likely to be among the most heavily affected. Both are profoundly reliant on foreign trade and global value chains, which deglobalisation is disrupting. Both economies depend fundamentally on imports of fossil fuels, for which supply has tightened; their rush to overcome this dependence through renewables has only resulted in different dependences. And last, but certainly not least, for both, potentially catastrophic military conflicts are looming right on their respective doorsteps.

In short, they, like all of us, are living in fabled – and cursed – 'interesting times'.

* * *

From the late 1940s, defeated Germany and Japan benefited disproportionately from the global capitalist order led by the United States. As manufacturing powerhouses with at times world-beating technological capabilities (developed somewhat later in Japan than in Germany), they were in a strong position to take advantage of the freeing up of trade restrictions championed by the United States to sell their wares on the world stage. Relatively unencumbered trade also allowed them to purchase goods, services, raw materials, and, not incidentally, supplies of oil and natural gas using growing surpluses of cash in their current accounts. The two countries, moreover, profited handsomely from the American willingness to furnish – perhaps better put: insistence on providing – military protection during the Cold War that characterised much of the period after 1945; and even, to a lesser degree, during the years since the end of the Cold War.

The social, political, and economic importance of this outsourced defence and national security burden is difficult to overestimate. Extensive stationing of US troops in both countries, for instance, has had profound and direct effects on Japanese and German society and culture. Politically, the troops and broader American security guarantees have not merely protected both countries from the dangers of military attack, even if there were times when this was touch and go, for instance, in the Berlin crisis of the late 1950s and early 1960s. Just as importantly, their neighbours and many of their citizens have by and large been spared anxiety about a resurgence of the German and Japanese economies possibly bringing with it a simultaneous reprise of the bellicosity and aggression that characterised the period prior to 1945. And the security umbrella provided by the Americans also entailed another enormous benefit for the economies of both countries: they have been able to devote the lion's share of their respective research and development expenditure (by government, universities, and business) to civilian rather than military R&D, in direct contrast to the United States (and, for instance, also the UK).

In these and other ways, both directly and indirectly, the United States has exercised unusually high levels of influence over the two countries. And, not surprisingly, this influence, along with widely admired (if also often despised) US business practices, economic performance, and consumerism, has frequently translated into a desire in both nations to emulate America. Still, in spite of many decades of undeniable 'Americanisation', they remain distinctly Japanese and German, as they will in the coming decades.

* * *

The outsized US influence in both countries began immediately after the conclusion of the Second World War in 1945, first in Europe and then in the Pacific. In defeated Japan and in much of former Nazi Germany, US military and civilian authorities became the de facto and de jure rulers of the country. And they arrived as occupiers with clear plans for realising the profound changes needed in each country – from deposing, and even jailing or executing, the nations' former rulers to recasting corporate governance; banning key military-related indus-tries; curtailing the military itself; overseeing the introduction of a new currency; and even, in the case of Japan, going as far as dictating an entirely new constitution.

This initial, unmediated set of jolts to German and Japanese politics, business, and society during the post-war military and civilian occupations gave way in the early 1950s to less direct, but still pervasive, American influence that has continued to the present day. In other words, to a degree unparalleled by any other advanced industrial nation, the United States has made a particularly heavy and often quite direct impression on Germany and Japan. In fact, it has operated as a crucial conduit linking, challenging, and shaping the two countries. And this shared transnational experience has provided a firm foundation for the comparative history pursued in these pages.

What is more, as the post-war period began, encouraged by the American and other Allied occupiers, German and Japanese elites responded in strikingly similar ways to fundamental deficiencies in their pre-war political economies. They accepted, and sometimes even embraced, industrial labour as a partner rather than adversary, and, in this way, redressed to a large degree the political and social effects of extreme pre-war economic inequality. They also proved energetic participants in the US-led system of relatively free trade, although they were somewhat less enthusiastic about abandoning their previous reliance on state-sanctioned cartels along with other, more informal, forms of regulation of industrial competition in favour of legally enforced industrial competition.

The resistance to American-style systems of corporate governance and regulation in Germany and Japan manifested itself in continued adherence to business and banking models based on interlocking shareholding; coordinated financing; and loose but ever-present guidance from the government and its bureaucracy. There would seem to be good reason, then, for adopting the popular and widespread, somewhat hyperbolic, shorthand of Deutschland AG and Japan, Inc. Both countries have pursued forms of cooperative capitalism, which is why proponents of the 'varieties of capitalism' (VoC) approach to analysing international political economy designate them as coordinated market economies (CMEs), in stark contrast to American- and British-style liberal market economies (LMEs).[1]

However, lumping post-1945 Germany and Japan together as CMEs is something of an exaggeration, for two reasons. One was recognised by a pioneer of the VoC approach, David Soskice, in an unpublished working paper from 1994. Soskice sought to tease out 'finer varieties' of CME capitalism by elaborating on the distinction between industry-based coordination in Germany compared with business group-based coordination in Japan. Using a different approach, Mark Metzler sees a major distinction between the two countries in the post-war period as arising from differences between Germany's export-led financing and Japan's industrial financing. We can quibble about which of these characterisations better captures the key distinctions between German-style and Japanese-style capitalisms as they developed after 1945. We might also discuss whether the differences require entirely separate categories of capitalism, adding to VoC's alphabet soup. But there is no question that there are fundamental differences in the institutions, processes, and central actors shaping the German and Japanese economic orders.[2]

The other reason why the CME category is problematic, however, is more fundamental: at base, it is static rather than dynamic. German and Japanese capitalisms were both undoubtedly heavily coordinated from the start of the post-war period, continuing many of the traditional institutions and mechanisms of pre-1945 coordination. But the actors involved constantly needed to adapt to new challenges, some anticipated but many unforeseen. In the process, by the twenty-first century, Germany and Japan have arguably become far less coordinated capitalist countries than they were in the middle of the twentieth century; and, insofar as they remain CMEs, there is no doubt that they have come to be coordinated in different ways from each other and from how they were coordinated in the past.

* * *

The adaptations and modifications of the coordinated market economies of Germany and Japan during the decades since 1945 have been impressive and fascinating. And leaders and opinion-shapers in many other countries would naturally like to emulate their success. The question is: how?

Some have suggested that one way might be to become more like them, to reproduce the practices, institutions, business organisation, and behaviours that make their economies successful. However, wholesale copying of the German or the Japanese coordinated market economy is impossible. As demonstrated in this book, each of the two combatants that emerged from defeat in war in 1945 (like many other nations, in fact) had highly developed and distinctive economic and technological capabilities, business organisations and practices, political traditions, social norms, and ways of behaving. In other words, each had a more or less peculiar history and culture. And these have conditioned their post-war development in important ways, not least since there have been strong strands of continuity in institutions, people, and behaviours.

Despite these continuities, however, there were also revolutionary changes to the German and Japanese versions of capitalism after 1945. Both abandoned aspirations for autarky, and instead embraced global market forces; opened up market coordination mechanisms by adding voices from organised labour to those of government, industry, and finance; overcame extreme inequality by promoting greater levels of economic equality; and abandoned militarism, relying instead on the United States for security. These quantum changes to German and Japanese capitalisms, however, almost certainly would not have occurred without the countries' abject defeat in the Second World War and subsequent Allied – and especially American – insistence on fundamental reform and reorientation.

The influence of these two 'peculiarities', of pre-1945 history and of post-war context, means that there is no template for other countries to follow should they wish to follow the German or Japanese path to prosperity. In this sense at least, German and Japanese post-1945 development is quite literally inimitable. And, in the light of the pivotal role of devastating military defeat in shaping reform of post-war German and Japanese capitalisms in the decades immediately after 1945, it is also not desirable.

Recognising this, however, does not mean that lessons cannot be learned from examining the post-war history of the two countries. They certainly can. In fact, there are two broad sets of lessons, both of which involve more narrow adaptations of specific aspects of German or Japanese capitalism to other countries.

The first involves a number of institutional and organisational innovations developed in the two countries after 1945, which can be – and in some cases have already been – imitated and adapted by other nations.

Codetermination in post-war West Germany is a case in point. Enshrined in law from 1951, codetermination, with its requirement for effective works councils in industry and trade-union representation on the non-executive boards of large enterprises, has played a key role in ensuring the relatively calm and consensual industrial relations underpinning post-war German prosperity. The practice has roots in 1918, in the period immediately after the First World War, and was elaborated upon in various ways during the Weimar and Nazi periods. But, as scholars pointed out in the mid-1950s, West Germany was itself a 'changeling', a country that was adapting to a dramatically changed context, which suggested it could be imitated elsewhere. And indeed it has been. Although the German version of codetermination has not been adopted exactly in other countries, the practice of direct worker involvement in corporate governance has become widespread in continental western Europe and serves as a model for would-be reformers in the United States and the UK.[3]

Japan, too, innovated organisationally and institutionally in response to its post-war context, partly on the basis of its previous history, for instance by developing just-in-time (JIT) production. A radical rejection of previous production systems (which have since been characterised as 'just-in-case'), JIT had its roots in 1930s Japan, where industrial innovators took inspiration from pioneering work in the area by Ford Motor Company, adapting it creatively to the Japanese context. JIT as developed in Japan ensured enormous savings on inventory costs and greater productive efficiency, while at the same time requiring other major innovations in supply chain management and demand forecasting, among other things. And the elaboration and industrial-scale application of the concept starting in the 1970s at Toyota resulted in its imitation – and adaptation – by companies the world over.[4]

Codetermination and JIT production systems are just two examples of organisational and institutional innovations in Germany and Japan after 1945 that are the specific products of prior historical development and post-war context, but which can also be usefully imitated by others. There are many more.

One of the most compelling and widely admired is Germany's dual vocational training system for apprenticeships, which is often hailed as a basis for reform elsewhere. The system has proven effective in training highly skilled workers for manufacturing and the trades to complement those educated in academic institutions. Given the global supply chain disruptions during and after the COVID-19 pandemic as well as indications that globalisation may have reached its political and economic limits – to the extent that it might in fact be reversing – it has become increasingly clear that there are also limits to the extent to which it is wise, or even possible, to rely primarily on the service economy for growth and job creation. What is more, realising targets to decarbonise the economy to counter climate change depends crucially on having enough qualified electricians, plumbers, and other tradespeople to install heat pumps, electric vehicle charging points, and other green technology infrastructure. If anything, Germany's dual vocational training system has become even more relevant than ever as a model for other countries.[5]

Another case in point is the Bank of Japan's pioneering financial innovation, quantitative easing (QE), which it introduced in spring 2001. QE involved the large-scale purchase of Japanese government bonds by the Bank with the aim of combatting recession and deflation by, in effect, printing large sums of money in the hope of kick-starting economic growth and modest inflation. In doing so, Japan, unique among the world's rich countries in suffering a prolonged period of deflation since the early 1990s, broke ranks with most of the rest of the developed world, where curbing inflation continued to be the bugbear of fiscal policymakers, as it had been since the 1970s. With the start of the 'Great Recession' that resulted from the financial crises that engulfed the world from 2007–2008, ushering in sluggish growth and ultra-low interest rates in all developed countries, Japan's pathbreaking use of QE and other unconventional fiscal tools became a model to be widely imitated rather than a mere curiosity.[6]

There are many other examples of institutional and organisational innovations that have been pioneered in Germany and Japan since 1945. Since 1945, for instance, Germany's Fraunhofer institutes have provided effective applied R&D support for the enterprises of the country's *Mittelstand*. In the light of the fact that small- and medium-sized enterprises (SMEs) are increasingly recognised in all countries as crucial motors of economic development, Fraunhofer-like institutions could underpin them elsewhere. Another, more well-known, example is Japan's adaptation and extension of statistical quality-control techniques developed originally in the United States during the Second World War. In every one of these cases, there have been admirers and imitators around the world. But these organisational and institutional innovations have also invariably needed to be adapted to different national, regional, corporate, and social contexts.

There is a second set of lessons to be learned from the history of German and Japanese capitalisms since 1945. Analysis of their responses to issues that confront many other countries – and indeed often continue to face Germany and Japan – can yield useful insights for other nations as they address similar challenges. Many of these responses can be characterised as simply making the best of a bad situation. One example involves the reactions by automakers and other manufacturers from both countries to pressure from the United States to locate factories there. More recently, there have been parallel overseas foreign direct investments by German and Japanese firms in emerging markets, most prominently China. Both actions have had many positive impacts on the investing country as well as the target of its investment, but have also had drawbacks by strengthening potential competitors, among other things. All countries engaged in overseas direct investment – which now include China, for instance – can learn from studying these experiences.

Another example, of a completely different type, was the controversial, difficult, but largely successful German acceptance in 2015–2016 of over a million refugees from multiple countries, including Syria, Afghanistan, and Iraq,[7] something experienced in many other countries, if usually on a much smaller scale. And Japan, by virtue of being the first of many highly industrialised economies to experience long-term economic doldrums from the 1990s onwards, has been a trailblazer in the establishment of a 'gig economy', with all of the often quite negative social and economic fallout that entails, and which has now spread to many other developed nations.

Both Germany and Japan, furthermore, have had to make difficult decisions on their evolving energy mix, seeking to optimise trade-offs between availability, cost, and environmental and national security implications. These, too, provide grist for the mill for most other countries, which face similar dilemmas. Both Germany and Japan have got it very wrong at times – witness Germany's overreliance on natural gas from the Russian Federation and Japan's continuing heavy reliance on nuclear power despite being on a dangerous geological fault-line – but they have also been among the world's leaders in their commitment to the energy transition towards renewables.

Finally, Germany and Japan have also had to make painful adjustments in relation to their national security stance at times. The legacy of their military aggression in the Second World War has conditioned this to some degree, as has the military umbrella and nuclear shield provided by the United States. Consequently, there has been reluctance in both countries – which in the case of Japan is also constitutionally mandated – to establish armed forces on a grand scale and, even more so, to deploy them (or their military equipment) abroad. This seems to be changing fundamentally for both countries, however, in the wake of Russia's invasion of Ukraine and escalating tensions with China over Taiwan.

* * *

Two decades and a bit into the new millennium, Germany and Japan face intractable dilemmas. The threat of escalating war, as unthinkable as that may be, and the impact of climate change, as undeniable as it is uncertain, are two of the most daunting. For these titans of manufacturing and export, however, there are additional challenges that will have to be addressed in the near future. The global automobile industry in which both countries have long excelled provides a vantage point for considering some of them. German and Japanese carmakers have from the outset been fundamentally focused on internal-combustion-engine technology. As that industry and its technological basis veer towards electric vehicles, however, different capabilities, involving power storage and software, for example, will be required. The trick will be to train and develop people who can bring these new skills to bear on the industry while at the same time recasting company cultures that have been dedicated to date to internal-combustion engines to accommodate and enable the new capabilities.

Electric vehicles, it is true, will considerably reduce the extremely heavy dependence of both countries on imports of petroleum in particular. But they will also create new dependences on other strategic materials, especially rare earths, economically viable deposits of which are similarly located abroad. As Daniel Yergin has pointed out, big oil in the not-too-distant future will certainly be replaced by 'big shovels', which are required to mine the rare earths, iron ore, and other materials required for electric vehicles and other technologies underpinning the energy transition.[8] Neither the Germans nor the Japanese have ever been involved in big oil; nor will they control the resources mined by big shovels. They may design and manufacture some of these giant diggers, but the minerals mined with them lie far beyond their borders.

Then there are the interrelated problems of who will make the cars and the parts required for them as well as who will buy them. The populations of Germany and, even more so, Japan are becoming increasingly elderly, the outcome of persistently low birth rates, rising levels of affluence, and vastly improved healthcare. Unlike the United States or even Great Britain, neither has been a country of immigration. This may well have to change, and, given the extensive influx of refugees into Germany, perhaps it has already started. Japan has also loosened its approach to foreign workers coming into the country, primarily from India, mainly to provide desperately needed staff for its technology industries.[9] But, in any event, if and when widespread immigration occurs, both countries will face the far from trivial problem of effectively integrating incomers into existing culture and society.

* * *

In other words, problems galore, and no simple solutions. That, though, has been a persistent theme throughout this book. The other is the constant reinvention of society and the economy to address the problems, however late, improvised, incomplete, or imperfect the reinvention may be. Surveying the devastation in Germany or Japan in 1945, few could have predicted how rapidly reconstruction would ensue, or that it would be followed rapidly by breathtaking economic growth, characterised by many as miracles.

As the early chapters of this book indicate, the economic performance and accompanying increases in standards of living in both countries were worthy of wonder. But they can be explained, not least through observation and analysis of the economists, politicians, industrialists, workers, and consumers who recast business, banking, and society to make it all happen. Surely, then, they were not miracles if we can explain fully and fairly precisely how they came about and how they have been sustained, even if the post-war economic and technological performance of the two nations has generated marvels.

Another reason for questioning the miraculousness of the German and Japanese 'economic miracles' is precisely *because* economic performance in both cases has been sustained – admittedly imperfectly, and not without interruption – for decades during which prevailing conditions in business, foreign trade, finance, energy, and politics have changed, at times quite dramatically. Both for Germany and for Japan, largely successful adaptation in the face of dependence and fragility has been the name of the game from the start. And this might be the final lesson of this history of the two countries since 1945: adaptation to changing circumstances is an ongoing process, not least because there is no one fixed and unvarying solution to any problem.

As the law requires stockbrokers to tell us, of course, past performance does not guarantee future performance. After all, even though some might characterise the two countries' economic resurgence after 1945 as a 'meteoric rise', we should also consider the fact that meteors can eventually crash to the ground. There can be no certainty, then, but the track record of German and Japanese capitalisms as they have adapted to the vagaries of the global political economy since the end of the Second World War favours guarded optimism about the future.

NOTES

Introduction

1 Reginald Stuart, 'First VW Rolls Off Assembly Line in US', *New York Times* (11 April 1978), pp. 51, 55; Jerry Knight, 'Volkswagen Begins in American Plant Production of Cars', *Washington Post* (11 April 1978).

2 'Honda: A Driving Force in Ohio since 1982', available at https://ohio.honda.com/ our-story (accessed 16 February 2022); 'Honda's First US Car Rolls Out', *New York Times* (2 November 1982), Section D, p. 4. A picture of the car, the opening ceremony, and some members of the marching band is on the 'Honda: A Driving Force in Ohio since 1982' web page. Timothy J. Minchin, *America's Other Automakers: A History of the Foreign-Owned Automotive Sector in the United States* (Athens, GA: University of Georgia Press, 2021), p. 1.

3 Prableen Bajpal, 'The 5 Largest Economies in the World and Their Growth in 2020', 22 January 2020, available at www.nasdaq.com/articles/the-5-largest-economies-in-the-world-and-their-growth-in-2020-2020-01-22 (accessed 3 November 2022).

4 The phrase is widely used for the astonishing economic performance of both countries from the 1950s. See, most recently for Germany, Tamás Vonyó, *The Economic Consequences of the War: West Germany's Growth Miracle after 1945* (Cambridge and New York: Cambridge University Press, 2018); and for Japan, among others, Chalmers Johnson, *MITI and the Japanese Miracle: The Growth of Industrial Policy* (Stanford, CA: Stanford University Press, 1982); and Arthur J. Alexander, *In the Shadow of the Miracle: The Japanese Economy since the End of High-Speed Growth* (Lanham, MD: Lexington Books, 2002). See also (although this author avoids for the most part the phrase 'economic miracle'), Walter F. Hatch, *Asia's Flying Geese: How Regionalization Shapes Japan* (Ithaca, NY: Cornell University Press, 2011).

5 On the German institutionalisation of ingenuity, see Alan D. Beyerchen, 'On the Stimulation of Excellence in Wilhelmian Science', in Jack R. Dukes and Joachim Remak, eds., *Another Germany: A Reconsideration of the Imperial Era* (Boulder, CO: Westview Press, 1988), pp. 139–168. On national systems of innovation in general, and on the German and Japanese systems in particular, see the editor's introduction and relevant essays (by Hiroyuki Odagiri and by Akira Goto and Otto Keck, respectively) in Richard Nelson, ed., *National Systems of Innovation: A Comparative Analysis* (Oxford and New York: Oxford University Press, 1993).

6 The classic statement of this concept and analytical approach is Peter A. Hall and David Soskice, eds., *Varieties of Capitalism: The Institutional Foundations of Comparative Advantage* (Oxford and New York: Oxford University Press, 2001).

7 Thomas Parke Hughes, *Networks of Power: Electrification in Western Society, 1880–1930* (Baltimore, MD: Johns Hopkins University Press, 1983).

8 David Soskice, 'Finer Varieties of Capitalism: Industry versus Group-Based Coordination in Germany and Japan', unpublished paper presented at the conference on Varieties of Capitalism, Poitiers, September 1994.

1 From Foe to Friend: The Allied Military Occupation of Germany and Japan

1 Thomas Pynchon, *Gravity's Rainbow* (New York: Viking, 1973), Part 3, pp. 279–616. For a vivid account of Germany as the war ended and the occupation started, see Douglas Botting, *In the Ruins of the Reich* (London: George Allen & Unwin, 1985).

2 Samuel Goudsmit, *Alsos* (Los Angeles: Tomash, 1983); Dieter Hoffmann, *Operation Epsilon: Die Farm-Hall-Protokolle oder die Angst der Alliierten vor der deutschen Atombombe* (Berlin: Rowohlt, 1993).

3 Clarence G. Lasby, *Project Paperclip: German Scientists and the Cold War* (New York: Atheneum, 1971); Annie Jacobsen, *Operation Paperclip: The Secret Intelligence Program That Brought Nazi Scientists to America* (New York: Little, Brown and Company, 2014).

4 Monique Laney, *German Rocketeers in the Heart of Dixie: Making Sense of the Nazi Past in the Civil Rights Era* (New Haven, CT: Yale University Press, 2015).

5 The most recent and best overview of the effort by all four Allies to collect information on German science and technology is Douglas O'Reagan, *Taking Nazi Technology: Allied Exploitation of German Science after the Second World War* (Baltimore, MD: Johns Hopkins University Press, 2019).

6 Marie-France Ludmann-Obier, 'Un aspect de la chasse aux cerveaux: Les transferts de techniciens allemands en France: 1945–1949', *Relations internationales* 46 (1986): 195–208.

7 Ulrich Albrecht, Andreas Heinemann-Grüder, and Arend Wellmann, *Die Spezialisten: Deutsche Naturwissenschaftler und Techniker in der Sowjetunion nach 1945* (Berlin: Dietz, 1992).

8 For this and the next paragraphs, see for instance Carolyn Eisenberg, *Drawing the Line: The American Decision to Divide Germany, 1944–1949* (Cambridge and New York: Cambridge University Press, 1996).

9 Raymond G. Stokes, *Constructing Socialism: Technology and Change in East Germany, 1945–1990* (Baltimore, MD: Johns Hopkins University Press, 2000), p. 18.

10 John Gimbel, *The American Occupation of Germany: Politics and the Military, 1945–1949* (Stanford: Stanford University Press, 1968), pp. 16–23.

11 For Japan's wartime economic situation, see Alan Milward, *War, Economy and Society, 1939–1945* (Berkeley, CA: University of California Press, 1979), especially pp. 30–36; for the situation immediately after the war's end, see John Dower, *Embracing Defeat: Japan in the Wake of World War II* (London: Allen Lane, 1999), especially Part 1.

12 Mark Metzler, *Capital as Will and Imagination: Schumpeter's Guide to the Postwar Japanese Miracle* (Ithaca, NY: Cornell University Press, 2013), p. 76.

13 Morris Low, 'Japan's Secret War? "Instant" Scientific Manpower and Japan's World War II Atomic Bomb Project', *Annals of Science* 47 (1990): 347–360.

14 The phrase comes from John Dower, *War without Mercy: Race and Power in the Pacific War* (London: Faber, 1986).

15 Eisenberg, *Drawing the Line*.

16 Joseph Borkin and Charles Walsh, with an introduction by Thurman Arnold, *Germany's Master Plan: The Story of an Industrial Offensive* (New York: Duell, Sloan, and Pearce, 1943).

17 Joseph Borkin, *The Crime and Punishment of I.G. Farben* (New York: Pocket Books, 1978), p. ix.

18 Raymond G. Stokes, *Divide and Prosper: The Heirs of IG Farben under Allied Authority, 1945–1951* (Berkeley, CA: University of California Press, 1988).

19 Raymond G. Stokes, 'The Development and Significance of IG Farben i.A. for the Post-war West German Economy', in Alexander Jehn, Albrecht Kirschner, and Nicola Wurthmann, eds., *IG Farben zwischen Schuld und Profit: Abwicklung eines Weltkonzerns* (Marburg: Historische Kommission für Hessen, 2022), pp. 47–59.

20 Stephan H. Lindner, *Aufrüstung – Ausbeutung – Auschwitz: Eine Geschichte des I.G.-Farben-Prozesses* (Göttingen: Wallstein, 2020).

21 Josiah E. DuBois, Jr, *The Devil's Chemists: 24 Conspirators of the International Farben Cartel Who Manufacture War* (Boston: Beacon Press, 1952), p. 339. DuBois refers to twenty-four rather than twenty-three defendants. This is because one of those charged died and therefore did not go to trial in the end. For McCloy's pardons in 1951, see Benjamin B. Ferencz, *Less Than Slaves: Jewish Forced Labor and the Quest for Compensation* (Bloomington, IN: Indiana University Press, 2002), especially pp. 32, 192.

22 BASF Unternehmensarchiv, Ludwigshafen, W 1/2/8.

23 For this and the following, see E. Sydney Crawcour, 'Industrialization and Technological Change, 1885–1920', in Peter Duus, ed., *The Cambridge History of Japan*, vol. VI: *The Twentieth Century* (Cambridge and New York: Cambridge University Press, 1988), pp. 385–450; Tessa Morris-Suzuki, *The Technological Transformation of Japan* (Cambridge and New York: Cambridge University Press, 1994).

24 For the following, see Michael A. Cusumano, '"Scientific Industry": Strategy, Technology, and Entrepreneurship in Pre-war Japan', in William D Wray, ed., *Managing Industrial Enterprise: Cases from Japan's Pre-war Experience* (Cambridge, MA: Harvard University Council on East Asian Studies, 1989), pp. 269–315.

25 See, for instance, Jacobsen, *Operation Paperclip*; Tom Bower, *The Paperclip Conspiracy: The Hunt for Nazi Scientists* (Boston: Little Brown, 1986); John Gimbel, *Science, Technology and Reparations: Exploitation and Plunder in Post-war Germany* (Stanford: Stanford University Press, 1990); O'Reagan, *Taking Nazi Technology*; Albrecht, Heinemann-Grüder, and Wellmann, *Die Spezialisten*.

26 Bower, *The Paperclip Conspiracy*, p. 6.

27 See Jonas Scherner, Jochen Streb, and Stephanie Tilly, 'Supplier Networks in the German Aircraft Industry during World War II and Their Long-Term Effects on West Germany's Automobile Industry during the "Wirtschaftswunder"', *Business History* 56, No. 6 (2014): 996–1020.

28 See William M. Tsutsui, *Manufacturing Ideology: Scientific Management in Twentieth-Century Japan* (Princeton, NJ: Princeton University Press, 1998).

29 See Takashi Nishiyama, 'Cross-disciplinary Technology Transfer in Trans-World War II Japan: The Japanese High-Speed Bullet Train as a Case Study', *Comparative Technology Transfer and Society* 1, No. 3 (December 2003): 305–325, p. 311.

30 Nishiyama, 'Cross-disciplinary Technology Transfer in Trans-World War II Japan', quotation p. 311.

31 Tamás Vonyó, *The Economic Consequences of the War: West Germany's Growth Miracle after 1945* (Cambridge and New York: Cambridge University Press, 2018); Herbert Giersch, Karl-Heinz Paqué, and Holger Schmieding, *The Fading Miracle: Four Decades of Market Economy in Germany* (Cambridge and New York: Cambridge University Press, 1992).

2 The Miracle Makers: (Re-)Constructing Cooperative Capitalism

1 John Stuart Mill, *Principles of Political Economy*, 7th ed. (London: Longmans, Green and Co., 1909), pp. 74–75. A facsimile edition is available at https://oll.libertyfund.org/title/mill-principles-of-political-economy-ashley-ed (accessed 19 August 2021).

2 The classic statement of the reconstruction thesis as applied to post-1945 recovery is Ferenc Janossy, *The End of the Economic Miracle: Appearance and Reality in Economic Development* (White Plains, NY: International Arts and Sciences Press, 1971). A recent overview and refinement of thesis can be found in Tamás Vonyó, *The Economic Consequences of the War: West Germany's Growth Miracle after 1945* (Cambridge and New York: Cambridge University Press, 2018). On the reconstruction thesis applied to Covid-19, see Michael Cembalest, 'John Stuart Mill and the Road from Ruin to Recovery', Eye on the Market, J. P. Morgan, available at https://privatebank.jpmorgan.com/content/dam/jpm-wm-aem/global/pb/en/insights/eye-on-the-market/john-stuart-mill-and-the-road-from-ruin-to-recovery.pdf (accessed 19 August 2021).

3 Mill, *Principles of Political Economy*, 7th ed., p. 75.

4 Denis Martin, 'At Last Erhard Gets the Job', *Daily Mirror* (24 April 1963). The article refers to Erhard succeeding Adenauer as German chancellor following his long stint as Economic Minister.

5 This paragraph and the following draw on Meinhard Knoche, 'Ludwig Erhard and the Ifo Institute: In the Service of German Reconstruction', *CESIfo Forum* 20, No. 2 (June 2019): 32–46.

6 Eckhard Wandel, 'Historical Developments Prior to the German Currency Reform of 1948', *Zeitschrift für die gesamte Staatswissenschaft/Journal of Institutional and Theoretical Economics* 135 (September 1979): 320–331.

7 Herbert Giersch, Karl-Heinz Paqué, and Holger Schmieding, *The Fading Miracle: Four Decades of Market Economy in Germany* (Cambridge and New York: Cambridge University Press, 1992), Chapters 2 and 3.

8 Rainer Karlsch and Raymond G. Stokes, *Faktor Öl: Die Mineralölwirtschaft in Deutschland 1859–1974* (Munich: Beck, 2003), pp. 280–281.

9 James van Hook, *Rebuilding Germany: The Creation of the Social Market Economy* (Cambridge and New York: Cambridge University Press, 2004).

10 Richard Hiscocks, *The Adenauer Era: Germany's Miraculous Post-war Renaissance and the Man Who Created It* (Philadelphia: J. B. Lippencott, 1966); Charles Williams, *Adenauer: The Father of the New Germany* (New York: John Wiley & Sons, 2000).

11 Volker Berghahn, *The Americanisation of West German Industry, 1945–1973* (Cambridge and New York: Cambridge University Press, 1986); Lionel Fulton, 'Code-termination in Germany: A Beginner's Guide', in *Mitbestimmungspraxis*, No. 32, Hans-Böckler-Stiftung, Institut für Mitbestimmung und Unternehmensführung (I.M.U.), Düsseldorf, 2020; available at http://hdl.handle.net/10419/246911 (accessed 14 March 2023).

12 S. Jonathan Wiesen, *West German Industry and the Challenge of the Nazi Past, 1945–1955* (Chapel Hill, NC: University of North Carolina Press, 2001), p. 15.

13 Kim Christian Priemel, *The Betrayal: The Nuremberg Trials and German Divergence* (Oxford and New York: Oxford University Press, 2016).

14 Wiesen, *West German Industry and the Challenge of the Nazi Past*.

15 'W. Alexander Menne', Munzinger Archiv, available at www.munzinger.de/search/ portrait/W+Alexander+Menne/0/6344.html (accessed 31 August 2021).

16 'W. Alexander Menne', Munzinger Archiv; Raymond G. Stokes, *Divide and Prosper: The Heirs of IG Farben under Allied Authority, 1945–1951* (Berkeley, CA: University of California Press, 1988), pp. 175–176. For more on the early history of the BDI as seen through the lens of one of its presidents, see Volker R. Berghahn, *Hans-Günther Sohl als Stahlunternehmer und Präsident des Bundesverbandes der Deutschen Industrie 1906–1989* (Göttingen: Wallstein, 2020).

17 'W. Alexander Menne', Munzinger Archiv.

18 Werner Abelshauser, 'BASF since Its Refounding in 1952', in Werner Abelshauser, Wolfgang von Hippel, Jeffrey Allan Johnson, and Raymond G. Stokes, *German Industry and Global Enterprise: BASF: The History of a Company* (Cambridge and New York: Cambridge University Press, 2004), pp. 363–365. On Abs in the Third Reich, see Lothar Gall, 'Hermann Josef Abs and the Third Reich: "A Man for All Seasons"?', *Financial History Review* 6 (1999): 147–202.

19 John Dower, *Embracing Defeat: Japan in the Aftermath of World War II* (London: Penguin, 1999), pp. 33–38; quotation from p. 36.

20 Mark Metzler, *Capital as Will and Imagination: Schumpeter's Guide to the Postwar Japanese Miracle* (Ithaca, NY: Cornell University Press, 2013), pp. 69–70; Laura E. Hein, 'In Search of Peace and Democracy: Japanese Economic Debate in Political Context', *The Journal of Asian Studies* 53, No. 3 (August 1994): 752–778, here p. 757.

21 Hein, 'In Search of Peace and Democracy', p. 757; Saburo Okita, *Japan in the World Economy* (Tokyo: The Japan Foundation, 1975), pp. 1–2; Metzler, *Capital as Will and Imagination*, pp. 69–70, quotation from p. 70.

22 Okita, *Japan in the World Economy*, p. 2.

23 Hein, 'In Search of Peace and Democracy', p. 758; Metzler, *Capital as Will and Imagination*, pp. 66–81, quotation from p. 66.

24 Okita, *Japan in the World Economy*, p. 5; Johannes Hirschmeier and Tsunehiko Yui, *The Development of Japanese Business*, 2nd ed. (London: George Allen & Unwin, 1981), pp. 290–291.

25 For this and the following paragraph, see Chalmers Johnson, *MITI and the Japanese Miracle: The Growth of Industrial Policy, 1925–1974* (Stanford: Stanford University Press, 1982), especially Chapter 2; quotation from p. 41.

26 Toshihiro Kodama, 'Role of Government (Industrial Policy)', in Japan Commission on Industrial Performance, ed., *Made in Japan: Revitalizing Japanese Manufacturing for Economic Growth* (Cambridge, MA: MIT Press, 1997), pp. 359–389.

27 P. K. Hall claims that things were not as bad as most scholars have portrayed them, but he admits that landlords and politicians at the time were also circulating the idea that there was an agrarian crisis. See P. K. Hall, 'Japan's Farm Sector, 1920–1940: A Need for a Reassessment', *Agricultural History* 58, No. 4 (October 1984): 595–616.

28 Ronald P. Dore, 'The Japanese Land Reform in Retrospect', *Far Eastern Survey* 27 (December 1958): 183–188; James Babb, 'Making Farmers Conservative: Japanese Farmers, Land Reform, and Socialism', *Social Science Japan Journal* 8 (2005): 175–195.

29 Hirschmeier and Yui, *The Development of Japanese Business*, pp. 284–288, quotation from p. 287.

30 Mark Metzler, 'The Occupation', in W. M. Tsutsui, ed., *A Companion to Japanese History* (Oxford: Blackwell, 2007), pp. 265–280, quotation from p. 269.

31 Mill, *Principles of Political Economy*, 7th ed., p. 75.

32 Metzler, *Capital as Will and Imagination*, pp. 78–81; Hirschmeier and Yui, *The Development of Japanese Business*, pp. 288–290.

33 Metzler, *Capital as Will and Imagination*, p. 79.

3 Manufacturing Miracles I: Forging Alternative Fordisms

1 On Arisawa, see Mark Metzler, *Capital as Will and Imagination: Schumpeter's Guide to the Post-war Japanese Miracle* (Ithaca, NY: Cornell University Press, 2013); Laura E. Hein, 'In Search of Peace and Democracy: Japanese Economic Debate in Political Context', *The Journal of East Asian Studies* 53, No. 3 (August 1994): 752–778, especially pp. 768–769; Raymond G. Stokes, *Divide and Prosper: The Heirs of IG Farben under Allied Authority, 1945–1951* (Berkeley, CA: University of California Press, 1988), pp. 42–49.

2 Michael Hughes, *The Anarchy of Nazi Memorabilia: From Things of Tyranny to Troubled Treasure* (London: Routledge, 2022), pp. 65–66.

3 Adam Tooze, *The Wages of Destruction: The Making and Breaking of the Nazi Economy* (London: Allen Lane, 2006), especially pp. 20–23. For more on the pre-1945 admiration and attempted implementation of Fordism internationally, including in Nazi Germany, see Stefan J. Link, *Forging Global Fordism: Nazi Germany, Soviet Russia, and the Contest over the Industrial Order* (Princeton, NJ: Princeton University Press, 2020).

4 Wolfgang König, 'Adolf Hitler vs. Henry Ford: The Volkswagen, the Role of America as Model, and the Failure of a Nazi Consumer Society', *German Studies Review* 27, No. 2 (May 2004): 249–268; Bernhard Rieger, *The People's Car: A Global History of the Volkswagen Beetle* (Cambridge, MA: Harvard University Press, 2013); Hans Mommsen with Manfred Grieger, *Das Volkswagenwerk und seine Arbeiter im Dritten Reich* (Düsseldorf: Econ, 1996); Steven Tolliday, 'Enterprise and State in the West German *Wirtschaftswunder*: Volkswagen and the Automobile Industry, 1939–1962', *Business History Review* 69, No. 3 (Autumn 1995): 273–350.

5 König, 'Adolf Hitler vs. Henry Ford', p. 256.

6 Tolliday, 'Enterprise and State in the West German *Wirtschaftswunder*', especially pp. 279–285; 'Es läßt sich nachrechnen. Volkswagen-Sparer', *Der Spiegel* 8/1952 (19 February 1952).

7 Figures on vehicle density in 1935 and estimated increases in employment for the motor industry in 1938 from Richard J. Overy, 'Cars, Roads and Economic Recovery in Germany, 1932–1938', *Economic History Review* 28, No. 3 (August 1975): 466–483, Table 3, p. 470 and Table 8, p. 478.

8 Tolliday, 'Enterprise and State in the West German *Wirtschaftswunder*', pp. 277–278; Rieger, *The People's Car*, pp. 28–29.

9 Tolliday, 'Enterprise and State in the West German *Wirtschaftswunder*', pp. 285–311.

10 Ralf Richter, *Ivan Hirst: British Officer and Manager of Volkswagen's Post-war Recovery* (Wolfsburg: Volkswagen AG, 2003), pp. 35–36, 46–47.

11 Tolliday, 'Enterprise and State in the West German *Wirtschaftswunder*', pp. 301–308.

12 Richter, *Ivan Hirst*, pp. 73–85.

13 Richter, *Ivan Hirst*; 'Heinrich Nordhoff', citation for induction into the Automotive Hall of Fame, www.automotivehalloffame.org/honoree/heinrich-nordhoff (accessed 15 October 2021).

14 Quotations from interview with Ivan Hirst, 21–23 October 1997, pp. 70, 118–120, 132. Cited in Richter, *Ivan Hirst*, pp. 87–88. See also Richter, *Ivan Hirst*, pp. 86–92.

15 Richter, *Ivan Hirst*, pp. 82–84; Nordhoff quoted in Tolliday, 'Enterprise and State in the West German *Wirtschaftswunder*', p. 330.

16 Tolliday, 'Enterprise and State in the West German *Wirtschaftswunder*', p. 329.

17 Tolliday, 'Enterprise and State in the West German *Wirtschaftswunder*', Table 1, p. 326.

18 Tolliday, 'Enterprise and State in the West German *Wirtschaftswunder*', pp. 331–333, quotation from p. 331.

19 Quoted in Tolliday, 'Enterprise and State in the West German *Wirtschaftswunder*', p. 323.

20 This paragraph and the two that follow are based on Tolliday, 'Enterprise and State in the West German *Wirtschaftswunder*', especially pp. 340–345; and Katje Fuder, 'No Experiments: Federal Privatisation Politics in West Germany 1949–1989', PhD Thesis, London School of Economics, 2017.

21 Rüdiger Strempel, 'Kleinsparer gegen VW – ein Prozessmarathon. Käfer-Klagen', *Der Spiegel* (1 May 2018); available at www.spiegel.de/geschichte/vom-kdf-wagen-zum-kaefer-warum-kleinsparer-vw-verklagten-a-1203308.html (accessed 18 October 2021).

22 Tolliday, 'Enterprise and State in the West German *Wirtschaftswunder*', pp. 337–340.

23 Herbert Giersch, Karl-Heinz Paqué, and Holger Schmieding, *The Fading Miracle: Four Decades of Market Economy in Germany* (Cambridge and New York: Cambridge University Press, 1992), especially Chapters 1, 3, and 4.

24 Tolliday, 'Enterprise and State in the West German *Wirtschaftswunder*', Table 2, p. 329.

25 Michael Cusumano, '"Scientific Industry": Strategy, Technology, and Entrepreneurship in Pre-war Japan', pp. 269–315, in William Wray, ed., *Managing Industrial Enterprise: Cases from Japan's Pre-war Experience* (Cambridge, MA: Harvard University Council on East Asian Studies, 1989), quotation from p. 284. For German commitments to technocracy, see Thomas Parke Hughes, 'Technology', in Henry Friedlander and Sybil Milton, eds., *The Holocaust: Ideology, Bureaucracy, and Genocide* (Millwood, NY: Kraus International, 1980), pp. 165–181; Kees Gispen, 'Visions of Utopia: Social Emancipation, Technological Progress, and Anticapitalism in Nazi Inventor Policy, 1933–1945', *Central European History* 32 (1999): 35–51.

26 Cusumano, '"Scientific Industry"'.

27 Toshihiro Kodama, 'Role of Government (Industrial Policy)', in Japan Commission on Industrial Performance, ed., *Made in Japan: Revitalizing Japanese Manufacturing for Economic Growth* (Cambridge, MA: MIT Press, 1997), pp. 359–389.

28 Takahiro Fujimoto, *The Evolution of a Manufacturing System at Toyota* (Oxford and New York: Oxford University Press, 1999), pp. 32–33; J. Hirschmeier and T. Yui, *The Development of Japanese Business*, 2nd ed. (London: George Allen & Unwin, 1981), p. 307; share of production in the early 1980s from Takahiro Fujimoto and Akira Takeishi, 'Automobile Industry', in Japan Commission on Industrial Performance, ed., *Made in Japan: Revitalizing Japanese Manufacturing for Economic Growth* (Cambridge, MA: MIT Press, 1997), pp. 71–95, Figure 3.1, p. 74.

29 This evolution is the subject of Fujimoto, *The Evolution of a Manufacturing System at Toyota*, especially Chapters 2 and 3.

30 Kazuo Wada, 'Koichiro Toyoda and the Birth of the Japanese Automobile Industry: Reconsideration of Toyoda–Platt Agreement', CIRJE Discussion Paper

CIRJE-F-288 (2004), quotation from p. 7. Available at https://core.ac.uk/down
load/pdf/6341781.pdf (accessed 25 October 2021).

31 Hirschmeier and Yui, *The Development of Japanese Business*, p. 308.

32 For this and the next paragraph, Hirschmeier and Yui, *The Development of
Japanese Business*, p. 308; Fujimoto, *The Evolution of a Manufacturing System at
Toyota*, pp. 60–61.

33 Fujimoto, *The Evolution of a Manufacturing System at Toyota*, Chapters 2 and 3,
quotation from p. 61. See also Taiichi Ohno's somewhat rambling account of his
role in developing the Toyota system, where he makes the points about the need
to adapt US-style mass-production methods and about the influence of his experience in loom production on his work with automobiles, in Taiichi Ohno, 'How
the Toyota System Was Created', in Kazuo Sato and Yasuo Hoshino, eds., *The
Anatomy of Japanese Business*, 2nd ed. (Abingdon: Routledge, 2011), pp. 133–134.

34 Fujimoto, *The Evolution of a Manufacturing System at Toyota*, Chapters 2 and 3
and appendix B, especially p. 287.

35 See William M. Tsutsui, 'W. Edwards Deming and the Origins of Quality Control in
Japan', *Journal of Japanese Studies* 22, No. 2 (Summer 1996): 295–325, especially
pp. 296–298.

36 Peter M. Leitner, 'Japan's Post-war Economic Success: Deming, Quality, and
Contextual Realities', *Journal of Management History* 5, No. 8 (1999): 489–505,
especially pp. 490–491.

37 'Editorial: Giants of Quality – W. Edwards Deming', *Quality, Reliability, and
Engineering International* 28 (2012): 247–248.

38 Leitner, 'Japan's Post-war Economic Success: Deming, Quality, and Contextual
Realities'. For a careful and critical overview of Deming's contributions to Japanese
and American quality-control efforts, see Tsutsui, 'W. Edwards Deming and the
Origins of Quality Control in Japan'.

39 Leitner, 'Japan's Post-war Economic Success: Deming, Quality, and Contextual
Realities'; J. Richard Hackman and Ruth Wageman, 'Total Quality Management:
Empirical, Conceptual and Practical Issues', *Administrative Science Quarterly* 40,
No. 2 (June 1995): 309–342.

4 Manufacturing Miracles II: From Humble Craftsmen to World Beaters

1 E. K. Neumann and Walter Dorn, 'Conversation', 4 June 1949, pp. 28–30, Records
of the US Military Government for Hesse, 8/187-2/11, in Hauptstaatsarchiv Hessen,
649, Wiesbaden.

2 Walter L. Dorn, 'Zur Entstehungsgeschichte des Landes Hessen' [in English],
Vierteljahrshefte für Zeitgeschichte 6 (April 1958): 191–196; Lutz Niethammer,
'Einleitung', in Walter L. Dorn, *Inspektionsreisen in der US-Zone: Notizen,
Denkschriften und Erinnerungen aus dem Nachlaß* (Stuttgart: Deutsche Verlags-
Anstalt, 1973), pp. 8–17; 'Ernst Karl Neumann', *Who's Who in America* 26
(1950/1951), p. 2010, and *Who's Who in America* 30 (1958/1959), p. 2034.
Additional information is from 'COL Ernest Karl "Doc" Neumann', available
at www.findagrave.com/memorial/66171294/ernest-karl-neumann (accessed 29
September 2021).

3 See, for instance, Guy Hartcup, *The Effect of Science on the Second World War*
(Basingstoke: Macmillan, 2000).

4 Jürgen Kocka, 'The Rise of the Modern Industrial Enterprise in Germany', in Alfred
D. Chandler, Jr, and Herman Daems, eds., *Managerial Hierarchies: Comparative
Perspectives on the Rise of the Modern Industrial Enterprise* (Cambridge,

MA: Harvard University Press, 1980), pp. 77–116, quotation from p. 110. For works that explore this industrial and technological dualism in Germany and the symbiotic relationship between the two sectors of the economy, see Gary Herrigel, *Industrial Constructions: The Sources of German Industrial Power* (Cambridge and New York: Cambridge University Press, 1996); and Raymond G. Stokes, 'Technology and the West German *Wirtschaftswunder*', *Technology and Culture* 32 (1991): 1–22.

5 Laura E. Hein, 'In Search of Peace and Democracy: Japanese Economic Debate in Political Context', *The Journal of Asian Studies* 53, No. 3 (August 1994): 752–778, here pp. 767–769, quotation from p. 768.

6 Hein, 'In Search of Peace and Democracy', p. 768. Hein is summarising insights from Alexander Gerschenkron, *Economic Backwardness in Historical Perspective* (Cambridge, MA: Belknap Press of Harvard University Press, 1962).

7 'How Germany Became Europe's Richest Country', 9 February 2012, available at www.youtube.com/watch?v=Uad1Ma5DSMA (accessed 9 November 2022). On the *Mittelstand*, see Hermann Simon, *Hidden Champions of the 21st Century: The Success Strategies of Unknown World Market Leaders* (New York: Springer, 2009); Jeffrey Fear, 'Straight outta Oberberg: Transforming Mid-sized German Family Firms into Global Champions, 1970–2010', *Jahrbuch für Wirtschaftsgeschichte/ Yearbook for Economic History* 53, No. 1 (2012): 125–169; David Paulson, *Family Firms in Postwar Britain and Germany: Competing Approaches to Business* (London: Boydell Press, 2023).

8 'How Germany Became Europe's Richest Country'.

9 Quotations from E. K. Neumann and Walter Dorn, 'Conversation', 4 June 1949, pp. 28–30, Records of the US Military Government for Hesse, 8/187-2/11, in Hauptstaatsarchiv Hessen, 649, Wiesbaden.

10 Much of the following draws on the excellent monograph by Frederick L. McKitrick, *From Craftsmen to Capitalists: German Artisans from the Third Reich to the Federal Republic, 1939–1953* (New York and Oxford: Berghahn Books, 2016).

11 For an excellent overview of this process, which includes attention to both Germany and Japan among other countries, see Jeffrey Fear, 'War of the Factories', in Michael Geyer and Adam Tooze, eds., *The Cambridge History of the Second World War*, vol. III: *Total War: Economy, Society, and Culture* (Cambridge and New York: Cambridge University Press, 2015), pp. 94–121.

12 'Automobile History in the Making', available at www.draexlmaier.com/en/company/ history (accessed 11 November 2021).

13 Fear, 'Straight outta Oberberg', pp. 144–145. See also www.trumpf.com/en_GB/ company/history (accessed 11 November 2021).

14 See the brief overview of the company's history at www.kaercher.com/de/inside-kaercher/unternehmen/ueber-kaercher/innovativ-von-anfang-an.html (accessed 11 November 2021).

15 See Fear, 'Straight outta Oberberg', especially pp. 142–143; and Stihl, *90 Years Stihl, 1926–1916* (Waiblingen: Stihl, 2016), especially pp. 4–7, available at www .stihl.com/history.aspx (accessed 11 November 2021).

16 David B. Audretsch and Julie A. Elston, 'Financing the German *Mittelstand* ', *Small Business Economics* 9, No. 2 (April 1997): 97–110, especially pp. 102–103.

17 See, for instance, Hartmut Berghoff and Ingo Köhler, *Varieties of Family Business: Germany and the United States, Past and Present* (Frankfurt am Main and New York: Campus, 2021).

18 See, for instance, 'Fraunhofer Chronicle', available at www.fraunhofer.de/en/ about-fraunhofer/profile-structure/chronicles/fraunhofer-chronicle/1949-1954.html #756514608 (accessed 12 November 2021).

19 'Under Pressure: Japan's *Mittelstand*', *The Economist* (8 March 2008): 81–82.

20 Yoshio Sato, 'Small Business in Japan: A Historical Perspective', *Small Business Economics* 1, No. 2 (1989): 121–128.

21 Sato, 'Small Business in Japan'. Quotations from the Law to Establish the Small and Medium Enterprise Agency of August 1948, p. 126.

22 Sato, 'Small Business in Japan', p. 126. The point about the extreme proportion of the Japanese economy devoted to the war effort comes from Alan Milward, *War, Economy, and Society, 1939–1945* (Berkeley, CA: University of California Press, 1977), especially pp. 30–36.

23 Sato, 'Small Business in Japan', pp. 122–123, 126.

24 Sato, 'Small Business in Japan', p. 127.

25 Robert E. Cole, 'Permanent Employment in Japan: Fact and Fantasies', *ILR Review* 26, No. 1 (October 1972): 615–630, quotation from p. 617.

26 Sato, 'Small Business in Japan', p. 126.

27 www.toyota-global.com/company/history_of_toyota/75years/data/automotive_business/production/purchasing/member_companies/kyohokai.html (accessed 17 November 2021); www.dnb.com/business-directory/company-profiles.aichi_hikaku_industry_coltd.c28b253e0f131ad5bf18126ca973afoe.html (accessed 17 November 2021); www.dnb.com/business-directory/company-profiles.aichi_hikaku_industry_coltd.c28b253e0f131ad5bf18126ca973afoe.html (accessed 18 November 2021); www.aisin-chem.co.jp/english/company/outline.html (accessed 17 November 2021).

28 'Tokai Rika Co. Ltd', *Financial Times*, https://markets.ft.com/data/equities/tearsheet/profile?s=6995:TYO (accessed 18 November 2021).

29 www.tokai-rika.co.jp/en/company/history/special (accessed 17 November 2021).

30 NBK, 'Corporate History', available at www.nbk1560.com/en/company/history/#com_nav02 (accessed 15 November 2021).

31 NBK, 'Corporate History'; 'Under Pressure: Japan's *Mittelstand*', *The Economist* (8 March 2008): 81–82, quotation from p. 82.

32 Demachi Yuzuru, 'How Traditional Metalworker Nousaku Created a Unique Brand', 27 January 2020, available at www.nippon.com/en/japan-topics/g00805/how-traditional-metalworker-nousaku-created-a-unique-brand.html (accessed 17 November 2021); www.nousaku.co.jp/en/about (accessed 17 November 2021).

33 Audretsch and Elston, 'Financing the German *Mittelstand*', p. 97.

5 Consuming Miracles

1 Roy Tomizawa, 'The Three Sacred Treasures of Post-war Japan: A Television, a Refrigerator and a Washing Machine', *The Olympians 1964 to 2020*, available at https://theolympians.co/2015/07/18/the-three-sacred-treasures-of-post-war-japan-a-television-a-refrigerator-and-a-washing-machine (accessed 21 November 2022).

2 Simon Partner makes this point convincingly with regard to the development of the Japanese consumer electronics industry prior to its export drive in the 1960s. Simon Partner, *Assembled in Japan: Electrical Goods and the Making of the Japanese Consumer* (Berkeley, CA: University of California Press, 1999).

3 James Bartholomew, *The Formation of Science in Japan: Building a Research Tradition* (New Haven and London: Yale University Press, 1989), especially pp. 73, 76–77, 80–82, 100–103, 206–208.

4 Data from statistics in spreadsheet compiled by Maddison Project, Maddison Project Database 2020, available at www.rug.nl/ggdc/historicaldevelopment/maddison/releases/maddison-project-database-2020 (accessed 16 March 2023).

5 Percentages calculated on basis of statistics in spreadsheet compiled by Maddison Project, Maddison Project Data 2020. The figures are based on constant 2011 prices.

6 Donna Hirsch, 'Industrialization, Mass Consumption, Post-industrial Society', in Helmut Walser Smith, ed., *The Oxford Handbook of Modern German History* (Oxford and New York: Oxford University Press, 2011), pp. 727–755, here p. 734.

7 Cissie Fairchilds, 'Consumption in Early Modern Europe: A Review Article', *Comparative Studies in Society and History* 35, No. 4 (October 1993): 850–858.

8 S. Jonathan Wiesen, *Creating the Nazi Marketplace: Commerce and Consumption in the Third Reich* (Cambridge and New York: Cambridge University Press, 2011).

9 See, for instance, Jan Logemann, *Trams or Tailfins: Public and Private Prosperity in Post-war West Germany and the United States* (Chicago: University of Chicago Press, 2012); Sean Vanatta, 'Citibank, Credit Cards, and the Local Politics of National Consumer Finance, 1968–1991', *Business History Review* 90, No. 1 (2016): 57–80.

10 Sue Bowden and Avner Offer, 'Household Appliances and the Use of Time: The United States and Britain since the 1920s', *Economic History Review*, New Series, 47, No. 4 (November 1994): 725–748, Table A1, pp. 745–746.

11 Bowden and Offer, 'Household Appliances and the Use of Time', Table A1, pp. 745–746.

12 David Landes, *The Unbound Prometheus: Technological Change and Economic Development in Western Europe from 1750 to the Present*, 2nd ed. (Cambridge and New York: Cambridge University Press, 2003 [1969]), pp. 427–430, especially p. 428.

13 Heather Chappells and Hiroki Shin, 'Making Material and Cultural Connections: The Fluid Meaning of "Living Electrically" in Japan and Canada, 1920–1960', *Science Museum Group Journal* (Spring 2018), available at https://journal.science museum.ac.uk/article/living-electrically/#abstract (accessed 9 September 2023). For adoption rates of radios in the late 1950s and early 1960s, see Susumu Ishii, 'A Research Note: Diffusion of Durable Consumer Goods in Japan', *Gakushuin Economic Papers* 36, No. 1 (April 1999): 1–26, p. 5, Figure 1.5.

14 Bowden and Offer, 'Household Appliances and the Use of Time', Table A1, pp. 745–746. For more on US householders' love affair with the refrigerator, see Jonathan Rees, *Refrigeration Nation: A History of Ice, Appliances, and Enterprise in America* (Baltimore, MD: Johns Hopkins University Press, 2013).

15 Bowden and Offer, 'Household Appliances and the Use of Time', Table A1, pp. 745–746; US Department of Commerce, Business and Defense Services Administration, *Major Household Appliances: Production; Consumption; Trade. Selected Foreign Countries* (Washington, DC: US Government Printing Office, 1960), p. 111; Chappells and Shin, 'Making Material and Cultural Connections'.

16 See, for instance, Victoria de Grazia, 'Changing Consumption Regimes in Europe, 1930–1970: Comparative Perspectives on the Distribution Problem', in Susan Strasser, Charles McGovern, and Matthias Judt, eds., *Getting and Spending: European and American Consumer Societies in the Twentieth Century* (Cambridge and New York: Cambridge University Press, 1998), pp. 59–83; Jan Logemann, *Trams or Tailfins*, especially Chapter 3.

17 Bowden and Offer, 'Household Appliances and the Use of Time', Table A1, pp. 745–746; Rees, *Refrigeration Nation*, p. 179; Ishii, 'A Research Note', Figure 1.3, p. 3; US Department of Commerce, Business and Defense Services Administration, *Major Household Appliances*, pp. 105, 111.

18 Bowden and Offer, 'Household Appliances and the Use of Time', Table A1, pp. 745–746; Rees, *Refrigeration Nation*, p. 179; Ishii, 'A Research Note', Figure 1.2, p. 3; US Department of Commerce, Business and Defense Services Administration, *Major Household Appliances*, p. 111; Hirsch, 'Industrialization, Mass Consumption, Post-industrial Society', Table 29.1.

19 Logemann, *Trams or Tailfins*, Table 5, p. 82. Figures on Japan are from Japanese Economic Planning Agency, *Economic Manual* (1986), cited in *The Japan of Today* (Tokyo: International Society for Educational Information, 1989).

20 Bosch refrigerator advertisement from 1965, available at www.bsh-group.com/about-bsh/history-of-bsh/advertising-through-the-ages (accessed 19 January 2022); Chappells and Shin, 'Making Material and Cultural Connections', Figure 4; Ruth Schwartz Cowan, *More Work for Mother: The Ironies of Household Technology from the Open Hearth to the Microwave* (New York: Basic Books, 1983).

21 Logemann, *Trams or Tailfins*, Chapter 3, especially Table 4, p. 81; Charles Yuji Horioka, 'Consuming and Saving', in Andrew Gordon, ed., *Post-war Japan as History* (Berkeley, CA: University of California Press, 1993), pp. 259–292, especially pp. 264–273.

22 Logemann, *Trams or Tailfins*, especially Chapter 3; Horioka, 'Consuming and Saving'.

23 Logemann, *Trams or Tailfins*, esp. Chapter 3; Horioka, 'Consuming and Saving'; Andrew Gordon, 'Consumption, Consumerism, and Japanese Modernity', in Frank Trentmann, ed., *The Oxford Handbook of the History of Consumption* (Oxford and New York: Oxford University Press, 2012), pp. 485–504.

24 US Department of Commerce, Business and Defense Services Administration, *Major Household Appliances*, quotations from pp. iii, 1.

25 US Department of Commerce, Business and Defense Services Administration, *Major Household Appliances*, pp. 1–2, quotations from p. 2.

26 US Department of Commerce, Business and Defense Services Administration, *Major Household Appliances*, pp. 3–6.

27 US Department of Commerce, Business and Defense Services Administration, *Major Household Appliances*, pp. x, 3, 112–114, quotation from p. 114.

28 US Department of Commerce, Business and Defense Services Administration, *Major Household Appliances*, p. 116, my emphasis.

29 US Department of Commerce, Business and Defense Services Administration, *Major Household Appliances*, pp. 137–142, quotations from pp. 137 and 142.

30 The point here with regard to white goods is reinforced by the evidence and argument in relation to consumer electronics (now called black goods) in Partner, *Assembled in Japan*.

31 US Department of Commerce, Business and Defense Services Administration, *Major Household Appliances*, pp. 140–141; Kei Takeuchi, 'Home Electric Appliance Industry', in Japan Commission on Industrial Performance, ed., *Made in Japan: Revitalizing Japanese Manufacturing for Economic Growth* (Cambridge, MA: MIT Press, 1997), pp. 51–70, especially pp. 57–59.

32 Herbert Giersch, Karl-Heinz Paqué, and Holger Schmieding, *The Fading Miracle: Four Decades of Market Economy in Germany* (Cambridge and New York: Cambridge University Press, 1992), p. 14, Figure 7.

33 'Exports and Imports as Proportion of GNP in 1966', in Jon Livingston, Joe Moore, and Felicia Oldfather, eds., *Post-war Japan: 1945 to the Present* (New York: Pantheon, 1973), p. 439.

6 Exporting Wonders

1 For this and the following paragraph, see Mark Hamilton, 'The Ad That Changed Advertising: The Story behind Volkswagen's Think Small Campaign', Medium (20 March 2015), available at https://medium.com/theagency/the-ad-that-changed-advertising-18291a67488c (accessed 2 December 2021). See also Christian

Kleinschmidt, 'Driving the West German Consumer Society: The Introduction of US Style Production and Marketing at Volkswagen, 1945–1970', in Akira Kudo, Matthias Kipping, and Harm G. Schröter, eds., *German and Japanese Business in the Boom Years: Transforming American Management and Technology Models* (London and New York: Routledge, 2004), pp. 75–92. Quotation from Hamilton.

2 Sebastian Bell, 'Top 10 Most Memorable VW Ads Ever Created', AutoGuide. com (24 October 2021), available at www.autoguide.com/auto-news/2016/10/top-10-most-memorable-volkswagen-ads-ever-created.html (accessed 2 December 2021).

3 Overall production and exports from Steven Tolliday, 'Enterprise and State in the West German *Wirtschaftswunder*: Volkswagen and the Automobile Industry, 1939–1962', *Business History Review* 69, No. 3 (Autumn 1995): 279–350, here Table 1, p. 326. Regarding exports to the United States, see Kleinschmidt, 'Driving the West German Consumer Society', Table 4.2, p. 87.

4 Walter Henry Nelson, *Small Wonder: The Amazing Story of the Volkswagen Beetle* (Cambridge, MA: Bentley Publishers, 1970).

5 Robert J. Simcoe, 'The Revolution in Your Pocket', *Invention & Technology Magazine* 20, No. 4 (Fall 2004). Purchasing power equivalents calculated at this site: www.measuringworth.com/calculators/ppowerus (accessed 21 November 2022).

6 Increases in exports from 1950 to 1960 calculated on the basis of figures in Tables XII and XV of UN, 'International Trade Statistics 1900–1960' (May 1962), which also provides percentages of world exports. The document is available at https://unstats.un.org/unsd/trade/imts/Historical%20data%201900-1960.pdf (accessed 1 December 2021). Increases from 1960 to 1970 calculated on the basis of data extracted from the dataset 'Trade in Value, Classified by Sections of SITC', in OECD.Stat, extracted 6 December 2021. The latter figures for 1960 are close, but not identical, to those for the same year in the May 1962 document. Exports as percentage of GNP are from Louis Kraar, 'How the Japanese Mount That Export Blitz', *Fortune* 32, No. 3 (September 1970), pp. 127–130, 170, 172, reproduced in Jon Livingston, Joe Moore, and Felicia Oldfather, eds., *Post-war Japan: 1945 to the Present* (New York: Pantheon, 1973), pp. 432–438, figures on p. 438.

7 Federal Ministry for Economic Affairs and Energy, 'Facts about German Foreign Trade' (Berlin, September 2019), Figure 11, p. 9. Available at www.bmwk.de/Redaktion/EN/Publikationen/facts-about-german-foreign-trade.pdf?__blob=publicationFile&v=10 (accessed 7 December 2019).

8 Rainer Vollmer, Wolfgang F. Stolper, and Michael Hudson, 'The Structure of West German Foreign Trade', *Zeitschrift für die gesamte Staatswissenschaft/Journal of Institutional and Theoretical Economics* 137 (September 1981): 575–589. Here, Table 5, p. 583.

9 Bo Carlsson, 'The Machine Tool Industry: Problems and Prospects in an International Perspective', IUI Working Paper No. 96, The Research Institute of Industrial Economics (IUI), Stockholm (1983), p. 1.

10 Carlsson, 'The Machine Tool Industry', pp. 1–2.

11 Raymond G. Stokes, *Constructing Socialism: Technology and Change in East Germany, 1945–1990* (Baltimore, MD: Johns Hopkins University Press, 2000).

12 Axel Wieandt, 'Innovation and the Creation, Development and Destruction of Markets in the World Machine Tool Industry', *Small Business Economics* 6, No. 6 (December 1994): 421–437, Table I, p. 428.

13 Carlsson, 'The Machine Tool Industry', pp. 9–11.

14 Robert Forrant, 'The Cutting-Edge Dulled: The Post-Second World War Decline of the United States Machine Tool Industry', *International Contributions to Labour Studies* 7 (1997): 37–58, here pp. 55–57, quotation from MIT study on p. 56.

15 See Stokes, *Constructing Socialism*; André Steiner, *The Plans That Failed: An Economic History of the GDR* (Oxford and New York: Berghahn Books, 2010).

16 Frank C. Englmann [sic] et.al., 'The German Machine-Tool Industry', in David Finegold, ed., *The Decline of the U.S. Machine-Tool Industry and Prospects for Its Sustainable Recovery*, vol. II: *Appendices* (Santa Monica, CA: RAND, 1994), pp. 23–68, especially pp. 25, 29–32, 48–52.

17 Chris Bryant, 'German Printing Press Makers Struggle', *Financial Times* (18 January 2012).

18 Information on the firm's history is available from www.krones.com/en/company-history (accessed 14 December 2021).

19 '100 Years of thyssenkrupp Uhde', available at www.thyssenkrupp-industrial-solutions.com/en/media/press-releases/100-years-of-thyssenkrupp-uhde (accessed 14 December 2021).

20 Raymond G. Stokes and Ralf Banken, *Building on Air: The International Industrial Gases Industry, 1886–2006* (Cambridge and New York: Cambridge University Press, 2016). See also Hans-Liudger Dienel, *Die Linde AG: Geschichte eines Technologiekonzerns 1879–2004* (Munich: Beck, 2004).

21 Gary Herrigel makes this point about the opportunities for specialist machine firms afforded by mass production (although not the point about mass consumption). Gary Herrigel, *Industrial Constructions: The Sources of German Industrial Power* (Cambridge and New York: Cambridge University Press, 1996), especially Chapter 5. Herrigel also indicates that servicing mass producers initially involved a large degree of dependence on larger companies – and therefore surrendering of independence of action – for the specialist machine producers.

22 Raymond G. Stokes, *Opting for Oil: The Political Economy of Technological Change in the West German Chemical Industry, 1945–1961* (Cambridge and New York: Cambridge University Press, 1994).

23 Günther Daumillier and Rudolf Keller, 'Eindrücke einer Reise in den Vereinigten Staaten … im Herbst 1953', in BASF Unternehmensarchiv, Ludwigshafen F9/39, p. 3, quoted in Stokes, *Opting for Oil*, p. 116.

24 Raymond G. Stokes, *Divide and Prosper: The Heirs of IG Farben under Allied Authority, 1945–1951* (Berkeley, CA: University of California Press, 1988), pp. 204–205.

25 Claudia H. Deutsch, 'A Campaign for BASF', *New York Times* (26 October 2004).

26 'Japan and Gatt [sic]', *The Economist* (26 July 1952): 252.

27 For instance, 'Trade with Japan', *The Economist* (6 February 1954): 407–408.

28 'Heartbreak of a Salesman: Where Are the Japanese to Sell Their Goods? So Many Doors Are Shut to Them', *The Economist* (8 March 1958): 23–24, quotation p. 23.

29 Kraar, 'How the Japanese Mount That Export Blitz', quotation from pp. 432–433.

30 Tessa Morris-Suzuki, *The Technological Transformation of Japan: From the Seventeenth to the Twenty-First Century* (Cambridge and New York: Cambridge University Press, 1994), pp. 128, 134. For more detail on the pre-war state of the machine-tool industry in Japan, see David Friedman, *The Misunderstood Miracle: Industrial Development and Political Change in Japan* (Ithaca, NY: Cornell University Press, 1988), Chapter 2.

31 Morris-Suzuki, *The Technological Transformation of Japan*, pp. 199–200.

32 See Friedman, *The Misunderstood Miracle*.

33 Morris-Suzuki, *The Technological Transformation of Japan*, pp. 199–202.

34 Wieandt, 'Innovation and the Creation, Development, and Destruction of Markets in the World Machine Tool Industry', Table I, p. 428.

35 David Noble, 'Social Choice in Machine Design: The Case of Automatically Controlled Machine Tools, and a Challenge for Labor', *Politics & Society* 8, No. 3–4 (1978): 313–347, quotation from p. 329.

36 Leonard H. Lynn, 'The Commercialization of the Transistor Radio in Japan: The Functioning of an Innovation Community', *IEEE Transactions on Engineering Management* 45, No. 3 (August 1998): 220–229, especially pp. 220–222.

37 '1956 Nobel Prize in Physics: John Bardeen, Walter H. Brattain, and William Shockley', available at www.bell-labs.com/about/awards/1956-nobel-prize-physics/#gref (accessed 16 December 2021).

38 Lynn, 'The Commercialization of the Transistor Radio in Japan', pp. 221–222.

39 'Sony History', Chapters 1 and 2, available at www.sony.com/en/SonyInfo/CorporateInfo/History/SonyHistory (accessed 17 December 2021).

40 On IG Farben's development of tape technology in cooperation with AEG, see Raymond G. Stokes, 'From the IG Farben Fusion to BASF AG (1925–1952)', in Werner Abelshauser, Wolfgang von Hippel, Jeffrey Allan Johnson, and Raymond G. Stokes, *German Industry and Global Enterprise: BASF: The History of a Company* (Cambridge and New York: Cambridge University Press, 2004), pp. 268–269. For the use of technical information gleaned from BASF and AEG after the war by Ampex and others, see Douglas M. O'Reagan, *Taking Nazi Technology: Allied Exploitation of German Science after the Second World War* (Baltimore, MD: Johns Hopkins University Press, 2019), pp. 61–63.

41 'Sony History', Chapter 2; Leonard H. Lynn, 'MITI's Successes and Failures in Controlling Japan's Technology Imports', *Hitotsubashi Journal of Commerce and Management* 29, No. 1 (December 1994): 15–33, here pp. 27–29.

42 Steve Schickel, 'Regency Markets Pocket Transistor Radio', *Billboard* (30 October 1954), p. 26; Simcoe, 'The Revolution in Your Pocket'.

43 Brian Santo, 'The Consumer Electronics Hall of Fame: Sony Trinitron', *IEEE Spectrum* (20 December 2018), available at https://spectrum.ieee.org/the-consumer-electronics-hall-of-fame-sony-trinitron (accessed 21 November 2022).

44 Lynn, 'The Commercialization of the Transistor Radio in Japan', pp. 224–225.

45 Morris-Suzuki, *The Technological Transformation of Japan*, pp. 166–168.

46 Helen Macnaughton, *Women, Work, and the Japanese Economic Miracle: The Case of the Cotton Textile Industry, 1945–1975* (London and New York: RoutledgeCurzon, 2005), especially pp. 211–214; Partner, *Assembled in Japan*, Chapter 4, pp. 193–224: 'Nimble Fingers: The Story of the Transistor Radio'. For the importance of unskilled and semi-skilled labour in general in the electronics industry, see John A. Alic and Martha Caldwell Harris, 'Employment Lessons from the Electronics Industry', *Monthly Labor Review* 109, No. 2 (February 1986): 27–36.

47 Brian Reinbold and Yi Wen, 'Understanding the Roots of the U.S. Trade Deficit', Federal Reserve Bank of St Louis Regional Economist (9 October 2018), available at www.stlouisfed.org/publications/regional-economist/third-quarter-2018/understanding-roots-trade-deficit (accessed 20 December 2021).

48 Lawrence A. Fox and William F. Averyt, 'The U.S. Trade Deficit: A Hard Look at Bad News', *Business Economics* 14, No. 2 (March 1979): 1–17, especially pp. 12–13.

7 The Wages of Construction

1 Adam Tooze, *The Wages of Destruction: The Making and Breaking of the Nazi Economy* (London: Allen Lane, 2006); John Dower, *Embracing Defeat: Japan in the Wake of World War II* (London: Allen Lane, 1999). Tooze deals exclusively with Germany, and Dower with Japan, but each book makes general points applicable to both countries.

2 Richard Pearson, 'Former Ala. Gov. George C. Wallace Dies', *Washington Post* (14 September 1998), p. A1 (first quotation); Glenn T. Eskew, 'George C. Wallace (1963–67, 1971–79, 1983–87)', *Encyclopedia of Alabama* (8 September 2008; revised 10 June 2021), available at http://encyclopediaofalabama.org/article/h-1676 (accessed 28 January 2022) (second quotation); William Boyd, *The Slain Wood: Papermaking and Its Environmental Consequences in the American South* (Baltimore, MD: Johns Hopkins University Press, 2015), introduction and p. 149 (third quotation, from p. 14).

3 Helmut Weidner, '25 Years of Modern Environmental Policy in Germany: Treading a Well-Worn Path to the Top of the International Field', *WZB Discussion Paper* No. FS II 95–301 (1995), p. 1. Quotation from current version of civil code is from Section 906, available at www.gesetze-im-internet.de/englisch_bgb/englisch_bgb .html (accessed 31 January 2022).

4 Harold James, *A German Identity, 1770–1990* (London: Weidenfeld and Nicolson, 1989), especially Chapter 9; Ezra Vogel, *Japan's New Middle Class*, 3rd ed. (Lanham, MD: Rowman and Littlefield, 2013 [1963]), especially Chapter 1.

5 Eric Pace, 'Countries That Touch the Fabled Rhine Take Steps to Clean Up the "Sewer of Europe"', *New York Times* (22 March 1970), p. 14; Nil Disco, '"The Power of Positive Thinking": From the Chemicals Convention to the Rhine Action Plan, 1970–1990', in Ralf Banken and Ben Wubs, eds., *The Rhine: A Transnational Economic History* (Baden-Baden: Nomos, 2017), pp. 355–378.

6 Tokyo Metropolitan Government, *Tokyo Fights Pollution* (Tokyo: Tokyo Metropolitan Government, 1977 [1971]), p. 75; quoted in Simon Avenell, *Transnational Japan in the Global Environmental Movement* (Honolulu: University of Hawai'i Press, 2017), p. 29.

7 Franz-Josef Brüggemeier, 'A Nature Fit for Industry: The Environmental History of the Ruhr Basin, 1840–1990', *Environmental History Review* 18, No. 1 (Spring 1994): 35–54, pp. 43–44.

8 Raymond Dominick, 'Capitalism, Communism, and Environmental Protection: Lessons from the German Experience', *Environmental History* 3, No. 3 (July 1998): 311–332, quotation from p. 316.

9 Avenell, *Transnational Japan*, p. 29.

10 'Tokyo Official Predicts Need for Gas Masks', *New York Times* (24 July 1970), p. 36.

11 Avenell, *Transnational Japan*, especially pp. 27–29; Science for Environmental Policy, *Tackling Mercury Pollution in the EU and Worldwide*, In-Depth Report 15, produced for the European Commission, DG Environment, by Science Communication Unit, UWE, Bristol (2017), p. 16, available at http://ec.europa .eu/science-environment-policy (accessed 4 February 2022); Government of Japan, Ministry for the Environment, 'Minamata Disease: The History and Measures' (2002), available at www.env.go.jp/en/chemi/hs/minamata2002/index.html (accessed 4 February 2002).

12 Government of Japan, Ministry for the Environment, 'Minamata Disease'; Avenell, *Transnational Japan*, p. 29.

13 Science for Environmental Policy, *Tackling Mercury Pollution*, pp. 16, 60–62, quotation from p. 16.

14 Andrea Westermann, *Plastik und politische Kultur in Westdeutschland* (Zurich: Chronos, 2007); A. M. Thiess and R. Frentzel-Beyme, 'Retrospective Survey of Alleged Diseases Associated with Vinyl-Chloride in the Federal Republic of Germany', *Journal of Occupational Medicine* 17, No. 7 (July 1975): 430–432; Gerald Markowitz and David Rosner, 'Monsanto, PCBs, and the Creation of a "World-Wide Ecological Problem"', *Journal of Public Health Policy* 39 (2018): 463–540.

15 Raymond G. Stokes, Roman Köster, and Stephen Sambrook, *The Business of Waste: Great Britain and Germany, 1945 to the Present* (Cambridge and New York: Cambridge University Press, 2013), pp. 160–161.

16 Rachel Carson, *Silent Spring* (New York: Houghton Mifflin, 1962).

17 Mark Stoll, '*Silent Spring*, an International Bestseller', *Environment & Society Portal* (2021), available at www.environmentandsociety.org/exhibitions/rachel-carsons-silent-spring/silent-spring-international-best-seller (accessed 7 February 2022); Avenell, *Transnational Japan*, p. 2.

18 Samuel Hays, *Beauty, Health, and Permanence: Environmental Politics in the United States, 1955–1985* (Cambridge and New York: Cambridge University Press, 1987).

19 Stokes, Köster, and Sambrook, *The Business of Waste*, pp. 60–61, 139–155; Joel A. Tarr, *The Search for the Ultimate Sink: Urban Pollution in Historical Perspective* (Akron, OH: University of Akron Press, 1996). For a more detailed overview of the German case, see Roman Köster, *Hausmüll: Abfall und Gesellschaft in Westdeutschland 1945–1990* (Göttingen: Vandenhoeck & Ruprecht, 2017).

20 'Scherbelino-Weiher', available at https://frankfurt.de/themen/umwelt-und-gruen/orte/stadtgewaesser/teiche-seen-tuempel/scherbelino-weiher (accessed 14 February 2022).

21 Japanese Government Ministry of the Environment, *History and Current State of Waste Management in Japan* (Tokyo: Ministry of Environment Office of Sound Material-Cycle Society, 2014), p. 4.

22 Tarr, *The Search for the Ultimate Sink*; Stokes, Köster, and Sambrook, *The Business of Waste*, pp. 81–85.

23 Stokes, Köster, and Sambrook, *The Business of Waste*, pp. 82–85; Japanese Ministry of the Environment, *History and Current State of Waste Management in Japan*, p. 4. Photos of the Glasgow and Tokyo facilities are on p. 82 of the former and p. 4 of the latter.

24 Stokes, Köster, and Sambrook, *The Business of Waste*, Chart 4.5, p. 142; Japanese Ministry of the Environment, *History and Current State of Waste Management in Japan*, p. 5.

25 Stokes, Köster, and Sambrook, *The Business of Waste*, pp. 207–208, 246–249; Jonathan R. Zatlin, *The Currency of Socialism: Money and Political Culture in East Germany* (Cambridge and New York: Cambridge University Press, 2007), p. 261.

26 Stokes, Köster, and Sambrook, *The Business of Waste*, p. 249.

27 Environmental Investigation Agency, *The Truth behind Trash: The Scale and Impact of the International Trade in Plastic Waste* (September 2021), pp. 4, 18–19, 24–28, available at https://rethinkplasticalliance.eu/wp-content/uploads/2021/09/EIA_UK_Plastic_Waste_Trade_Report.pdf (accessed 17 February 2022); Leslie Hook and John Reed, 'Why the World's Recycling System Stopped Working', *Financial Times FT Magazine* (25 October 2018).

28 Carl A. Zimring, *Cash for Your Trash: Scrap Recycling in America* (New Brunswick, NJ and London: Rutgers University Press, 2005); Susan Strasser, *Waste and Want: A Social History of Trash* (New York: Henry Holt, 1999). On salvage versus recycling, see Stokes, Köster, and Sambrook, *The Business of Waste*, especially pp. 301–302.

29 On enthusiasm for separation, see, for instance, Melissa Eddy, 'Germany Gleefully Leads List of World's Top Recyclers', *New York Times* (28 November 2016); Grace Dobush, 'The Brutal Reality of Being the World's "Best" Recycler', Huffington Post (19 July 2019), available at www.huffingtonpost.co.uk/entry/germany-recycling-reality_n_5d30fccbe4b004b6adad52f8 (accessed 18 February 2022); Norimitsu

Onishi, 'How Do Japanese Dump Trash? Let Us Count the Myriad Ways', *New York Times* (12 May 2005). On the impact of recycling and reduction on incineration, see Stokes, Köster, and Sambrook, *The Business of Waste*, pp. 275, 281–282; David Cyranoski, 'One Man's Trash …', *Nature* 44 (November 2006): 262–263.

30 European Court of Auditors, *Special Report: The Polluter Pays Principle: Inconsistent Application across EU Environmental Policies and Actions* (Brussels: European Union, 2021), pp. 6–7, available at www.eca.europa.eu/en/publications?did=58811 (accessed 18 February 2022); United Nations Environmental Program, *The Japanese Industrial Waste Experience: Lessons for Rapidly Industrializing Countries* (Osaka: UNEP, 2013), p. 18, available at https://wedocs.unep.org/handle/20.500.11822/27294 (accessed 18 February 2022); PREVENT Waste Alliance, 'Germany: How Germany's EPR System for Packaging Waste Went from Single PRO to Multiple PROs with a Register' (2021), p. 1, available at https://prevent-waste.net/wp-content/uploads/2023/06/Germany.pdf (accessed 4 October 2023); Mahajan Niyati, 'A Comparative Study of Municipal Solid Waste Management in India and Japan' (2015), p. 50, available at https://core.ac.uk/download/pdf/144446327.pdf (accessed 22 February 2022).

31 Stokes, Köster, and Sambrook, *The Business of Waste*, pp. 274–276; PREVENT Waste Alliance, 'Germany'; United Nations Environmental Program, *The Japanese Industrial Waste Experience*, p. 30; Christine Yolin, *Waste Management and Recycling in Japan: Opportunities for European Companies (SMEs Focus)* (Tokyo: EU–Japan Centre for Industrial Cooperation, 2015), available at www.eu-japan.eu/sites/default/files/publications/docs/waste_management_recycling_japan.pdf (accessed 18 February 2022).

32 This section uses the title of Andrew Hoffman's book about the rise of corporate environmentalism to make a more general point about the move in Germany and Japan from the 1960s onwards away from economic growth at any price and towards recognition of the necessary limits to growth through environmentalism. See Andrew J. Hoffman, *From Heresy to Dogma: An Institutional History of Corporate Environmentalism* (Stanford, CA: Stanford Business Books, 2001).

33 Avenell, *Transnational Japan*, pp. 1–3, 27–29, 162, quotation for Jun Ui, p. 1; Frank Uekötter, *The Greenest Nation? A New History of German Environmentalism* (Cambridge, MA: MIT Press, 2014), especially Chapter 3; quotation about implications of the *Lucky Dragon V* incident from p. 76.

34 United Nations, 'Germany', www.un.org/en/about-us/member-states/germany (accessed 21 February 2022); Philippe Boudes, 'United Nations Conference on the Human Environment [1972]', *Britannica*, available at www.britannica.com/topic/United-Nations-Conference-on-the-Human-Environment (accessed 21 February 2022). The barring of East German participation in the conference led to a boycott by the entire Soviet bloc, but Chinese delegates did attend in their first ever participation in a major UN conference.

35 Uekötter, *The Greenest Nation?*, especially Chapters 3 and 4.

36 Avenell, *Transnational Japan*; Uekötter, *The Greenest Nation?*, especially pp. 101–111.

37 Christopher Allen, 'Political Consequences of Change: The Chemical Industry', in Peter Katzenstein, ed., *Industry and Politics in West Germany: Toward the Third Republic* (Ithaca, NY: Cornell University Press, 1989), pp. 157–184; Uekötter, *The Greenest Nation?*, p. 110; Cyranoski, 'One Man's Trash …'; Japanese Ministry of the Environment, *Solid Waste Management and Recycling Technology of Japan: Toward a Sustainable Society* (Tokyo: Ministry of Environment Waste Management and Recycling Department, 2012), p. 10, available at www.env.go.jp/en/recycle/

smcs/attach/swmrt.pdf (accessed 25 February 2022); Ephrat Livni, 'Japan Wants to Become Southeast Asia's Trash Manager', *Quartz* (23 June 2019), available at https://qz.com/1650893/japan-wants-to-become-southeast-asias-trash-manager (accessed 24 February 2022).

8 The Hauntings of the Past

1 Justin McCurry, 'Japan and South Korea in Row over Mines That Used Forced Labour', *The Observer* (19 February 2022); UNESCO, 'The Sado Complex of Heritage Mines, Primarily Gold Mines' (22 November 2010), available at https://whc.unesco.org/en/tentativelists/5572 (accessed 2 March 2022).

2 The agreement is in United Nations Treaty Series, No. 8473, 'Agreement on the Settlement of Problems Concerning Property and Claims and on Economic Co-operation between Japan and the Republic of South Korea', signed in Tokyo on 22 June 1965, available at https://treaties.un.org/doc/Publication/UNTS/Volume%20583/volume-583-I-8473-English.pdf (accessed 10 March 2022).

3 Sourina Bej and Prakash Pannerselvam, 'Forced Labour and the Impact of History of Japan–South Korea Relations', Institute of Peace and Conflict Studies (27 March 2019), available at www.ipcs.org/comm_select.php?articleNo=5571 (accessed 2 March 2022); McCurry, 'Japan and South Korea in Row over Mines That Used Forced Labour'; Choe Sang-Hun and Motoko Rich, 'The $89,000 Verdict Tearing Japan and South Korea Apart', *New York Times* (13 February 2019).

4 EVZ Foundation pages, available at www.stiftung-evz.de/en (accessed 2 March 2022); International Court of Justice (ICJ), 'Jurisdictional Immunities of the State (Germany v. Italy: Greece Intervening)', 2008–2012, available at www.icj-cij.org/case/143 (accessed 2 March 2022).

5 ICJ, 'Jurisdictional Immunities of the State (Germany v. Italy: Greece Intervening)', 3 February 2012, especially pp. 59–61.

6 On the wartime origins of these concepts, see Phillipe Sands, *East–West Street: On the Origins of Genocide and Crimes against Humanity* (London: Weidenfeld & Nicolson, 2016).

7 Kim Christian Priemel, *The Betrayal: The Nuremberg Trials and German Divergence* (Oxford and New York: Oxford University Press, 2016), especially Chapters 3 and 4; John Dower, *Embracing Defeat: Japan in the Aftermath of World War II* (London: Allen Lane, 1999), Chapter 15.

8 On other trials of war criminals after 1945 and their outcomes, see, for instance, Riesenfeld Rare Books Research Center, University of Minnesota, 'A Witness to Barbarism: Horace R. Hansen and the Dachau War Crimes Trials' (Digital Exhibition, n.d.), available at http://moses.law.umn.edu/hansenwitness/index.html (accessed 7 March 2022); Donald Bloxham, 'British War Crimes Trial Policy in Germany, 1945–1957: Implementation and Collapse', *Journal of British Studies* 42, No. 1 (January 2003): 91–118; Yuma Totani, *Justice in Asia and the Pacific Region, 1945–1952: Allied War Crimes Prosecutions* (Cambridge and New York: Cambridge University Press, 2015), Introduction, especially pp. 8–11.

9 Rainer Schulze, 'Trial of 100-Year-Old Man in Germany: Why Nazi War Crimes Take So Long to Prosecute', *The Conversation* (5 October 2021), available at https://theconversation.com/trial-of-100-year-old-man-in-germany-why-nazi-war-crimes-take-so-long-to-prosecute-166001 (accessed 9 March 2022).

10 Frank Smith, 'Survivor of Forced Labor in Japan Seeks True Apology', *DW* (8 February 2021), available at www.dw.com/en/south-korea-japan-forced-labor-wwii/a-56497264 (accessed 10 March 2022); 'Under Japanese Law, 14 at Yasukuni

Not War Criminals: Abe', *The Japan Times* (7 October 2006). Quotation from second source.

11 For this and the following paragraph, Wolfgang Benz, 'Der Wollheim-Prozeß. Zwangarbeit für die I.G. Farben in Auschwitz', in Ludolf Herbst and Constantin Goschler, eds., *Wiedergutmachung in der Bundesrepublik Deutschland* (Munich: Oldenbourg, 1989), pp. 303–326; 'Wollheim v. I.G. Farben', Wollheim Memorial Website, available at www.wollheim-memorial.de/en/das_verfahren_wollheim_gegen_ig_farben (accessed 8 March 2022). Quotation from second source.

12 'Wollheim v. I.G. Farben'.

13 S. Jonathan Wiesen, *West German Industry and the Challenge of the Nazi Past, 1945–1955* (Chapel Hill, NC: University of North Carolina Press, 2001).

14 Ian Buruma, *The Wages of Guilt: Memories of War in Germany and Japan* (London: Jonathan Cape, 1995).

15 United Nations, 'Rome Statute of the International Criminal Court', n.d., available at https://legal.un.org/icc/general/overview.htm (accessed 10 March 2022); Timothy Webster, 'Recent Attempts at Reparations Show That World War II Is Not Over', *The Conversation* (23 May 2019), available at https://theconversation.com/recent-attempts-at-reparations-show-that-world-war-ii-is-not-over-114655 (accessed 10 March 2022); EVZ Foundation pages.

16 US Library of Congress Law Library, 'Japan: WWII POW and Forced Labor Compensation Cases', LL File No. 2008-000158 (2008), p. 3, available at www.loc.gov/item/2018298796 (accessed 8 March 2022); Webster, 'Recent Attempts at Reparations Show That World War II Is Not Over'.

17 United Nations Treaty Series, No. 8471, 'Treaty on Basic Relations between Japan and the Republic of Korea', signed in Tokyo on 22 June 1965, available at https://treaties.un.org/doc/Publication/UNTS/Volume%20583/volume-583-I-8471-English.pdf (accessed 10 March 2022); United Nations Treaty Series, No. 8473, 'Agreement on the Settlement of Problems Concerning Property and Claims and on Economic Co-operation between Japan and the Republic of South Korea'. Quotations from the first (p. 46) and second source (p. 260, emphasis added).

18 Mari Yamaguchi, 'Japan Urges South Korea to Drop Wartime Compensation Demands', *The Diplomat* (19 January 2021), available at https://thediplomat.com/2021/01/japan-urges-south-korea-to-drop-wartime-compensation-demands (accessed 10 March 2022); Kenji Kawase, 'Japan–South Korea Dispute Has Roots in 1965 Post-war Agreement', Nikkei Asia (31 July 2019), available at https://asia.nikkei.com/Spotlight/The-Big-Story/Japan-South-Korea-dispute-has-roots-in-1965-post-war-agreement (accessed 10 March 2022).

19 Sarah Parsons, director of consultancy Japan In Perspective, quoted in Justin McCurry, 'Nissan Crisis Sheds New Light on Japan Inc's Awkward Secrets', *The Observer* (24 November 2018).

20 Peter A. Hall and David Soskice, eds., *Varieties of Capitalism: The Institutional Foundations of Comparative Advantage* (Oxford and New York: Oxford University Press, 2001).

21 Paul Lersch and Hartmut Palmer, 'Die geflegte Landschaft', *Der Spiegel* (12 December 1999); 'Die Flick-Affäre. Ein Mann kaufte die Republik', *Der Spiegel* (6 October 2006). The following relies heavily on the Lersch and Palmer report from 1999. Unless otherwise noted, quotations in what immediately follows are from that source.

22 On the elder Flick's background and activities in the Third Reich, see Tim Schanetzky, *Regierungsunternehmer: Henry J. Kaiser, Friedrich Flick und die Staatskonjunkturen in den USA und Deutschland* (Göttingen: Wallstein, 2015).

23 Unless otherwise noted, the following is drawn largely from Robert Shaplen, 'Annals of Crime: The Lockheed Incident – I', *The New Yorker* 53 (23 January 1978), pp. 48–74.

24 'Kodama, Yoshio, Rightist Leader', CIA Intelligence Report (15 October 1963) (Secret: No Foreign Dissemination), declassified under the Nazi War Crimes Disclosure Act, quotations from p. 1, available at www.cia.gov/readingroom/docs/KODAMA,YOSHIO%20%20 VOL.1_0002.pdf (accessed 17 October 2023).

25 'Kodama, Yoshio, Rightist Leader', quotation p. 2. Information on Kodama's wartime drug trafficking is from Shaplen, 'Annals of Crime: The Lockheed Incident – I', p. 49.

26 'Kodama, Yoshio, Rightist Leader', quotation from p. 2.

27 'Kodama, Yoshio, Rightist Leader', p. 2; information on Kodama's personal wealth from Shaplen, 'Annals of Crime: The Lockheed Incident – I', p. 49.

28 'Kodama, Yoshio, Rightist Leader', p. 3. For Kodama's work for American intelligence, see Hans H. Baerwald, 'Lockheed and Japanese Politics', *Asian Survey* 16, No. 9 (September 1976): 817–829, p. 817.

29 'Proof of Lockheed Bribes in Germany Held Lacking', *New York Times* (11 March 1976), p. 57; Shaplen, 'Annals of Crime: The Lockheed Incident – I'.

30 Shaplen, 'Annals of Crime: The Lockheed Incident – I', especially pp. 48, 60, 62–64, 66.

31 Wolfgang Saxon, 'Yoshio Kodama; Was Rightist', *New York Times* (18 January 1984); Shaplen, 'Annals of Crime: The Lockheed Incident – I', p. 66.

32 Baerwald, 'Lockheed and Japanese Politics', p. 824; Shaplen, 'Annals of Crime: The Lockheed Incident – I', p. 50. Quotations from Baerwald.

33 Levin Center for Democratic Oversight, 'Portraits in Oversight: Frank Church and the Church Committee', www.levin-center.org/frank-church-and-the-church-committee (accessed 24 November 2022).

34 Eiichiro Tokumoto, 'The Man Who Pulled the Trigger on a Scandal', *The Blue Review* (17 October 2016), available at www.boisestate.edu/bluereview/man-pulled-trigger-scandal (accessed 23 March 2022). Quotation is from an interview by Tokumoto with Jack Blum, an associate counsel of Church's subcommittee and a leading investigator in the Lockheed case.

35 Blum interview as quoted in Tokumoto, 'The Man Who Pulled the Trigger on a Scandal'.

36 A. Carl Kotchian, as quoted in Robert Lindsey, 'Kotchian Calls Himself the Scapegoat', *New York Times* (3 July 1977), p. 73.

37 First interchange as quoted in Baerwald, 'Lockheed and Japanese Politics', p. 817; Shaplen, 'Annals of Crime: The Lockheed Incident – I', p. 66.

38 Shaplen, 'Annals of Crime: The Lockheed Incident – I'.

39 Baerwald, 'Lockheed and Japanese Politics', pp. 818–819. The Arthur Young accountant is quoted by Baerwald from the transcript of the subcommittee hearing.

40 'Japan Arrests 17th Official in the Lockheed Bribe Scandal', *New York Times* (21 August 1976), p. 33; Steve Lohr, 'Tanaka Is Guilty in Bribery Trial', *New York Times* (12 October 1983), p. 1; Sam Jameson, 'Conviction of Former Japanese Leader Tanaka Upheld', *Los Angeles Times* (29 July 1987); Junko Takahashi, 'Voters put Tanaka, Kato Scandals Behind', *The Japan Times* (31 October 2003).

41 Frank Badua, 'Laying Down the Law on Lockheed: How an Aviation and Defense Giant Inspired the Promulgation of the Foreign Corrupt Practices Act of 1977', *The Accounting Historians Journal* 42, No. 1 (June 2015): 105–126.

42 'The Corporate Scandals That Rocked Japan', *BBC News Online* (20 November 2018), available at www.bbc.co.uk/news/business-46267868 (accessed 24 March

2022); McCurry, 'Nissan Crisis Sheds New Light on Japan Inc's Awkward Secrets'; Hartmut Berghoff, '"Organised Irresponsibility"? The Siemens Corruption Scandal of the 1990s and 2000s', *Business History* 60, No. 3 (2018): 423–445; Hartmut Berghoff, 'From the Watergate Scandal to the Compliance Revolution: The Fight against Corporate Corruption in the United States and Germany, 1972–2012', *Bulletin of the German Historical Institute Washington DC* 53 (Fall 2013): 7–30, especially pp. 16–20.

43 Walter Sim, 'Japan Inc Hit by Two Corporate Governance Scandals in as Many Months', *The Straits Times* (10 July 2021).

44 'The Corporate Scandals That Rocked Japan'; McCurry, 'Nissan Crisis Sheds New Light on Japan Inc's Awkward Secrets'.

45 On themes in the literature on white collar crime in general, see Hartmut Berghoff and Uwe Spiekermann, 'Shady Business: On the History of White-Collar Crime', *Business History* 60, No. 3 (2018): 289–304; Hugo van Driel, 'Financial Fraud, Scandals, and Regulation: A Conceptual Framework and Literature Review', *Business History* 61, No. 8 (2019): 1259–1299.

46 This point about the differences between Germany and Japan in coming to terms with their respective pasts is made with great eloquence in Ian Buruma, *The Wages of Guilt: Memories of War in Germany and Japan* (London: Jonathan Cape, 1994).

9 Fragile Strength: Coping with Currency and Oil Crises

1 Richard Nixon, 'Address to the Nation Outlining a New Economic Policy: "The Challenge of Peace"', 15 August 1971, available at www.presidency.ucsb.edu/documents/address-the-nation-outlining-new-economic-policy-the-challenge-peace (accessed 29 November 2022).

2 US Department of State, Office of the Historian, 'Nixon and the End of the Bretton Woods System, 1971–1973', available at https://history.state.gov/milestones/1969-1976/nixon-shock (accessed 5 December 2022).

3 Tsuchiya Hideo, 'The Nixon Shock of 1971 and Today's "Cheap Japan"', *Nippon.com* (23 August 2021), available at www.nippon.com/en/in-depth/d00743 (accessed 29 November 2022).

4 Winston Lord, Memorandum for Henry A. Kissinger, Subject: Memcon of Your Conversations with Chou En-Lai, 19 July 1971, p. 1, document from US National Archives, reproduced as facsimile in William Burr, ed., 'The Beijing–Washington Back-Channel and Henry Kissinger's Secret Trip to China', Document 34, National Security Archive, available at https://nsarchive2.gwu.edu/NSAEBB/NSAEBB66/#docs (accessed 5 April 2022).

5 Hans-Joachim Spanger, 'The Perils of Path Dependency: Germany's Russia Policy', *Europe–Asia Studies* 72, No. 6 (2020): 1053–1072.

6 For this paragraph and the following two, see Peter Kugler, 'The Bretton Woods System: Design and Operation', in David Fox and Wolfgang Ernst, eds., *Money in the Western Legal Tradition: Middle Ages to Bretton Woods* (Oxford and New York: Oxford University Press, 2016), pp. 611–630.

7 Barry Eichengreen, *Golden Fetters: The Gold Standard and the Great Depression* (Oxford and New York: Oxford University Press, 1992).

8 Otmar Emminger, *The D-Mark in the Conflict between Internal and External Equilibrium* (Princeton: Princeton University Department of Economics International Finance Section, 1977), pp. 3–4.

9 Emminger, *The D-Mark in the Conflict between Internal and External Equilibrium*, pp. 1, 6–10, 42–53.

10 Emminger, *The D-Mark in the Conflict between Internal and External Equilibrium*;
    Hugh M. Kaufmann, 'A Debate over Germany's Revaluation 1961: A Chapter in
    Political Economy', *Weltwirtschaftliches Archiv* 103 (1969): 181–212.

11 For inflation differentials, see Emminger, *The D-Mark in the Conflict between
    Internal and External Equilibrium*, p. 7, Table 2; William Glenn Gray, '"Number
    One in Europe": The Startling Emergence of the Deutsche Mark', *Central European
    History* 39, No. 1 (March 2006): 56–78, pp. 59–60.

12 United Nations, 'Case Concerning the Revaluation of the German Mark', *Reports
    of International Arbitral Awards* XIX (16 May 1980): 67–145, here, pp. 81–83;
    quotation from Kaufmann, 'A Debate over Germany's Revaluation 1961', p. 209.

13 Gray, 'Number One in Europe'.

14 Gray, 'Number One in Europe'.

15 Harold James, 'The Nixon Shock Revisited', Project Syndicate (1 April 2010), avail-
    able at www.project-syndicate.org/commentary/the-nixon-shock-doctrine-revisited
    (accessed 11 April 2022).

16 Masahiko Takeda and Philip Turner, 'The Liberalisation of Japan's Financial
    Markets: Some Major Themes', Bank for International Settlements (BIS) Economic
    Papers, No. 34 (November 1992), p. 12; OECD, *Economic Surveys – Japan* (Paris:
    OECD, 1969), quotation from p. 5.

17 Mark Metzler, *Capital as Will and Imagination: Schumpeter's Guide to the Post-
    war Japanese Miracle* (Ithaca, NY: Cornell University Press, 2013), especially
    Chapter 12.

18 Metzler, *Capital as Will and Imagination*, especially pp. 12, 20–21, 212. Quotation
    from p. 212.

19 'Timeline: Milestones in the Yen's History', Reuters (27 October 2008), available
    at www.reuters.com/article/us-yen-idUSTRE49Q1AN20081027 (accessed 12 April
    2022).

20 Richard Nixon, 'Address to the Nation about Policies to Deal with the Energy
    Shortages', 7 November 1973, text online through Gerhard Peters and John T.
    Wooley, eds., *The American Presidency Project*, available at www.presidency.ucsb
    .edu/documents/address-the-nation-about-policies-deal-with-the-energy-shortages
    (accessed 12 April 2022).

21 'Oil Production by Country', *Our World in Data*, available at https://ourworld
    indata.org/grapher/oil-production-by-country (accessed 13 April 2022); Council
    on Foreign Relations, 'Oil Dependence and U.S. Foreign Policy' (2022), available
    at www.cfr.org/timeline/oil-dependence-and-us-foreign-policy (accessed 13 April
    2022).

22 Nixon, 'Address to the Nation about Policies to Deal with the Energy Shortages'.

23 Joel Darmstadter, *Energy in the World Economy: A Statistical Review of Trends
    in Output, Trade, and Consumption since 1925* (Baltimore, MD: Johns Hopkins
    University Press, 1971).

24 BWM Abteilung IV to Minister and State Secretary, 'Betr.: Besprechungspunkte
    mit den Mineralölgesellschaften am 27. November 1956', BAK B102/5444, Heft
    3; BWM IV B (Neef), 'Vermerk', 17 December 1956. Generally, see Rainer Karlsch
    and Raymond G. Stokes, *Faktor Öl: Die Mineralölwirtschaft in Deutschland
    1859–1974* (Munich: Beck, 2003), especially Chapters 7–10.

25 Darmstadter, *Energy in the World Economy*.

26 BP, *Statistical Review of World Energy* (July 2021), available at www.bp.com/
    en/global/corporate/energy-economics/statistical-review-of-world-energy.html
    (accessed 15 April 2022). Note that data from this source are available only from
    1965 onwards. Darmstadter, *Energy in the World Economy* contains earlier data.

27 BP, *Statistical Review of World Energy* (July 2021).

28 Data on current account balances as percentage of GDP for 1971–2023 (forecasts for 2022 and 2023), available at OECD, 'Current Account Balance Forecast (Indicator)' (2022), www.oecd-ilibrary.org/trade/current-account-balance-forecast/indicator/english_38d572e4-en (accessed 30 November 2022).

29 Darmstadter, *Energy in the World Economy*. See also Satoru Kobori, 'Japan's Energy Policy during the 1950s: The Reasons for the Rapid Switch from Coal to Oil', (2009), available at https://apebhconference.files.wordpress.com/2009/09/kobori1.pdf (accessed 30 November 2022).

30 Darmstadter, *Energy in the World Economy*.

31 BP, *Statistical Review of World Energy* (July 2021).

32 OECD, 'Current Account Balance Forecast (Indicator)' (2022).

10 Managing in Major Markets: Selling and Making in the United States and China

1 'Columbus, Indiana Population 2022', https://worldpopulationreview.com/us-cities/columbus-in-population (accessed 3 May 2022).

2 'Guide to the Architecture of Columbus, Indiana', https://columbus.in.us/guide-to-the-architecture (accessed 3 May 2022).

3 Will Connors, 'Indiana Town Preserves Its Historical Architecture, without a Protective Law', *Wall Street Journal* (10 April 2017).

4 Greater Columbus Indiana Economic Development, 'FDI Preferred Destination' (4 September 2020), available at www.columbusin.org/advantages/fdi-preferred-destination (accessed 17 October 2023); Will Connors, 'An Indiana Town's Big Bet on International Business Pays Off', *Wall Street Journal* (10 April 2017). Quotation from Connors.

5 Kristen Bialik, 'Number of U.S. Workers Employed by Foreign-Owned Companies Is on the Rise', Pew Research Center (14 December 2017), available at www.pewresearch.org/short-reads/2017/12/14/number-of-u-s-workers-employed-by-foreign-owned-companies-is-on-the-rise (accessed 4 May 2022).

6 Santander Trade Markets, 'United States: Foreign Investment', available at https://santandertrade.com/en/portal/establish-overseas/united-states/foreign-investment (accessed 4 May 2022).

7 Mira Wilkins, *The Maturing of the Multinational Firm: American Business Abroad from 1914 to 1970* (Cambridge, MA: Harvard University Press, 1974), pp. 349–350.

8 Volker R. Berghahn, *American Big Business in Britain and Germany: A Comparative History of Two 'Special Relationships' in the 20th Century* (Princeton, NJ: Princeton University Press, 2014).

9 Wilkins, *The Maturing of the Multinational Enterprise*, pp. 343–344; Robert Fitzgerald, *The Rise of the Global Company: Multinationals and the Making of the Modern World* (Cambridge and New York: Cambridge University Press, 2015), especially pp. 283–297.

10 Robert Shaplen, 'Annals of Crime: The Lockheed Incident – I', *The New Yorker* 53 (23 January 1978), pp. 48–74.

11 Japan became the second-largest economy in the capitalist world in the late 1960s. See the graphic in www.visualcapitalist.com/animation-the-worlds-10-largest-economies-by-gdp-1960-today (accessed 1 December 2022).

12 'Former Governor Rhodes Returns to the Scene of One of His Greatest Triumphs 20 Years Later', Gongwer News Service, *Ohio Report* Vol. 66, No. 195 (8 October 1997), available at www.gongwer-oh.com/125/rhodeshonda.pdf (accessed 6 May 2022).

13 Greg Drevenstedt, 'Honda Celebrates 60 Years in America', *Rider Magazine* (8 November 2019), available at https://ridermagazine.com/2019/10/08/honda-celebrates-60-years-in-america (accessed 6 May 2022).

14 Drevenstedt, 'Honda Celebrates 60 Years in America'.

15 'Suppliers Join Honda in Ohio; Parts Plants Springing Up', *New York Times* (6 July 1984), p. D3.

16 'Suppliers Join Honda in Ohio; Parts Plants Springing Up', p. D3.

17 'Former Governor Rhodes Returns to the Scene of One of His Greatest Triumphs 20 Years Later'.

18 Justin Kocher, 'Ohio Welcomes Japanese Investment' (2021), available at www.jetro.go.jp/ext_images/world/n_america/us/grassroots-seminar/pdf/JETRO-OHIO.pdf (accessed 6 May 2022).

19 'Nissan Manufacturing in Tennessee' (October 2021), available at https://nissanmanufacturing.com/assets/pdf/Nissan-TN-Factsheet.pdf (accessed 17 October 2023); Choong Soon Kim, *Japanese Industry in the American South* (New York: Routledge, 1995); Timothy J. Minchin, *America's Other Automakers: A History of the Foreign-Owned Automotive Sector in the United States* (Athens, GA: University of Georgia Press, 2021).

20 David McHugh, 'Volkswagen to Stop Making the Beetle after 81 Years', *PBS News Hour* (9 July 2019), available at www.pbs.org/newshour/economy/volkswagen-to-stop-making-the-beetle-after-81-years (accessed 9 May 2022); Jerry Knight, 'Volkswagen Begins in American Production of Cars', *Washington Post* (11 April 1978).

21 Steven Tolliday, 'Enterprise and State in the West German *Wirtschaftswunder*: Volkswagen and the Automobile Industry, 1939–1962', *Business History Review* 69, No. 3 (Autumn 1995): 273–350, here pp. 337–340; Bernhard Rieger, *The People's Car: A Global History of the Volkswagen Beetle* (Cambridge, MA: Harvard University Press, 2013), especially Chapter 7; McHugh, 'Volkswagen to Stop Making the Beetle after 81 Years'.

22 'Autos: American-Made Rabbit', *Time* (3 May 1976); Knight, 'Volkswagen Begins in American Production of Cars'.

23 'Autos: American-Made Rabbit'.

24 'Autos: American-Made Rabbit'.

25 'Chrysler Plant Set South of Pittsburgh', *New York Times* (27 September 1968), p. 69; Matt Simmons, 'July 14, 1988: Last Volkswagen Built at Westmoreland County Factory', *WPXI News* (14 July 2020), available at www.wpxi.com/archive/this-day-july-14-1988-last-volkswagen-built-westmoreland-county-factory/4JHNJWFSF5AEJNKMPVUQCFA4HI (accessed 11 May 2022); Reginald Stuart, 'First VW Rolls off Assembly Line in U.S.', *New York Times* (11 April 1978), pp. 51, 55; Knight, 'Volkswagen Begins in American Production of Cars'; Len Boselovic, 'Sony's the 3rd Company to Fall Short in New Stanton', *Pittsburgh Post-Gazette* (16 March 2007).

26 Quoted by Stuart, 'First VW Rolls off Assembly Line in U.S.', p. 51. Armstrong actually said 'one giant leap'.

27 Knight, 'Volkswagen Begins in American Plant Production of Cars'; Tom Hundley, 'Tough Lessons Taught in VW Plant's Closing', *Chicago Tribune* (14 July 1988).

28 Hundley, 'Tough Lessons Taught in VW Plant's Closing'.

29 Erik Verg, *Milestones: The Bayer Story, 1863–1988* (Leverkusen: Bayer AG, 1988), pp. 50–51, 206, 485–489; 'Bayer USA and Subsidiaries to Change Name to Miles Inc.', *Journal of Commerce Online* (24 September 1991), available at www.joc.com/article/bayer-usa-and-subsidiaries-change-name-miles-inc_19910924.html (accessed 18 May 2022); Bayer, 'Transformation and Globalization (1988–2001)',

available at www.bayer.com/en/history/1988-2001 (accessed 18 May 2022). Quotation from last source.

30 Siemens, 'Crossing the "Big Pond": The History of Siemens in the USA', available at https://new.siemens.com/global/en/company/about/history/stories/siemens-in-the-usa.html (accessed 22 May 2022).

31 Hermann Simon, 'Lessons from Germany's Mid-sized Giants', *Harvard Business Review* (March–April 1992).

32 Simon, 'Lessons from Germany's Mid-sized Giants'; Jeffrey Fear, 'Straight outta Oberberg: Transforming Mid-sized German Family Firms into Global Champions, 1970–2010', *Jahrbuch für Wirtschaftsgeschichte/Yearbook for Economic History* 53, No. 1 (2012): 125–169; 'About Fraunhofer', available at www.fraunhofer.de/en/about-fraunhofer.html (accessed 18 May 2022).

33 BMW Group, 'Our Factory', n.d. [c. 2020 updated] available at www.bmwgroup-werke.com/spartanburg/en/our-plant.html (accessed 17 May 2022).

34 Volkswagen, 'Volkswagen Group of America Chattanooga', n.d., available at www.volkswagen-newsroom.com/en/volkswagen-group-of-america-chattanooga-4071 (accessed 17 October 2023).

35 Len Boselovic, 'Sony's the 3rd Company to Fall Short in New Stanton', *Pittsburgh Post-Gazette* (16 March 2007).

36 Barry Naughton, *Growing Out of the Plan: Chinese Economic Reform, 1978–1993* (Cambridge: Cambridge University Press, 1995), pp. 70–71.

37 Naughton, *Growing Out of the Plan*, pp. 75–76.

38 Mitsuru Obe, 'Decoupling Denied: Japan Inc Lays Its Bets on China', *Financial Times* [*Nikkei Asia*] (16 February 2021).

39 Quotations from Obe, 'Decoupling Denied'. See also Itsuro Fujino, 'Inspired by China, Panasonic Gets Back to Its Innovative Roots', *Nikkei Asia* (22 December 2019).

40 This and the following two paragraphs draw upon Barry Naughton, *The Chinese Economy: Transitions and Growth* (Cambridge, MA: MIT Press, 2007), pp. 349–374 and 402–402, especially pp. 356–361; the quotation in the third paragraph is from p. 360. On general development paths and mechanisms of technology acquisition, see Mozammel Huq, ed., *Building Technological Capability: Issues and Prospects. Nepal, Bangladesh, and India* (Dhaka: University Press Limited, 2003), especially Table 1 on p. 337.

41 Obe, 'Decoupling Denied'; Fujino, 'Inspired by China, Panasonic Gets Back to Its Innovative Roots'.

42 Obe, 'Decoupling Denied'; Fujino, 'Inspired by China, Panasonic Gets Back to Its Innovative Roots'. Quotation from Fujino.

43 On the cautious approach to market reform in China, see especially Isabella M. Weber, *How China Escaped Shock Therapy: The Market Reform Debate* (London: Routledge, 2021).

44 K. C. Fung, Hitomi Iizaka, and Alan Siu, 'Japanese Direct Investment in China', *China Economic Review* 14 (2003): 304–315; Santander Trade Markets, 'China: Foreign Investment', available at https://santandertrade.com/en/portal/establish-overseas/china/foreign-investment (accessed 1 December 2022).

45 Lord Russell of Liverpool, *The Knights of Bushido: A History of Japanese War Crimes during World War II* (Barnsley: Frontline Books, 2016 [1958]); Hui-Yi Katherine Tseng, 'China's Territorial Disputes with Japan', *Journal of Territorial and Maritime Studies* 1, No. 2 (July 2014): 71–95.

46 Kristin Vekasi and Jiwon Nam, 'Boycotting Japan: Explaining Divergence in Chinese and South Korean Economic Backlash', *Journal of Asian Security and International Affairs* 6, No. 3 (2019): 299–326.

47 Volkswagen Group, 'Carl Hahn Was, Is and Will Remain an Integral Part of the Volkswagen Family', 15 January 2023, available at www.volkswagen-newsroom .com/en/press-releases/carl-hahn-was-is-and-will-remain-an-integral-part-of-the-volkswagen-family-15413 (accessed 17 October 2023); Joe Miller, 'Volkswagen and China: The Risks of Relying on Authoritarian States', *Financial Times* (16 March 2022).

48 Volkswagen Group, 'Carl Hahn Was, Is and Will Remain an Integral Part of the Volkswagen Family'; Miller, 'Volkswagen and China'.

49 Miller, 'Volkswagen and China'.

50 China International Investment Promotion Agency/FDI Center, 'German Investment in China: Changing Opportunities and Trends 2019', especially Introduction and pp. iii, 2–3, 13–14, available at http://fdi-center.com/wp-content/uploads/2020/05/ German-Investment-in-China-English-Version.pdf (accessed 30 May 2022); German Chamber of Commerce in China in cooperation with KPMG, 'German Business in China: Business Confidence Survey 2019/20', especially pp. 52–53, available at https://china.ahk.de/fileadmin/AHK_China/Market_Info/Economic_ Data/BCS_2019_20.SEC.pdf (accessed 30 May 2022); Verg, *Milestones*, p. 592. For the experience of another German chemical firm in China, see Michael Grabicki, *Breaking New Ground: The History of BASF in China from 1885 to Today* (Hamburg: Hoffmann & Campe, 2015).

51 Personal communication to author, November 2015.

52 German Chamber of Commerce in China in cooperation with KPMG, 'German Business in China: Business Confidence Survey 2019/20', pp. 33–37; Miller, 'Volkswagen and China'; Obe, 'Decoupling Denied'.

11 Coping with the Close of the Cold War

1 'Günter Schabowski's Press Conference in the GDR International Press Center 6:53–7:01 p.m.', 9 November 1989, History and Public Policy Program Digital Archive, Transcript of television broadcast by Hans-Hermann Hertle. Translated for CWIHP by Howard Sargeant, available at http://digitalarchive.wilsoncenter .org/document/113049 (accessed 16 June 2022).

2 Katinka Barysch, 'Germany: The Sick Man of Europe?', Working Paper, Centre for European Reform, (December 2003), available at www.cer.eu/sites/default/ files/publications/attachments/pdf/2012/policybrief_germany_man_kb-5422.pdf (accessed 17 June 2022); Valentina Romei, 'Germany: From "Sick Man" of Europe to Engine of Growth', *Financial Times* (14 August 2017); Naoki Abe, 'Japan's Shrinking Economy', *Brookings* (12 February 2010), available at www.brookings .edu/articles/japans-shrinking-economy (accessed 21 July 2022).

3 Interview with Gerhard Lauter in 'The Berlin Wall: A Stroke of Fate That Changed History', *DW News*, n.d. (from about four minutes into the film), available at www .youtube.com/watch?v=DTBnOoBEJPo (accessed 17 June 2022).

4 For a case study, see Rainer Karlsch and Raymond G. Stokes, *The Chemistry Must Be Right: The Privatization of BSL GmbH, 1990–2000* (Leipzig: Edition Leipzig, 2001).

5 Rupert Wiederwald, 'Privatizing the GDR', DW.com (20 September 2010), available at www.dw.com/en/treuhand-took-the-heat-for-privatization-of-east-german-economy/a-5985015 (accessed 6 December 2022).

6 Michael Sauga, Stefan Simons, and Klaus Wiegrefe (*Der Spiegel*, Hamburg), 'You Get Unification, We Get the Euro', *Voxeurop_English* (1 October 2010), available at https://voxeurop.eu/en/you-get-unification-we-get-the-euro (accessed 17 June 2022).

7 Estimate of cost from Stephen Beard, 'Itemizing Germany's $2 Trillion Bill for Reinification', *Marketplace* (5 November 2019), available at www.marketplace .org/2019/11/05/itemizing-germanys-2-trillion-bill-for-reunification (accessed 6 December 2022); quotation from Barysch, 'Germany: The Sick Man of Europe?', p. 1.

8 S. J. Silvia, 'The Fall and Rise of Unemployment in Germany: Is the Red–Green Government Responsible?", *German Politics* 11 (2002): 1–22, here pp. 2, 5.

9 Romei, 'Germany: From "Sick Man" of Europe to Engine of Growth'; Barysch, 'Germany: The Sick Man of Europe?', p. 1. Quotation from Barysch.

10 Mike M. Mochizuki, 'Japan after the Cold War', *SAIS Review* 10, No. 2 (Summer–Fall 1990): 121–137, quotations from p. 122.

11 Mark Metzler, *Capital as Will and Imagination: Schumpeter's Guide to the Postwar Japanese Miracle* (Ithaca, NY: Cornell University Press, 2013), pp. 219–220; Naoyuki Yoshino and Farhad Taghizadeh-Hesary, 'Causes and Remedies for Japan's Long-Lasting Recession: Lessons for the People's Republic of China', Asian Development Bank Institute, ADBI Working Paper No. 554 (December 2015), pp. 2–10, available at www.adb.org/sites/default/files/publication/177252/adbi-wp554.pdf (accessed 20 June 2022).

12 Mark Metzler, 'Toward a Financial History of Japan's Long Stagnation, 1990–2003', *Journal of Asian Studies* 67, No. 2 (2008): 653–666; Yoshino and Taghizadeh-Hesary, 'Causes and Remedies for Japan's Long-Lasting Recession', pp. 2–10; Paul Krugman, 'Japan's Trap' (May 1998), available at https://web.mit .edu/krugman/www/japtrap.html (accessed 20 June 2022).

13 This and the following two paragraphs are based on Ethan Devine, 'What Americans Should Understand about Japan's 1990s Economic Bust: The Slacker Trap', *The Atlantic* (May 2013), available at www.theatlantic.com/magazine/archive/2013/05/the-slacker-trap/309285 (accessed 24 October 2023).

14 On the profound changes for Japanese business between the late 1990s and 2006, see Ulrike Schaede, *Choose and Focus: Japanese Business Strategies for the 21st Century* (Ithaca, NY: Cornell University Press, 2008). On the resulting economic distress for many Japanese, including the freeters, that all too frequently resulted in suicide, see especially pp. 22–24.

15 Jack E. Triplett, 'The Solow Productivity Paradox: What Do Computers Do to Productivity?', *The Canadian Journal of Economics* 32, No. 2 (April 1999): 309–334, quotation from p. 309.

16 There is debate about the extent to which malls have this effect. See Francesco Chiodelli and Stefano Moroni, 'Do Malls Contribute to the Erosion of the Public Sphere? Reconsidering the Role of Shopping Centres', *City, Culture and Society* 6 (2015): 35–42.

17 Oberste Bauehörde im Bayerischen Staatsministerium des Innern (OBBSI), 'Forschungsbericht Innerstädtische Einkaufszentren' (March 2003), p. 6, available at www.stmb.bayern.de/assets/stmi/buw/staedtebaufoerderung/iic6_oeff_forsc hung_ekz.pdf (accessed 4 July 2022).

18 Evgenia Koptyung, 'Number of Shopping Centres in Germany 1965–2022' (27 June 2022), available at www.statista.com/statistics/523100/number-of-shopping-centers-in-germany (accessed 4 July 2022); OBBSI, 'Forschungsbericht Innerstädtische Einkaufszentren' (March 2003), pp. 6–7. Quotation from OBBSI, p. 7.

19 Matthias Finger, 'No Money in Post, so Why Was Royal Mail a Good Buy?', *The Conversation* (12 November 2012), available at https://theconversation.com/no-money-in-post-so-why-was-royal-mail-a-good-buy-20110 (accessed 4 July 2022); Andreas Schwilling and Stephan Bunge, Roland Berger Strategy Consultants, *20 Years of German Rail Reform and Deutsch Bahn AG* (n.d., c. 2013), p. 1

(emphasis in original), available at www.deutschebahn.com/resource/blob/692580 4/8a392129dc76ee3525d0e87e7953a85a/20-years_summary-data.pdf (accessed 4 July 2022).

20 Sigurt Vitols, 'Negotiated Shareholder Value: The German Variant of Anglo-Saxon Practice', *Competition & Change* 8, No. 4 (December 2004): 357–374; Lazaros Goutas and Christel Lane, 'The Translation of Shareholder Value in the German Business System: A Comparison of DaimlerChrysler and Volkswagen AG', *Competition & Change* 13, No. 4 (December 2009): 327–346; Christian Odendahl, 'The Hartz Myth: A Closer Look at Germany's Labour Market Reforms', Centre for European Reform Policy Brief (July 2017), available at www.cer.eu/publications/ archive/policy-brief/2017/hartz-myth-closer-look-germanys-labour-market-reforms (accessed 6 July 2022).

21 Vitols, 'Negotiated Shareholder Value', pp. 358, 367–368; Odendahl, 'The Hartz Myth'.

22 Odendahl, 'The Hartz Myth'; Will Hutton, 'The Slick Man of Europe', *The Guardian* (23 November 2003).

23 Katsumu Shimotsu, 'The Effect of Large-Scale Retailers on Price Level: Evidence from Japanese data for 1977–1992', RIETI Discussion Paper Series 14-E-013 (March 2014), available at www.rieti.go.jp/jp/publications/dp/14e013.pdf (accessed 20 July 2022); Tokumi Odagiri and Paul Riethmiller, 'Japan's Large Scale Retail Store Law: A Cause of Concern for Food Exporters?', *Agricultural Economics* 23 (2000): 55–65.

24 Quotation from C. H. Kwan, 'Revitalizing the Japanese Economy', Brookings Institution Working Paper (1 June 2000), available at www.brookings.edu/articles/ revitalizing-the-japanese-economy (accessed 14 July 2022).

25 Chul Ju Kim and Michael C. Huang, 'The Privatization of Japan Railways and Japan Post: Why, How, and Now, in Farhad Taghizadeh-Hesary, Naoyuki Yoshino, Chul Ju Kim, and Kunmin Kim, eds., *Reforming State-Owned Enterprises in Asia* (Singapore: Springer, 2021), pp. 133–155, quotation from p. 134.

26 Kazuo Ueda, 'Japan's Experience with Zero Interest Rates', *Journal of Money, Credit and Banking* 32, No. 4 (November 2000): 1107–1109.

27 Kwan, 'Revitalizing the Japanese Economy'; Justin McCurry, 'Japan Lifts Interest Rates from Zero and Tries to Forget "Lost Decade" of Stagnation', *The Guardian* (15 July 2006); Abe, 'Japan's Shrinking Economy'; Kana Inagaki and Leo Lewis, 'Global Inflation: Japan Faces a Moment of Truth', *Financial Times* (4 July 2022). Quotation from Kwan.

28 This paragraph and the following draw upon Mercedes-Benz Group, '1995–2007: "World Corp." Vision', available at https://group.mercedes-benz.com/company/ tradition/company-history/1995-2007.html (accessed 14 July 2022); John Rankin Wood Riach and Martin R. Schneider, 'The DaimlerChrysler Takeover Failure Revisited from a Varieties-of-Capitalism Perspective', Cross Cultural and Strategic Management (2022), https://doi.org/10.1108/CCSM-12-2020-0250; Goutas and Lane, 'The Translation of Shareholder Value in the German Business System'; Michael D. Watkins, 'Why DaimlerChrysler Never Got into Gear', *Harvard Business Review* (18 May 2007).

29 Edmund L. Andrews, 'DaimlerChrysler Abandons Talks about Buying Control of Nissan', *New York Times* (11 March 1999), pp. C-1, C-4; Kwan, 'Revitalizing the Japanese Economy'. Schrempp statement quoted in Andrews, p. C-4.

30 Graeme Wearden, 'From $35bn to $7.4bn in Nine Years', *The Guardian* (14 May 2007); Watkins, 'Why DaimlerChrysler Never Got into Gear'; Mercedes-Benz Group, '1995–2007: "World Corp." Vision'. Quote from Watkins.

31 Stephanie Strom, 'Wondering What It Will Take to Get Nissan a Mate', *New York Times* (11 March 1999), p. C-4; Andrews, 'DaimlerChrysler Abandons Talks about Buying Control of Nissan'. Quote from Strom.

32 Andrews, 'DaimlerChrysler Abandons Talks about Buying Control of Nissan'.

33 This and the follow draw on Carlos Ghosn, 'Saving the Business without Losing the Company', *Harvard Business Review* (January 2002); 'The Renault–Nissan Alliance', in *Nissan Sustainability Report 2012*, available at www.nissan-global .com/EN/SUSTAINABILITY/LIBRARY/SR/2012/ASSETS/PDF/SR12_E_P014.pdf (accessed 14 July 2022); 'Renault and Nissan Rule Out Merger as They Unveil Survival Plan', Reuters (27 May 2020), available at www.cnbc.com/2020/05/27/ renault-and-nissan-rule-out-merger-as-they-unveil-survival-plan.html (accessed 15 July 2022).

34 Ghosn, 'Saving the Business without Losing the Company'.

35 Ghosn, 'Saving the Business without Losing the Company'.

36 Watkins, 'Why DaimlerChrysler Never Got Into Gear'.

37 Neil Winton, 'Renault–Nissan Alliance, Faced with Existential Problems, Tries to Tweak Current Deal', *Forbes* (27 May 2020).

38 Theo Leggett and Rupert Wingfield-Hayes, 'The Fall of the God of Cars', BBC News (n.d. [2020]), available at www.bbc.co.uk/news/extra/Bi5xGc7SIj/the_fall_of_the_ god_of_cars#group-Next-ouZWKdgLyW (accessed 15 July 2022); Dearbail Jordan and Simon Jack, 'Ex-Nissan Boss Carlos Ghosn: How I Escaped Japan in a Box', BBC News (13 July 2021), available at www.bbc.co.uk/news/business-57760993 (accessed 31 October 2023).

39 Winton, 'Renault–Nissan Alliance'.

12 The Shock of the New Century: Three Crises (and a Near Miss)

1 For this and the following paragraph, see Martyn Thomas, 'The Millennium Bug Was Real – and 20 Years Later We Face the Same Threats', *The Guardian* (31 December 2019); Luke Jones, 'How the UK Coped with the Millennium Bug 15 Years Ago', *BBC News* (31 December 2014), available at www.bbc.co.uk/news/ magazine-30576670 (accessed 27 July 2022).

2 Will Hutton, 'The Slick Man of Europe', *The Guardian* (23 November 2003).

3 For this and the following, see the excellent overview of the financial (and related other) crises that started in 2007 by Adam Tooze, *Crashed: How a Decade of Financial Crises Changed the World* (London: Penguin, 2018).

4 Gautam Mukunda, 'The Price of Wall Street's Power', *Harvard Business Review* (June 2014).

5 Harald Hau and Marcel Thum, 'Subprime Crisis and Board (In-)Competence: Private versus Public Banks in Germany', *Economic Policy* 24, No. 60 (October 2009): 701–752, especially pp. 703–707.

6 Stefan Theil, 'German Banks Worst Hit by Financial Crisis', *Newsweek* (11 June 2009); Hans-H. Bleuel, 'The German Banking System and the Global Financial Crisis: Causes, Developments and Policy Responses', *Düsseldorf Working Papers in Applied Management and Economics*, No. 8 (2009), available at www.econstor .eu/bitstream/10419/30798/1/593928032.pdf (accessed 31 October 2023).

7 Martin Hellwig, 'Germany and the Financial Crises, 2007–2017' (June 2018) available at www.bundesbank.de/en/bundesbank/research/germany-and-the-financial-crises-2007-2017-759000 (accessed 29 July 2022); quote from Michael Lewis, *Boomerang: The Meltdown Tour* (London: Penguin, 2011), p. 137.

8 Mark Copelovitch, Jeffry Frieden, and Stefanie Walter, 'The Political Economy of the Euro Crisis', *Comparative Political Studies* 49, No. 7 (2016): 811–840; Mark Blyth, *Austerity: The History of a Dangerous Idea* (Oxford and New York: Oxford University Press, 2013), especially Chapter 7.

9 IMF Survey Online, 'Germany's Impressive Recovery Presents Reform Opportunity' (12 July 2011), available at www.imf.org/en/News/Articles/2015/09/28/04/53/socar071211a (accessed 1 August 2022).

10 For this and the following paragraph, see graphic by UNCTAD, 'Evolution of the World's Top 25 Trading Nations' (2021), available at https://unctad.org/topic/trade-analysis/chart-10-may-2021 (accessed 8 December 2022).

11 Leo Lewis and Kana Inagaki, 'Shinzo Abe, Influential Japanese Prime Minister, 1954–2022', *Financial Times* (8 July 2022).

12 Kana Inagaki and Leo Lewis, 'Global Inflation: Japan Faces a Moment of Truth', *Financial Times* (4 July 2022); Robin Harding, 'Six Abenomics Lessons for a World Struggling with "Japanification"', *Financial Times* (2 September 2020). Quotation from Inagaki and Lewis.

13 Casey Baseel, 'Abe Says He Didn't Want to Cosplay as Mario at 2016 Olympics', *Japan Today* (24 October 2020), available at https://japantoday.com/category/politics/abe-says-he-didn%E2%80%99t-want-to-cosplay-as-mario-at-2016-olympics (accessed 3 August 2022); Adam K. Raymond, 'Japan's Prime Minister Gave Trump a $3,800 Golden Golf Club', *New York Magazine* (21 November 2016); 'Donald Trump Plays Golf with Shinzo Abe Using Golden Driver', *Golf.com* (13 February 2017), available at https://golf.com/lifestyle/celebrities/donald-trump-plays-golf-with-shinzo-abe-using-a-golden-driver (accessed 3 August 2022); Francesca Chambers, 'It Is the Most Beautiful Weapon I've Ever Seen', *Daily Mail Online* (6 November 2017), available at www.dailymail.co.uk/news/article-5053517/Japanese-PM-claims-game-Trump-golf-pro-close.html (accessed 3 August 2022); Inagaki and Lewis, 'Shinzo Abe'. Quote from Inagaki and Lewis.

14 BBC News, 'Japan's PM Falls into Golf Bunker' (10 November 2017), available at www.youtube.com/watch?v=ZaAHT83XC2s&t=29s (accessed 28 March 2023).

15 Zeke J. Miller, 'Japan's Prime Minister Showed the Way to President Trump's Heart: Flattery', *Time* (10 February 2017); David Langbart, 'Golf Diplomacy', The Text Message, US National Archives (20 May 2015), available at https://text-message.blogs.archives.gov/2015/05/20/golf-diplomacy-1957 (accessed 3 August 2022).

16 'Japan PM Shinzo Abe Visits Yasukuni WWII Shrine', *BBC News* (26 December 2016), available at www.bbc.co.uk/news/world-asia-25517205 (accessed 3 August 2022); Peter Landers, 'Shinzo Abe Visits Tokyo War Shrine Linked to Militarist Past', *Wall Street Journal* (19 September 2020); Shin Ji-hye, 'Shinzo Abe Visits Controversial Shrine, Sparks Fury in Seoul', *Korea Herald* (21 April 2022).

17 This and the following paragraphs draw on Hiroko Yoda, 'Shinzo Abe's Assassin and Japan's Complicated Spirituality', *The New Yorker* (26 July 2022); Ben Dooley and Hisako Ueno, 'In Japan, Abe Suspect's Grudge against Unification Church Is a Familiar One', *New York Times* (23 July 2022).

18 Becky Oskin, 'Japan Earthquake & Tsunami of 2011: Facts and Information', *Live Science* (25 February 2022), available at www.livescience.com/39110-japan-2011-earthquake-tsunami-facts.html (accessed 4 August 2022); Alan Taylor, '10 Years since the Great East Japan Earthquake', *The Atlantic* (10 March 2021) (photo essay); 'Fukushima Disaster: What Happened at the Nuclear Power Plant?', *BBC News* (10 March 2021), available at www.bbc.co.uk/news/world-asia-56252695 (accessed 4 August 2022).

19 Daniel Kaufmann and Veronika Penchlakova, 'Japan's Triple Disaster: Governance and the Earthquake, Tsunami, and Nuclear Crises', Brookings (16 March 2011), available at www.brookings.edu/articles/japans-triple-disaster-governance-and-the-earthquake-tsunami-and-nuclear-crises (accessed 4 August 2022); Justin McCurry, 'Fukushima Nuclear Disaster: Ex-bosses of Owner Tepco Ordered to Pay ¥13 tn', *The Guardian* (13 July 2022); 'Fukushima: Japan Court Finds Government Liable for Disaster', BBC News (17 March 2017), available at www.bbc.co.uk/news/world-asia-39303178 (accessed 4 August 2022).

20 World Nuclear Association, 'Nuclear Power in Japan' (updated October 2023), available at https://world-nuclear.org/information-library/country-profiles/countries-g-n/japan-nuclear-power.aspx (accessed 24 October 2023).

21 BP, *Statistical Review of World Energy* (July 2021), available at www.bp.com/en/global/corporate/energy-economics/statistical-review-of-world-energy.html (accessed 15 April 2022); World Nuclear Association, 'Nuclear Power in Japan'; US Energy Information Administration, 'Japan' (last updated 7 July 2023), available at www.eia.gov/international/analysis/country/JPN (accessed 24 October 2023).

22 US Energy Information Administration, 'Japan'.

23 World Nuclear Association, 'Nuclear Power in Germany' (updated January 2022), available at https://world-nuclear.org/information-library/country-profiles/countries-g-n/germany.aspx (accessed 5 August 2022). The most recent version of the information on the site dates from April 2023 (accessed 31 October 2023); Joanna Partridge, '"It's a Shame to Turn It Off." Mixed Feelings over the Ending of Germany's Nuclear Dream', *The Guardian* (9 December 2022).

24 Patrick Wintour, '"We Were All Wrong": How Germany Got Hooked on Russian Energy', *The Guardian* (2 June 2022).

25 Katrin Bennhold, 'The Former Chancellor Who Became Putin's Man in Germany', *New York Times* (23 April 2022).

26 Melissa Eddy and Stanley Reed, 'Germany Counts on Chilled Gas to Keep Warm over Winter', *New York Times* (27 July 2022).

27 US Centers for Disease Control and Prevention, 'CDC Museum Covid-19 Timeline', n.d., available at www.cdc.gov/museum/timeline/covid19.html (accessed 9 August 2022); European Centre for Disease Control, 'ECDC Response to the Covid-19 Pandemic', n.d., available at www.ecdc.europa.eu/en/covid-19/timeline-ecdc-response (accessed 9 August 2022).

28 Christine Farr, 'Germany's Coronavirus Response: A Master Class in Science Communication', CNBC (21 July 2020), available at www.cnbc.com/2020/07/21/germanys-coronavirus-response-masterful-science-communication.html (accessed 27 July 2022); Yuri Okina, Ortwin Renn, and Anshar Lohse, 'What Can We Learn from Germany's Response to Covid-19? Medical Preparedness/Flexible Responses/Management of Public Funds', Nippon Institute for Research Advancement, NIRA Opinion Paper No. 54 (October 2020), available at www.nira.or.jp/paper/e_opinion54.pdf (accessed 26 July 2022).

29 Holly Ellyatt, 'Germany Was Once Praised for Its Covid Response', CNBC (11 November 2021), available at www.cnbc.com/2021/11/11/germany-covid-cases-hit-50000-a-day-prompting-100000-deaths-warning.html (accessed 27 July 2022); Johns Hopkins University Coronavirus Resource Center, 'Mortality Analyses' (last updated 16 March 2023), available at https://coronavirus.jhu.edu/data/mortality (accessed 31 October 2023).

30 For a sophisticated attempt to develop methodologies to evaluate the effectiveness of these policies, see J. Stokes, Alex James Turner, Laura Anselmi, Marcello Morciani, and Thomas Hone, 'The Relative Effects of Non-pharmaceutical Interventions on

Wave One Covid-19 Mortality: Natural Experiment in 130 Countries', *BMC Public Health* 22 (2022): article 1113, doi:10.1186/s12889-022-13546-6.

31 Johns Hopkins University Coronavirus Resource Center, 'Mortality Analyses'; Hisako Ueno and Shashnk Bengali, 'Japan Tries a New Tactic as Virus Surges: Public Shaming', *New York Times* (3 August 2021); Dyani Lewis, 'Where Covid Contact-Tracing Went Wrong', *Nature* 858 (17 December 2020): 384–388; Motoko Rich and Ben Dooley, 'Japan's Secret to Taming Coronavirus: Peer Pressure', *New York Times* (2 July 2022). The following paragraph also draws on Rich and Dooley.

32 Quoted in Rich and Dooley, 'Japan's Secret to Taming the Coronavirus'.

Conclusion: Deutschland AG and Japan, Inc. – Lessons and Limits

1 The classic statement of this concept and analytical approach is in Peter A. Hall and David Soskice, eds., *Varieties of Capitalism: The Institutional Foundations of Comparative Advantage* (Oxford and New York: Oxford University Press, 2001).

2 David Soskice, 'Finer Varieties of Capitalism: Industry- versus Group-Based Coordination in Germany and Japan', unpublished working paper, Wissenschaftszentrum Berlin, 1994; Mark Metzler, *Capital as Will and Imagination: Schumpeter's Guide to the Postwar Japanese Miracle* (Ithaca, NY: Cornell University Press, 2013), p. 212.

3 On the development of codetermination in Germany starting in 1918, see Edwin F. Beal, 'Origins of Codetermination', *ILR Review* 8, No. 4 (July 1955): 483–498; Hedwig Wachenheim, 'Communication: Origins of Codetermination', *ILR Review* 10, No. 1 (October 1956): 118–126. On admiration of codetermination in the United States and UK, see, for instance, Steven Hill, *Europe's Promise: Why the European Way Is the Best Hope in an Insecure Age* (Berkeley, CA: University of California Press, 2010); Will Hutton, 'Davos Man Survives While the Rest of Us Pay for His Excesses', *The Guardian* (20 January 2013).

4 Peter B. Petersen, 'The Misplaced Origin of Just-in-Time Production Methods', *Management Decision* 40, No. 1 (2002): 82–88.

5 Simone R. Hassler, 'The German System of Vocational Education and Training: Challenges of Gender, Academisation, and the Integration of Low-Achieving Youth', *Transfer: European Review of Labour and Research* 26, No. 1 (2020): 57–71; David Owen, 'The Great Electrician Shortage', *The New Yorker* (24 April 2023).

6 Mark Metzler, 'Toward a Financial History of Japan's Long Stagnation, 1990–2003', *Journal of Asian Studies* 67, No. 2 (2008): 653–666; Ugo Fasano-Filho, Qing Wang, and Pelin Berkmen, 'Bank of Japan's Quantitative and Credit Easing: Are They Now More Effective?', IMF Working Paper WP/12/2 (January 2012), available at www.imf.org/en/Publications/WP/Issues/2016/12/31/Bank-of-Japan-s-Quantitative-and-Credit-Easing-Are-they-Now-More-Effective-25483 (accessed 4 May 2023).

7 Sekou Keita and Helen Dempster, 'Five Years Later, One Million Refugees Are Thriving', Center for Global Development Blog (4 December 2020), available at www.cgdev.org/blog/five-years-later-one-million-refugees-are-thriving-germany (accessed 29 March 2023).

8 Daniel Yergin, *The New Map: Energy, Climate, and the Clash of Nations* (London: Penguin, 2020), quotation from p. 422.

9 Joseph Coleman, 'Japan Needs Indian Tech Workers. But Do They Need Japan?', *New York Times* (12 December 2022).

INDEX

shopping centres, development in
Germany after unification,
240–242
Showa Denko Company, 143
Siemens, 95, 108, 166
corporate scandal, 179
operations in China, 227
operations in the United States, 217
Silesia, 12, 41
Small and Medium Enterprise Agency
(Japan), 86
small and medium-sized enterprise (SME)
Germany (*Mittelstand*), 79–86, 93
operations in China, 228
operations in the United States,
217–218
orientation towards global
markets, 259
research and development support,
85, 218, 280
Japan, 86–93
SMH Corporation, 247
Smithsonian Agreement, 195
Smyrna assembly plant (Nissan), 211
Social Democratic Party of Germany
(SPD), 66, 166, 168, 192, 242,
267–269
social market economy, 41, 48
Solow, Robert, 240
Solow paradox, 239
Soni-Tape, 130
Sony, 129–132
location of factory in the United
States, 219
transistor radio, 114–116, 131
Soskice, David, 277
South German Institute for Economic
Research, 40
South Korea, 263
dependence on foreign trade, 225
restitution from Japan, 156–157,
163–164
Soviet Union
assent to German unification, 185, 235
declaration of war on Japan, 17

exodus of German refugees to, 12
gas supply, 199, 268
occupation of Germany, 11, 14–16,
20, 23–24
response to the German currency
reforms, 32–33
utilisation of German aeronautical
expertise, 28–29
Spain
labourers from, 191
spread of the financial crisis to, 258
Sparkassen (local savings banks), 85
stagflation, 93, 186, 199
Stalin, Josef, 15, 16
Standard Oil of New Jersey (Esso), 22
steel production, 7
decline in Japanese, 47
production of air gases for, 122
Sterling Winthrop, 217
Steyler (Catholic missionary order),
167–168
Strauss, Franz Josef, 168, 192
Strauss-Mark, 192
Strughold, Hubertus, 14
subprime crisis, 256–258
Suez crisis, 198
Sumida River, 140
Sun Myung Moon, Reverend, 264
Suzuki, 248

Taiwan, 6, 184, 210, 224, 229,
274, 282
Takata Corporation, 179
Tanaka, Kakuei, 177–179, 193, 207
Tarr, Joel, 146
television
domination of Japanese
technology, 131
ownership of, 94–95, 101, 103
Termumo corporation, 96
Texaco, 207
Texas Instruments (TI), 114
Theil, Stefan, 257
Three Sacred Treasures, 94–95
Thyssen-Krupp, 79